Money
and
Financial Intermediation

PAUL F. SMITH

Professor of Finance
The Wharton School
University of Pennsylvania

Money
and
Financial Intermediation

The theory and structure
of financial systems

PRENTICE-HALL, INC., Englewood Cliffs, New Jersey 07632

Library of Congress Cataloging in Publication Data

SMITH, PAUL F (date)
  Money and financial intermediation.

  Bibliography: p.
  Includes index.
  1. Financial institutions. 2. Money. I. Title.
HG153.S533 1978   332   77-21636
ISBN   0-13-600288-9

© 1978 by Prentice-Hall, Inc., Englewood Cliffs, New Jersey 07632

Printed in the United States of America

10   9   8   7   6   5   4   3

PRENTICE-HALL INTERNATIONAL, INC., *London*
PRENTICE-HALL OF AUSTRALIA PTY. LIMITED, *Sydney*
PRENTICE-HALL OF CANADA, LTD., *Toronto*
PRENTICE-HALL OF INDIA PRIVATE LIMITED, *New Delhi*
PRENTICE-HALL OF JAPAN, INC., *Tokyo*
PRENTICE-HALL OF SOUTHEAST ASIA PTE. LTD., *Singapore*
WHITEHALL BOOKS LIMITED, *Wellington, New Zealand*

To my parents

Contents

Preface

This book is designed to integrate the many new developments in the theory of financial decisions and behavior into the story of the financial process in its role in supporting and shaping economic activity. It was developed to meet a perceived need for an approach that extended the traditional subject matter of money and banking into a broader view of the financial system. It views money as part of a system of monetary aggregates that play a complex role in determining the level of interest rates and economic activity. It views banks as one of a set of financial institutions that convert savings into usable loan funds. The financial system is seen as the servant of the real economic needs of businesses and consumers that are recorded in their demands for loans. The emphasis of the book is on the structure and organization of the private financial system as it has developed to supply these needs. The monetary and regulatory authorities are introduced as external influences that shape and alter the financing process.

The book assumes that the reader is familiar with elementary economics and statistics. If it is used for students who are not familiar with the features of financial institutions and markets, it should be supplemented by descriptive readings. For more advanced students, it should be supplemented with readings from the original sources and from empirical work and with discussions of the theoretical issues. Readings of both types are suggested at the end of each chapter.

The impact on the book of conversations and contacts with many financial experts and specialists over many years cannot be adequately acknowledged. The author has been fortunate to work in an environment and with colleagues that have continuously provided the stimulus of new ideas and perspectives. Specific acknowledgment can be made to the following people who have directly commented on or contributed to the manuscripts that were used in developing this book: Jamshed K. S. Ghandhi, Jack Guttentag, Edward S. Herman, John M. Mason, Anthony M. Santomero, and Susan M. Wachter.

MICROECONOMICS OF FINANCE

Part ONE

Role of Financial Markets

1

On any day, the *Wall Street Journal* carries announcements of new security issues of corporations and governments totalling billions of dollars. On the same day, thousands of businessmen and individuals contact their local banks about new loans, and hundreds of thousands of individuals use their credit cards. These events have one feature in common—they are attempts to raise funds for expenditures. They are motivated by economic needs and desires that require credit or that are made easier by the use of credit. These transactions link the real world of goods and services with the financial world of money and credit. Spending decisions are motivated by real economic objectives but the availability of credit may play an essential role in the achievement of those objectives.

Three Types of Financial Markets

The markets used by businessmen and consumers to raise funds for expenditures are called *primary markets*. They serve as the interface between the demand for funds and the complex structure of financial markets and institutions that has developed to serve these needs. The demand orientation of the definition of primary markets leaves the supply side unidentified. The natural source of funds would appear to be the surplus funds and savings of households and businesses, but as a practical matter these funds are seldom placed directly into primary markets. Individual savers almost never lend directly to borrowers. The needs of individual borrowers and savers are too difficult to match.

A second type of market serves as an outlet for savings and an elaborate system of financial intermediaries has developed to move the funds from these *savings markets* into the primary markets. Since some savings find their way into the primary markets directly, the term *institutional savings markets* will be used for markets that supply the funds for financial intermediaries.

Financial intermediaries operate in two sets of markets. They appear on the demand side of the institutional savings markets and on the supply side of primary markets (see Figure 1-1). Institutional savings markets supply the funds that appear as liabilities and capital on the accounting statements of financial institutions. Primary markets provide the outlets that appear as assets. The cost of financial intermediation appears as the spread between the rates that financial institutions pay for funds and the rates that they charge for loans.

The New York Stock Exchange, the best known financial market, does not enter directly into the flow of savings into primary loans at all. It

FIGURE 1-1

FINANCIAL MARKETS AND THE FLOW OF FUNDS

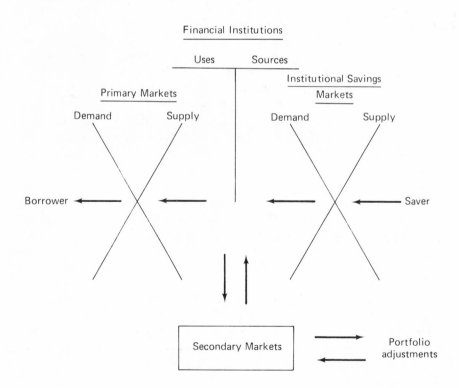

and other less well-known *secondary markets* provide a place to buy or sell the financial contracts and securities that have been issued as part of the primary borrowing and lending process. The term *seasoned securities* is used to distinguish the securities that are traded in secondary markets from the *newly issued* securities that originate in the primary markets. The transactions in secondary markets only involve shifts in the ownership of securities. They do not generate new funds nor do they create any new obligations. But the availability of these markets adds to the attractiveness of new security issues and greatly facilitates the primary financing process.

Two Views of Financial Markets

The microeconomic approach to financial markets goes to the sources of the borrowing and lending decisions. It examines the motives and objectives of households, governments, and corporations in seeking the determinants of the demand and supply of funds. It also looks at the institutions and markets that serve these borrowers and lenders. It views the financial process from the perspective of the individual participants, and judges it by its effectiveness in meeting their needs and objectives. The first part of the book deals with these issues.

The macroeconomic approach to financial markets looks at the aggregate sources and uses of funds and the implications of events in financial markets for the aggregate level of economic activity. Financial aggregates can be viewed, in many cases, as the simple summation of the decisions of individual households and businessmen. In such cases, aggregate theory is a simple extension of microeconomics; but in other cases, aggregate events cannot be interpreted as simple analogies of individual behavior. Individual actions may set in motion other actions that offset or accentuate the effects of the initial act. The principal problems and controversies of aggregate theory arise from conclusions that are not intuitive extensions of individual actions. Understanding the aggregate results requires an overview of the financial process which provides for the interaction of individual events that may be partly or totally offsetting in their aggregative effects.

In addition, the aggregate view reveals the monetary authorities as a new participant in the financial process. Additions to the money supply affect the level of interest rates and conditions in financial markets as well as the level of economic activity. An understanding of the role of monetary policy is essential for the interpretation of financial events. The second part of the book deals with the role of the financial process in determining the level of interest rates, the structure of interest rates, and the aggregate level of economic activity.

Formation of Financial Assets

The existing structure of financial assets stands as a record of financial transactions that have taken place in the past. This edifice of wealth depends not only on the total real wealth of the economy but on the way expenditures are financed. In socialist countries, where a substantial proportion of the productive resources and housing are owned by the government, the ratio of financial assets to real wealth may be quite small. In capitalist countries, where capital expenditures and private housing are financed by borrowing or security issues, the ratio financial assets to real wealth reflects the complexities of the private financing process.

The structure of financial assets is constantly changing as new loans are made and old loans are repaid. The total grows as long as part of income is allocated to financial savings. Financial assets are most likely to grow when income is expanding, but their growth is not necessarily tied to income growth. Some growth is possible without an increase in income. Either an increase in the importance of external financing or an increase in the number of steps in the financing process can add to the growth of financial assets without adding to the aggregate supply of funds.

Flow of Funds Accounts

The flow of funds data published by the Federal Reserve System give the most comprehensive view of the financial process in the United States. These data record changes in the financial assets and liabilities of the major sectors of the economy and provide details on all of the major types of financing.

Figure 1-2 looks at the financial process from the demand side of the primary markets. All the primary financial markets are covered by the information in lines 2 to 11. Corporate borrowing is distributed among several classifications, depending on the features of the instruments used and on the source of funds. It appears in the figures for bonds, equities, mortgages, bank loans, and open market paper (lines 4, 5, 7, 9, and 10, respectively). Household demand for funds appears primarily in home mortgages and in consumer credit. The total amounts raised by borrowing sectors are summarized in the bottom part of the table (lines 12 to 18). There is no direct way of reconciling these figures with the classifications used in the top part of the table.

Figure 1-3A shows the amounts raised in primary markets from 1950 to 1975. Despite the size, $197 billion in 1975, these figures measure only the additions to financial assets. They fall far short of measuring the total amount of borrowing and lending activity. Most new loans are financed with the payments on old loans.

FIGURE 1-2
FUNDS RAISED IN U.S. CREDIT MARKETS, 1975

		(Billions of dollars)
1.	Total funds raised (nonfinancial sectors)	197.3
	By type of obligation	
2.	U.S. government and agency obligations	85.2
3.	State and local government obligations	15.4
4.	Corporate bonds	27.0
5.	Corporate equities	9.6
	Mortgages:	
6.	Home	35.9
7.	Other	16.5
8.	Consumer credit	5.3
9.	Bank loans (not elsewhere classified)	−12.6
10.	Open-market paper	−1.6
11.	Other[a]	16.6
	By borrowing sector	
12.	U.S. government and agencies	85.2
13.	State and local governments	13.2
14.	Households	43.3
	Nonfinancial business:	
15.	Farm	6.7
16.	Nonfarm, noncorporate	2.5
17.	Corporate	34.2
18.	Foreign	12.0

[a]Including foreign credit, which is not classified by type of obligation.
Source: Board of Governors of the Federal Reserve System, *Flow of Funds Accounts*, 4th Quarter 1975 (February 10, 1976) pp. 2–3.

Figure 1-4 looks at the financing process from the supply side. The total amounts supplied in 1975 are equal to the total funds raised (except for the exclusion of equities from the total supplied) but it is impossible to match the individual items on the demand and supply sides. Funds typically move through complex paths where each step in the process creates a new asset and a new liability. The accounting records of financial transactions may show several dollars of new financial assets and liabilities for every dollar of new funds that moves through the system. Many of these potential duplications are eliminated from the moneyflows data, but some remain. For example, the purchases of government agency securities by financial institutions appear as funds advanced by financial institutions, and the loans made by the government agencies with these funds appear as funds advanced by the agency sector. The amount of these duplications and other discrepancies for 1975 is shown in item 6 in Figure 1-4.

FIGURE 1-3

A. FUNDS RAISED IN PRIMARY MARKETS

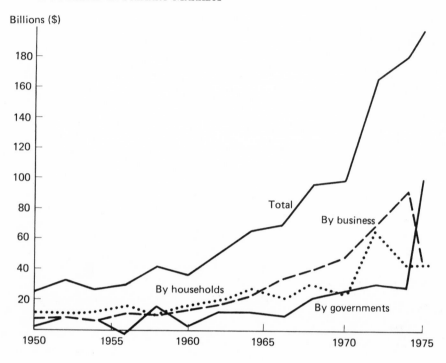

B. FUNDS ADVANCED IN PRIMARY MARKETS

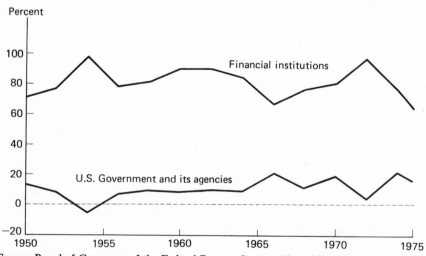

Source: Board of Governors of the Federal Reserve System, *Flow of Funds Accounts*.

FIGURE 1-4
DIRECT AND INDIRECT SOURCES OF FUNDS
IN U.S. CREDIT MARKETS, 1975

			(Billions of dollars)
1.	Total funds advanced (excluding equities):		187.7
2.	By public agencies:		30.6
	U.S. government	10.6	
	Sponsored credit agencies	11.5	
	Monetary authorities	8.5	
3.	Foreign sources		3.9
4.	Private financial institutions		121.7
	Commercial banks	26.6	
	Savings institutions	56.1	
	Insurance and pension funds	39.7	
	Other	−0.6	
5.	Direct lending in credit markets		40.8
6.	Duplications and discrepancies		(−9.3)

Source: Board of Governors of the Federal Reserve System, *Flow of Funds Accounts*, 4th Quarter (February 10, 1976), pp. 4–5.

The dominant role of private financial institutions in the financing process is illustrated in Figure 1-3B. Their share of the total funds advanced ranged from a low of 75 percent in 1975 to a high of 98 percent in 1954. The U.S. government and its agencies also provide substantial amounts in most years. The role of the federal government in the financing process takes two forms. First, the Federal Reserve System provides the banks with reserves for the growth of the money supply. These funds and the demand deposits that they support supplement the normal savings process. Second, the federal government makes some direct loans to various sectors of the economy, and the federally sponsored credit agencies play the same role as their private counterparts in attracting savings and making loans. The share of the total funds advanced by the federal government and its sponsored agencies ranged from minus 3 percent in 1954 to 21 percent in 1974.

It is impossible to make a good estimate of the share of the funds placed directly into primary markets by households and corporations. A substantial share of the moneyflows estimates of direct lending in credit markets (line 5, Figure 1-4) falls into three types of transactions that involve financial intermediation. First, some of these funds are used to purchase the securities of financial institutions. Second, some of the funds are used to purchase the securities issued by government credit agencies. Third, most of the addition to the holdings of households are obtained in secondary markets as purchases of seasoned issues rather than as direct purchases of newly issued securities. When adjustments are made to exclude these transactions, the funds supplied directly by savers to borrowers represent a very small share of the total.

Summary

The financial process is motivated by the real economic needs and objectives of borrowers. These needs appear as the demand for funds in primary markets. Although these demands must ultimately be met by the surpluses of other households or businesses, the barriers to the direct interaction of borrowers and lenders give rise to the complex process of financial intermediation that characterizes the U.S. financial system. Most of the funds in primary markets are supplied by financial institutions that, in turn, must raise the funds in the institutional savings markets. The story of the financing process lies in the techniques that have been developed to match the needs of borrowers with needs and objectives of the supplier of funds. What appears to be a simple problem of demand and supply turns out to be a complex set of problems where the success or failure of the solutions affects the level of real economic activity.

QUESTIONS FOR DISCUSSION

1. What are the advantages and disadvantages of borrowing money?
2. What are the advantages and disadvantages of saving money?
3. Why are most savers unwilling to make direct loans to other individuals or businessmen who need loans?
4. Give an illustration of an act of saving that can lead to the creation of financial assets equal to several times the amount originally saved.

Nature of Financial Decisions

2

Businesses and consumers make their current decisions with one eye on the future. Modern organization theory recognizes the role of long-run considerations in current business decisions and modern consumption theory recognizes the role of life cycle planning in current spending decisions. In modern theory, current economic behavior is accepted as the first stage of longer-run plans that attempt to reconcile hopes and desires with economic realities. Financial markets are important to this long-run planning process because they permit businesses and consumers to shift their resources through time. Spending needs are seldom perfectly synchronized with cash flows. Retailers need funds for inventories before they receive the income from sales and receivables. Farmers need funds for fertilizer and seed before they get the cash for their crops. Financial markets make it possible for some businesses and consumers to spend their expected income before they receive it and for others to earn money on funds that they want to hold for future expenditures. Both the borrowers and lenders gain by their cooperative participation in the financial process. The existence of financial markets adds a flexible time dimension to the decision process and gives businesses and consumers greater freedom in selecting the time pattern of expenditures that best suits their long-run needs.

Time Preferences and Decisions to Borrow or Lend

Borrowing involves the decision to divert future resources into current expenditures. Lending reverses the process and postpones the use of resources that are currently available. Both decisions involve a choice between the current and future use of resources. Businesses are continually faced with this choice. Current outlays must be balanced against future outlays. Many current outlays must be given a high priority in this decision process. Wages and salary payments, purchases of essential materials and services, and the payment of contractual commitments may be essential for the continued operation of the business. Other outlays, such as dividend payments and advertising, may be less urgent. A graph of all potential current cash outlays, measured and ranked by urgency and accumulated by amounts, would look like a staircase with steps decreasing in height as the urgency of expenditures decreases. A continuous curve drawn through this graph would resemble the diminishing marginal utility function of the classical theory of demand.

Businesses must also make judgments about the urgency of anticipated expenditures. The urgency of some future expenditure may be slightly less than that of a similar current expenditure, but many future expenditures are essential for the survival of the company and may therefore be more important than some of the less urgent current outlays. Businesses must allocate the funds that they currently have available and those that they expect to receive in a way that provides the best overall pattern of expenditures. This allocation may involve either investing current surplus or borrowing to cover current shortages.

Consumers face the same type of decision in adjusting their current and expected income flows to the time pattern of expenditures that they regard as most desirable. At a minimum, some current expenditures are necessary for survival. Others are hard to postpone because of their regular or contractual nature. However, as consumers move up the scale of expenditures, current expenditure alternatives become less and less urgent and easier to postpone. A cumulative chart of these expenditures would be similar to that described for businesses.

The nature of the choice faced by businesses and consumers can be illustrated by assuming that all outcomes are known with certainty and that plans are being made for only two periods. The decision maker must try to find the best combination of expenditures over both periods when his choice is constrained by current resources, expected cash flows, and the financial alternatives that are available. The choice requires a comparison of the desirability of different levels of expenditures in both periods. This comparison is simplified by combining the urgency or utility functions into an indifference map that reflects the decision maker's attitude toward various combinations of expenditures in the two time periods. The derivation of an indifference map of this type is illustrated in Figure 2-1. The utility function $U(X_1)$ on the right vertical face of the three-dimensional diagram represents the utility of various levels of expenditure in the current period (X_1) and the utility function $U(X_2)$ represents the utility of

FIGURE 2-1
UTILITY AND INDIFFERENCE MAPS

A. Utility Surface

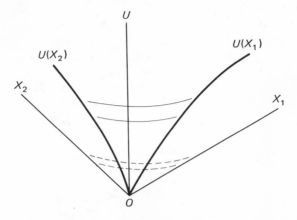

B. Derived Indifference Map

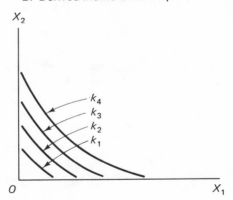

various levels of expenditures in the second period (X_2). The utility of all combinations of expenditures in X_1 and X_2 is represented by the surface formed by the two functions. This surface can be thought of as a hill between the two vertical planes. If this utility surface is cut by a plane drawn parallel to the base, the intersection of the plane and the hill will leave a line on the surface of the hill that measures all points on the surface that are the same distance from the base or all combinations of expenditures in periods X_1 and X_2 that have the same combined utility. On a hill, this would be a contour line representing points with the same altitude. When these contour lines are projected onto the base of the diagram, they form a set of indifference curves that indicate combinations of expenditures in the two periods that have the same combined utility. Figure 2-1A shows the contour lines on the utility surface as solid lines and the same lines projected on the base as dotted lines. Figure 2-1B shows the base of the three-dimensional diagram and several of the projected indifference curves.[1] Since the best combination of expenditures is the one that places the decision maker on the highest level of total utility, he will try to reach the highest possible point on the utility surface or move as far as possible from the origin of the indifference map.

After the indifference map is obtained, the utility superstructure is unnecessary. The individual's preferences are recorded in his indifference map. Three general classes of indifference maps can be identified for purposes of this discussion. First, there are those that indicate a preference for a stable pattern of expenditure in the two periods. These maps will be symmetrical around the 45° line that is the locus of points indicating equal expenditures in both periods. The slopes of the indifference curves at the 45° line will be equal to 1 (in absolute terms) because at that point an exchange of a unit of expenditures in either period will be a matter of indifference ($|\Delta X_2/\Delta X_1| = 1$). Second, there are those that indicate a general bias toward current period expenditures. The slopes of these indifference curves at the 45° line will be greater than 1 (in absolute terms) because the loss of current expenditures would have to be offset by a larger gain in future expenditures to maintain constant total utility ($|\Delta X_2/\Delta X_1| > 1$). Third, there are those that indicate a general bias toward future expenditures. The slopes of these indifference curves at the 45° line will be less than 1 (in absolute terms) because the loss of current expenditures can be offset by a smaller gain in future expenditures to maintain constant total utility ($|\Delta X_2/\Delta X_1| < 1$).

Mathematical note: This presentation assumes that cardinal utility functions can be obtained for successive time periods (i) that satisfy the following conditions:

$$dU = U_{x_i} > 0 \qquad \text{(nonsatiability of wants)} \qquad (1)$$

$$d^2U = U_{x_ix_i} < 0 \qquad \text{(diminishing marginal utility)} \qquad (2)$$

The total utility (U) for the two periods is a function of the amounts spent in the two periods:

$$U = U(X_1, X_2) \qquad (3)$$

[1]Indifference maps may also be constructed directly from the "revealed preferences" of the decision makers. This approach avoids assumptions about the existence and nature of utility functions but other assumptions have to be introduced to avoid the possibilities of indeterminant or multiple solutions. The resulting analysis is much the same.

The indifference map is made up of a series of indifference curves (k_j) that represent the locus of points or combinations of expenditures that give constant utility:

$$k_j = U(X_1, X_2) \tag{4}$$

Indifference curves derived from utility functions satisfying conditions in (1) and (2) will meet the nonsatiation and convexity conditions that are required for predictable behavior.

The nonsatiation requirement rules out any positively sloped segments of indifference curves which would imply indifference to an increase in expenditures in both periods. This possibility is excluded by the first condition applied to the utility function. Since no utility is added by movement along an indifference curve, the derivative with respect to total utility is equal to zero,

$$dU = U_{x_1} d_{x_1} + U_{x_2} d_{x_2} = 0 \tag{5}$$

and the slopes of the indifference curves are equal to

$$\frac{d_{x_2}}{d_{x_1}} = \frac{-U_{x_1}}{U_{x_2}} \tag{6}$$

Since both of the partial derivatives of the utility functions are positive by (1), the slopes of the indifference curves will be negative.

The convexity requirement, which rules out the possibility of the existence of a higher level of total utility on a lower order indifference curve than on a higher order curve, is assured by the second condition applied to the utility functions.

Choice Subject to Constraints

An indifference map provides a picture of time preferences. However, the problem remains of reconciling these preferences with the constraints imposed by the individual's wealth and by the market alternatives. An individual's wealth or endowed position can be represented on the coordinates used for the indifference map as a point or an ordered pair of values measuring the resources available for current expenditures in the first period (X_1) and the expected income (with certainty in this example) in the second period (X_2). This point (a_1, a_2) is usually called the *endowed position* (p_0) (see Figure 2-2). The funds available in the first period can be in the form of either current income or accumulated wealth. The funds expected in the second period represent a new source of funds not

FIGURE 2-2

ALLOCATION OF FUNDS WITHOUT ACCESS TO FINANCIAL MARKETS

A.

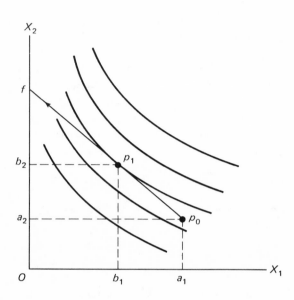

B.

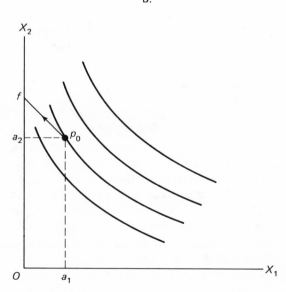

currently accessible. The sum of the two amounts represents the total resources that are available for expenditures in both periods.

The total expenditures that can be made during the two periods are constrained by the total endowment but the utility that is gained from the expenditure of this amount may be improved by shifting some of the funds from one period to another. In the absence of financial markets or investment opportunities, expenditures in the two periods are restricted to combinations that can be achieved by postponing the use of current resources until the second period. The set of potential expenditure combinations can be shown as a straight line running from the endowed position (p_0) to a point (f) on X_2 that is equal to the total amount of wealth and income that is available for both periods of time:

$$f = a_1 + a_2 \qquad (7)$$

The individual can select any combination of expenditures along this opportunity line that gives him the most desirable combination of expenditures (maximizes his utility). This position is reached at the point on the opportunity line that touches the highest indifference curve or at the point of tangency with an indifference curve.

Two cases of this simplest type of financial adjustment are illustrated in Figure 2-2. In Figure 2-2A, an individual with an endowment that gives him a relatively large share of his total resources in the first period will find it to his advantage to save some of his current resources for use in the second period. The amount he will save is determined by the shape of his indifference map. His best combination of expenditures will occur at the point (p_1) where his opportunity line is tangent to an indifference curve. This will place him at the highest possible position on his indifference map —the position that maximizes his total utility. He will save the amount a_1b_1 and spend the amount ob_1 in the first period. He will spend ob_2 in the second period, some share of which (a_2b_2) was saved for that purpose. The individual in Figure 2-2B cannot improve his position by saving money and will spend the funds that are currently available to him.

Financial and Investment Opportunities

The range of alternatives available to businesses and consumers is greatly expanded by the existence of financial markets and productive investment opportunities. The features of the opportunities can be captured by the slope and direction of the opportunity lines that they create. The simplest opportunity for shifting funds from one period to another consists of holding cash and spending it later (as in Figure 2-2A). This alternative results in an opportunity line that extends from the endowed position to the left (since funds can only be transferred from the current to future periods) and that has a negative slope of 1. The slope indicates that one dollar of funds from the current period will generate one dollar of expenditures in the second period ($\Delta X_2/\Delta X_1 = -1$) (see Figure 2-3).

Financial markets add the options of lending and borrowing. When the borrowing and lending rates are assumed to be the same, the slope of the opportunity line reflects the addition of interest payments on loans. The individual can convert his endowed position to the point f' by lending the entire amount of his current resources. The maximum expenditure he

FIGURE 2-3

Financial and Investment Opportunities

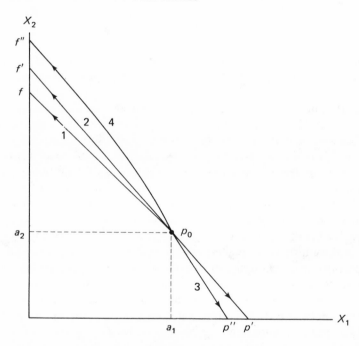

	Direction	Equation	Slope
1. Holding cash	$X_2 \leftarrow X_1$	$f = a_1 + a_2$	-1
2. Borrowing and lending at the same rate (r)	$X_2 \leftrightarrow X_1$	$f' = a_1(1 + r) + a_2$	$-(1 + r)$
Present value form		$p' = a_1 + a_2/(1 + r)$	
3. Different borrowing rate (b) (present value form)	$X_2 \rightarrow X_1$	$p'' = a_1 + a_2/(1 + b)$	$-(1 + b)$
4. Investment opportunities e = marginal yield i = average yield	$X_2 \leftarrow X_1$	$f'' = a_1(1 + i) + a_2$	$-(1 + e)$

can achieve will be equal to his initial endowed position plus the interest he can obtain by lending his current resources (a_1):

$$f' = a_1(1+r) + a_2 \tag{8}$$

The maximum current expenditure that he can make with his given endowment will be equal to the sum of his current resource plus the discounted value of his expected income:

$$p' = a_1 + \frac{a_2}{(1+r)} \tag{9}$$

Note that the value of p' corresponds to the concept of the discounted present value of the endowed position (p_0) when r is used as the discount rate.

For most borrowers, the borrowing rate (b) is higher than the lending rate (r) and the actual opportunity set will consist of a kinked curve made up of separate borrowing and lending segments. The lending segment will permit movement of funds from the current to future periods at the lending rate. The borrowing segment will permit the movement of resources from the future into current expenditures at the borrowing rate.

In the discussion of borrowing and lending rates it has been assumed that the individual's actions do not affect the existing market rates and that he can borrow or lend any amount at the applicable market rate (i.e., the opportunity lines have a constant slope). In discussions of real investment opportunities it is usually assumed that the available set of investment opportunities will produce different yields. In the construction of the investment opportunity curve, these opportunities are arranged in order by their yields so that the resultant function indicates diminishing marginal returns. If the unlikely but convenient assumption is made that these investment opportunities are infinitely divisible, the investment opportunities can be drawn as a continuous function that originates at the endowed position and has a gradually decreasing slope. The slope of the function at any point is an index of the marginal return (e). The slope of an arc drawn between any point in the curve and the endowed position is an index of the average return (i).

A simple model that combines the relevant opportunity functions with an indifference map and an endowed position can be used to illustrate a wide variety of financial behavior. It can also be used to demonstrate a number of important propositions about the economic role of financial markets. The original version of this model was developed by Irving Fisher in 1907. It was reintroduced into the mainstream of economic discussion by Hirshleifer in 1958.[2] It will be referred to in the following discussions as the Fisher–Hirshleifer (F–H) model.

Social Contributions of Financial Markets

Financial markets contribute to the aggregate level of economic activity by the "intermediation effect." They also contribute directly to the welfare of borrowers and lenders by adding to the utility that they can get from a given set of resources. Both of these results can be demonstrated with the F–H model by comparing the financial adjustments that can be made in the absence of financial markets (see Figure 2-2) with those that can be made when financial markets are available.

Figure 2-4 reproduces the results presented in Figure 2-2 but with the addition of an opportunity line that provides for borrowing and lending at the same rate. An individual with a relatively large current endowment (panel A) will still want to save a share of his current resources but he will be able to lend it when financial markets are available. The new opportunity line will make it possible for him to reach a higher preference level and to increase the utility that he can get from his given resources. An individual with scarce current resources (panel B) can adjust his unbalanced moneyflows position by borrowing and can increase his expenditures in the current period. This reduces the funds he has available for the combined periods by the amount of interest payments, but this cost is more than offset by the utility he gains from the timing of the expenditures. He, too, moves to a higher preference level. Both sides of the market benefit.

Whenever a borrower uses funds that would not otherwise have been spent, the aggregate level of expenditures is increased and the intermediation effect is observed. Any expenditures based on borrowed funds offers a potential illustration of the intermediation effect because the borrower could not make the expenditure without the loan and the lender would not use the funds for current expenditures. The full effect is reduced, however, by any side effects of the market interest rate on the lender's current expenditures. The amount of new expenditures is measured by the distance a_1c_1 of Figure 2-4B. But some contraction in current expenditures by the suppliers of funds is indicated in the model by the amount b_1c_1 in panel A. The aggregate intermediation effect would be the net of all such changes.

Any spread between borrowing and lending rates reduces the

---

[2]Irving Fisher, *The Role of Interest* (Macmillan Company, New York, N. Y., 1907). Jack Hirshleifer, "On the Theory of Optimal Investment", *Journal of Political Economy* (August 1958).

FIGURE 2-4
FINANCIAL MARKETS AND SOCIAL GAINS

A. Lender's Gain

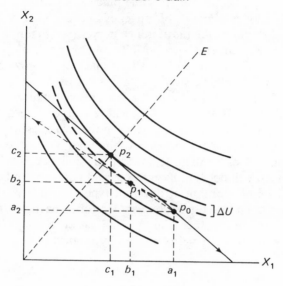

B. Borrower's Gain

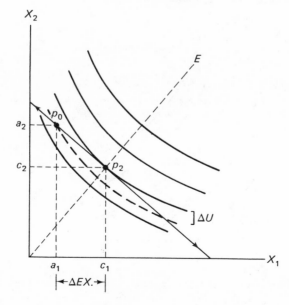

theoretical benefits obtained from financial markets. If it is assumed, for purposes of illustration, that borrowers and lenders have the same indifference maps and that borrowing and lending rates are the same, they will find their respective best positions some place along an equilibrium line *E* that represents a locus of points of tangency between the market opportunity line and the slopes of the indifference curves (see Figure 2-5). In such a world, everyone with an endowed position on either side of the equilibrium line will gain by the existence of financial markets. If, however, there is a spread between borrowing and lending rates, the set of equilibrium borrowing positions (E_b) will be to the left of the equilibrium lending line while the equilibrium lending positions will remain on line *E*. Those whose endowed position falls in the space between the two lines will be unable to take advantage of financial markets. Attempts to adjust their positions in either direction will move them to lower preference levels. The size of the excluded segment will depend upon the spread between the borrowing and lending rates, the distribution of different types of indifference maps, and the distribution of endowed positions. Any reforms or improvements in the financial process that reduce the spreads between the borrowing and lending rates expand the benefits offered by financial markets.

FIGURE 2-5
DIFFERENTIAL BORROWING AND LENDING RATES
AND EXCLUSIONS FROM FINANCIAL MARKETS

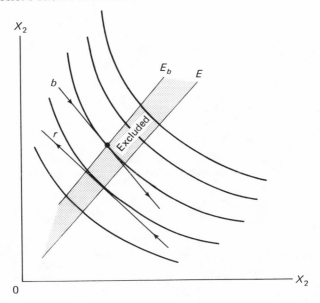

Financing Capital Outlays

The most important demands for funds arise in the financing of capital outlays and real investments of all types. Productive opportunities in the real world are not available to everyone. They may depend on an established economic position, on the skills and expertise needed to exploit the possibilities, or merely on the ability to see the opportunities for profit. These opportunities, when they occur, are not necessarily matched with the funds needed to take advantage of them. Some businesses with opportunities may not have the money. Others with money may not have the opportunities. Financial markets can bring the two together.

For those with excess funds, investment opportunities are a competitive alternative to lending opportunities offered by the financial markets. In this model, the decision to invest is simply a matter of the best yield. An investor will continue to invest as long as the return on the investment (e) is higher than the market rate of interest (r). In Figure 2-6A, he will invest to point p_1 where the marginal return on investment (e) is equal to the market rate (r). This level of investment (a_1b_1) may or may not result in the best combination of expenditures and may or may not lead to the highest preference level, but it maximizes the present value of his potential wealth. When the market rate (r) is used as the discount rate, the discounted present value of point p_1 is measured at p^* on the X_1 axis. This amount is greater than the present value of his endowed position and exceeds the present value of any other position on his investment opportunity function. This conclusion can be confirmed by drawing market opportunity lines through other points on the investment opportunity function. In all cases, it will be seen that the intersection of these lines with the X_1 axis (which measures the present value) will be to the left of p^*.

If the optimum level of investment does not provide the best pattern of cash flows, the pattern of cash flows can be adjusted by borrowing or lending. In the example in Figure 2-6A, the investor has more funds than he can profitably invest. He will lend any excess funds at the market rate (r) which exceeds the return he could get on additional investments until he reaches an equilibrium at p_2. Note that the discounted present value of p_2 is equal to that of p_1. His additional savings do not add to the present value of his fully invested position but they add to the utility he gets from the time pattern of his expenditures.

When the investor has surplus funds, he will finance the investment with his own funds. A corporation, for example, may use retained earnings for *internal financing*. The availability of surplus funds may depend in part upon dividend policies but these policies are implicit in the shape of the indifference map. A change in dividend policies may affect the source of funds used to finance investment but it will not affect the level of investment.

FIGURE 2-6
FINANCING CAPITAL OUTLAYS

A. Internal Financing

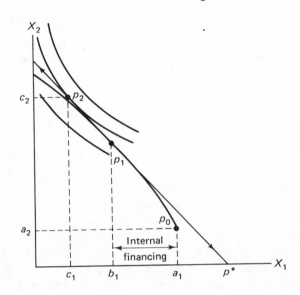

B. External Financing

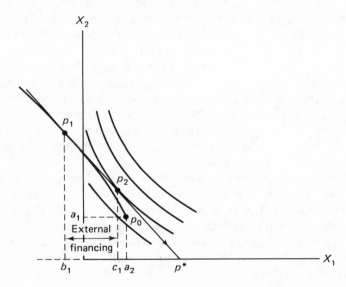

If an investor does not have the funds he needs for investments, he will have to borrow them. Figure 2-5B illustrates the role of *external financing* in the investment process. An investor with the same investment opportunities as in Figure 2-5A, but without the funds required to finance the investment, will invest the same amount. He will invest as long as the marginal return (e) covers the market rate (r) because he knows that this action will maximize the discounted present value of his combined resources and that he can borrow the funds he needs to finance the investment and to balance his cash flows. He will borrow the amount b_1c_1 which will give him the best allocation of his combined resources at point p_2.

Under the assumptions used in these examples, the level of investment will be independent of the investor's endowed position and his indifference map. In the real world, uncertainties and risks complicate this simple theoretical result but the model serves to identify the motives underlying investment decisions and the nature of the decisions involved.

Sources of Demand and Supply

The demand for and supply of funds in financial markets arise from a lack of synchronization between the expenditures of corporations, governments, or individuals and the flow of funds to be used for these expenditures. In the absence of any new money, the supply of funds for the economy as a whole is limited to the sum of the current endowments of all segments of the economy. A large share of these funds will be used for consumption and for internal financing but the surpluses, temporary or long-run, can be made available for loans to other segments of the economy.

The irregular patterns of cash flows reflected in the endowed positions of individual participants in financial markets give rise to both the demand for and supply of funds. The role of different endowed positions can be illustrated by assuming that all businesses, governments, and individuals have the same indifference map (see Figure 2-7A). At any given market interest rate, a line (E) can then be drawn on this map that represents the locus of equilibrium points, i.e., points of tangency between the market opportunity line and the indifference curves. Anyone with an endowed position to the right of this equilibrium locus will be a supplier of funds. Anyone to the left of the line will be able to improve his position by borrowing.

The role of real investment opportunities can be introduced by adjusting all the endowed positions of those who have investment opportunities to include the effects of investments on their cash flow positions (p_1 positions in Figure 2-6). These fully invested positions will be to the

FIGURE 2-7
SOURCES OF DEMAND AND SUPPLY

A. Different Endowments (similar time preferences)

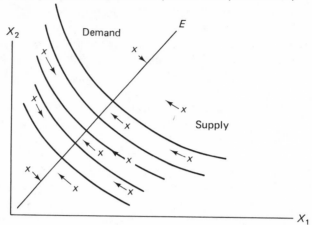

B. Endowments Adjusted for Investment Outlays

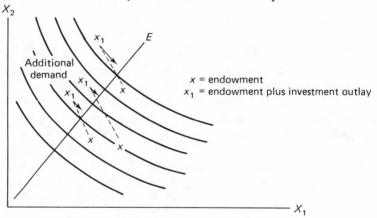

x = endowment
x_1 = endowment plus investment outlay

C. Different Time Preferences (stable cash flows)

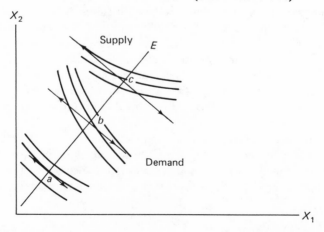

left of the equilibrium line for all those who require external financing. They will need funds to finance their investment outlays and to obtain the best allocation of their resources.

The equilibrium line assumes that the demand for and supply of funds is in balance. If the demand exceeds the supply, an increase in the market rate will serve to (1) reduce the demand for funds to finance investments and (2) increase the supply of funds by shifting the locus line to the left. If the supply exceeds the demand, the process will be reversed.

Some of the simplicity of this illustration is lost when the assumption of uniform indifference maps is dropped. Differences in time preferences can also affect the demand for and supply of funds. The role of variations in time preferences can be illustrated by examining the effects of different time preferences on the demand for and supply of funds of individuals whose endowed positions fall on the equilibrium line in the previous example. With a stable pattern of time preferences, they will neither borrow nor lend (see case *a*, Figure 2-7C). With a strong preference for current expenditures, as in case *b*, they will be able to improve their position by borrowing. With a strong preference for future expenditures, as in case *c*, they will be willing to supply funds. The real world includes variations in time preferences as well as variations in endowments.

The F–H model gives a comprehensive picture of the economic and financial decisions of businesses, governments, and individuals under the assumptions of the model. It indicates the amount that will be invested, the amount that will be spent for current consumption or current operating expenses, and the amount that will be borrowed or supplied in financial markets. But the student is warned that the sum of these individual solutions cannot be used as the aggregate demand and supply functions for the economy as a whole. When the process is in equilibrium, the sum of individual current endowments represents the total supply of funds for all internally and externally financed expenditures. But this does not provide for any elasticity in the supply of funds—either expansion or contraction. Under the assumption of certainty, all of the funds received will be spent or placed in financial markets. No one will hold cash balances for precautionary and speculative reasons. Thus, the assumption of certainty excludes the variations in holdings of money balances that provide for much of the elasticity in aggregate money supply function under the Keynesian liquidity preference approach. It also, of course, does not provide for the actions of the monetary authorities.

Inflation and Financial Adjustments

The role of expected inflation on the decision process and on the level of interest rates can be illustrated by the F–H model. The inputs into the model from the current period (X_1) will be unchanged but the inputs for the second period (X_2) will have to be adjusted to reflect the expected (with certainty) changes in prices. Investment opportunities have to be reappraised. Higher prices imply inventory profits and higher returns on fixed components of the productive process so that the investment opportunities function will shift upward. This upward shift will lead to a high level of investment (at the given market rate) and to an increase in the demand for funds in financial markets (see Figure 2-8A). Or, if the expanded investment is financed internally, it will lead to a decrease in the supply of funds placed into financial markets. Commodity speculation either for inventories or for hoarding should be treated as an investment opportunity for this purpose.[3]

The impact of inflationary expectations on endowments depends upon the nature of the income source. Some gain by inflation and others lose. The overall effect should be to shift the endowed positions in nominal terms upward by the amount of the expected inflation, i.e., to p'_0 in Figure 2-8B. This shift will put upward pressure on the interest rates but this effect will be largely offset by the changes in indifference maps that will accompany inflationary expectations. If it is assumed that real preferences for goods and services are unchanged, the same allocation of real resources will require a larger allocation of nominal resources to the second period to cover the higher prices. The nominal time preference map will shift toward future preferences or the slopes in absolute terms will be reduced. This shift will reduce the pressure on interest rates (see Figure 2-8C).

Summary

Financial markets and institutions permit businesspeople and consumers to use their resources more efficiently to achieve the long-run time patterns of expenditures that best suit their needs and objectives. The financial decisions faced by economic units of all types involve choices between current and future expenditures. These choices are influenced by long-run objectives and are constrained by available resources. The existence of financial markets is assured by the diversity of the opportunities and objectives among various sectors of the economy and by the irregular patterns of the cash flows that must be used to support their plans. Nearly every economic unit can at one time or another improve its time pattern of expenditures by borrowing or lending. The resultant pressures of demand and supply are brought into balance by changes in the interest rate. This process sets the underlying pattern of adjustments in financial markets. In

---

[3]The same results could be obtained by shifting the time preference curves toward current expenditures to indicate hoarding, but this is a less desirable treatment because the economic intent is clearly to provide for future gains rather than for current expenditure benefits.

FIGURE 2-8
INFLATION AND THE DEMAND AND SUPPLY OF FUNDS

A. Shifts in Investment Opportunities

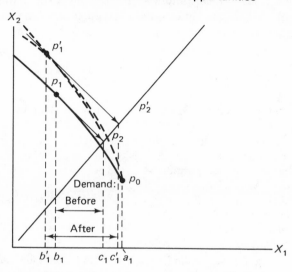

B. Shifts in Endowed Position
C. Shifts in Nominal Time Preferences
(real unchanged)

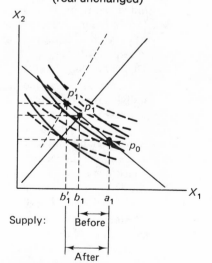

the real world, uncertainties and risks remove some of the precision from the theoretical solutions, and the complexities of individual financing needs and objectives introduce nonprice considerations into the process, but the central behaviorial tendencies remain. The next six chapters are devoted to a closer look at the practical financial needs and objectives of various sectors of the economy and to the identification of the complexities that they introduce into the theoretical discussion of the financing process.

QUESTIONS AND PROBLEMS

1. Give an example of an event that could shift an individual's indifference map toward a preference for future expenditures.

2. a. Plot an individual's two-period endowed position when he expects an income of $15,000 in both periods. Calculate and plot the discounted present value of that position when the borrowing and lending rate is 5 percent. (Ans. $29,285.71)
    b. Calculate the value of his position after he has invested $10,000 at an average return of 10 percent. (Ans. $29,761.90)
    c. Calculate the value of his position when he borrows $5,000 at the market rate to finance the investment.

3. a. Illustrate and describe the financial situation of an individual (or firm) who is in an equilibrium position without borrowing or lending.
    b. Show how a change in his endowed position would convert him to a supplier of funds.

4. a. Show how a decrease in the market interest rate would convert the individual in question 3a into a borrower.
    b. Derive the individual's demand curve for funds. (*Suggestion:*—unrealistically large changes in interest rates will simplify the graphic problems.)
    c. Derive his supply curve.

5. a. Illustrate and describe the equilibrium level of investment for an individual that involves neither borrowing nor lending in financial markets but assumes that one exists. Comment on the likelihood that this position is a realistic one.
    b. Show that the position in part (a) maximizes the discounted present value of the individual's potential wealth alternatives.
    c. Illustrates the effects of an increase in the market interest rate on (1) the level of investment and (2) the discounted present value of the individual's wealth position.

6. a. Demonstrate the implication of a change in an individual's endowed position for the amount of his investment.
    b. Demonstrate the implications of a change in his indifference map for the amount of his investment.

c. Comment on the implications of your answers to (a) and (b) for the relationship between an individual's financial situation and the amount he invests.

SELECTED REFERENCES

FAMA, EUGENE F., and MERTON H. MILLER, *The Theory of Finance*. New York: Holt, Rinehart and Winston, 1972.

FISHER, IRVING, *The Theory of Interest*. New York: Augustus M. Kelly, 1965. Reprinted from 1930 edition.

HIRSHLEIFER, JACK, "On the Theory of Optimal Investment Decision," *Journal of Political Economy* 66 (August 1958), 329–52.

———, *Investment, Interest, and Capital*. Englewood Cliffs, N.J.: Prentice-Hall, Inc., 1970.

Financing Corporate Needs

3

A free enterprise system looks to its citizens for its economic growth and development. When its markets are working successfully, it controls their activities by offering profits and by imposing losses. The view of capitalism that sees the money and initiative as coming from a few extremely wealthy and powerful individuals does not accurately describe modern industrial society. Business leaders must take the initiative in planning and developing products and ventures but, in the modern version of capitalism, they are seldom using their own money. Their financing comes largely from the retained earnings of corporations and from the savings of the public. As Berle and Means pointed out in their classic book on the modern corporation, professional managers are at the center of the decision process and their decisions and choices are directly influenced by their sources of funds.[1]

Corporate financial activities penetrate every phase and form of financing. Their long-run needs are reflected in new debt issues, new stock issues, in directly placed loans with insurance companies and other financial institutions, and in specialized instruments such as mortgages and equipment certificates. Their short-run needs are served by bank loans, by sales of money market instruments, and by intra-business financing. The outstanding amount of corporate financing, including all forms of debt and equity but excluding intra-business financing, had a market value at the end of 1973 of $1,711 billion. This was about $500 billion larger than the sum of financial claims against all other nonfinancial sectors of the

[1]Adolf A. Berle, Jr., and Gardiner C. Means, *The Modern Corporation and Private Property* (New York: Macmillan, 1933).

economy. In addition to being users of credit, corporations are suppliers of funds on many occasions. They hold substantial amounts in money market securities. They are also active in the use of credit as a promotional tool to expand and support their sales.

The financing problems of a corporation can be divided into the long-run problems of raising funds for growth and expansion and the day-to-day problems of handling cash flows. The first set of problems appeared in the F–H model in the financing of investment opportunities. The second set appeared as the financial adjustments needed to obtain optimal use of available resources. The first two sections of this chapter deal with these two sets of problems. The third section examines the use of credit as a promotional or sales tool.

Financing Capital Outlays

Corporate investment in a free enterprise economy is often the cutting edge of social and economic change. These changes may not always please social reformers, but the initiative rests with those who see and take investment opportunities. Even the most powerful businessman, however, must be responsive to the needs of his potential customers, and the most successful business ventures are those that have successfully captured the moods and wishes of the public. A social reformer may have doubts about the social contribution of Disneyland or of overpowered and luxurious automobiles, but few people are content to let anyone else decide how their money should be spent or how their "dollars should be voted."

In the F–H model, a business will take any and all investment opportunities that have an expected return equal to or larger than the borrowing rate. If it cannot finance the investment from the corporation's funds it will turn to external sources to obtain the funds. In practice, both the decision to invest and the problem of raising the funds is more complex. All investment alternatives involve some risks and the amounts are discrete, so that the actual investment opportunities function is likely to be discontinuous in a way that complicates both the decision process and the financing. The external sources of funds are likely to be quite different from the perfectly competitive markets assumed by the F–H model. In the real world, borrowers and lenders are distinct economic units with specific financial needs and objectives. A corporation trying to raise money is only one of many potential borrowers. It must compete with the U.S. Treasury, with state and local governments, and with households in its search for mortgage loans or consumer credit. The corporation must convince potential suppliers that the risks and potential rewards are actually as the corporation sees them.

There are several considerations in practical financial management that are not implicit in theoretical models: (1) the potential for differences in opinion between the borrowers and lenders on the risk and return on a given venture; (2) imperfections in financing markets; (3) the existence of financial target ratios, such as debt-to-equity ratios, that reduce the range of alternatives; and (4) specialized financing needs of both the borrower and the lender that require special contract features. These considerations lead to a complex range of financial contracts with a variety of features and rates. One of the essential skills of a corporate treasurer is the ability to raise funds at the lowest cost in ways that are consistent with needs of the corporation. This might mean the use of leasing agreements, mortgages, or other instruments, as well as stocks and bonds.

There is some empirical evidence that the independence of the investment decision from the related financing problem, which was implicit in the F–H model, does not realistically describe the financing process. For example, Dhrymes and Kurz found a significant degree of interdependence between dividend and investment policies.[2] This result would not be observed if conditions in external financing markets permitted the corporation to achieve its objectives in terms of the optimal level of both investment and dividend payout. The actual level of investment is influenced by the ability of the corporation to find appropriate financing. These results should not be interpreted as undermining the usefulness of the F–H model, but as extensions of the implication of the model to the practical realities of financial behavior.

Internal sources of funds, principally undistributed profits and depreciation allowances, provide a large share of funds for corporate investment. But a financing gap of varying size always exists (see Figure 3-1). This gap has to be filled with external funds of various types. The amounts raised by stock, bonds, and mortgages provided the funds for one-sixth to one-half of their total fixed outlays (see Figure 3-1B). Other needs were financed with short-term funds.

The composition of long-term financing since 1950 has varied from year to year (see Figure 3-2). Long-term bonds provided the largest share of the total throughout this period, with the amounts of new equity issues varying widely. Mortgages became a relatively more important source of funds in the early 1970's.

The statistics on corporate financing do not give the full story of the scope and complexity of the process. Several sources of funds are not included in either the corporate statements or the aggregate statistics. Leasing arrangements and other forms of "off-statement financing" may not be included. In addition, the classifications used for statistical purposes

---

[2]Phoebus J. Dhrymes and Mordecai Kurz, "Investment, Dividends and External Finance Behavior of Firms," *Determinants of Investment Behavior* (New York: Columbia University Press, 1967), pp. 427–67.

FIGURE 3-1

A. Internal Financing and External Financing Needs

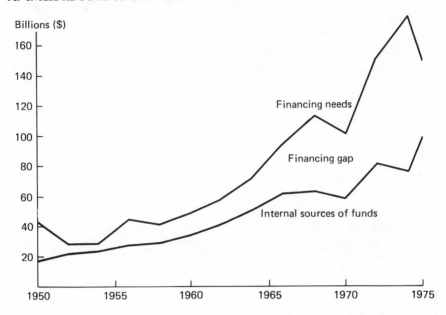

B. Selected Financing Ratios

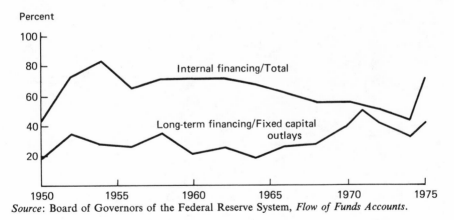

Source: Board of Governors of the Federal Reserve System, *Flow of Funds Accounts*.

conceal the diversity and variety of the instruments and techniques that are actually used.

A variety of different instruments and different sources of funds provide important alternatives in practice. Although they may not be perfect substitutes, they are competitive alternatives. For example, a small corporation may find it difficult or expensive to try to sell securities to the

FIGURE 3-2

A. Sources of New Long-Term Funds

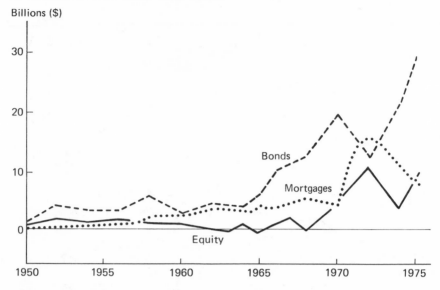

B. Percentage Distribution of Long-Term Sources

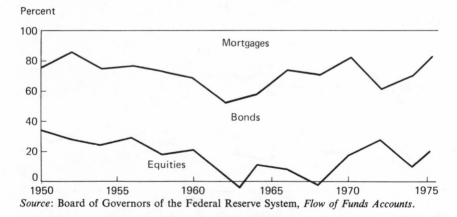

Source: Board of Governors of the Federal Reserve System, *Flow of Funds Accounts*.

public and may prefer to place them directly with large insurance compan-ies or pension funds. The practical field of finance is concerned with identifying the needs of both the borrower and the lender and with tailoring financing arrangments to fit those needs.

Figure 3-3 shows the principal suppliers of long-term funds for corporations. Households, including private trusts and nonprofit institu-tions, hold the largest share of corporate equities. The holdings of financial

FIGURE 3-3

HOLDERS OF CORPORATE SECURITIES, SELECTED DATES
(PERCENTAGE DISTRIBUTION)

Holder	1950	1960	1970	1975
Equities[a]:	100.0	100.0	100.0	100.0
Households	91.6	87.8	81.5	75.4
Life insurance companies	1.4	1.1	1.7	3.1
Pension and retirement funds	.8	3.8	8.4	12.3
Open-end investment companies	2.0	3.3	4.4	3.7
All others	4.2	4.0	4.0	5.5
Corporate Bonds[a]:	100.0	100.0	100.0	100.0
Households	13.0	12.1	19.9	19.5
Commercial and savings banks	11.0	5.3	5.3	8.3
Life insurance companies	63.2	53.1	36.0	32.9
Pension and retirement funds	8.7	24.9	30.9	31.5
All others	4.1	4.6	7.9	7.8

[a]Includes the securities of foreign and financial corporations.
Source: Board of Governors of the Federal Reserve System, *Flow of Funds Accounts*.

institutions and pension funds have been growing in importance and have become an important consideration in the markets for those securities. Financial institutions have always been the largest holders of corporate bonds and mortgages, and, as principal sources of corporate financing, they are in a very real way the partners of the large corporations in shaping and determining the course of investment plans and objectives.

Financing Current Needs

We can think of an established corporation as a self-perpetuating unit. Its capital provides the output and sales that generate a stream of cash flows. If the cash flows provide for the replacement of capital, the firm does not need long-term funds unless it decides to expand. But unless it is in the most unusual position, it still faces a wide range of short-term financing problems. The problems of short-term financing have traditionally not attracted the attention of economists because they represent day-to-day routine activities that do not normally affect the level of output or employment. They are, however, of considerable interest to observers of financial markets because of their implications for interest rates and for the elasticity of the aggregate supply of funds.

The current assets of a corporation are distinguished from fixed assets or capital by the fact that they are continuously turning over. The total amount may or may not vary appreciably but the individual items are continuously being replaced. This churning feature gives them a type of "turnover liquidity" that is used as a justification for financing these assets with short-term loans. From the lender's point of view the funds generated by reductions in inventories or receivables automatically provide for the repayment of the loans that are secured by these assets. However, these assets are essential to a firm's day-to-day operations, and, despite the fact that they may vary widely in amounts from time to time, they are a permanent feature of the financial needs of a corporation.

Some share of current assets is usually held in liquid form to enable a firm to meet its current payment obligations and to provide longer-run liquidity. These assets include currency and demand accounts and various types of money market securities. Since all of the current assets provide some liquidity, they are used in measures of a firm's liquidity. An excess of current assets over current liabilities is regarded as one measure of the ability of a corporation to withstand adverse cash drains.

To the extent that an excess of current assets over current liabilities is maintained, the excess (sometimes called *working capital*) has to be financed. Figure 3-4 shows the short-term financing needs of corporations since 1950 and the internal funds available to support them. The difference between these two amounts represents the short-term financing gap that had to be filled by funds obtained from other corporations in the form of trade credit or from other banks, other financial institutions, or directly

FIGURE 3-4
SHORT-TERM FINANCING NEEDS OF CORPORATIONS

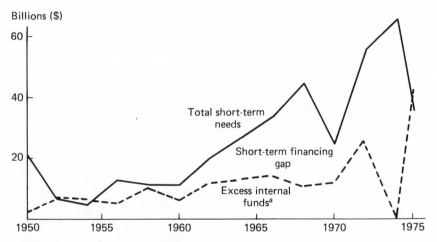

[a] Over and above the amounts needed to finance fixed capital outlays.
Source: Board of Governors of the Federal Reserve System, *Flow of Funds Accounts*.

from the money markets. Trade credit and bank loans provide most of these funds (see Figure 3-5). In the late 1960's and early 1970's money market instruments began to appear as a significant source.

The share of current assets held for payment and liquidity purposes depends on a corporation's approach to the cash management problem. The need for cash arises from lack of synchronization between cash inflows and outflows. The nature and extent of the problem depends upon the characteristics of these two sets of cash flows. If the pattern of flows is known with certainty, precise financial adjustments can be made. If pattern of flows is unpredictable, financial arrangements must provide for flexibility.

An endless variety in the pattern of cash flows can be observed in practice. A retail store will have outlays for inventories in advance of the seasonal sales peaks, with inflows related to the pattern of sales and to credit provisions. A corporation engaged in processing agricultural products may have a fairly stable cash inflow but will have large outflows when it has to buy the crops. For purposes of examining the financing problems that these variations create, two assumptions will be used. First, it will be assumed that over some period of time, perhaps a year, the total inflows

FIGURE 3-5
SOURCES OF SHORT-TERM FUNDS

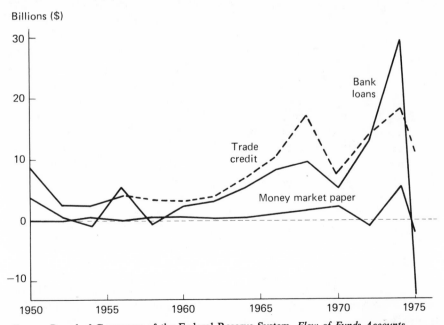

Source: Board of Governors of the Federal Reserve System, *Flow of Funds Accounts*.

will exactly match the outflows. This assumption merely distinguishes the problems of synchronization from those involving permanent or long-run financing. Second, it will be assumed that the pattern of cash flows is given and cannot be adjusted to reduce or solve the financial problems it creates. This assumption assigns fairly realistic priorities to the decision process and indicates that the given pattern of cash flows is dictated by needs and objectives of the corporation and that those objectives have higher priorities than any gains or losses involved in the day-to-day management of cash balances.

The lack of synchronization in cash flows can theoretically be handled with an average closing cash balance of zero by investing any surplus or by borrowing to cover any deficit. In practice, several considerations disrupt this perfect solution. First, satisfactory outlets for funds or sources of funds may not be available for the amounts and time involved. Second, transaction costs may exceed the potential income from lending out the surplus or the opportunity costs of holding funds idle to cover deficits. Third, uncertainty about the amount and timing of the cash flows introduces the possibility that potential transaction costs or market risk may offset expected returns. These barriers to the potentially perfect solution reflect the nature of the available financing alternatives.

In modern money markets, a large corporation that is paying out and receiving millions of dollars a day can come close to the theoretical zero balance in its checking accounts. It can achieve this position by two entirely different techniques or by some combination of both. It could theoretically manage its cash position without any short-term money market assets by lines of credit that could be reduced by the amount of surplus or be increased by enough to cover deficits. This approach depends upon the willingness of banks to accommodate variations of this type in its loan accounts. In the extreme and unlikely case, the corporation would not need to carry any current assets for payment or liquidity purposes. It could handle these problems entirely by variations in its credit lines. No firm needs to worry about a deficit if it can be sure that someone will lend it money.

It could also maintain a zero cash balance without borrowing by setting up a liquid asset portfolio large enough to cover any cash flow deficit and by buying and selling securities to adjust the cash account to zero. Modern money markets can accommodate adjustments of this type when the amounts are large. If the corporation adopts this approach, it is assuring its own liquidity and is not dependent on its ability to borrow. But it must also provide the funds from its equity or from debt financing. The cost of funds used to provide liquidity of this type will normally be higher than the return that can be earned on the portfolio, but the net cost can be justified as a legitimate business precaution.

In practice, corporations are seldom able to maintain zero cash balances (although they can come surprisingly close); and even if they could, it is unlikely that they would adopt either of these extreme approaches to handling their cash flow problems. Corporations typically hold cash balances and some money market assets as part of their current assets. The cash balances, however, may be held largely to satisfy the compensating balance requirements of their banks. The size of money market asset portfolios varies from company to company. Liquidity is a business cost. Some find it more important than others and some are in a better position to incur it than others. Those who can best afford it are probably least in need of it.

Inventories and receivables of various types are essential for business operations. The amounts involved are a matter of business policy. All current assets must be financed and the cost of the supporting funds is directly related to the size of the assets. Figure 3-6 shows the annual changes in principal types of current assets from 1950 to 1975.

The credit items that appear as current assets are often an essential feature of a firm's sales program. It may be to the advantage of a large firm with stable sources of funds to provide credit to its customers, particularly if the buyers do not have access to credit. Credit in this form is

FIGURE 3-6

GROWTH IN CURRENT ASSETS OF CORPORATIONS—ANNUAL CHANGES

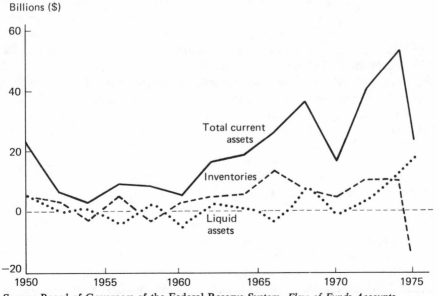

Source: Board of Governors of the Federal Reserve System, *Flow of Funds Accounts*.

an integral part of merchandising and can be used to create loyalty among customers or to expand sales volume. The costs of these asset items may often be justified by their role in merchandising and selling operations.

Credit as a Promotional Tool

Credit can be a powerful sales tool and an important competitive device. Inventories and productive equipment have to be purchased before they can be used to generate sales and cash flows. Someone has to finance these purchases. The financing can be handled by either the buyer or the seller. The choice depends largely on the comparative financial position of the two. The one with the best source of funds can use that advantage in negotiations for the sale. If the seller has good credit sources, he can provide the financing and thus reduce potential credit problems for the buyer. If the buyer has better credit arrangements, he can press for price concessions in lieu of credit. Any seller with a comparative money cost advantage over his competitors can use credit, or more favorable credit terms, as an alternative to price competition. In the business world, where inventories and capital equipment must be obtained before cash inflows can begin, the need for financing is clear. The uneven distribution of resources places the holders of these resources, or the ones with access to them, in a stronger bargaining position than those who need them.

The terms of credit may be as important as credit availability. Large capital outlays may be impossible for small businesses unless credit terms can be arranged that permit them to repay the loans in small periodic payments. Installment financing of the type used for financing automobiles and houses is widely used in financing equipment sales to small businesses. The size of the periodic payments can be adjusted to the income stream of the borrower by extending the maturity of the contract. Lease-purchase and pure leasing agreements are extensions of this principle, with different ownership arrangements. Financial implications are much the same as on long-term credit contracts, although legal and tax considerations may be different.

The use of credit as a sales tool has attracted the most attention at the final stage of the distribution process, as the goods move into the hands of the consumer. A retailer is likely to be in a stronger credit position than most of his customers. He is also likely to be in a position of decreasing operating costs so that additions to his sales volume can add significantly to his profits. Any costs of extending credit can therefore be justified by the improvement in his sales.

The most important use of consumer credit centers around sales of expensive durable items, such as houses and automobiles, where the cost of the item exceeds by sizable amounts the funds that are available to the purchaser from his current cash flows. Among lower income groups this condition may apply even on purchases of clothing or small household items. In many cases, these items can only be sold when they are accompanied by credit terms that provide for monthly payments small enough to be handled by the purchaser's budget. The credit terms have to be geared to the price of the item and to the purchaser's income.

Marketing experts also cite the role of credit in encouraging impulse buying and in creating customer loyalty as arguments for the use of credit plans. For all these reasons, credit has become an essential feature of the selling process. The availability of credit is the starting point. Special types of contracts and special credit terms can be used as additional inducements that can, in many cases, serve as effective alternatives to price concessions in the competition for sales.

The use of credit as a promotional tool creates a related set of financial and managerial problems for the corporation. The current assets generated by credit sales have to be financed. The extension of credit involves risks, collection problems, and the whole range of costs associated with lending operations. These specialized problems usually do not fit very well into the firm's regular production and sales operations. The company must, therefore, either obtain its own specialists or make arrangements for the credit function to be handled outside of the company. Various techniques and institutions have been developed to relieve businesses of some of these problems. Commercial banks and sales finance and factoring companies are active in assisting with credit operations. They may merely lend the funds needed to finance the receivables that credit sales generate. Or, they may purchase the credit contracts under various arrangements for sharing the risks and operating problems. In the extreme case, the financial institution may buy the contracts without recourse to the seller, and may take complete responsibility for all of the risks and management problems associated with providing credit. Some companies establish their own subsidiaries to handle credit operations. General Motors Acceptance Corporation, General Electric Credit Corporation, and International Harvester Credit Corporation are examples of credit subsidiaries. The separation of the credit function from the parent company makes it possible to obtain different types of financing and larger amounts of debt financing.

QUESTIONS FOR DISCUSSION

1. Financial ratios, such as debt-to-equity ratios, are often used by financial institutions in appraising the credit worthiness of corporations and as the basis for policy targets by the corporations themselves. How might this approach to financial decisions affect the actual level of investments undertaken by a corporation as compared to the level of investment indicated by the F–H model?

2. How would the reluctance of lenders to provide funds to a corporation be reflected in the financial policies of that company? In the level of investment? In the types of financial contracts used?

3. How would the sources of funds and financial policies of a very small corporation differ from those of a very large corporation?

4. What are the most important types of current assets? Why are these assets regarded as a source of liquidity when they are a relatively stable and permanent part of the corporation's asset structure?

5. What are the advantages to a corporation of extending trade credit to its customers? What are the disadvantages?

6. In an industry that is composed of a small number of large and well-known manufacturers and a large number of small wholesalers or retailers, what pattern of intra-industry financing would you expect? Why?

7. Why does the importance of internal financing by corporations vary widely from year to year? Is depreciation a source of funds?

8. Why does the relative importance of various sources of long-term funds vary widely from year to year?

9. Suggest a financial approach to increasing sales that does not require price reductions. What are the disadvantages of this approach?

10. Discuss the implications of the risks, uncertainties, and imperfections that are observed in day-to-day financial decisions for the equilibrium solutions indicated by the F–H model.

SELECTED REFERENCES

BERLE, ADOLF A., and GARDINER C. MEANS, *The Modern Corporation and Private Property*. New York: Macmillan, 1933.

FERBER, ROBERT, ed., *Determinants of Investment Behavior*. New York: Columbia University Press, 1967.

GOLDSMITH, RAYMOND W., *The Flow of Capital Funds in the Postwar Economy*. New York: Columbia University Press, 1965.

HICKMAN, BERT G., *Investment Demand and U.S. Growth*. Washington, D.C.: The Brookings Institution, 1965.

KUZNETS, SIMON S., *Capital in the American Economy: Its Formation and Financing*. Princeton, N.J.: Princeton University Press, 1961.

MEYER, JOHN R., and ROBERT R. GLAUBER, *Investment Decisions, Economic Forecasting and Public Policy*. Boston: Harvard University Press, 1964.

Financing Social
and Governmental Needs

4

Public debt, like private debt, must be judged by the tradeoff between the benefits of current expenditures and the disadvantage of future obligations. But the analysis of the benefits cannot be based solely on the analogy between public and private spending. The traditional reasons for public borrowing have been supplemented by the use of federal debt as a tool of economic policy. Economic policy objectives add a second set of criteria to the budgeting process that may or may not be consistent with the traditional objectives. Both sets of criteria enter into the shaping of the federal budget, and in the complexity of the process it is impossible to disentangle the two.

Everyone worries about the potential misuse of public financing. The political motives for borrowing are persuasive. Social reforms or other political goals are much easier to achieve when a direct confrontation with the taxpayers can be avoided. Government borrowing can be a powerful force for social change but it also offers temptations. The limits to public borrowing are elusive. They center around the willingness of creditors to accept the obligations and the ability of the government to raise the taxes to support the debt costs. Former Mayor Lindsay of New York City may have been right in saying that the financial problems of his successor were created by the failure of the city to retain the confidence of the financial community. Financial problems are easily solved if someone is willing to provide the money, but the limit to the relationship between the growth of debt and the ability of the tax base to support the expenditures is reached when creditors lose their confidence.

The U.S., state, and local governments are regular and active participants in a variety of financial markets. They sell long-term securities to finance schools, highways, wars, or mere deficits. They buy and sell short-term money market securities to adjust their cash positions, and they occasionally make loans in specialized markets. Most of the practical financing problems of governmental units are similar to those of corporations. The long-term debt issues of state and local governments are typically tied to some specific long-term construction or improvement project that can be treated as a form of public capital outlay. Shorter term borrowing and lending activities arise from the lack of synchronization between tax receipts and expenditures and are very similar to the cash management problems faced by corporations.

The federal government also uses a variety of credit programs to achieve special social objectives. Although these programs differ widely in form, they are all designed to encourage or subsidize expenditures that are "socially desirable." They all serve to modify the priorities in credit markets so that (1) borrowers who might otherwise be excluded from these markets can get loans and/or (2) the cost of borrowing to selective groups, or for selective purposes, is reduced.

The principal types of credit programs are:

1) *Direct loans*. The most direct method of making sure that some borrower or class of borrower gets a loan is to make it directly from government funds. The loans may be made directly from the funds of some department or agency that is under the federal budget, as in the case of loans for defense production or the emergency loan to the Lockheed Aircraft Corporation in 1971. The Federal Reserve's moneyflows statistics recorded $65 billion in loans of various types on the books of the U.S. government and agencies included in the federal budget at the end of 1973. These direct loans usually carry rates and terms that are more favorable than similar loans by private financial institutions.

2) *Sponsored credit agencies*. The Federal Land Banks were established in 1916 to assist farmers with mortgage loans. The Reconstruction Finance Corporation was established in 1932 to provide loans to businesses that were faced with financial difficulties, and the Federal Housing Administration was established in 1934 to support and stimulate the housing industry. These, and a variety of other agencies, have been used to provide credit or credit insurance for select purposes or to select groups. These agencies resemble private financial intermediaries in many ways except that they have specialized objectives and have direct or indirect governmental support or aid. The government's role in these agencies varies from direct capital contributions to sponsorship without guarantees. Even in cases where the government's role is largely supervisory, the credit markets have tended to assume that the government would accept responsibility in case of default, and the sponsored agencies get many of the benefits of the federal government's credit rating.

3) *Loan guarantee programs.* The federal government has many extensive programs of loan guarantees. It guarantees the securities of some of its sponsored agencies, of some private corporations, of some local governments, and of some foreign governments. It even guarantees the debts of a great many individuals under the Veterans Administration's mortgage program.

4) *Insurance programs.* The federal government has also developed a variety of insurance programs to give financial contracts covered by these programs an added element of safety, which improves their competitive standing in the money and credit markets. The most familiar are the Federal Housing Administration's (FHA) program for insuring mortgages and the Federal Deposit Insurance Corporation's (FDIC) program for insuring bank deposits.

5) *Income tax exemptions.* By exempting the income from selected securities from federal income taxes, the federal government can indirectly subsidize the issuers of the securities. This exemption, which applies to the securities issued by state and local governments, has given them a preferred position in the money and capital markets. Some of these advantages may be passed on to private corporations by the use of public borrowing authority to finance industrial facilities. The hidden cost of this program to the federal government is the amount of the tax loss. The benefits to the issuers of the securities arise in the spread between the market rates on securities of comparable quality and the rates on tax-exempt issues. An unwelcome side effect of these programs has been to provide a tax shelter for individuals with accumulated wealth.

Federal credit programs are an important feature of present day money and capital markets. The beneficiaries of the programs hold a preferred position in the market. Their gains are at the expense of the nonbeneficiaries who find credit more expensive and more difficult to get. The obvious solution for the marginal borrower who is being crowded out of the market is to turn to Congress for some form of assistance that will boost his credit status. But not all borrowers have equal access to Congress. Aid of this type is painless in that it does not involve public cash outlays, but it implies a redistribution of costs that are borne by those who must pay higher rates. Figure 4-1 shows the funds raised by the U.S. government and by federally sponsored or subsidized borrowers as a percentage of total funds raised in credit markets from 1950 to 1975. In the peak year, 1975, they accounted for 65 percent of all the funds raised. These tabulations do not include some types of funds raised under guarantee insurance programs, but they illustrate the magnitude of the potential impact of federal credit activities on primary credit markets.

The first two sections of this chapter deal with the direct financing needs of the U.S. government and of state and local governments. The

FIGURE 4-1

FUNDS RAISED BY THE U.S. GOVERNMENT AND FEDERALLY
SPONSORED OR SUBSIDIZED BORROWERS
AS A PERCENTAGE OF TOTAL FUNDS RAISED*

*Excluding amounts raised by equities.

[a] Includes funds raised by tax exempt securities of state and local governments,
Federally sponsored credit agencies and mortgages insured by the FHA or
guaranteed by the VA.

[b] Net increase in liabilities.

Source: Board of Governors of the Federal Reserve System, *Flow of Funds Accounts.*

third section deals with the special role of the federally sponsored credit agencies and their credit programs.

Financing the Needs of the U.S. Government

The financial needs of the U.S. government appear as the spread between expenditures and other cash outlays and tax revenues. A small share of this gap can be traced to financing needs that arise from increases in financial assets that appear in the federal budget. These items include holdings of the securities of credit agencies, and direct loans or advances made under various credit programs. Since there are no provisions for capital assets on the books of the federal government, long-run financing needs cannot be related directly to the growth in physical assets. The financing activities of the U.S. government have to be justified in terms of desirability of permitting current expenditures to exceed revenues. Ideally, the economic impact of deficit financing should serve as a dominant consideration in the decision to permit this imbalance, but the realities of the legislative and administrative process that determines the level of tax revenues and expenditures suggest that other considerations frequently play the dominant role in the size of the financing gap. The annual gap averaged about 6 percent of total expenditures from 1950 through 1975, and ranged from −7 percent in 1956 to 24 percent in 1975 (see Figure 4-2).[1]

The preferred credit status of the U.S. government places it in a unique position in the credit markets. The scale of its financing operations and the safety of its securities give it a wide range of financial options. In practice, the U.S. Treasury handles most of its financing by offering its securities in the private financial markets where they are purchased initially by large financial institutions or by dealers in government securities. It is one of a very small number of borrowers in primary markets that can deal directly with the individual suppliers of funds as well as with the major financial institutions and markets. It has taken advantage of its access to individual savers by issuing savings bonds that give the purchaser the liquidity and safety of a redeemable security and a fixed rate of return. Individuals held about 60 billion of these bonds at the end of 1973 (see Figure 4-3).

The daily impact of Treasury financing on the money and capital markets is much more important than the size of the annual financing gap would suggest. The short-run financing problems of the U.S. Treasury center around the day-to-day management of its transactions balances and of the refinancing problems arising from an outstanding federal debt that

---

[1]Since the formation of the Federal Financing Bank in 1973, the Treasury borrowing needs may be larger than the financing gap indicated by the official budget. The F.F.B. borrows from the Treasury to make loans to departments and agencies of the government, which appear as "off budget financing."

FIGURE 4-2
GOVERNMENTAL FINANCING NEEDS, 1950 TO 1975

A. Dollar Financing Gap

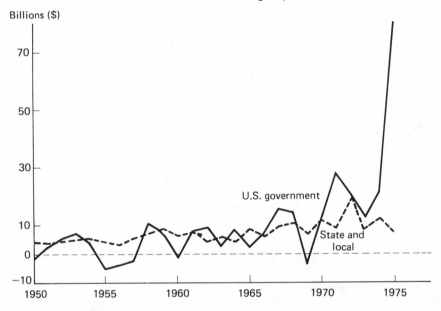

B. Financing Gap as a Percentage of Total Outlays*

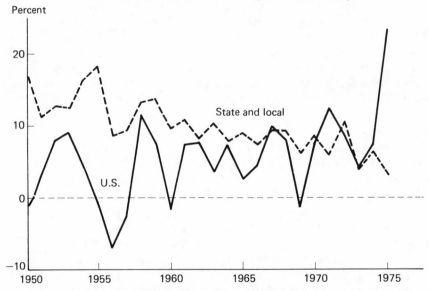

*Total expenditures minus receipts plus additions to social insurance and retirement accounts and net additions to financial assets.

Source: **Board of Governors of the Federal Reserve System,** *Flow of Funds Accounts.*

FIGURE 4-3

OWNERSHIP OF U.S. GOVERNMENT SECURITIES, END OF 1973
(BILLIONS OF DOLLARS)

| Sector | Total | Treasury issues | | | Other debt[a] |
		Short-term	Savings bonds	Other	
Total outstanding	422.1	153.1	59.8	125.6	83.6
Households	105.3	19.2	59.8	5.2	21.1
Corporations	5.4	.7	—	.4	4.3
State and local governments	31.0	15.7	—	11.4	3.9
Commercial banks	88.8	28.5	—	30.7	29.6
Other financial institutions	52.4	13.4	—	16.3	22.7
Foreign	54.8	21.0	—	33.8	—
Federal Reserve System	80.5	50.6	—	27.9	2.0
Other	4.0	4.0	—	—	—

[a]Includes agencies issues and loan participations.
Source: Board of Governors of the Federal Reserve System, *Flow of Funds Accounts*.

amounted to over $500 billion at the end of 1975. The Treasury's operations in the money and capital markets are followed closely by all other participants in those markets because of the temporary effects of these large operations on the daily markets. The daily public debt transactions of the U.S. Treasury for one week, picked at random, are shown in Figure 4-4. Although the Treasury reduced its outstanding debt by $1.1 billion

FIGURE 4-4

DAILY PUBLIC DEBT TRANSACTION, SAMPLE WEEK

| Date | (In millions of dollars) | | |
	Issues	Redemptions	Net change in public debt
March 1, 1976	2,016	2,270	− 254
March 2	402	395	7
March 3	3,198	6,442	− 3,244
March 4	7,456	7,287	169
March 5	2,765	598	2,167
Daily Average	3,167	3,398	− 231

Source: U.S. Treasury Department, *Daily Statement of Cash and Debt Operations of the U.S. Treasury*.

during the week, it issued new securities at a rate of more than $3 billion a day. New corporate issues of stocks and bonds for the entire month of March amounted to $4 billion.

Financing the Needs of State and Local Governments

Long-term financing needs of state and local governments are most closely associated with special bond issues for schools, highways, or other long-term projects. This type of financing is usually justified in terms of the stream of services that these projects produce, and the analogy with private capital outlays is appropriate.

Short-term financing is less commonly used by state and local governments and accounted for less than 10 percent of the net funds raised from 1950 through 1975. Most of this financing is in the form of tax anticipation notes that are frequently sold to the local banks. Some bond anticipation notes have also been used to obtain funds for the construction costs on capital projects. These notes are then funded when the long-term financing for the projects is completed. The proportion of the total outlays of state and local governments that have been supported by debt issues has declined somewhat from the high levels of the early 1950's (see Figure 4-2).

Most state and local bonds are sold by competitive bidding to investments bankers who reoffer the securities to the ultimate buyer. The cost of the issue to the borrower is determined by the market price and the underwriter's spread. The underwriter's risk is assumed by the investment banker or syndicate of investment bankers submitting the lowest bid for the issue. The tax exempt status of state and local issues makes them particularly attractive to individuals and institutions subject to relatively high income tax rates. Commercial banks and insurance companies are the major institutional holders of state and local government securities, with households also holding a substantial share (see Figure 4-5).

FIGURE 4-5

OWNERSHIP OF STATE AND LOCAL SECURITIES, SELECTED DATES
(PERCENTAGE DISTRIBUTION)

Sector	1950	1960	1970	1973
Total	100.0	100.0	100.0	100.0
Households	36.9	43.5	31.3	26.6
Corporations	2.7	3.4	1.5	2.1
Banks	34.8	25.9	48.8	50.8
Insurance companies	9.4	16.5	14.6	17.8
Other[a]	16.2	10.7	3.8	2.7

[a]Includes holdings of state and local government retirement funds.
Source: Board of Governors of the Federal Reserve System, *Flow of Funds Accounts*.

Federal Credit Agencies

The last half century has seen the development of a number of federally sponsored credit agencies that play an important role in the financing process. These institutions are similar to private financial intermediaries except for their specialized charter objectives and their sponsorship by the federal government, which gives them a preferred credit status in the money and capital markets. The extent of government sponsorship varies from agencies that are under the federal budget to agencies that are owned and financed entirely from private sources. The role of the federal government in the latter case is largely supervisory, but the implied protection of the debts of these agencies usually persists in the eyes of the purchasers of their securities. The purposes and functions of the federally sponsored agencies differ and can best be understood by examining the circumstances associated with their origins and subsequent development.

Farm credit agencies

The financing of agriculture has always presented difficult problems. The amounts needed are large. Mortgage funds are needed for the land and buildings. Intermediate-term credit is needed for the financing of equipment, machinery, and livestock. Short-term credit is needed for feed, fertilizer, and other cash flow problems that arise from the irregular pattern of income from farm crops. Those needs are accompanied by the high risk associated with the volatility of the prices on farm products, the variability of the weather, and the small specialized nature of single farms. Bank failures in the United States in the Eighteenth and early Nineteenth Centuries were closely related to problems with loans to farmers and on farm land. Federal assistance with farm credit problems began with the Federal Farm Loan Act of 1916. This act established 12 Federal Land Banks. They were financed by sales of stock to the public but with the understanding that the Treasury would purchase any unsubscribed stock and waive dividends on its subscription. These banks made loans on first mortgages through the National Farm Loan Association. The borrowers were required to subscribe to capital stock in the amount of 5 percent of their loans.[2] The capital obtained from the borrowers provided for reduction and eventual elimination of the Treasury's stock holdings.

The federal farm credit system has been expanded and modified by numerous legislative changes over the years. It evolved into three independent systems, under the supervision of the Farm Credit Administration, that offer a full range of credit facilities to farmers. The Federal Land Banks provide mortgage loans. The Federal Intermediate Credit Banks,

---

[2]Paul Studenski and Herman E. Kroos, *Financial History of the United States* (New York: McGraw-Hill, 1963), p. 262.

through local Production Credit Associations, provide short-term and intermediate-term credit. The Banks for Cooperatives provide the financing for farm cooperatives that have grown up as service organizations for farmers. All three systems are owned by the farmers. The U.S. Treasury no longer has any funds invested in the farm credit agencies and does not formally guarantee their securities. The system obtains its funds by selling debentures and notes in the money and capital markets. The successful credit record of these agencies and the implicit assumption by investors that the U.S. Treasury will stand by their securities in the event of default gives them a preferred credit rating in financial markets. Their borrowing costs are only a fraction above those of the U.S. Treasury.

Mortgage-related agencies

The depression of the early 1930's stimulated the federal government's efforts in the mortgage credit field. The Home Loan Bank system was established in 1932 with authority to rediscount mortgages for lending institutions and the Home Owner's Loan Corporation was established in 1933 to assume the mortgages of distressed homeowners who could not obtain accommodation from other sources.[3] Later, in 1934, as part of an effort to stimulate economic recovery and to direct funds toward housing, the Federal Housing Administration was established; it had a wide range of credit functions, including insuring mortgages made by private lenders.[4]

The role of the federal government in sponsoring and encouraging the flow of credit into mortgages has continued since that time. Numerous changes in the structure and organization of the agencies involved have occurred. The Federal Home Loan Bank System has been expanded and strengthened. It now serves as a central bank for savings and loan associations. As a lender of last resort it rediscounts the mortgages of these associations when they are pressed for funds and sells its own securities to obtain the funds it needs for this purpose. This process illustrates the role of the federal credit agencies in helping the housing industry find funds. The securities of the Federal Home Loan Banks, which have a preferred credit status, are, in effect, substituted for the savings deposits of savings and loan associations that for various reasons may be unable to obtain or hold their deposits. The process is reversed when credit conditions are eased.

The Federal National Mortgage Association was chartered to create a secondary market for home mortgages. Its operations were converted into private ownership in 1968. Its primary purpose is to provide a

[3]*Ibid.*, p. 373.
[4]*Ibid.*, p. 417.

secondary market for FHA- and VA-insured mortgages. It held mortgage loans amounting to $32 billion at the end of 1975.

The Federal Housing Administration and the Veterans Administration administer their respective mortgage insurance and mortgage guarantee programs within the federal budget. Neither agency is currently engaged in large-scale direct financing activities or in raising funds independent of the Treasury. The private mortgage loans backed by these two programs amounted to $135 billion at the end of 1973 and accounted for 21 percent of all outstanding mortgage credit.

Business-related agencies

Recent efforts of the federal government in supporting business credit needs have been on a relatively small scale. They have been limited primarily to the sponsorship of the Small Business Investment Corporations, the Export–Import Bank, and to some direct loan or guarantee efforts under special circumstances that seem to require federal intervention or support.

The Export–Import Bank is owned by the government and aids in the sale of U.S. exports and the purchases of its imports. The bank makes loans to importers or exporters of U.S. goods and in addition guarantees private loans for this purpose. It sells participation certificates in its loans to raise funds. These certificates, which give the holder a share of the bank's assets, are also a general debt obligation of the bank.

The direct and indirect loan and credit operations of the federal government almost defy description. New provisions are made continuously and older provisions expire. The list includes loans to college students, lease-purchase loans for public buildings, a new Environmental Financing Authority, flood relief loans, and loans by the Bureau of Indian Affairs. The role of the federal government in the credit field is varied and complex and is continuously changing.

QUESTIONS FOR DISCUSSION

1. How are the decisions of governmental units to borrow and lend similar to those faced by corporations? How are they different?
2. What are the social benefits and the social costs of various governmental credit programs? How do these programs affect credit markets?
3. What are some of the features of governmental securities that make them attractive relative to similar securities issued by private corporations? How can some of the benefits of these features be passed on to private corporations?

4. Discuss the political advantages of the use of debt financing for public expenditures and comment on the nature of the limits to public indebtedness. Do state and local governments and the federal government face the same problems?

5. Why do state and local governments hold substantial amounts in time and savings accounts and in U.S. government securities or other money market instruments?

6. What are some of the pressures for increased expenditures by state and local governments? Which types of expenditures can or should be financed by borrowing?

7. Can the F–H model be used to describe the borrowing and lending decisions of governmental units?

SELECTED REFERENCES

COPELAND, MORRIS A., *Trends in Government Financing*. Princeton, N.J.: Princeton University Press, 1961.

GAINES, T. C., *Techniques of Treasury Debt Management*. Glencoe, Ill.: Free Press, 1962.

OTT, DAVID J., and ALLEN H. MELTZER, *Federal Tax Treatment of State and Local Securities*. Washington, D.C.: Brookings Institution, 1963.

PECHMAN, JOSEPH A., *Federal Tax Policy*. Washington, D.C.: The Brookings Institution, 1971.

Report on the President's Commission on Budget Concepts. Washington: U.S. Government Printing Office, 1967.

ROBINSON, ROLAND I., *Postwar Market for State and Local Government Securities*. Princeton, N.J.: Princeton University Press, 1960.

STEIN, HERBERT, *The Fiscal Revolution in America*. Chicago: University of Chicago Press, 1969.

Household Financial Activities

5

Our affluent society has brought the privileges and burdens of financial decisions to all but the poorest and most dependent of its members. The buildings and industries that symbolize our national wealth have been built with the savings accounts, investments, pension funds, and insurance reserves of millions of people. Individuals own and finance much of our housing and the principal component of our transportation system—automobiles. The expanding role of consumers as an economic force can be traced in part to their access to financial markets. George Katona, in describing the changing role of consumers, lists two financial changes as essential. First, "the larger amount of reserve funds," and second, "the fact that buying on credit is today a generally accepted and widely practiced form of behavior."[1]

Households, including the very wealthy, have always supplied the major share of savings. However, the forms of savings have changed. Modern financial markets include a wide variety of savings alternatives that are available to nearly every income group. They also provide a variety of borrowing alternatives, ranging from mortgages for home financing to credit cards for day-to-day expenditures. The modern consumer is required to make financial decisions that were once the exclusive domain of the financial expert. This chapter deals with the factors that affect the financial decisions of households and with specific financial instruments and alternatives that have been developed to meet their specialized needs.

[1]George Katona, *The Powerful Consumer* (New York: McGraw-Hill, 1960), pp. 12–13.

Households as Suppliers of Funds

Consumers prepare for the future by saving. But not all forms of household savings supply funds to financial markets, and those that do show very different behavioral patterns. *Saving* is defined in economic terms as the difference between current income and current consumption. It is defined in accounting terms as an increase in net worth. These two definitions are consistent when the definitions of consumption and of assets are consistent. If current expenditures for houses and consumer durable goods are regarded as part of savings rather than as current consumption, they must also be treated as assets for accounting purposes. When items such as clothing are included in current consumption, they must be written off in the current period for accounting purposes regardless of the fact that, in many cases, they may provide a stream of services for many years. The distinction between expenditures that should be regarded as consumption and those that are treated as additions to assets is somewhat arbitrary, and the amount of "savings" therefore depends on the definition used.

Within the accepted definition of savings, the different types of savings have very different implications for financial markets. For our purposes, the ideal household accounting records would include all income (including insurance, pension, and other benefits paid by employers that add to the individual's savings) and would show the disposition of income into (1) consumption expenditures, (2) expenditures for houses or durable goods, (3) additions to financial assets, (4) payments on debts, and (5) increases in holdings of money (currency or demand accounts). All but the first of these items add to the individual's net worth and are properly regarded as savings. But only two of them (items 3 and 4) supply funds to financial markets, and those two items behave in very different ways. Additions to financial assets (item 3) include the most familiar types of savings—additions to savings accounts, purchases of stocks and bonds, and additions to insurance or pension reserves. Debt repayments (item 4) are largely contractual. The supply of funds from repayments depends on the pattern of past expenditures and on the terms of the debt contracts.

Somewhat more than half the gross savings of the household sector appears in the aggregate statistics as outlays for purchases of houses and consumer durables (see Figure 5-1). These figures, however, give a misleading impression of the financing process. Only a small share of current income is spent directly on the original purchase of houses and other durables (item 2). Most of the money for the purchase price is borrowed. The funds for these loans come from the savings of other consumers, either

FIGURE 5-1

HOUSEHOLDS AS SUPPLIERS OF FUNDS

A. Percentage of Personal Income

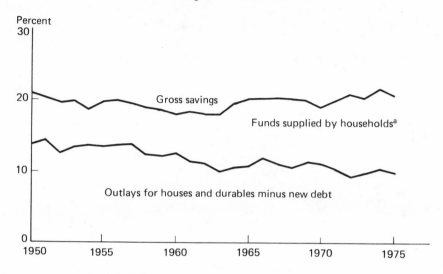

B. Percentage of Total Funds Raised (excluding equities)

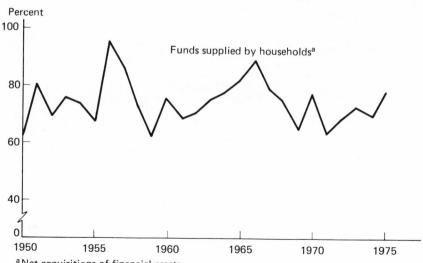

ª Net acquisitions of financial assets.

Source: Board of Governors of the Federal Reserve System, *Flow of Funds Accounts*.

in the form of deposits in financial institutions (item 3) or as payments on their loans (item 4). Payments on old loans provide most of the funds for new loans, but these amounts do not appear separately in the aggregate statistics. Good estimates of the volume of loan payments are not available, but they would, in all likelihood, amount to more than two-thirds of the total outlays for houses and consumer durables.

FIGURE 5-2

A. ANNUAL ADDITIONS TO HOUSEHOLD ASSETS

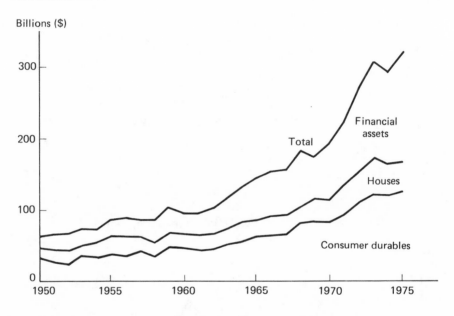

B. DISTRIBUTION OF ANNUAL CHANGES IN FINANCIAL ASSETS

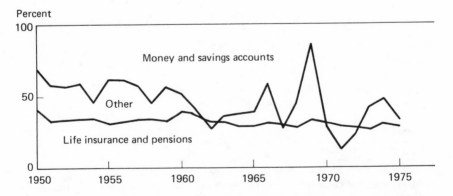

Source: Board of Governors of the Federal Reserve System, *Flow of Funds Accounts.*

The savings of the household sector not used to finance other consumers provide most of the funds for financing the needs of business and government. The net additions to the financial assets of the household sectors provided 60 percent or more of the total funds raised by all sectors from 1950 through 1975 (see Figure 5-1B). But only a small share of these funds is supplied directly to borrowers. The largest share goes into time and savings accounts at banks and other financial institutions (see Figure 5-2B). The next largest share goes into insurance and pension programs. This component of the savings stream is relatively stable from year to year and is, in many cases, beyond the direct day-to-day control of individual households. Only a small and highly volatile share of household savings is placed into credit market instruments, equities, or direct business ownership.

Studies indicate that consumer preferences for assets differ widely with age and wealth. The share of assets devoted to automobiles and liquid assets decreases with wealth, and the share devoted to business and investment assets increases with wealth.[2] The assets of the lowest income groups are dominated by automobiles and liquid assets. Houses increase in importance with wealth and age up to a certain level, and then decline in importance. Investment assets in the form of stocks, corporate bonds, and business ownership become an important share of wealth only for those with assets of $100,000 or more.

Decision to Save[3]

George Katona, in a summary of the results of a survey of the motives for saving, says, "There are only two motives to save which today are widely held by masses of the American population. They want to save, first, in order to accumulate a reserve fund against unforeseen contingencies and, second, in order to spend money later for specific purposes."[4] The specific plans included provisions for retirement or old age, educational funds for children, additions to houses, summer homes, long trips, and hobbies. Two potentially important reasons for savings—to provide an estate for one's heirs and for the income on savings—were seldom mentioned. In practice it may be hard to distinguish between savings that are

[2]Dorothy Projector, *Survey of Financial Characteristics of Consumers* (Washington, D.C.: Board of Governors of the Federal Reserve System, 1966), pp. 19–27.

[3]Discussions of the motives for saving usually focus implicitly on decisions to acquire financial assets. Some parts of these discussions, but not all, also apply to decisions to save through purchases of houses and other durable goods. The implications of these two forms of savings for the individual and for financial markets may be very different. The decision to purchase durable goods will be discussed in the last section of this chapter.

[4]Katona, *The Powerful Consumer*, p. 95.

accumulated for planned expenditures and those held for precautionary purposes. Various forms of savings can and do serve both purposes.

Saving is part of long-run financial planning, and the motives for saving can best be seen in the context of long-run expenditure needs and plans. Consumption theories provide complementary saving theories. Modern consumption theories have been concerned primarily with the problem of explaining the stability of consumption relative to income. The implicit savings theories have been concerned with the problem of explaining the relative volatility of saving. Keynes focused attention on the problem with his observation that

> The fundamental psychological law, upon which we are entitled to depend with great confidence both *a priori* from our knowledge of human nature and from the detailed facts of experience, is that men are disposed, as a rule and on the average, to increase their consumption as their income increases, but not by as much as the increase in their income.[5]

This statement has been interpreted to mean that the average and marginal propensities to save are greater than zero and that the marginal propensity to save is greater than the average propensity to save.

Behavioral explanations for the long-run stability of consumption have been advanced by Milton Friedman and Franco Modigliani. They both view the stability of consumption as arising from the consumer's attempts to achieve the best pattern of consumption over the long-run. Friedman considers current consumption as primarily a function of the consumer's *permanent income* where the amount of permanent income is measured as the discounted present value of the stream of future expected income receipts. The specific relationship between permanent consumption and permanent income is recognized to be a function of wealth, age, and tastes but, once determined, it is independent of transitory changes in income. The actual levels of consumption may deviate from the planned or permanent levels by the amount of transitory changes, but the permanent components remain to give the overall consumption its basic stability.

The Modigliani version is based on the "...notion that the purpose of savings is to enable the household to redistribute the resources it gets (and expects to get) over its life cycle in order to secure the most desirable pattern of consumption over life."[6] His life cycle version of long-run consumption theory is somewhat more flexible than Friedman's in that it

---

[5]J. M. Keynes, *The General Theory of Employment, Interest and Money* (New York: Harcourt, Brace and Co., 1955), p. 96.

[6]F. Modigliani and A. Ando, "Tests of the Life Cycle Hypothesis," *Bulletin of the Oxford University Institute of Statistics,* 19 (May 1957), p. 105.

provides for changes in the relationship between long-run income expectations and consumption through time.

The aggregate consumption theories suggest that the day-to-day variations in the flow of savings depend upon short-run changes in the level of economic activity. The longer-run variations in the supply of savings are also affected by the demographic and socioeconomic characteristics of the population. Studies show that the proportion of income saved (savings ratio) depends upon the demographic and financial characteristics of the household. The savings ratio increases with income. It is higher for self-employment households, including farmers, than for wage and salaried workers. Among self-employed households, the lower income groups may have large negative savings ratios while those in the higher income groups have exceptionally high ratios. Savings ratios also vary over the life cycle: they increase with age up to upper-middle age and then decline; they tend to be somewhat lower for those with higher levels of education; they tend to be higher among those with recent favorable changes in income; households that expect a decrease in income tend to save more; and so on. Structural changes in the financial characteristics or expectations of the population can affect the overall supply of funds.

A number of life cycle profiles have been presented by Fama and Miller to illustrate the relationship between income and expenditure patterns and changes in the household's financial position.[7] These illustrations provide examples of the potential socioeconomic variations in the pattern of household savings that can exist within an aggregate theory of savings related to individual life cycles. The simplest case of assumed stable income and stable expenditure needs is illustrated in Figure 5-3. This example also assumes a specific retirement date, the precise coordination of the amount of savings accumulated, and no need to leave an estate at the death of the consumer. It also assumes a zero interest rate.

The second case, somewhat more realistic, makes the same assumptions about the stability of expenditure needs (a symmetrical indifference map) but assumes a growth in income (see Figure 5-4). The maintenance of the desired level of expenditures in the early stages of a working career requires borrowing (at an assumed zero interest rate in the illustration) and the more rapid accumulation of savings just before retirement.

These examples are merely suggestive of the variety of savings-expenditure patterns. They emphasize the role of life cycle considerations in the decision process. Budget studies suggest a typical pattern of income growth with age. They also reveal the expenditure pressures associated with the early stage of family formation.

---

[7]Eugene F. Fama and Merton H. Miller, *The Theory of Finance* (New York: Holt, Rinehart & Winston, 1972), pp. 42–47. Adapted by permission of Holt, Rinehart & Winston.

FIGURE 5-3

A. LIFE CYCLE PROFILE OF STABLE INCOME AND EXPENDITURES (NO INTEREST RECEIVED)

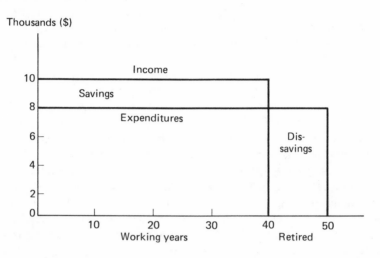

B. ASSET PROFILE

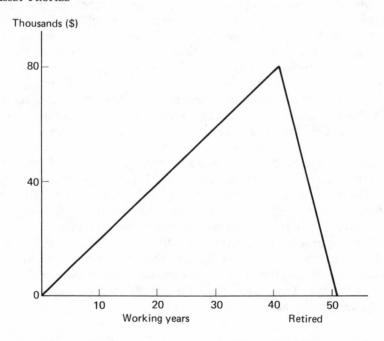

FIGURE 5-4

A. Life Cycle Profile of Growing Income and Stable
Expenditures (no interest received)

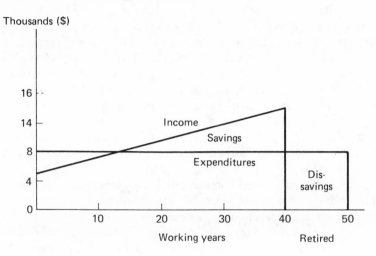

B. Asset Profile

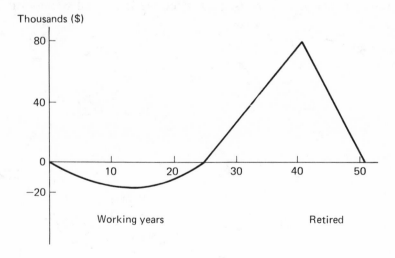

Households as Borrowers

Most consumer debt is not used to indulge current spending desires at the expense of future consumption. Most of the borrowing by households arises from purchases of houses or other durable goods that provide a future stream of consumption services. The consumer's decision is not a choice between current and future consumption. It is a choice about the source of his future consumption services and the method of payment for those services. Will he live in an apartment and pay rent, or will he buy a house and incur the costs of ownership including the payments on the mortgage and the interest charges? Most consumer borrowing decisions are easier to understand if they are regarded as analogous to business investment decisions where the stream of consumption services represents the expected return on the investment.

Debt is typically used for the purchase of houses and other major durables simply because the size of the expenditure is too large to be financed from the household's income stream. The purchase of a new house or other durable item adds to the assets of the household and the economy as a whole. But the amount of saving out of income at the time of the purchase may be very small. The purchase recorded as savings in the aggregate statistics for the household sector actually represents a demand for funds in financial markets. Saving for the individual begins with the

FIGURE 5-5
ANNUAL ADDITIONS TO HOUSEHOLD DEBTS

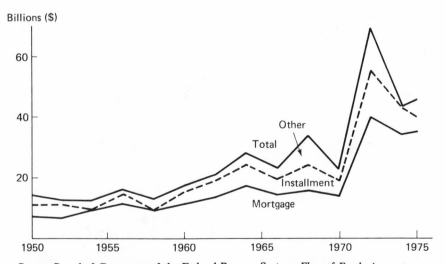

Source: Board of Governors of the Federal Reserve System, *Flow of Funds Accounts.*

first payment on the loan. The amount of the saving depends on the relationship between the payments and the depreciation of the asset. Debts are usually paid off faster than the asset depreciates so that some saving is likely to occur. The use of debt by consumers starts out as a demand for funds in financial markets, but it initiates a stream of repayments that provides the supply for most new loans. New funds have to be raised by lenders only when the demand for new loans exceeds the flow of funds from repayments. If the demand drops, the flow of repayments provides a supply of funds that can be diverted to other uses.

Some share of consumer credit may be used to accommodate simple time preferences for current expenditures. Households face cash management problems similar to those faced by corporations, and current cash shortages can be financed by the use of credit cards or other forms of short-term credit. Some share of longer-term personal loans may also be used for goods or services that are consumed immediately. Emergency medical expenses, Christmas spending, or vacations may be financed by installment credit. Credit cards and charge accounts are also used as a convenient alternative to using money as a means of payment. Credit used for this purpose reduces the transactions demand for currency and demand deposits. The cost of this type of credit may in many cases be absorbed by the retailer who provides the credit. In other cases, the user may be willing to pay for the convenience. Most modern credit cards and charge accounts offer the borrower the option of prompt payment with no service or finance charges, or delayed payment with charges.

Decision to Borrow

The decision to borrow is inseparable from the decision to purchase the house or automobile that leads to the need for funds. The loan itself has no separate utility. The unpleasant features of debt, such as the interest charges and the repayment obligations, are part of the basic purchase decision. Most buyers of houses and expensive durables do not have the option of paying cash. They do not have liquid assets that can be used, and the process of accumulating savings for the purchase involves a period of double costs for the services they are seeking. A renter who is trying to accumulate enough savings to buy a house for cash has to go through a period of paying for both current and future housing. Very few budgets permit large scale efforts of that type.

The discussion of factors that affect the demand for credit is therefore inseparable from the discussion of factors that affect the demand for houses and other durable goods. The list of factors includes income, changes in income, prices of houses and durable goods, and stock of houses and other durable goods. The demand for consumer durables is closely related to general economic conditions and to expectations about the future. It has some of the cyclical volatility associated with the demand for investment goods and inventories. The demand for new durables (including houses) is derived from the demand for the services that they generate. Any change in the demand for these services will create an accelerator effect in the demand for durables. For example, a 1-percent increase in the demand for the services of automobiles will require a 1-percent increase in the stock of automobiles. If it is assumed that automobiles are normally replaced every 10 years, 10 percent of the stock is being replaced every year. A 1-percent increase in the total stock represents an increase in the demand for new automobiles of 10 percent. The willingness to lengthen or shorten the life of durables also adds to the potential volatility of the demand for these assets and, indirectly, to the demand for credit.

The essential role of credit in purchase decisions creates a link between the supply of credit and the demand for houses and consumer durables. Changes in the supply of credit can affect the demand for houses and durables in a number of ways. Any reduction in interest rates reduces the cost of credit and therefore the overall cost of the item being purchased. But more importantly, changes in the supply of credit are likely to lead to changes in the availability of credit or to changes in credit terms. Consumers who do not have access to cash or credit cannot buy houses. They represent a demand potential but are not part of the market. Any expansion in the availability of credit brings some of these potential customers into the market, i.e., shifts the effective demand for houses and other durables. In the same way, potential customers who do not have enough cash for the down payment or who cannot afford the monthly payments are not part of the effective market for houses or expensive durables. A reduction in the required down payment or in the size of the monthly payment brings them into the market. Salespeople and real estate promoters are well aware of the role of credit in the selling process. Their practical and intuitive approach to the problem is supported by utility theory and by empirical evidence.

The use of credit varies widely among households and is closely related to the households' social, financial, and demographic characteristics. Surveys of the use of debt indicate the highest debt ratios among young families that are facing, for the first time, the problem of obtaining houses, automobiles, and all of the consumer durables that have become part of the American way of life. The proportion of households with debt is highest among young married families with children. It declines in higher age brackets and with household features that reduce expenditure burdens. The use of debt rises rapidly with income at the lower levels of income distribution and continues to increase until upper-middle income groups. The use of debt is lowest at the extreme ends of the income scale. Lower income groups cannot get credit. Higher income groups have better ways of paying for expensive durables. They can avoid the high interest costs and the burdensome contracts associated with consumer credit by liquidating securities or other assets. Purchases of houses and expensive durables by households with large investment portfolios can best be analyzed as a portfolio decision. They are, in effect, choosing among assets that produce different types of returns. The purchase will be financed by borrowing only if the return on their other assets is greater than the interest charges on the consumer credit contract or if there are reasons for not liquidating their assets.

Sources and Composition of Household Debt

Nearly all of the mortgage and installment debt incurred by households arises in connection with purchases of houses, automobiles, and other durables. The outstanding amount of these obligations amounted to 88 percent of their total obligations at the end of 1975 (see Figure 5-6). Since the data for households includes personal trusts and nonprofit organizations, these figures include some mortgages on multifamily dwellings and commercial properties. They also include a small amount of personal installment loans that are used for debt consolidation, medical emergencies, vacations, and other expenditures not directly related to purchases of homes and durable goods.

The relatively small share of "other consumer credit" arises from charge accounts, credit cards, and various types of service accounts. It is

FIGURE 5-6

HOUSEHOLD DEBT OBLIGATIONS, SELECTED YEARS*

(IN BILLIONS OF DOLLARS)

Type of debt	1950	1960	1970	1975
Total credit market instruments	71.9	216.3	459.3	722.1
Home mortgages	42.6	136.7	272.5	445.3
Other mortgages	2.4	9.2	20.5	27.2
Installment credit	14.7	43.0	102.1	159.8
Other consumer credit	6.8	13.2	25.1	35.5
All other	5.4	14.2	39.1	54.4

*Includes nonprofit organizations and personal trusts.

Source: Board of Governors of the Federal Reserve System, *Flow of Funds Accounts*.

often characterized as convenience credit. The remaining share of household indebtedness is related to the various types of household business activities and to borrowing by nonprofit organizations included in the data.

Savings institutions provide most of the home mortgage funds (see Figure 5-7). Commercial banks and insurance companies have substantial holdings, and in recent years ownership by federally sponsored credit agencies has become important as part of various mortgage and housing support programs.

Commercial banks dominate nearly all phases of consumer credit. They held about 43 percent of the outstanding amount of consumer credit at the end of 1975 (see Figure 5-7). In addition, they supply substantial amounts of funds indirectly through loans to finance companies and business organizations to help in the financing of their holdings of consumer credit. Since such a large share of consumer credit is related to consumer purchases, the initial credit arrangements are most conveniently made at the time of purchase. A wide variety of financing channels have

FIGURE 5-7

SOURCE OF CONSUMER AND HOME MORTGAGE FINANCING,
SELECTED YEARS (IN BILLIONS OF DOLLARS)

Source of funds	1950	1960	1970	1975
Home mortgages, total	45.2	141.3	280.2	458.2
Savings institutions	17.5	74.1	163.1	272.9
Commercial banks	9.5	19.2	48.0	76.4
Insurance companies	8.6	26.2	28.3	23.6
Sponsored credit agencies	9.6	21.8	16.1	51.1
Other			24.7	34.3
Consumer credit, total	21.5	56.1	127.2	195.4
Installment credit	14.7	43.0	102.1	159.8
Commercial banks	5.8	16.7	45.4	72.4
Finance companies	5.3	15.4	32.4	45.7
Credit unions	.7	4.4	13.0	25.3
Business	2.9	5.3	9.2	13.1
Other	.1	1.2	2.1	3.2
Noninstallment credit	6.8	13.2	25.1	35.5
Commercial banks	1.6	3.9	8.5	10.9
Business	5.0	8.7	15.5	23.1
Other	.2	.6	1.1	1.5

Source: Board of Governors of the Federal Reserve System, *Flow of Funds Accounts*.

developed to bring the basic sources of funds to the consumer at the point of purchase. The retailer may extend the credit and hold and service the obligations himself, sell the contracts to a bank or other financial institution, or offer bank financing in various forms directly to the customer. Or, in some cases, the customer may prefer to raise his own money and pay the retailer in cash. Regardless of the financing path, the funds must come ultimately from the savings of other households.

A close look at the loan contracts that arise from the various forms of household indebtedness reveals an almost endless variety of terms and features. The maturities range from 30 years to a few days. The loan may be secured by the object purchased, where the lender may actually hold the title, or it may be unsecured. The contract may provide for periodic payments, or it may require full payment on a single date. This variety can be traced in most cases to the attempt to adapt credit contracts to the specific needs of the borrower, while providing the lender with features he regards as essential. These arrangements represent an important part of the practical art of finance. The next chapter deals with the instruments and contracts that have been developed to handle the wide range of financial activities conducted by consumers and businesses.

QUESTIONS FOR DISCUSSION

1. Define savings and list the major types of household savings. Which types of household savings supply funds to financial markets? Which types do not?

2. Why does the purchase of a new house that appears in the aggregate statistics as gross savings sometimes not represent current savings of an equal amount for the household that makes the purchase? Why should it be regarded as savings for the economy as a whole?

3. What are some of the important considerations in the decision to save? How do these considerations affect the form of savings? What form of financial savings is most widely used? How does the pattern of financial saving change with wealth?

4. How does a household's decision to borrow money resemble the corporate decision to borrow? How does it differ?

5. Among what groups would you expect the use of consumer credit to be most common? Is this answer consistent with the life cycle theories of savings?

6. How do changes in the supply of credit affect the demand for houses and other durables?

7. It is sometimes said that the commercial banks supply a very large share (75 to 80 percent) of the funds for consumer credit. How can that statement be reconciled with the information in Figure 5-6, which shows the amount of consumer credit held by banks?

SELECTED REFERENCES

BEYER, GLENN H., *Housing and Society*. New York: Macmillan Co., 1965.

FRIEDMAN, MILTON, *A Theory of the Consumption Function*. New York: National Bureau of Economic Research, 1957.

GALBRAITH, JOHN KENNETH, *The Affluent Society*. Boston: Houghton Mifflin Co., 1958.

JUSTER, F. THOMAS, *Household Capital Formation and Financing, 1897–1962*. New York: National Bureau of Economic Research, 1964.

KATONA, GEORGE, *The Powerful Consumer*. New York: McGraw-Hill Book Co., 1960.

————, Burkhard Strumpel, and Ernest Zahn, *Aspirations and Affluence*. New York: McGraw-Hill Book Co., 1971.

KISSELGOFF, AVRAM, *Factors Affecting the Demand for Consumer Installment Sales Credit*. New York: National Bureau of Economic Research, 1952.

MAISEL, SHERMAN J., *Financing Real Estate*. New York: McGraw-Hill Book Co., 1965.

MCCRACKEN, PAUL W., JAMES C. MAO, and CEDRIC FRICKE, *Consumer Installment and Public Policy*. Ann Arbor, Mich.: University of Michigan, Bureau of Business Research, 1965.

MODIGLIANI, FRANCO, and A. K. ANDO, "Tests of Life Cycle Hypothesis of Savings." *Bulletin of the Oxford Institute of Statistics*, 19 (May 1957), 99–124.

Money

and

Other Financial Instruments

6

Money is one of those concepts which, like a teaspoon or an umbrella, but unlike an earthquake or a buttercup, are definable primarily by the use or purpose which they serve.[1]

This observation identifies the problem of defining money but does not solve it. The Federal Reserve System regularly publishes data for five versions of the money supply. Money serves many purposes. The traditional definitions focus on its role as a means of payment, a unit of account, a means of deferred payment, or a store of value. The more recent definitional problems center around its role as an economic variable.

Money as a Means of Payment

The most common definition of money focuses on its role as a means of payment. In this role, many things have served as money. Historical examples have included coconuts, cowry shells, rice, cattle, tobacco, cigarettes, and many other commodities, as well as gold and silver. The money role of a commodity has to be identified by the intent of the users. If the commodity is accepted with the intention of using it in exchange for something else, it is money. Despite the subjective nature of the criterion, the means-of-payment function provides a conceptually clear definition. The objects used as money may change, but the set of things included as

[1]R. G. Hawtrey, *Currency and Credit* (London: Longmans, Green, 1928), p. 1.

money can be distinguished from things that are not used as money. Things that are used as money can be used for other purposes. But the things that are not money cannot be used directly in exchange for other goods and services. They must first be exchanged for money. Modern savings accounts cannot be used at the grocery store. They have to be converted into money before they can be used to purchase goods and services. Under the means-of-payment definition of money, they are not money. The situation may change, however. Some savings institutions have been permitted to operate point-of-sale terminals that provide for transfers of funds from savings accounts. These accounts can be used for payments and would be classified as money under the means-of-payment definition.

Whether or not the means-of-payment function of money is accepted as the sole basis for the definition of money, it is one of the most important functions served by money. A good money system must provide an efficient means of payment. The best means of payment is one that is instantly accepted for any or all types of transactions and one that does not involve any transfer problems or costs. No single form of money is acceptable for all purposes: a New York cab driver won't take your check; a twenty-dollar Federal Reserve note is not very useful when you are trying to get a cup of coffee from a vending machine, and it would be extremely burdensome to purchase stock with coins. The U.S. system of payment provides for metallic coins, paper currency, and checks. All three have specific advantages and disadvantages. Together they cover the entire range of payment problems and provide a highly efficient payment system. Credit cards are not part of the means-of-payment system in their present form. They set up a debt obligation that must later be reduced by one of the official means of payment. But the payment system may change. If an electronic transfer system is developed that provides for transfers in bank accounts from the point of the transaction, an encoded card (literally a money card) might be used to replace the check as a transfer order, and credit cards could become a form of money under the means-of-payment definition.

A good money system reduces the search costs that are implicit in every stage of the economic process. The best system also minimizes the costs associated with the use of the medium of exchange itself, such as handling or transportation cost arising from the use of metallic currency, or the verification or inspection costs needed to establish the validity of some forms of money. The efficiency of a modern payment system can be appreciated only by looking at some of the historical problems that had to be solved.

The role of a medium of exchange in reducing search costs can be illustrated by looking at the exchange problems that arise in attempts to exchange two commodities in a barter system. The search costs can be expressed as a function of the probability of finding the correct match as part of a random search, and can be measured by the number of encounters that have to be undertaken to complete the exchange. It can be demonstrated that these search costs can be reduced by a two-stage exchange process when a third commodity exists that is more widely traded.[2] The third commodity becomes a medium of exchange. The gains to both traders can be measured by the reduction in number of encounters required for the exchange, and the corresponding economic gain can be identified. The analysis suggests that the most widely traded commodities will also be used as money in pre-money economies. This hypothesis is consistent with the information that is available for commodity money systems. Coconuts were used as money in tropical islands, tobacco was used in colonial Virginia and Maryland, and cattle were used in grazing societies.[3]

The ability of money to serve as the third commodity in the exchange process depends on its high exchange acceptability (low search cost, high encounter probability). The source of this acceptability is easy to see in the case of commodities that are widely used. The added role of serving as money can lead to changes in the commodity itself or to a differentiation of the commodity along the lines of its money and nonmoney functions. The use of tobacco as money in the American colonies led to changes in both the quantity and quality of the tobacco produced. Low-grade as well as high-grade tobacco served as money and the problems of variations in both the quality and quantity of tobacco eventually led to the adoption of more stable forms of money.[4] In ancient China, iron implements such as hoes and knives were used as currency. By the Seventh Century B.C., knives became a generally accepted medium of exchange, but the knives used as currency were very different from commodity knives. Holes were cut in the handles and they assumed a symbolic rather than a functional shape. They looked like coins with a hole in the middle and a short tail. The word *tao*, which meant knife, eventually lost its original meaning and was used to refer to a unit of currency.[5]

When a commodity money loses its commodity value its acceptance as a medium of exchange is harder to explain. There are historical examples of symbolic objects of little intrinsic value serving as money without any apparent official support. Acceptance as money in such cases

[2]Robert Jones, *A Theory of the Origin and Development of Media of Exchange*, Unpublished dissertation for Brown University.

[3]Paul Einzig, *Primitive Money* (London: Eyre and Spottiswoode, 1951).

[4]John K. Galbraith, *Money: Whence It Came, Where It Went* (Boston: Houghton Mifflin, 1975), pp. 48–49.

[5]Norman Angell, *The Story of Money* (New York: Frederick A. Stokes Co., 1929), pp. 80–81.

has to be traced to custom, tradition, or religious belief. The following quote from a Bantu farmer illustrates the potential distinction between the commodity and money value of cattle that were used as currency. He replied to an agricultural expert who was trying to persuade him to get rid of some diseased cattle:

> ...here are two pound notes. One is old and wrinkled and ready to tear—this one is a new one. But they are both worth a pound, aren't they? Well it's the same with cows. They are both a cow.[6]

The problem of maintaining the acceptability of paper currency and token coins is usually solved by (1) making the official forms of money legal tender for the settlement of debts and (2) making them acceptable for the payment of taxes. The acceptability of bank money, in the form of either notes (not permitted in the United States) or checking accounts, depends on the reputation of the bank and the banking system. In the days of "wildcat" banking in the Nineteenth Century, the notes of many banks were accepted only at sharp discounts or would not circulate at all in regions at some distance from the bank.[7] The possibility of long-run changes in the value of money does not normally affect its role as a means of payment. However, in periods of hyperinflation the standard means of payment may be replaced at least in part by commodity monies of some type.

Money as the Unit of Account

Everyone but the economic theorist uses monetary units as the measuring scale for economic transactions: food and clothing are priced in dollars; loan contracts are expressed in dollars; and pay contracts are negotiated in dollars. The use of monetary units as accounting units is dictated by its obvious convenience. Money is involved on one side of nearly all economic transactions. The use of any other measure would require an extra exchange rate conversion on all of these transactions.

The concept of value implies a comparison. The value of potatoes expressed in terms of their price provides a comparison with other commodities. The value of money can be expressed as the reciprocal of the price of a single commodity or group of commodities. The value of money expressed in terms of a single commodity is a specific measurable concept. When potatoes are 10 cents a pound, a dollar is worth 10 pounds of

---

[6]Einzig, *Primitive Money*, p. 127.

[7]Paul Studenski and Herman E. Krooss, *Financial History of the United States* (New York: McGraw-Hill, 1963), pp. 73–74.

potatoes. The value of money expressed in terms of more than one commodity becomes a statistical abstraction. The usefulness of the abstraction depends on the prices that are used in computing the index and on the statistical properties of the index. The value of money is usually calculated as the reciprocal of the consumer price index or of the price deflators used in the national income accounts (see Figure 6-1). These calculations are designed to obtain a generalized measure of the purchasing power of the dollar and to look behind the "monetary veil" at the real value of goods and services. By these measures, the 1975 dollar was worth 43 to 45 percent of the 1950 dollar.

The terms *value of money*, *purchasing power of money*, and *inflation* refer to the relationship between the standard monetary unit and real goods and services. Despite the conceptual and statistical difficulties of measuring this relationship accurately, some distinction needs to be made between price changes that result from changing conditions in specific

FIGURE 6-1
VALUE OF MONEY, 1950 TO 1975 (INDICES 1950 = 100.0)

markets and those that are somehow attributed to developments in the payment system. Instability in the value of money reduces its usefulness as a store of wealth and as a standard of deferred payment. The appearance of cost-of-living clauses in labor contracts is a sure sign of instability in the value of money. Some instability in value, however, does not seriously reduce the use of money as a means of payment. Money in this role can be turned over rapidly enough to avoid major changes in value and its comparative advantages over most of the alternative means of payment are usually considerable. Only in periods of hyperinflation do commodities appear as money substitutes.

Money as an Economic Variable

Control of the money supply is accepted as the responsibility of a modern government. This authority has such important economic and social implications that it cannot be treated merely as an administrative operation that involves the printing and coinage of money of various types. Any change in the supply of money is marked as an economic force, and the problems of controlling the supply must be solved in the context of overall economic policy.

Since the largest component of the money supply in the United States consists of demand deposits at commercial banks, the principal changes in the money supply can be traced to these accounts. The problem of defining money as an economic variable arises from the problem of differentiating economic effects of changes in demand deposits from economic effects of changes in similar accounts that are not included in the means-of-payment definition of money. New money is introduced into the economy through the loans and investments made possible by the growth in demand accounts. The growth in other accounts at banks and savings institutions also provides funds for loans and investments, and the economic implications of the two types of growth seem to be much the same. The recognition of this similarity has led to the argument that, for control purposes, the concept of the money supply should be broadened to include the deposits of banks and, perhaps, other financial institutions which are similar to money and appear to have similar economic effects.

What concept of money is most useful for control purposes? It is not obvious that the traditional means-of-payment concept is best for this purpose. The possibilities range from the traditional definition, which has been designated as M_1, to all short-term financial assets that serve as good money substitutes for portfolio purposes. Techniques that could be used to control the correct monetary aggregate if the best one could be identified are theoretically available. The search for the best concept is taking two forms. The first consists of attempts to identify impact similarities or differences that will serve as the basis for the best definition. The second consists of statistical tests of the relationship between various aggregate combinations and the level of economic activity. The issues in this search are complex and controversial. They will be considered in detail in the second part of the book.

Money in the United States

Money as a means of payment in the United States consists of metallic coin, paper currency, and accounts on which checks may be drawn. The administrative control of the supply is the responsibility of the Federal Reserve System. Some of the coinage functions rest with the Treasury Department and the U.S. Mint, but the issuance of currency and coin is in the hands of the Federal Reserve System. Nearly all the paper currency outstanding is in the form of Federal Reserve notes. An official description of the outstanding types of coin and currency is shown in Figure 6-2.

FIGURE 6-2
STATEMENT OF UNITED STATES CURRENCY AND COIN
DECEMBER 31, 1975

	Outstanding amounts in circulation[a] (In billions of dollars)
Total Currency and Coin	86.5
Currency:	
Federal Reserve notes	77.0
United States notes	0.3
Types no longer issued	0.3
Coin:	
Dollars	0.9
Fractional coin	8.1
Currency by denominations	
One dollar	2.8
Two dollars	0.1
Five dollars	3.8
Ten dollars	10.8
Twenty dollars	28.3
Fifty dollars	8.2
One hundred dollars	23.1
All other	0.4
Total	77.6

[a]Outside of the Treasury and the Federal Reserve Banks.
Source: Department of the Treasury, *Daily Statement of United States Currency and Coin.*

The procedures of the Federal Reserve System permit the public to decide how much and what type of coin and currency it wants. The system supplies coin and currency on demand and takes back any surplus that the public or the banks do not want to hold. Payments for the additions or reductions in currency holdings are made in the reserve accounts of member banks. Although, as will be seen later in Chapter 14, the changes in public holdings of currency can affect the total money supply, these effects can be offset by the actions of the Federal Reserve System. The variations in the coin and currency components of the money supply can be regarded primarily as an indication of the type of money that the public wants to hold.

The principal component of U.S. money defined as a means of payment consists of the demand accounts on which checks may be drawn. The official statistics on the money stock published by the Federal Reserve System avoid any attempt to endorse a single definition by supplying the components for most of the alternatives (see Figure 6-3).

FIGURE 6-3

COMPONENTS OF MONEY STOCK AND RELATED ITEMS
(AMOUNTS IN BILLIONS OF DOLLARS—NOT SEASONALLY ADJUSTED)

Item	Outstanding amount (End of December 1975)
Demand deposits and currency:	
Currency	75.0
Demand deposits:	
At member banks	162.1
At domestic nonmember banks	66.3
Time and savings deposits:	
CD's	83.5
Other	365.0
At nonbank thrift institutions	425.2
U.S. government deposits	4.2
Measure of the Money Stock	
M_1 (currency and demand deposits)	303.4
M_2 (M_1 plus savings and time accounts other than CD's)	668.4
M_3 (M_2 plus nonbank thrift deposits)	1,093.6
M_4 (M_2 plus large negotiable CD's)	751.8
M_5 (M_3 plus large negotiable CD's)	1,177.0

Source: Board of Governors of the Federal Reserve System, *Federal Reserve Bulletin* (April 1976), p. A12.

The money supply defined as a means of payment is approximated by the currency and demand deposit items shown in Figure 6-3 and corresponds to the M_1 concept shown at the bottom of the table. A conceptually accurate measure of all means-of-payment would also include small amounts of a variety of new types of accounts. Some savings institutions have checking accounts or payment systems that appear in a variety of forms and under a variety of names. Checking accounts have also appeared as the right to withdraw funds by draft from liquid asset mutual funds. These accounts illustrate the attempts by various types of institutions to attract funds by offering the payment advantages of money forms that earn interest. They also illustrate some of the dynamic forces that are continuously at work in shaping the payment system.

Financial Instruments

The financial wizardry that attracts attention in the popular press often takes the form of a particularly ingenious type of financial instrument or contract. Financial instruments serve as contractual arrangements between borrowers and lenders and have to provide for the complex needs of both groups. The supplier of funds wants safety, liquidity, and the best possible return. The borrower needs a specific amount of money for a specific period of time. He may not be able to guarantee either the safety or the liquidity of the loan. He may also have special repayment problems or needs. The successful loan officer is one who finds terms that are the most convenient and attractive for the customers and, at the same time, serve the best interests of the bank. The successful corporate treasurer is the one who designs instruments that are most attractive to the suppliers of funds but, at the same time, protect the interests of the company. The interest rate is only one of the features of a financing package; there is usually some tradeoff between the interest rate and various nonprice features. A good financial contract provides the mix of stated interest rate and contract features that is most attractive to the participants. This discussion will be concerned primarily with functional features of financial contracts and with techniques used to solve special financial problems.

Reduction of risk

Risk is one of the most persistent of financial problems. It serves as a potential and actual barrier to a wide range of financing activities. The supplier wants to be sure that he gets his money back, and a variety of contract features can be introduced to protect his interests. Some of these features limit the activities of the borrower and prevent him from taking actions that might endanger the supplier's funds. The indenture agreements on corporate bonds can contain a wide range of controls over the activities of managers. They are likely to restrict the type of business that the corporation can conduct and the sources of new funds that it can use. The restrictions may be designed specifically for special risk problems.

A wide variety of contract features has been developed to separate the lender's risk from the general risks faced by the borrower and to protect the lender's position in the event of default. Many of these arrangements give the supplier *collateral* in the form of a claim on some specific asset. Mortgages, equipment certificates, and various types of lease agreements provide this type of protection. A form of pass-through financing, sometimes used by financial institutions, gives the supplier of funds a claim on a specified group of the mortgages or loans held by the borrower. This gives the supplier the dual protection of both sets of borrowers. The financial agreements can also give the supplier a *preferred position among creditors* in case of default. The complete hierarchy of corporate financing ranges from senior debt to subordinated debt of varying degrees, to preferred stock, and eventually to common stock. The financing costs, as would be expected, are associated with the degree of subordination. *Guarantee arrangements* can be included where the borrower's contract is guaranteed by some public or private arrangement. The U.S. government guarantee programs have been extended to a wide range of private borrowing: loans for exports and imports, ship-building, housing, and many others. Banks may guarantee the special obligations of some borrowers. *Insurance programs* have also been developed to protect the supplier of funds. U.S. government programs cover the deposit liabilities of banks and savings institutions and various types of loans. Private credit insurance can be obtained on some types of contracts.

All of these techniques for reducing the supplier's risk tend to reduce the borrower's costs. Some of them may be unattractive from the borrower's point of view but they represent concessions that he may have to make to get funds or that he may be willing to make to get a reduction in borrowing costs.

Repayment provisions

As was seen earlier in the discussions of the financing needs of corporations, governments, and households, borrowed funds are used for many purposes. They may be used for the construction of a specialized factory that has an expected productive life of 40 years or they may be used for temporary shortages of funds that may last only a few days. Financial instruments have to be adapted to these specific purposes.

In practice, the maturities of financing arrangements range from common stock, which does not anticipate the repayment of the initial investment, to one-day notes. The maturity of the obligation may materially affect its attractiveness to suppliers of funds. They may have specific time horizons or they may have preferences for specific maturities. Many investors prefer to avoid long-term commitments; others may want them. The difficulties faced by savings institutions in adjusting to higher levels of interest rates illustrate some of the problems that may arise from long-term loan commitments. Many of these institutions were unable to pay savings rates high enough to hold their deposits because of the limitations imposed by the rates they were earning on their mortgages. The structure of interest rates on contracts with different maturities will reflect the borrower's needs and the investor's preferences. It is normally assumed that suppliers of funds will insist upon higher returns on long-term contracts. However, the problem of comparing rates on contracts with different maturities is complicated by expectations about changes in rates. These problems will be discussed in detail in Chapter 16.

It is frequently to the advantage of both borrower and lender to provide for some gradual schedule of repayments over the life of the loan. The stream of services or income generated by the assets purchased with the loan and the depreciation of the asset provide guides to the pattern of repayments. Lenders have found that periodic payments provide a type of budgetary discipline that may be important for some borrowers. Any break in the pattern of payments also serves as an early warning system for potential credit problems. Amortized contracts are standard for mortgages, automobile financing, and equipment financing. Sinking funds and serial bonds provide these features for municipal and corporate financing. The repayment pattern is an important feature of financing arrangements. Maturities that are too short can impose financial problems for the borrower that can add to the risk of the loan. Maturities that are longer than necessary reduce the flexibility of the supplier of funds.

Short-term loans may provide for specific repayment schedules or dates or may be made under open lines of credit. Bank credit lines give borrowers an important degree of flexibility and protection in their financing arrangements, but at the same time they impose commitments on the banks, which can create problems. Loan demands are usually at a peak when the market is tight and money is hard to find, and the bank is committed to raising the funds needed to honor its credit lines. The bank is usually in a better position to raise funds than the borrower, but its efforts may involve special costs. Banks are compensated for these risks by commitment fees or by compensating balance requirements that promise the bank deposit funds as a form of payment for the commitment.

Flexibility and liquidity

Plans and circumstances change. Either the borrower or the lender may find that he wants to get out of some financial arrangement. The borrower may want to repay before his loan is due, or the lender may want to be repaid before repayment is due. In either case it is unlikely that the other party to the contract will be enthusiastic about the change. The problem of reversibility is somewhat easier to solve for the borrower than it is for the lender. Loan contracts may specifically provide for early repayment and the lender's interests may be protected by a prepayment penalty. The size of the penalty will depend on the market conditions at the time the contract is written and on expectations about the future trend of interest rates. Call provisions, which give the issuer the right to call the bonds in advance of maturity at some specified price, are frequently added to corporate or government security issues. On many types of shorter-term loans, prepayment is permitted without penalty.

Providing the lender with liquidity, however, is a more difficult problem. Very few borrowers are in a position to repay their loans at the convenience of the supplier. They need the protection of specific maturities and repayment schedules. The U.S. government provides for redemption upon demand of its Series E Savings Bonds, but very few borrowers are in a position to offer this privilege. The inability of the borrower to provide the supplier with liquidity is one of the major barriers to direct borrowing–lending arrangements. Most loans are handled by financial institutions because they can offer their suppliers liquidity while, at the same time, they can give their borrowers the protection of specific maturities. The accounts of banks and savings institutions are almost perfectly liquid. Savings institutions can theoretically require notice of withdrawal, but that right is seldom enforced. Financial institutions incur some management and liquidity problems by promising to redeem debt on demand, but they are compensated for these problems by the lower rates they have to pay on contracts that provide liquidity.

The borrower can, in some cases, satisfy the supplier's need for liquidity by issuing marketable securities. This option only exists, however, for very large corporations and government units whose securities can command a good secondary market. The existence of a secondary market makes it possible for all those who can qualify for the market to offer liquidity in the form of marketability and to obtain the benefits of the reduced costs of funds. But most borrowers are not in a position to take advantages of this option.

Profile of a financial contract

Individual financial contracts and instruments may not display the diversity that is attributed to snowflakes but they are seldom identical. Any feature that is of importance to either the borrower or the lender will be reflected in the contract. The nonprice features, implicit in the financial contract itself, include size, maturity, prepayment penalties, redemption or call features, negotiability, schedule of payments, and collateral. The risk on the contract is inseparably tied to the financial characteristics of the borrower as well as to the protective provisions of the contract. The interest rate, one of the most flexible features, will be adjusted to reflect the other features. Each financial agreement has its own distinctive features, and one of the important arts of applied finance lies in designing contracts that best accomplish the objectives of the designer.

QUESTIONS FOR DISCUSSION

1. Why would you expect a commodity money system to develop if no better means of payment existed? What characteristics would be exhibited by the commodity selected for the role of commodity money?

2. Why is money without intrinsic value accepted in exchange for commodities of real value?

3. Comment on the following statement: "Instability in the value of money destroys the usefulness of money."

4. Compare the operations of a payment system that officially designated a share of A.T.&T. stock as the standard unit of account with a system that uses the dollar as a unit of account.

5. What information is provided by an index of the value of money based on the consumer price index? Is it a good measure of the impact of inflation on a specific company or individual?

6. In what way do the economic effects of a growth in the money supply appear to be similar to those of a growth in savings accounts?

7. Discuss the techniques that can be used to protect the lender from some of the risks of lending money. How does the use of these techniques affect the other features and terms of financial contracts?

8. Why is the call privilege sometimes provided on bonds? How are the suppliers of funds persuaded to accept this feature?

9. Can you think of any circumstances in which changes in contract features might affect the level of spending and therefore the level of economic activity?

SELECTED REFERENCES

ANGELL, NORMAN, *The Story of Money*. New York: Frederick A. Stokes Co., 1929.

EINZIG, PAUL, *Primitive Money*. London: Eyre and Spottiswoode, 1951.

FEDERAL RESERVE BANK OF CLEVELAND, *Money Market Instruments*, 1964.

FEDERAL RESERVE BANK OF RICHMOND, *Instruments of the Money Market*, 1968.

GALBRAITH, JOHN KENNETH, *Money: Whence It Came, Where It Went*. Boston: Houghton Mifflin Company, 1975.

HAWTREY, R. G., *Currency and Credit*. London: Longmans and Green, 1928.

KEYNES, J. M., *A Treatise on Money*. New York: Harcourt, Brace and Company, 1930.

ROBERTSON, D. H., *Money*. New York: Harcourt, Brace and Company, 1929.

Nature of Financial Risk

7

The desire for safety and liquidity creates a major barrier to the movement of savings into loans. In the F–H model, where certainty was assumed, the alternative of holding surplus funds in money balances was rejected as being inferior to market opportunities that paid interest. In practice, the alternative of holding money balances cannot be so easily rejected. The potential supplier of funds may prefer the liquidity and safety of money balances to financial alternatives that involve either risk or the loss of liquidity. The success of financial markets depends on the availability of financial alternatives that provide the potential supplier of funds with combinations of safety, liquidity, and return that will induce him to give up his money balances. This chapter deals with the problems of identifying and measuring financial risk and with the role of risk as a barrier to financial activity. Chapter 8 examines the concept of liquidity and the techniques that have been developed to provide potential suppliers of funds with liquid alternatives to their money balances.

Two types of risk are found in financial contracts. *Default risk*, or credit or lender's risk as it is sometimes called, is present to some degree in all financial contracts. It arises from the possibility that the borrower will not repay the loan. The potential losses range from 100 percent of the interest and principal to zero percent. The best abstract description of default risk is the frequency distribution that describes this full range of possible outcomes. *Market risk* arises from the possibility that the contract will have to be sold at a loss. It is measured by the variations in the sale price of the contract. It includes the pleasant possibility of a capital gain, as well as the unpleasant possibility of a loss. Losses are limited to the amount of the investment (possibly with some provision for the opportunity costs of the funds involved), and the gains are, theoretically at least, unlimited.

Default Risk

The binomial distribution serves as a simple model of the frequency distributions associated with default risk. It gives the probability that a given number of loans (x) in a portfolio of n loans will be bad:

$$f(x) = \binom{n}{x} p^x q^{n-x} \tag{1}$$

where:

p = probability of a bad loan
q = probability of a good loan
$p + q = 1.0$

The sum of the probabilities of all possible outcomes equals 1:

$$\sum_{x=0}^{n} \binom{n}{x} p^x q^{n-x} = (p+q)^n = 1.0 \tag{2}$$

The distribution of the default risk on any given type of loan depends on the expected rate (p) and on the number of loans in the portfolio (n). In practice, loss rates are developed from experience with a particular type of loan time. If the expected loss rate were 0.5, the distribution would resemble a normal frequency distribution (see Figure 7-1). As the loss rate decreases, the mean of the distribution shifts toward the favorable end of the scale and the distribution becomes very skewed. Since, in practice, the loss rates tend to be very small (usually less than 0.01), the distributions that describe default risk are extremely skewed and are almost impossible to illustrate graphically. The distributions for a single loan and a portfolio of 10 loans with bad debt ratios ranging from 0.5 to 0.01 are shown in Figure 7-1. When only one loan is involved, the expected loss rate or the mean of the distribution does not measure a realizable outcome. The loan is either good or bad.

An increase in the number of loans increases the variety of possible outcomes and introduces three important changes in the features of the probability distribution that describe default risk. First, the possibility of a total loss becomes less as the number of loans increases. Second, the possibility of no losses also becomes less as the number of loans increases, or the likelihood that some losses will be incurred increases as the number of loans increases. Third, the density of the distribution around the mean increases as the number of loans increases.

FIGURE 7-1
Expected Loss Rate and Distribution of Default Risk

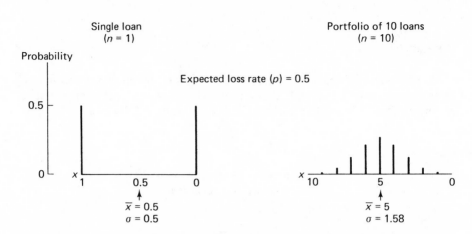

Single loan
(*n* = 1)

Portfolio of 10 loans
(*n* = 10)

Expected loss rate (*p*) = 0.5

$\bar{x}$ = 0.5
σ = 0.5

$\bar{x}$ = 5
σ = 1.58

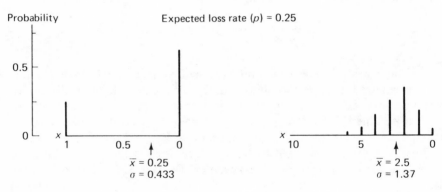

Expected loss rate (*p*) = 0.25

$\bar{x}$ = 0.25
σ = 0.433

$\bar{x}$ = 2.5
σ = 1.37

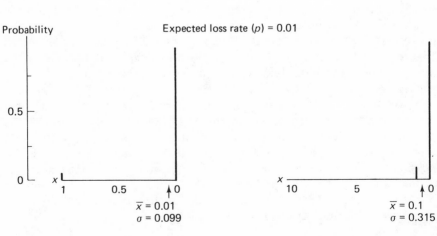

Expected loss rate (*p*) = 0.01

$\bar{x}$ = 0.01
σ = 0.099

$\bar{x}$ = 0.1
σ = 0.315

When the expected loss rate is high and the frequency distribution is close to normal, the standard deviation can be used to measure the concentration of the distribution. In a binomial distribution the standard deviations (σ) can be calculated as follows:

$$\sigma = \sqrt{npq} \tag{3}$$

The relative standard deviation is obtained by dividing equation (3) by n,

$$\frac{\sigma}{n} = \frac{\sqrt{npq}}{n} \tag{4}$$

From equation (4), it can be seen that the relative standard deviation will decrease as n increases and will approach zero as n approaches infinity. As the number of loans increases, the expected loss rate becomes an increasingly accurate measure of actual loss.[1]

On very large portfolios, three statements can be made about default risk: (1) the number of loans that will go bad can be predicted with considerable accuracy, (2) the possibilities of a total loss are very remote, and (3) some losses are almost certain. The predictability of the amount of the loss removes much of the uncertainty associated with default risk. Reliable estimates of losses can be treated as a cost of doing business. Figure 7-2 illustrates the implications of portfolio size for the possibilities of extreme outcomes (a total loss or no loss) and for the standard deviation of the distribution.

The dollar amount of losses depends on the size distribution of loans, the proportion of the loan amount that has to be charged off, and the number of bad loans. An accurate description of the dollar losses requires a joint distribution of the number of bad loans and the dollar amounts of the associated losses. For simplicity it will be assumed in the following discussion that all the loans are the same size and that the dollar losses on bad loans are the same.

Since all loans involve some default risks, all lending operations have to provide for these risks. In practice the provisions take two forms. First, the rates charged on loans have to be large enough to provide a risk premium to cover losses. Second, some provisions have to be made for the variability in actual year-to-year loss experience. The statistical features of the default risk distributions provide a basis for estimating the protection needed.

The risk premium (k) charged on loans must at least cover the expected losses to give the lender a statistical "fair gamble." The expected

---

[1]Although the standard deviation loses its accuracy as a measure of fixed proportion of the total distribution as the distribution becomes more skewed, it can be used as an index of the variations around the mean.

FIGURE 7-2

INFLUENCE OF EXPECTED LOSS RATE (p) AND PORTFOLIO SIZE (n) ON
PORTFOLIO RISK FEATURES

Number of loans (n)	Expected loss rate (p)			
	0.5	0.25	0.01	0.0025
	Relative standard deviation (σ/n)			
1	0.50	0.43	0.099	0.050
2	0.35	0.31	0.070	0.035
3	0.29	· 0.25	0.057	0.029
4	0.25	0.22	0.050	0.025
5	0.22	0.19	0.044	0.022
10	0.16	0.14	0.031	0.016
100	0.05	0.043	0.010	0.005
1000	0.02	0.014	0.0031	0.0016
	Probability of total loss ($x = n$)			
1	0.5	0.25	0.01	0.0025
2	0.25	0.063	0.0001	0.000006
3	0.13	0.016	0.000001	*
4	0.063	0.0039	*	*
5	0.031	0.00098	*	*
10	0.00098	0.000001	*	*
100	*	*	*	*
1000	*	*	*	*
	Probability of some losses ($x > 0$)			
1	0.5	0.25	0.01	0.0025
2	0.75	0.44	0.02	0.0050
3	0.88	0.58	0.03	0.0075
4	0.94	0.68	0.039	0.010
5	0.97	0.76	0.049	0.012
10	1.00	0.94	0.096	0.025
100	1.00*	1.00*	0.63	0.221
1000	1.00*	1.00*	1.00	0.92

*Probabilities of less than 1 in a million of total loss ($x = n$) or of no losses ($x = 0$).

dollar losses $E(L)$ are equal to the expected loss rate (p) times the number of loans (n) times the average dollar amount of losses (A).

$$E(L) = pnA \qquad (5)$$

This amount can be considered as a cost that has to be deducted from the contracted interest income (I_c) to get the expected return $E(R)$ on the portfolio:

$$E(R) = I_c - E(L) \tag{6}$$

Equation (6) can be expressed in rates by dividing by the outstanding amount of the loan portfolio to obtain

$$r_e = r_c - k \tag{7}$$

where: r_e = expected yield
            r_c = contract rate

              k = expected default rate or minimum risk premium

A contract rate of 7 percent would be required to obtain an effective yield of 6 percent when the default rate is 1 percent.[2]

The risk premium has its accounting counterpart in a cost item that appears in the income and expense statements of financial institutions and is sometimes called *provisions for losses on loans*. If the amounts of these annual provisions were actually calculated by multiplying the expected dollar default rate by the outstanding amount of loans, the provision for losses should be exactly equal to actual losses averaged over a period of time. In a world without deviations from the mean, the amount of the losses each year would be equal to the amount of the provisions for losses. No additions to reserves for losses would occur, and the net income would never be smaller than expected because of larger-than-expected charge-offs. In practice, even when the average losses over time conform to expectations, the pattern of losses may be erratic. Delayed losses present no problem. The yearly provisions for losses prevent the overstatement of earned income and these provisions accumulate so that they will be available to cover the expected losses when they occur. Premature losses are another matter. Large premature losses can disrupt the normal cash flows and create payment problems for the lender. Statistics may tell us that there is no real problem because the losses will be smaller in subsequent years so that the future flows of funds from risk premium payments will replace the losses. But creditors or others who are expecting current payments may not be consoled by statistical arguments. Most lenders find it desirable to protect themselves from possible variations in the pattern of losses by setting up special reserves for losses. These reserves are likely to

---

[2]This statement of the relationship between the contract rate and expected rate assumes that there is no loss of interest income on the loans charged off. This may be a realistic assumption in some cases. On some types of loans interest is collected in advance. If some interest is lost, a term for the actual rate, r_a, has to be substituted for the contract rate (r_c) in equation (7). When the full amount of the interest is lost on bad loans, the relationship between the actual rate (r_a) and the contract rate (r_c) becomes

$$r_a = r_c(1 - k)$$

be larger than those that would be developed by the mere accumulation of a "fair gamble" risk premium. The actual size depends on the manager's attitude toward risk and on the alternative needs for the funds. The variance or dispersion of the frequency distribution of losses gives some indication of the need for protection of this type. Since the dispersion of the loss distribution decreases with the number of loans in the portfolio, the reserve required to obtain a given degree of protection decreases as the number of loans in the portfolio increases. Large and small portfolios face the same default costs on loans of similar quality, but a large lender can obtain a given degree of protection from variations in losses with a relatively smaller reserve.

Market Risk

Market risk, as the name implies, is associated with the possibility that a financial contract will have to be sold at a price that is different from the purchase price or the maturity value. It exists on any contract that can be sold and, despite the unattractive connotation of the term *risk*, it is associated with a desirable feature—marketability. The option of being able to sell a security gives it a form of liquidity. The degree of liquidity depends on the speed and convenience with which the security can be sold and on the costs associated with the sale. The risk of a capital loss at the time of sale is one of the costs of liquidity. The liquidity of the asset is inversely related to the potential size of the loss.

The size of the variations in the prices of marketable securities depends on the features of the secondary market for the securities and on the features of the security itself. Short-term U.S. treasury securities trade with price variations that seldom exceed 1 percent of the maturity value; long-term government securities vary over a wider range, and variations of 50 to 100 percent of the purchase price are not unusual on common stocks. Price variability provides an index of the potential capital losses. It is one of the features of a contract that have to be considered in the decision to acquire the contract.

The statistical features of market risk are very different from those of default risk. The maximum loss that can be sustained is 100 percent of the purchase price, as in the case of default risk, but there may not be an upper limit to the potential capital gain. The frequency distribution associated with market risk is two-sided. Objective frequency distributions can be developed from historical price data but any distributions used to describe future events imply some subjective judgments about the future. The normal distribution is usually used to illustrate market risks, but the actual distributions are likely to show some skewness or other irregularities. Figure 7-3 compares the actual frequency distributions of a small

FIGURE 7-3
FREQUENCY DISTRIBUTIONS OF SELECTED MARKETABLE SECURITIES,
MEASURED BY STANDARD DEVIATION (σ)

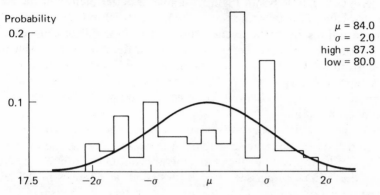

A. U.S. Government Bond (4%, 1980)

μ = 84.0
σ = 2.0
high = 87.3
low = 80.0

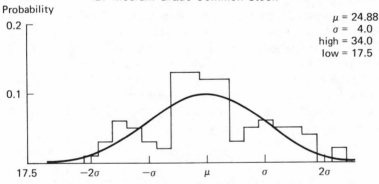

B. Medium Grade Common Stock

μ = 24.88
σ = 4.0
high = 34.0
low = 17.5

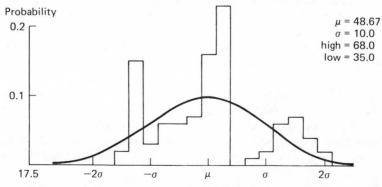

C. Ba Convertible Corporate Bond (5.5%, 1996)

μ = 48.67
σ = 10.0
high = 68.0
low = 35.0

sample of prices on three types of securities with the normal distribution. In these examples, the actual prices nearly all fell within the range of plus or minus two standard deviations. The standard deviation, which is frequently used as a measure of market risk, ranged from $2 on the U.S. government bond to $4 on the medium-grade common stock to $10 on the long-term convertible bond. Figure 7-4 gives a better picture of the relative risks involved. It shows the same frequency distributions measured in dollar variations from the average price. The bimodal tendencies of the two bond distributions reflect the variations in the interest rates during the period from which the sample was drawn (1973 and 1974). The lowest prices represent losses relative to the average prices of 5 percent on the government security and about 30 percent on both the common stock and the convertible bond.

A distinction is frequently made between the systematic and unsystematic risk on marketable securities. *Systematic risk* refers to the variability that can be traced to changes in general economic conditions and to the factors that affect all classes of securities, such as changes in the level of interest rates or prices. *Unsystematic risk* refers to the share of price variability that is unique for the particular class of security or for the securities of a particular company or agency. Unsystematic risk can be reduced by portfolio diversification; systematic risk cannot. The terms are defined more precisely in terms of the statistical regression between price changes of some general class of security (X) and the price changes of a specific issue (Y). The term *systematic risk* refers to the variations from the mean of the specific security (Y) that are explained by the fitted regression equation between the two variables. The term *unsystematic risk* refers to the variations that are unexplained by the regression equation. In a regression equation in the following form

$$Y = \alpha + \beta X + e \tag{8}$$

the residual (e) which measures the amount of the variation of a specific observation of Y from the regression line is also the measure of the unsystematic risk (or the unexplained error in statistical terms). This distinction is most frequently applied to comparisons of changes in the prices of common stocks where a specific stock (Y) is compared with the changes of some general index of stock prices (X). The regression equation is referred to as the *characteristic line* for stock Y where the β in equation 8 is the *beta coefficient* or the slope of the regression line. The beta coefficient has attracted the attention of stock analysts as a useful measure of the behavior of the stock relative to the market in general. If the beta value of a stock is above 1, the prices of the stock are likely to be more volatile than those of the index used for the comparison. If the beta value is below 1, prices are likely to be less volatile than the market. Although

FIGURE 7-4

FREQUENCY DISTRIBUTIONS OF SELECTED MARKETABLE SECURITIES
MEASURED BY DOLLAR DEVIATIONS

A. U.S. Government Bond (4%, 1980)

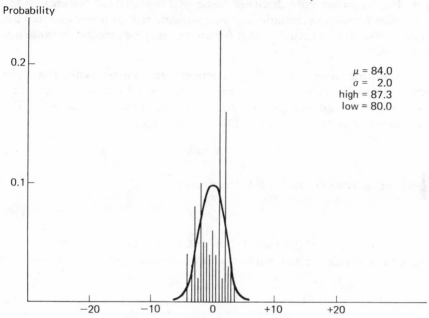

μ = 84.0
σ = 2.0
high = 87.3
low = 80.0

B. Medium Grade Common Stock

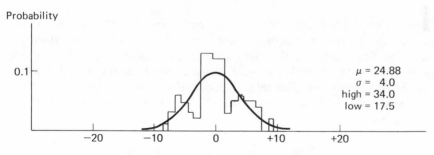

μ = 24.88
σ = 4.0
high = 34.0
low = 17.5

C. Ba Convertible Corporate Bond
(5.5%, 1996)

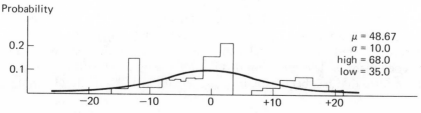

μ = 48.67
σ = 10.0
high = 68.0
low = 35.0

the distinction between systematic and unsystematic risk is used primarily in the analysis of the prices of common stock, it is a useful distinction for other types of marketable securities. Individual issues may have distinctive patterns of price behavior that can be analyzed by the use of this distinction. The following note discusses some of the statistical features of the distinction between systematic and unsystematic risk. It is not essential for an understanding of materials that follow and may be omitted by those not interested.

Statistical note—measuring systematic and unsystematic risk: The terms *systematic risk* and *unsystematic risk* can be substituted for the terms *explained error* and *unexplained error* used in correlation analysis. The regression line of two sets of variables can be expressed as

$$\mu_{yx} = a + bX \tag{9}$$

where the individual values of Y are equal to

$$Y = \mu_{yx} + e \tag{10}$$

The deviation of individual values of Y from the average of Y values (μ_y) can be divided in two parts in relation to the regression line

$$\underset{\substack{\text{Total} \\ \text{risk}}}{(Y - \mu_y)} = \underset{\substack{\text{Unsystematic} \\ \text{risk}}}{(Y - \mu_{yx})} + \underset{\substack{\text{Systematic} \\ \text{risk}}}{(\mu_{yx} - \mu_y)} \tag{11}$$

The term on the left side of (11) is the total error or total risk. The second term on the right of the equation is the explained error or the systematic risk. The first term on the right side is the unexplained error or the unsystematic risk. It measures the distance between the individual Y values and the regression line. The values for equation (11) for individual Y's can be squared, summed and divided by the number of observations to obtain the following:

$$\frac{\Sigma(Y - \mu_y)^2}{n} = \frac{\Sigma(Y - \mu_{yx})^2}{n} + \frac{\Sigma(\mu_{yx} - \mu_x)^2}{n} \tag{12}$$

The first term will be recognized as the total variance of $Y(\sigma_y^2)$. The second term is the variance of Y around the regression line (σ_{yx}^2). The third term measures the reduction in total variation achieved by the regression line. The coefficient of determination (ρ^2) is obtained by dividing the amount of the variance that has been explained (systematic risk) by the total variance (total risk):

$$\rho^2 = \frac{\sum (\mu_{yx} - \mu_y)^2}{\sum (Y - \mu_y)^2} \qquad (13)$$

Dividing equation (12) by the total variance gives

$$1.0 = \frac{\sum (Y - \mu_{yx})^2}{\sum (Y - \mu_y)^2} + \rho^2 \qquad (14)$$

Equation (14) shows the allocation of risk between the systematic and unsystematic components. If the coefficient of determination is equal to 0.9, 90 percent of the total variance (total risk) is explained by systematic risk and 10 percent by unsystematic risk.

Subjective Aspects of Risk

The importance of risk as a barrier to financial transactions can be measured by the premium that has to be paid to induce suppliers to accept risky contracts. The mathematics of risk suggest that a rational investor will purchase a financial contract whenever the expected value is equal to or greater than the price. This approach, however, ignores the potential importance of a large gain or a loss for the budget position of the supplier of funds. The outcome for the supplier is almost never equal to the expected value on a single contract. It may fall in any position that ranges from a complete loss to a sizable capital gain. The lender's decision will reflect the possibilities of the extreme outcomes, and the advantages and disadvantages of these outcomes may affect the premium he requires for accepting risk.

Traditional utility theory suggests that the supplier's reaction to risk will not be symmetrical but that a given dollar loss will be more damaging to his financial position than an equal dollar gain would be helpful. This expectation arises from the assumption that the supplier of funds has a utility function for wealth that is characterized by diminishing marginal utility. The utility added by a given increase in wealth will be less than that lost by a given decrease of the same amount. No one with such a utility function would accept a fair gamble in statistical terms because the potential loss of utility would be greater than the potential compensation.

The traditional utility function implies a subjective premium for risk that exceeds that implied by the mathematics of risk. However, the willingness of people to gamble, particularly with unfavorable odds, seems inconsistent with this interpretation of attitudes toward risk. A number of solutions have been offered to this apparent contradiction, and an examination of these alternatives gives some insight into subjective attitudes toward risk and the implications of different attitudes for the pricing of financial assets.

The role of the subjective evaluation of the extreme possibilities that are involved in risk taking can be illustrated by a simple example. If two students (A and B) are given the opportunity of paying three dollars to gamble by flipping a coin to obtain six dollars or nothing, the expected value of the gamble will be three dollars:

$$\bar{X} = p_1 X_1 + p_2 X_2 \tag{15}$$
$$3 = (0.5)0 + (0.5)6$$

Since the price is equal to the expected value, it is a fair gamble. But we cannot tell whether the students will accept the gamble or not until we know something about their personal situations (their utility functions). If we know (1) that both students have only three dollars, (2) that student A plans to spend the evening with his friends drinking beer, and (3) that student B wants to attend a basketball game that costs five dollars, we can anticipate their reactions. Student A will not accept the gamble because if he loses he will have no money to cover his expenses and if he wins he may have more than he needs. Student B is unable to go to the game with only three dollars but if he wins he will have enough money to pay for the ticket. He will accept the gamble and A will reject it.

In a more formal way, we can say that for A the utility of the possession of three dollars is greater than the utility of the expected value of the gamble,

$$U'_a(\$3) > U_a(\bar{X}) \tag{16}$$

However, for B the utility of the possession of three dollars is less than the utility of the expected value of the gamble,

$$U'_b(\$3) < U_b(\bar{X}) \tag{17}$$

The decisions of these two students can be used to illustrate the nature of their utility functions within the range of the simple choice. In Figure 7-5, X_1 is the cash position of either student if he takes a gamble and loses. X_2 is a position equal to six dollars or the position of either student if he wins. Since we know that six dollars will have a higher utility than zero we can arbitrarily plot two points on the utility curves for both students. A straight line drawn between these two points on their utility curves serves as a reference line. The midpoint on the reference line gives the weighted average utility $[U(\bar{X})]$ of the two alternatives (six dollars or

FIGURE 7-5
UTILITY AND RISK

A. Risk Averter

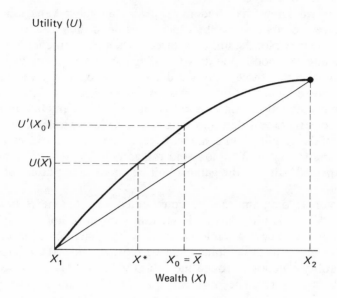

B. Risk Seeker

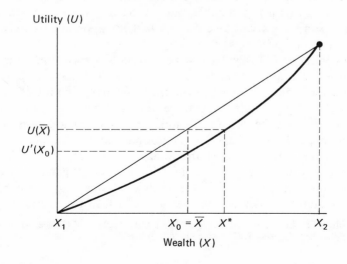

zero) when the probability of each alternative is 0.5. This line also represents the imaginary utility function for someone who is indifferent to the extreme alternatives, i.e., where the absolute value of the utility added by winning three dollars is exactly equal to the absolute value of the utility lost by losing three dollars.

Since we know that student A places a higher value on actually holding three dollars than on the expected value of the game (equation 16), we can arbitrarily plot the utility of three dollars above the midpoint of the reference line. A smooth line drawn through the three points that indicate the utility of zero, three, and six dollars, respectively, gives his utility function. Since his utility function is above the reference line throughout the range of this simple wealth situation, he will reject any fair gamble that can be constructed within the zero-to-six-dollar extremes. If the risk implied by the gamble is in some way forced on him, he will be willing to pay any amount up to $X^*\overline{X}$ to avoid the gamble. At that point the utility of the expected value of the gamble will be equal to the utility of his cash position.

A similar diagram can be constructed for student B (see Figure 7-5B). We know that he places a lower utility on three dollars in cash than he does on the expected value of the gamble (equation 17). The utility position assigned to three dollars can be plotted below the reference line, and the utility function, through the values for zero, three, and six dollars, will fall below the reference line. Student B is a *risk seeker* who would be happy to take any fair gamble and would be willing to pay the amount $\overline{X}X^*$ as a premium to take the gamble.

These two examples illustrate the role of subjective factors in the approach to risk. Traditional theory assumes that individuals are risk averse. The example of risk seeking, illustrated by student B in the context of this example, seems reasonable, but it is hard to imagine a consumer or businessperson who would take the risk seeker's approach to a very broad range of financial decisions.

Friedman and Savage have suggested an S-shaped utility function as a solution to the apparent inconsistencies in individuals' reaction to risk.[3] The same individuals who buy insurance and pay for protection against risk may also engage freely in unfair games such as lotteries. Friedman and Savage suggest that the individual's utility function for wealth may assume a special shape that provides for the normal diminishing marginal utility throughout the early ranges of the function but that shifts to increasing marginal utility at levels above the individual's current position (see Figure 7-6). The cords drawn around the individual wealth position represent simple, two-outcome risk alternatives and can take two forms. First, they

---

[3]Milton Friedman and L. J. Savage, "The Utility Analysis of Choices Involving Risk," *Journal of Political Economy* LVI (1948), pp. 279–304.

FIGURE 7-6
FRIEDMAN-SAVAGE UTILITY FUNCTION

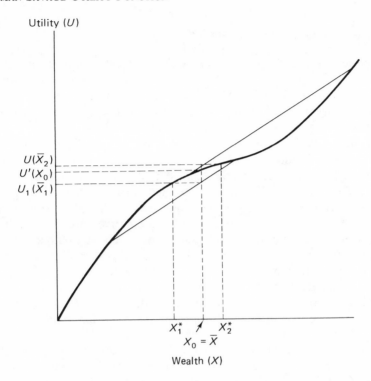

Utility (*U*)

$U(\bar{X}_2)$
$U'(X_0)$
$U_1(\bar{X}_1)$

X_1^* X_2^*
$X_0 = \bar{X}$

Wealth (*X*)

can be drawn below the individual's utility function where they describe fair risk alternatives that the individual, as a risk avoider, would reject. The subjective risk premium, measured by $X_1^*\bar{X}$, is the amount that the individual would pay for insurance against the risk. Second, cords can be drawn above the individual's utility function where they represent alternatives that the individual, as a risk seeker, would accept. The subjective risk premium $\bar{X}X_2^*$ measures the premium that he would pay for a chance on a gamble that promises a very large but unlikely return for a relatively small outlay.

Risk seeking in the Friedman–Savage model is limited to a relatively small set of theoretically troublesome types of risk behavior. The unfavorable odds are recognized by most of the gamblers and their decision has to be explained either by the pleasure or enjoyment that they associate with gambling or as risk seeking. The odds on many other types of risk alternatives are so uncertain that what may appear to be risk seeking may be only excessive optimism or misinformation. A stock that appears too

risky to one investor may appear to offer a premium that justifies the risk
to another.

Risk Aversion as a Financial Barrier

Subjective reactions to the possibilities of extreme outcomes add to
any purely mathematical barriers that risk imposes on financial transactions. The implication of subjective attitudes toward risk can be illustrated
by the construction of indifference lines (or maps) that measure the
individual's tradeoff between the rate of return and risk.

Figure 7-7 illustrates the derivation of an indifference line which
indicates the individual's tradeoff between return and risk on loans that
involve default risk. Relatively high default rates have been used to
simplify the illustration. It is assumed that an individual is offered two
loans that are of the same dollar amount (X_1X_0) but that have different
default ratios $(p_a$ and $p_b)$. When both alternatives are plotted as fair
gambles on the individual's utility function, a default premium of X_0X_{2i}
has to be offered on these loans in addition to the riskless interest rate r to
convert them into fair gambles.[4] The fair gamble return is plotted as a
function of the default rate in Figure 7-7B. Any lender with an aversion to
risk will reject both of these loans because the utility of his initial wealth
position X_0 is greater than the utility of the expected returns from the
loans.

The lender can be induced to make the loans only if an additional
subjective risk premium is added. The addition of this premium increases
the loan payoff and shifts the right end of the cord to the right. The
increased payoff also shifts the expected value of the loan $(\overline{X_i'})$ to the right
along the cord. The loan becomes acceptable at the point where the utility
of the expected value of the loan option equals the utility of the initial
position. The amount of the subjective risk premium is equal to $X_{2_i}X_{2_i}'$. The
actual loan transactions illustrated by this example represent the obligation
of the borrower to repay the principal on the loan (X_1X_0) plus the riskless
interest charge (not shown on the chart) plus the two risk premiums. His
annual interest charges (I) would be equal to

$$I = r(X_1X_0) + \underset{\substack{\text{fair gamble}\\\text{default}\\\text{premium}}}{X_0X_{2_i}} + \underset{\substack{\text{subjective}\\\text{risk}\\\text{premium}}}{X_{2_i}X_{2_i}'} \tag{18}$$

$$\underset{\substack{\text{riskless}\\\text{interest}\\\text{charge}}}{}$$

These amounts can be converted to rates by dividing by the principal of
the loan (X_1X_0).

---

[4]The illustration assumes that the amount of the riskless interest is received with
certainty and is not subject to risk on the principal. The assumption is not essential but it
simplifies the calculations.

FIGURE 7-7
Subjective Premium on Default Risk

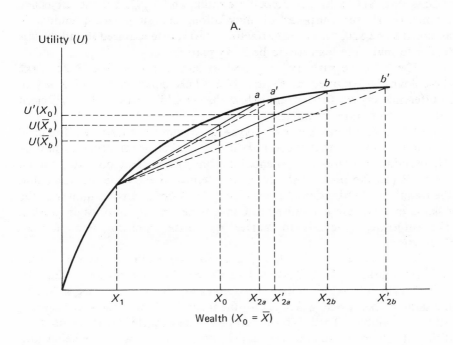

A.

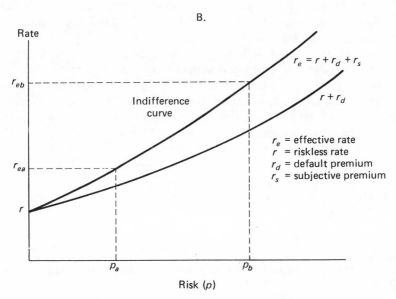

B.

A $100 loan with a potential default ratio of 0.1 and a riskless interest rate of 5 percent would involve annual interest charges of $5 for the riskless rate, $11.11 for the default premium, and $X_{2i}X'_{2i}$ for the subjective premium.[5] If, for purposes of illustration, the subjective premium is assumed to be $20, the annual effective interest rate required to induce this lender to make the loan would be 36.11 percent.

The effective rates (r_e) required to induce a risk avoider to make these loans are plotted in Figure 7-7B. This curve is one of a set of indifference curves for the individual that would correspond to different riskless market rates of interest.

The role of market risk serves as a similar barrier to financial transactions except that the variability of market prices provides part of the premium because the potential capital gains offset potential capital losses. When the price of the contract is equal to the expected value and the frequency distribution of price changes is normal, no premium over the riskless interest rate is required to convert the security into a fair gamble. The subjective reactions to market risk arise from the size of price fluctuations.

The implication of risk aversion for the yield on securities with different market risk is illustrated in Figure 7-8. It is assumed that the individual is offered a choice of two investments (a,b) that are selling at the same market price, which is also the price that makes them mathematically fair gambles. They differ only in that the expected market prices are different. The possible outcomes consist of only two prices, one below and one above the purchase price, that are indicated by the ends of the cords (a,b). It is assumed, for simplicity, that these outcomes are equally likely, that the potential losses $(X_{1i}\overline{X})$ are equal to the potential capital gains $(\overline{X}X_{2i})$ and that the securities will be sold a year after they are purchased. The expected return on both alternatives is zero (excluding dividends). However, the potential losses and gains on b would be greater than those on a $(\sigma_b > \sigma_a)$. It is also assumed that both of the securities pay dividends (not shown in the chart) equal to the riskless rate (r). No mathematical premium is required for the differences in risks because the possibilities of gains exactly offset the possibilities of losses. In a world of people indifferent to risk, the market yields would be equal to the riskless rate (r). However, the investor with the utility function illustrated in Figure 7-8 would reject both alternatives because the utility of his wealth position (X_0) is greater than it would be after accepting either of the alternatives. He could be induced to accept the securities by a reduction in their prices.

---

[5]When the amount of the riskless interest is received with certainty, the maximum loss on the loans will be the amount of the principal $(X_{1i}X_0)$ which equals $(1-p)(X_{1i}X_{2i})$. The default premium of X_0X_{2i} equals $p(X_{1i}X_{2i})$, so the default premium expressed as a percentage of the loan amount will be $100p/(1-p)$.

FIGURE 7-8
Subjective Premium on Market Risk

A.

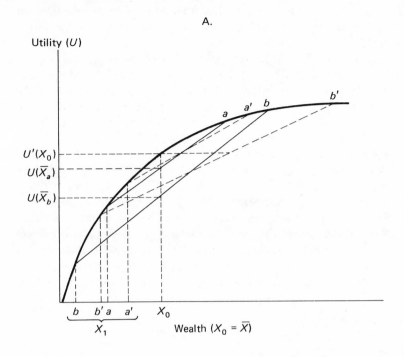

B.

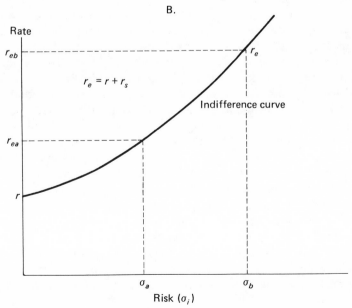

A market price reduction would reduce the maximum loss he could take and increase the maximum gain. It is represented in the chart as a shift of the cord to the right. The securities become acceptable to the investor when the utility of expected value is equal to the utility of his initial position (X_0).

The amount of the subjective premium can be measured by the required decline in prices $(X_{1i}X'_{1i})$. The returns required to compensate him for the risks (r_s) can be calculated by dividing the premiums by the new prices $(X'_{1i}X_0)$. The rates can be added to the riskless rate to obtain an indifference curve that measures the individual's subjective tradeoff between risk and return (see Figure 7-8B). It is one of a set of such curves that can be constructed for different riskless rates.

Some subjective premium must be paid to a risk avoider to induce him to accept either market or default risk. In addition, on default risk a premium must be paid to compensate him for the purely mathematical risks. The combined premiums represent a major barrier to direct lending activities. The illustration of the potential size of the premiums on direct loans in Figure 7-7 gives some insight into the extreme rates that arise in loan shark operations and go a long way in explaining the virtual absence of direct lending by individual suppliers of funds to individual borrowers.

Risk Aversion and Insurance

The analysis of a risk avoider's decision to buy insurance involves a slightly different approach than the analysis of his decision to accept risk. Instead of starting in a certainty position that can be measured by a single point on his utility function, the individual who is a candidate for insurance starts with a position that has some inherent risks. His accountant can give him the total dollar value of his current wealth (X_0), but if he is realistic about the potential risk of fire or other damage, his actual total utility will not be equal to the utility of his wealth position when there are no risks involved. The actual utility of his current position will be the weighted average utility of the possible values of his wealth position. For purposes of illustration, it has to be assumed that there are only two possible outcomes (see Figure 7-9), one (X_0) where the current value of his wealth remains intact and the other (X_1) where some major asset, his house for instance, is totally destroyed. His actual utility is measured by the utility of the mean of the risk inherent in his wealth position $(U(\bar{X}))$. If he can buy insurance that will protect him completely from the loss, he will be able to improve his current utility. The purchase of insurance will permit him to move along his utility function to a position of certainty that reduces his current wealth by the amount he has to pay for the insurance.

FIGURE 7-9
RISK AVERSION AND THE WILLINGNESS TO BUY INSURANCE

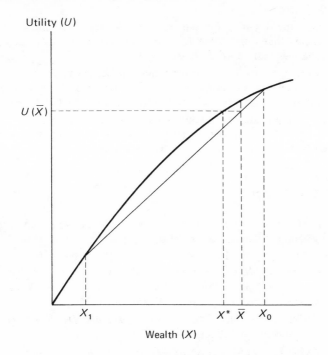

Wealth (*X*)

A premium equal to $X_0\overline{X}$ would represent the statistically fair gamble, but he will be willing to pay even more. He would pay any premium up to the amount X_0X^*. If the distance $X_0\overline{X}$ represents the actuarial risk of a fire that will destroy his house, a premium of that amount would cover the pure insurance risk for an underwriter. The remaining amount that the risk avoider is willing to pay provides a margin for the related costs of insurance operations and provides an economic basis for private insurance operations.

QUESTIONS AND PROBLEMS

1. Why is a purely statistical premium required on default risk and not on market risk?
2. If the default risk on very large loan portfolio can be estimated with considerable accuracy, why do financial institutions set up reserves for losses that are larger than needed to cover the expected losses?
3. Regulatory agencies frequently set maximum size limits on loans that can be

made to any one borrower. Discuss the implications of a large loan for portfolio risk where the loan is equal to half the amount of a portfolio of 1000 loans.

4. Discuss the day-to-day behavior of a risk seeker and indicate the potential problems that might arise from this approach to a full range of financial alternatives that he might face.

5. Consider the apparent inconsistencies between the reaction to risk implied by the assumption that consumers are risk averse and the gambling behavior that is actually observed. How can these inconsistencies be resolved?

6. What interest rate would you ask on a loan that was relatively safe (bad debt ratio of 0.001) when the amount of the loan represented 75 percent of your total financial assets? How would you arrive at the figure?

SELECTED REFERENCES

CHERNOFF, HERMAN, and LINCOLN E. MOSES, *Elementary Decision Theory*. New York: John Wiley and Sons, 1959.

FRIEDMAN, MILTON, and L. J. SAVAGE, "Utility Analysis of Choices Involving Risk," *Journal of Political Economy*, LVI (August 1948), 279–304.

KEYNES, J. M., *The General Theory of Employment, Interest and Money*, chapter 12. New York: Harcourt, Brace and Company, 1935.

LUCE, R. DUNCAN, and HOWARD RAIFFA, *Games and Decisions: Introduction and Critical Survey*. New York: John Wiley and Sons, 1958.

VON NEUMANN, JOHN, and OSKAR MORGENSTERN, *Theory of Games and Economic Behavior*. Princeton, N.J.: Princeton University Press, 1953.

SAVAGE, LEONARD J., *The Foundations of Statistics*. New York: John Wiley and Sons, 1954.

Motives for Liquidity

8

Keynes gave the desire to hold money balances a new role in economics and finance. He identified it as a barrier to the more efficient use of the money stock and as a potential source of elasticity in the supply of funds. He originally suggested four reasons for holding money balances.[1] The first two of these, the income and business motives, have since been combined in modern discussions into the transactions motive. The *transactions motive* refers to the balances required by households, governments, and corporations to meet their day-to-day obligations or, in Keynes' words, "to bridge the interval between the receipt of income and its disbursement."[2] The *precautionary motive* refers to the desire to hold funds to meet unforeseen needs. The *speculative motive* refers to the use of money as part of investment strategy to avoid losses on securities when interest rates are expected to increase.

Funds held in money balances are at the same time withheld from financial markets. The Keynesian motives for liquidity identify the barriers to the movement of these funds into the money market. The discussion in this chapter is concerned primarily with techniques to overcome the desire to hold money balances and with a closer examination of the factors that affect the demand for money balances.

[1]J. M. Keynes, *The General Theory of Employment, Interest and Money* (New York: Harcourt, Brace and Co., 1935), pp. 195–7.

[2]*Ibid.*, p. 195.

Substitutes for Money Balances

The obvious advantages of money balances lie in their complete flexibility as a means of payment and in their almost complete freedom from default or credit risk. Their only disadvantage lies in the fact that they do not earn interest (or, in cases where interest can be paid on money forms, the rates are below those on other instruments). These funds can be drawn into the loan market by offers of attractive substitutes at rates that are high enough to induce the holders of money balances to buy them.

The term *liquidity* has been used to describe the ease with which an asset can be converted into money. This feature can be given to financial instruments in two ways: (1) by making them redeemable for money and (2) by making them negotiable. Both techniques have been used in developing substitutes for money balances. The deposits of various types of financial institutions that are redeemable on demand come very close to money in meeting the liquidity preference motives. They are also, in many cases, as safe as checking accounts because they are offered by the same or similar institutions and they may be insured by the U.S. government. They are inferior to checking accounts only because they cannot be used directly for payments. They have to be transferred to a checking account or converted into currency before payments can be made. The institutions offering these accounts can improve their substitutability for money by making transfers easier and quicker. Provisions for automatic transfers from savings to checking accounts in event of an overdraft on the checking accounts convert savings accounts into money. This privilege is not generally available and cannot be offered by some institutions, but savings accounts are naturally good substitutes for money and can be made into nearly perfect substitutes.

The differences in the degree of liquidity in various types of savings accounts may be subtle. They center on the ease and convenience of transferring funds into means-of-payment forms and on the costs of these transfers in time, convenience, and loss of interest. Electronic or telephone transfers are easier and quicker than mail transfers, and mail transfers are usually more convenient than transfers that require personal visits.

Financial institutions can give their depositors the right to withdraw their funds without notice, but in doing so they incur the problems of providing the liquidity that they have promised. As will be seen later, the liquidity that makes the deposits of an institution attractive to suppliers of funds introduces risks and liquidity problems into the affairs of the institution. Financial institutions are designed to handle these problems, but other borrowers are not. Few borrowers are in a position to give their creditors the right to call their funds either with or without notice. This technique for providing liquidity can seldom be used by borrowers other than financial institutions.

Liquidity is also provided by the marketability of financial instruments. Some of the essential ingredients of marketability can be supplied by the issuers of the instruments, but others cannot. The issuers can offer instruments that meet the requirements of the negotiable instrument laws, but they cannot create a market for the instruments. A good secondary market depends on many factors, nearly all of which are beyond the control of the issuer.

The economic role of secondary markets and the conditions essential for their existence will be discussed in Chapter 15. In the United States, the existence of various good secondary markets has made possible the development of a large variety of alternatives to money. Large and relatively efficient secondary markets exist for U.S. government securities, negotiable certificates of deposit, commercial paper, and the securities of large state and local governments and government agencies. These markets make it possible for anyone who has access to them to issue securities that are also good substitutes for money.

The liquidity of marketable securities depends not only on the speed and convenience with which they can be converted into money but also on the transactions costs and the market risks. The market risk on money market instruments can be measured by their day-to-day price variations, and the scale of price variations becomes an inverted measure of liquidity. The price stability and roll-over features of short-term securities give them a dual advantage over longer-term issues. The term *money market securities* is sometimes used to describe the set of marketable securities that serve as good substitutes for money.

Close substitutes for money balances are the interface between idle money balances and the demand for loan funds. The holders of money balances can release them to meet loan demands by shifting to money substitutes without losing much in the way of safety or liquidity. Money substitutes are at the cutting edge of the Keynesian liquidity preference function. The rates on these instruments are the relevant rates for money balance decisions and the availability and features of the substitutes determine the extent to which the liquidity preference motives can be satisfied by money substitutes.

Demand for Money as Asset Balances

All money balances appear as assets in financial statements, but it is useful to distinguish between money that is held as a component of an asset portfolio and money that will be used for transactions purposes. The reasons for holding the two types of accounts are different, and the resultant behavior of the accounts is different. Asset balances are sometimes called *idle* balances in contrast to the *active* balances being held for transactions purposes, which are constantly turning over as they are spent and replenished.

Traditional discussions of the demand for money attributed most of the interest elasticity to the demand for asset balances. More recently, however, both theoretical and empirical evidence has suggested that the demand for transactions purposes may also be interest elastic. The interest elasticity of the demand for asset balances has been attributed to opportunity costs, to the nature of the speculative motive, to risk, and to changes in wealth. All of these approaches relate to the choice of financial assets and to the composition of asset portfolios rather than to changes in the amounts of financial assets. These shifts from money into other types of assets are likely to involve the close substitutes described in the previous section.

Opportunity costs

In the decision to hold money balances, the advantages of money have to be balanced against the interest lost on less attractive types of financial assets. The opportunity costs of holding money will be directly related to the level of interest rates. The existence and nature of these opportunity costs suggest an inverse relationship between interest rates and demand for money balances. The opportunity–costs argument applies to all of the motives for holding money.

Speculative motives

Keynes' speculative motive traditionally has been given the dominant role in shaping the inverse relationship between interest rates and the demand for money. It views speculative money balances as an alternative to holding fixed income securities where the individual's choice is affected by his expectations about changes in interest rates. The purchaser of a bond expects to receive income from the interest on the bond and from any capital gains that would accompany an increase in bond prices. The amount of the fixed annual interest income (I) is given by multiplying the coupon rate (c) by the face amount of the bond. The current yield (r) on the bond can be obtained by dividing the interest income by the market price,[3]

$$r = \frac{I}{P} \tag{1}$$

---

[3]This simple ratio assumes that the bond is in the form of a consol with no maturity date. The market yield of a bond with a fixed maturity would have to be obtained by finding the discount rate that sets the market price equal to the discounted present value of the income stream.

The market price of a bond can be expressed as a ratio of the interest income rate to the yield:

$$P = \frac{I}{r} \tag{2}$$

The expected capital gain (g) from an expected change in the market interest rate to r_e can be written as the percentage change in market prices,

$$g = \frac{P_e - P}{P} \tag{3}$$

or, in terms of rates, as

$$g = \frac{\dfrac{I}{r_e} - \dfrac{I}{r}}{\dfrac{I}{r}}$$

or

$$g = \frac{r}{r_e} - 1 \tag{4}$$

If the individual is making the simple choice between money balances and fixed income obligations, he will hold money when he expects the interest rate to rise ($r < r_e$) and hold bonds when he expects it to fall ($r > r_e$). If he has some opinion about the normal level of interest rates, he will want to hold bonds when the market rates are above normal and will want to hold money balances when rates are below normal. His behavior results in an inverse relationship between the demand for money and the interest rate. Tobin has shown that if the individual's view of the normal rate is precise, his demand function would appear as a step function with all of his funds in bonds at rates above the critical rate and all of his funds in cash at rates below the critical rate.[4] The continuity of any aggregate demand function would be maintained by the fact that different individuals would have different ideas about the normal rates and would be induced to act at different critical interest rates.

Risk

Tobin has also demonstrated that the changes in portfolio composition that arise from the individual's efforts to avoid risk can result in an inverse relationship between the interest rate and the demand for money. He assumes that the portfolio can be distributed between only two assets, money and bonds, which are represented as proportions of the total as M

[4]J. Tobin, "Liquidity Preferences as Behavior Toward Risk," *Review of Economic Studies*, 25 (February 1958), 65–86.

and B:[5]

$$M + B = 1.0 \tag{5}$$

The total return $(\bar{R})$ on the portfolio will be equal to

$$\bar{R} = B(r+g) \tag{6}$$

where r is the yield on the bonds and g is the expected value of the capital gain. The risk on a bond is measured by the standard deviation of the distribution of capital gains and losses (σ_g) and the total portfolio risk is equal to the proportion of the portfolio held in bonds times the risk:

$$\sigma_T = B\sigma_g \tag{7}$$

The individual can increase the return on his portfolio $(\bar{R}_T)$ by increasing the share of bonds, but in doing so he increases the portfolio risk (σ_T). The possible combinations of return and risk at a market rate r can be expressed by substituting the value for B in equation (7) into equation (6):

$$\bar{R} = \frac{\sigma_T}{\sigma_g}(r+g) = \frac{r+g}{\sigma_g}\sigma_T \tag{8}$$

The investor knows the current market rate (r) and must decide how much risk (σ_T) he is willing to take to improve the portfolio return. The return opportunities and the implications for the distribution of his total portfolio are shown in Figure 8-1. Equation (8) is plotted in the top part of Figure 8-1A and equation (7) is plotted in the lower part. The choice of the portfolio return $(\bar{R})$ carries with it a specified risk (σ_T) and a given portfolio share of bonds (B).

His choice will depend upon his attitude toward risk. If he is indifferent toward risk, he will try to maximize the return on his portfolio and will invest the entire portfolio in bonds, and the demand for money balances will be zero. If he is risk averse, his attitude can be shown by his indifference map (see Figure 7-7). When his indifference map is superimposed on the portfolio alternatives as indicated in Figure 8-1A, he will select the combination of money and bonds that places him on the highest preference level. At the market rate (r_0), he will invest B_0 of his portfolio in bonds with the total portfolio risk of (σ_{T^0}). As the interest rate increases, he will be willing to increase his risk and reduce his holding of money balances. The derived demand for money function is plotted in Figure 8-1B.

[5]For simplicity he assumes that the bonds are consols. See footnote 3.

FIGURE 8-1

A. Market Risk and Portfolio Choice

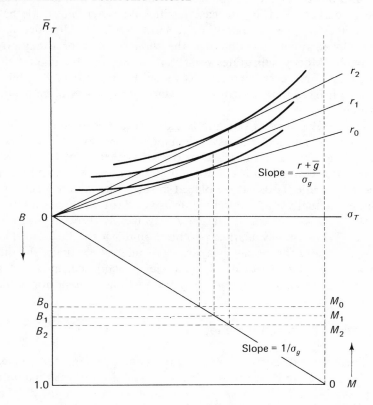

B. Derived Demand for Money

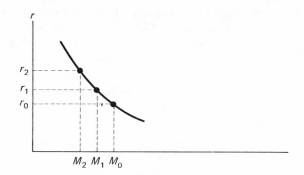

This approach specifically recognizes the individual's preference for safety and illustrates the role of risk as a barrier to the flow of funds into financial markets. Risk in this case justifies the retention of idle balances and becomes a specific factor in the individual's liquidity decisions. In well-developed financial economies, the choice in this form may not have to be made. Money substitutes exist that do not involve market risk but pay interest, and even market risks can be significantly reduced (or eliminated if fixed time horizons are given) by purchases of money market instruments.

The development of safe and liquid alternatives to money reduces the potential importance of the asset demand for money as a financial and economic variable. Even speculative decisions that involve the postponement of purchases of bonds are unlikely to increase the demand for money balances. The idle funds can be placed in substitute money forms until the purchase is actually made. Purchase delays of this type do not interrupt the flow of funds into financial markets; they merely direct it into different channels. When money market practices diminish the theoretical role of the asset demand for money as a source of interest elasticity, the question arises as to whether the demand for money function becomes inelastic or whether there is some elasticity in the transactions demand for money.

Transactions Demand for Money

Theoretical discussions of the transactions demand for money have their practical counterpart in the applied discussions of cash management. The priorities and objectives are the same in both problems. The top priority in both cases is assigned to having money available as a means of payment to meet the desired schedule of expenditures and payments. The secondary objective, which is implicit in the name *cash management*, is to achieve the primary objective as efficiently as possible. The first objective, together with the time pattern of receipts and expenditures, determines the temporary surplus of funds available. The second objective determines the distribution of this surplus between money balances and money substitutes. The cash management problem is a specialized portfolio problem, characterized by a very short time horizon and the existence of some uncertainties. The shortness of the potential investment period and the need for liquidity even during that period are the constraints that must be faced by cash managers.

The dollar amount of money required for payments during any period of time is determined by the level of expenditures. For the economy as a whole when income also measures expenditures, it has become customary to express the demand for transactions balances (L_1) as some proportion (k_1) of income (Y).

$$L_1 = k_1 Y \tag{9}$$

For individual firms and households the size of k_1 depends on the pattern of cash flows. If income receipts and expenditures are perfectly coordinated, large amounts can be spent with average daily money balances of close to zero. For example, assume that someone uses a credit card for all of his daily expenditures and pays his credit card bill and all other bills with checks on the same day that he deposits his paycheck. He could show a zero balance in his checking account at all times, and his money balances would be close to zero except for the small amounts of currency and coin that he might need. At the other extreme, he might deposit his paycheck at the beginning of the period and pay all bills at the end of the period, and his transactions money balance would be approximately equal to the level of expenditure $(k_1 = 1)$. Most cases fall somewhere between these extremes and it is often assumed in the short run that the value of k_1 will be relatively stable and that it depends upon customary patterns of payments.

When money substitutes are available, the assumption of stability in k_1 is not justified even for the short run. If money substitutes are available that have short enough maturities to fit the time horizons of the payment schedules or that can be converted to cash without excessive risk, some share of the funds needed for transactions purposes can be invested in money substitutes. The total balances required may be stable but the money share can change and the ratio k_1 will change with it. If the ratio a_1 is introduced to measure the ratio of total asset balances (T) required to support a given level of expenditure, equation (9) can be reformulated as

$$T = a_1 Y \tag{10}$$

The ratio a_1 can be expected to show the stability that arises from the institutional arrangements for payments, but the composition of a_1 and of the liquid asset portfolio may vary with the availability of money substitutes and with the interest rate. The relationship between money and money substitutes can be examined by dividing the transactions balances portfolio into money balances (L_1) and balances of money substitutes (L_3)

$$T = L_1 + L_3 \tag{11}$$

and dividing the liquidity requirements ratio into money (k_1) and money substitute (k_3) requirements

$$a_1 = k_1 + k_3 \tag{12}$$

Equation (11) can then be expressed as

$$T = L_1 + L_3 = (k_1 + k_3)Y \tag{13}$$

The cash manager needs liquid assets of T to meet his payment require-ments. But he will try to maximize the share that is invested in money substitutes (L_3). The total pool of funds (T) represents a potential source of funds for financial markets that can be tapped only if the cash manager is offered the safety and convertibility that he needs to meet his first priorities—the required schedule of payments. All of the transactions demand funds (T) could theoretically be invested if the income was enough to cover the costs and the inconvenience of converting these balances into money substitutes and back into money.

The income from money substitutes is a direct function of the duration of the investment and the amounts involved. The transactions costs of investing cash balances, including inconvenience, tend to be independent of both the duration and the amount. They take the form of fixed costs with respect to time and size. As fixed costs, they establish minimums on both the time availability intervals and the account size for purposes of converting money balances into money substitutes (L_3) (see Figure 8-2). The average transactions costs (c) decrease as the fixed total is spread over the number of days that the funds are invested, and the costs will exceed the expected return (r) on balances available for only a short time period.

Any increase in the market rate (r) or any decrease in transactions costs (c) will reduce the constraints on the conversion of funds into money substitutes and will increase the share of transactions balances that can be moved into the money markets. The magnitude of these effects will depend on the distribution of individual accounts by size and availability time. Figure 8-3 illustrates the role of changes in interest rates on the residual demand for money balances and on the supply of money market funds obtained from transactions balances. The top half of Figure 8-3A shows the role of the interest rate and transactions cost in determining the minimum period of availability. The bottom half of Figure 8-3A gives a hypothetical example of the expected distribution of aggregate transactions balances at a given time by their availability time. At an interest rate (r_0) only the share of balances with an availability time period of more than 20 days can be invested (L_3^0). The residual amount (measured from L_3^0 to T) has to be held in money balances (L_1). An increase in the interest rate to r_1 reduces the minimum expected time interval required for investment, increases the share of the total that can be invested, and reduces the residual demand for L_1 balances. The derived supply of funds that can be generated by changes in the interest rate is plotted in Figure 8-3B, and the

FIGURE 8-2

NATURE OF COST CONSTRAINTS ON CASH MANAGEMENT

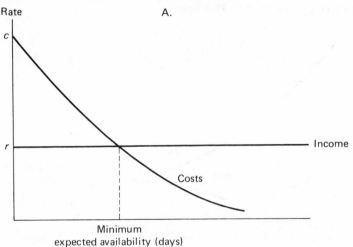

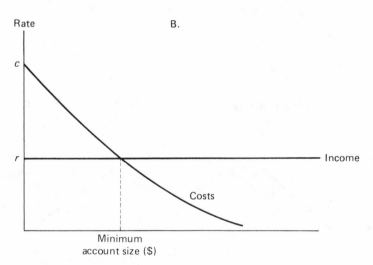

residual demand for transactions balances in money form is plotted in Figure 8-3C.

Figure 8-4 illustrates the effects of changes in transactions costs on the demand for money balances (L_1) and the supply of funds for money market substitutes (L_3). Similar illustrations could be used to show that the distribution of transactions balances by size will also introduce some interest elasticity and cost elasticity into the residual transactions demand for money balances. The demand for transactions balances (L_1) and the supply of investable transactions balances (L_3) are functions of the market

FIGURE 8-3
INTEREST RATES AND THE RESIDUAL DEMAND FOR MONEY FOR TRANSACTIONS PURPOSES

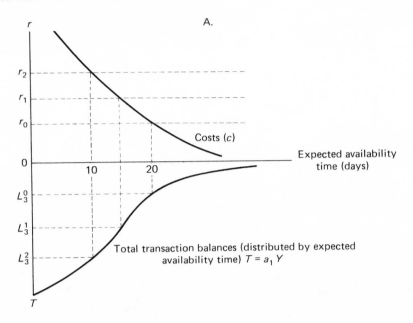

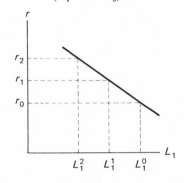

B. Funds Invested (L_3)

C. Residual Demand for Money Balances
$(L_1 = T - L_3)$

interest rate (r), transactions costs (c), including inconvenience, and the distributions of balances by time-availability (t) and size (s).

$$L_1 = f(r,c,t,s)$$

$$L_3 = f(r,c,t,s)$$

If the investable share of transactions balances is assumed to be a linear

FIGURE 8-4

TRANSACTIONS COSTS AND THE RESIDUAL DEMAND
FOR MONEY FOR TRANSACTIONS PURPOSES

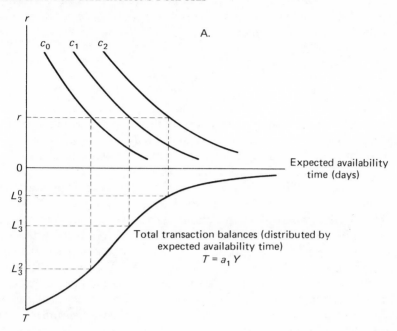

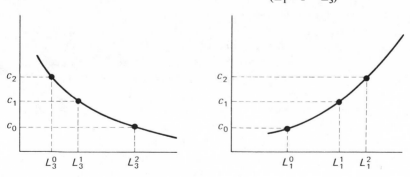

B. Funds Invested (L_3)

C. Residual Demand for Money Balances
($L_1 = T - L_3$)

function of the interest with a slope m_1,

$$L_3 = m_1 r \tag{14}$$

the transactions demand equation (10) can be expressed as

$$T = a_1 Y = L_1 + m_1 r \tag{15}$$

or
$$L_1 = a_1 Y - m_1 r \tag{16}$$

The total demand for money balances in the form of a means of payment (M_1) can be expressed as the sum of the asset demands (L_2) and the residual transactions demands (L_1):

$$M_1 = L_2 + L_1$$

or

$$M_1 = L_2 + a_1 Y - m_1 r \tag{17}$$

where: $L_2 = f(r)$

The L_1 term represents only a fraction of the total transactions balance requirement ($a_1 Y$) where the rest of the needs have been invested in money substitutes (L_3). The demand for money substitutes arising from cash management of transactions balances is not the total demand for those instruments. They are also useful as alternatives to longer-term investment as a part of regular asset portfolios.

The residual share of transactions balances represents a potential source of funds for the money market that can be tapped by the right combination of rate, safety, and liquidity and by lower transactions costs. Illustrations of all these approaches can be found in the period after World War II. Savings institutions that originally computed and paid interest only on accounts that had been on deposit for six months have gradually moved to payment of interest on a daily basis. New short-term instruments, such as negotiable certificates of deposit, have been introduced. Transactions and trading costs have been reduced, and transactions have been made more convenient and faster by the use of telegraphic transfers. The managers of large transactions balances can come close to operating with zero money balances in modern money markets.

The development of money market mutual funds has extended the advantage of money market operations to the holders of smaller cash balances that would otherwise be excluded. These funds accept and pay out funds on demand by telegraphic transfers or checks. They invest the funds for their shareholders in money market instruments and credit interest daily to the share accounts. Most of them permit withdrawal by checking privileges or by telegraphic transfers to the shareholder's bank. Since the fees are deducted from the interest payments, the costs do not have fixed cost features that establish minimum size and time limits on transactions. The funds themselves, however, impose limits on transaction sizes, but those limits are much smaller than those imposed by direct operations in the money market. They may be as small as $200 or $300.

The techniques for tapping the transactions balances have been developed by the mid-1970's to the point where it is possible for anyone to reduce the money share of his transactions balances to a few hundred dollars. He can maintain virtually complete liquidity and receive daily interest on invested balances with the only constraint being in the form of the size of the adjustments. The development of such good substitutes for money balances raises an empirical question about the remaining elasticity of funds from this source.

QUESTIONS FOR DISCUSSION

1. List the most common forms of money substitutes and compare their relative advantages and disadvantages.
2. Why is marketability as a technique for providing liquidity limited to such a small group of borrowers?
3. Can you distinguish the money that you hold for asset purposes from the money that you hold for transactions purposes? How would you go about trying to make the same distinction between the money balances of a corporation?
4. How do money balances reduce the holder risk? Do money balances have unique features for risk reduction?
5. Is it theoretically possible for a large corporation to maintain a daily zero close-of-business money balance? What institutional arrangement might interfere in practice with achieving such a target? What policy considerations might make it undesirable?
6. What changes in the features of financial instruments would you expect to find during a period of tight money? Why?

SELECTED REFERENCES

BAUMOL, WILLIAM J., "Transactions Demand for Cash: An Inventory Theoretic Approach," *Quarterly Journal of Econometrics*, LXVI (November 1952), 545–56.

LAIDLER, DAVID E. W., *The Demand for Money: Theories and Evidence.* Scranton, Penn.: International Textbook Company, 1969.

MILLER, M. H., and D. ORR, "Model of the Demand for Money by Firms," *Quarterly Journal of Economics*, LXXX (August 1966), 413–35.

———, "Mathematical Models for Financial Management," *Frontiers of Financial Management*, eds. Serraino, Singhvi and Soldofsky. Cincinnati, Ohio: South-Western Publishing Co., 1971.

NADIRI, M. I., "The Determinants of Real Cash Balances in the U.S. Total Manufacturing Sector," *Quarterly Journal of Economics*, LXXXIII (May 1969), 173–96.

TOBIN, JAMES, "The Interest Elasticity of Transactions Demand for Cash," *Review of Economics and Statistics*, XXXVIII (August 1956), 241–47.

———, "Liquidity Preference as Behavior Towards Risks," *Review of Economic Studies* 25 (February 1958), 65–86.

Financial Intermediation

9

Financial intermediation is an essential feature of the borrowing–lending process. It bridges the gap between borrowers and lenders and reconciles their often incompatible needs and objectives. Two types of barriers to the financing process can be identified. The first type arises from the difficulty and expense of matching the complex needs of individual borrowers and lenders. Financial institutions reduce these costs by providing centralized markets for borrowers and lenders of all types. Their role in handling these problems is similar to that played by economic markets of all types. The second type of barrier arises from the incompatibility of the financial needs and objectives of borrowers and lenders. The lender is looking for safety and liquidity, and the borrower can't promise either. Financial institutions can reconcile these needs by offering suppliers of funds safety and liquidity and by using the funds for loans and investments with varying degrees of risk and liquidity. They can give their suppliers long-term contracts and lend on short-term contracts, or they can borrow short and lend long. Their ability to match apparently inconsistent types of financial contracts is sometimes called the *transmutation effect.*

The secret of the transmutation effect lies in the structure of financial institutions. These institutions are made up of two large pools of financial contracts—their sources of funds and their assets. Their successful operations depend upon the overall performance of these pools. The performance of these pools is shaped by individual contracts, but the overall performance of the pool is much more dependable and predictable than that of individual contracts. The pools have the statistical advantages of large numbers. The average loss rates and the average liquidity requirements can be predicted with considerable accuracy even when the prospects for individual contracts are uncertain. The art of managing a financial institution lies in combining individual contracts into asset and liability portfolios that have compatible statistical features. The first three sections of this chapter discuss the relationships between individual financial contracts and their combined statistical features that make possible the reduction of risk and the provision of liquidity. The last section discusses the problems of compatibility between asset and liability portfolios.

Reduction of Default Risk

The reduction of default risk by financial institutions is made possible by the supplier of funds trading the risk he would face on a single loan for a share of the risk of a portfolio of those loans. In statistical terms, he trades a risk that is describable by a frequency distribution for one loan for a $1/n$th share of a frequency distribution for n loans where n may be a very large number. The changes in the nature of his risk arise from the changes in the nature of the frequency distributions that accompany an increase in n (see Chapter 7). The possibilities of a total loss are virtually eliminated and the amount of the expected loss can be predicted with considerable accuracy. Since the amount of the expected loss can be predicted, it can be treated as a cost of doing business and handled as an expense. The only risk that the supplier faces arises from the possibility that the losses may exceed expectations. But even in this case, his maximum loss is limited to $1/n$th of the total loss of the institution and is likely to be only a fraction of his initial investment. If the standard deviation (σ) is used as the measure of dispersion, $1/n$th of the potential variation from the expected loss approaches zero as the number of loans increases as indicated by the following equation (see Figure 9-1):

$$\frac{\sigma}{n} = \frac{\sqrt{npq}}{n} \tag{1}$$

where: $p =$ default rate

$q = (1-p)$

In practice, this purely theoretical approach to default risk has to be modified in two ways. First, the theoretical version assumes that the losses on individual loans are statistically independent, and the possibility of some covariance has to be introduced. Second, a number of institutional features have been developed by financial institutions and their regulators, which can be used to protect some or all of the suppliers of funds from unexpected variations in losses.

FIGURE 9-1
NUMBER OF LOANS AND PORTFOLIO RISK

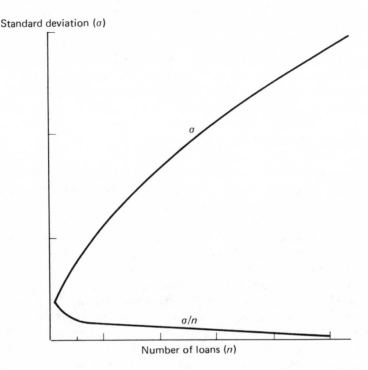

Standard deviation (σ)

σ

σ/n

Number of loans (n)

The loans in a typical loan portfolio may not be completely independent in statistical terms. Borrowers from the same industry, who work at the same factory, or who live in the same region may be affected in much the same way by selective economic events. An individual financial institution cannot escape some elements of positive covariance among its loans, and the possibility of covariance has to be taken into consideration in judging the portfolio risk of the institution.

Positive covariance reduces the theoretical advantages of pooling as a device for reducing risks. Its implications for the frequency distribution of losses are similar to those of decreasing the number of loans in the portfolio (n). At the extreme, perfect positive covariance implies that if one loan goes bad they will all go bad. A $1/n$th share of the total loss would be equal to the total loss on a single loan, and there would be no advantages in sharing a pool of loans. The potential sources of positive covariance can often be identified and taken into consideration in calculating portfolio risk.

A number of techniques have been developed to protect the supplier of funds from losses. First, reserves for loans are usually larger than those dictated by the expected default rates. These reserves are available to absorb unexpected losses and to shield the supplier from these risks. Second, priorities that provide for different degrees of protection from risk may be assigned to the suppliers of funds. In view of the skewed nature of the frequency distributions associated with default risk, the suppliers in the senior positions may be assured of substantial freedom from risk. Third, insurance programs of various types can be used to protect the supplier from these unexpected losses. The insurance of commercial bank deposits by the FDIC is an example of this type of protection.

The system of financial intermediaries as it currently exists in the United States provides the suppliers of funds with a wide variety of savings alternatives that are virtually free of default risk. Insurance programs and capital and loss reserves provide back-up protection, but the basic risk reduction arises from the statistical features of the pooling opportunities offered by financial institutions.

Reduction of Market Risk

The frequency distributions associated with market risk in general show a much wider potential variance than those for default risk. But the role of financial institutions in reducing these potential risks and, in particular, the extreme variations that are so important in subjective reactions to risk, is much the same. The risk reduction is possible because the supplier of funds can trade the frequency distribution that describes the risk on a single security for a share of the risk on a portfolio of securities. The portfolio risk, where the standard deviation (σ_p) is used as the measure of risk, can be calculated as follows:

$$\sigma_p = \sqrt{\sum_{i=1}^{n} \sum_{j=1}^{n} X_i X_j C_{ij}} \tag{2}$$

where: X_i = proportion of the portfolio held in security i.

C_{ij} = covariance between the expected returns (or changes in prices) on securities i and j.

The calculations for a portfolio of a large number of securities are obviously quite involved, but we can see the implications of the formula for the portfolio risk by applying it to two securities (a,b). Equation (2) becomes

$$\sigma_p = \sqrt{X_a^2 \sigma_a^2 + X_b^2 \sigma_b^2 + 2 X_a X_b C_{a,b}} \tag{3}$$

and, where ρ equals the coefficient of correlation, the covariance becomes

$$C_{a,b} = \rho\sigma_a\sigma_b \tag{4}$$

Three alternatives can be used to illustrate the relationship between covariance and portfolio risk.

1) When the returns on the securities are perfectly correlated ($\rho = 1$), equation (3) becomes

$$\sigma_p = \sqrt{X_a^2\sigma_a^2 + X_b^2\sigma_b^2 + 2X_aX_b\sigma_a\sigma_b} \tag{5}$$

and the standard deviation of the portfolio can be obtained by taking the square root of equation (5)

$$\sigma_p = X_a\sigma_a + X_b\sigma_b \tag{6}$$

The standard deviation of this portfolio is equal to the weighted average standard deviations of the individual securities. No risk reduction is gained by combining the securities. An increase in the share of the riskier security (X_b) will increase the portfolio risk proportionally to the amount added (see line (1) in Figure 9-2).

2) When the returns on the securities are independent ($\rho = 0$), equation (3) becomes

$$\sigma_p = \sqrt{X_a^2\sigma_a^2 + X_b^2\sigma_b^2} \tag{7}$$

Since the first two terms of equation (7) are the same as those of equation (5) and the last term of equation (5) is positive, combination of the two securities into a portfolio will achieve some risk reduction compared to a portfolio with positively correlated securities (see line (2) in Figure 9-2).

3) When the returns on the securities are negatively correlated ($\rho = -1$), the capital gain on one will be exactly offset by the losses on the other. Equation (3) becomes

$$\sigma_p = \sqrt{X_a^2\sigma_a^2 + X_b^2\sigma_b^2 - 2X_aX_b\sigma_a\sigma_b} \tag{8}$$

A portfolio of two securities that are negatively correlated would have zero market risk when the correct mix of securities is reached. In the illustration in Figure 9-2, the risk of b is twice that of a; and in a portfolio of one-third b and two-thirds a, the changes in the market prices of the securities would

FIGURE 9-2

COVARIANCE AND PORTFOLIO RISK—TWO SECURITIES

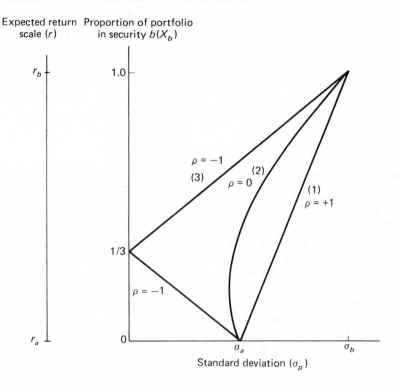

be offsetting and the standard deviation of the portfolio would be equal to zero ($\sigma_p = 0$).

If the expected return on security b is higher than the expected return on security a, the illustration in Figure 9-2 can be converted to the standard graph of expected return and risk. The portfolio return of

$$r_p = r_a X_a + r_b X_b \tag{9}$$

is proportional to the share of the portfolio invested in b and can be measured by a scale that runs from r_a, when X_b is equal to zero, to r_b, when X_b equals one.

In practice, the control of the market risk on securities is less exact than these illustrations suggest, but a pool of securities that shows anything less than perfect positive covariance permits some risk reduction. An individual with a relatively small amount of funds to invest can reduce his market risk by buying a share in a portfolio of stocks or by placing his funds in a financial institution that gives him a share of its assets. A very wealthy individual can diversify his own holdings and may not need a financial institution to achieve this type of risk reduction. But diversification of market risk is one of the features that a pool of funds can provide.

Provision of Liquidity

Banks promise their depositors perfect liquidity, yet a close look at the assets of a bank at any given time may not show any free cash at all. The techniques used by banks to handle their liquidity problem will be discussed in the next chapter. The immediate problem is to identify the statistical properties of a bank's deposits that produce manageable stability in the combined totals. The observed stability in the total demand deposits of an individual bank appears even more remarkable when the fluctuations in the size of individual accounts are examined. The frequency distributions of the daily balances of a typical checking account are likely to be highly skewed with a standard deviation that is several times the average size of the account. The extreme positive variations may be hundreds of times larger than the mean of the account.

The conventional explanation of the stability in total deposits assumes the statistical independence of the accounts. The layman's explanation that "not everyone wants their money at the same time" is essentially correct, but it does not identify a second source of stability that is important for understanding the role of banks in the financing process. A strong element of *perfect negative covariance* can also be identified in the behavior of checking accounts. Perfect negative covariance is a rare statistical phenomenon, but it appears in bank checking accounts as a by-product of the use of these accounts as a means of payment. A check drawn on one account is deposited in another account, and the variations in the two accounts are offset exactly. When the two accounts are held by the same bank, the bank's total deposits are unaffected by the activity in those accounts.

The negative covariance in the total deposits of all banks is nearly complete and perfect. A money system comprised of checking accounts is basically a bookkeeping arrangement. Funds are shifted from one account to another without affecting the aggregate total. This element of negative covariance is *not* present in the savings accounts of institutions that do not have checking accounts. The ability of savings institutions to promise their account holders almost complete liquidity has to be traced to the statistical independence of their accounts and not to the presence of any significant element of negative covariance.

Individual financial institutions may also be exposed to some elements of positive covariance. Regional flows of funds, such as those that can be observed in resort areas or in agricultural communities, create liquidity problems for individual banks. Many banks are faced with seasonal or other periodic flows of funds that are evidence of positive covariance. An extreme case of positive covariance is observed in a "run on the bank" when all of the depositors want their money. The statistical advantages of a pool of funds disappears with the appearance of perfect positive covariance. The term *disintermediation* describes a type of positive covariance that can be traced to money market conditions.

The identification of the potential sources of positive covariance among the accounts of an institution also identifies the institution's liquidity management problems. Under normal conditions, commercial banks can depend on elements of negative covariance and independence for considerable stability in their total deposits. Their practical liquidity problems are further reduced by the practice of requiring compensating balances, which introduce an element of stability into the individual accounts, and to the growth of aggregate deposit funds. The commercial banks only have to be concerned with their ability to handle the special cases of positive covariance. Savings institutions without the built-in stability of negative covariance in their accounts generally have greater stability in their individual accounts.

Compatibility of Asset and Liability Portfolios

The assets and liabilities of a financial institution are constantly changing. The statistician sees them as ever-changing sets of values that can be described by frequency distributions. The accountant captures one point in the distribution when he produces the institution's asset and liability statement. Double entry accounting assures equality of assets and liabilities, but the two sets of accounts are subject to very different types of economic and financial pressures that can create problems for the institution. The art of management of financial institutions centers around the maintenance of financial and statistical compatibility between asset and liability portfolios.

Default or market losses reduce the value of an institution's assets, and these reductions must be accompanied by an appropriate reduction in the value of the claims against those assets. The bookkeeping transactions are automatic, but the implications for the institution may be serious. Losses will normally be deducted from loss reserves or earnings. If they are larger than the loss reserves, they have to be deducted from equity. If they should exceed the combined value of reserves and equity, they will impinge on the value of the fixed dollar claims against the institution. The term *insolvency* is used to describe this unpleasant state of affairs.

The management problems associated with default and market risk depend on the statistical features of the institution's assets. No one ever draws the frequency distribution for default risk on a financial institution's assets because, in many cases, the standard deviation is so small that the distribution itself would be difficult to draw. But the features of that distribution identify the problems of risk management. When the distribution is superimposed on the structure of liabilities, it indicates the range of losses that can be absorbed easily and the probabilities associated with those losses. It indicates the critical amounts associated with insolvency and the chances of losses of that size. Figure 9-3 uses the frequency distribution for an unrealistically high default rate ($p = 0.1$) to illustrate the relationship between the frequency distribution of assets and the structure of liabilities.

The assets of a financial institution are usually reported in accounting statements as *net of reserves for losses*. The gross value of its assets includes reserves for losses and measures the upper limit of asset values (assuming no capital gains). The spread between the institution's gross assets and its net assets measures the amount of its loss reserves. The proportion of the frequency distribution over that range of assets measures

FIGURE 9-3

FREQUENCY DISTRIBUTION OF LOSSES
AND THE STRUCTURE OF LIABILITIES

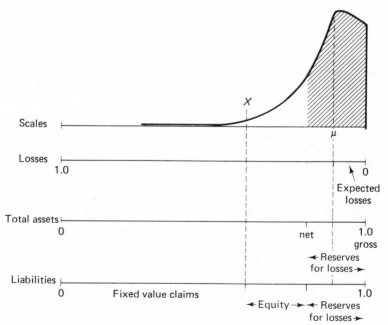

the likelihood that the institution will incur losses without impairing its capital (shaded area in Figure 9-3). The share of the frequency distribution over the combined amount of reserves and equity (up to point X) gives the likelihood that losses can be absorbed without leading to insolvency.

The techniques for safeguarding the institutions from insolvency fall into two obvious classes. First, the nature of frequency distribution of risks can be controlled by the selection of assets. Second, the structure of liabilities can be adjusted to reduce the likelihood of insolvency by increasing reserves and equity. Note that an institution without fixed claims does not face a specific danger point in the size of its losses. Risk management in such an institution becomes largely a question of the reactions of the shareholders of the institution.

The liabilities of financial institutions that provide liquidity are also a source of uncertainty. The variations in the total liabilities of these institutions can be described by frequency distributions that indicate the likelihood of various changes. These distributions will be unrestrained on the growth side and limited on the contraction side. The comparison of such a distribution with the structure of the institution's assets identifies its liquidity problems (see Figure 9-4). Any loss of funds requires a contraction of assets. These adjustments may be easy and normal when liquid

FIGURE 9-4
FREQUENCY DISTRIBUTION OF DEPOSIT CHANGES
AND THE STRUCTURE OF ASSETS

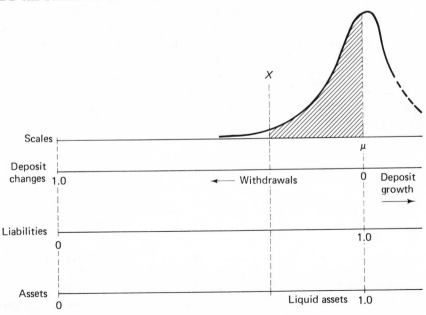

assets are available. The problems become potentially more serious, however, when the loss of funds exceeds the available liquid assets. The forced liquidation of less marketable assets is likely to produce market losses, which give the institution the joint problem of adjusting for both losses and liquidity. The danger point is not as precise in liquidity problems as the insolvency point, but the dangers increase as the size of the adjustment increases. The specific techniques for handling liquidity problems will be discussed in the next chapter, but it can be seen from this discussion that they fall into two classes: those that involve changes in the structure of the institution's assets to provide better liquidity, and those designed to reduce variations in liabilities.

Liquidity and cash flow problems can be reduced in some cases by matching the maturities of asset and liability contracts. Although matches of this type are theoretically not essential, they introduce a helpful element of covariance into the cash flows of asset and liability portfolios. A portfolio of 20-year loans could be financed with short-term funds or a portfolio of short-term loans could be financed with long-term debt. But management problems are intensified by mismatches of this type. The short-term contracts are subject to continuous renegotiation and changes in market conditions can lead to rate changes that may be incompatible with contractual rates on long-term contracts. The savings institutions with long-term mortgage loans and short-term sources of funds faced serious problems when short-term rates rose above the rates they could afford to pay. It is generally assumed that commercial banks should limit their loans and investments to short-term commitments despite the relative stability of their deposits. When they venture into longer maturities, the practice is often rationalized by some sort of internal matching of the long asset with savings funds thought to provide greater stability than demand deposit accounts. The direct pairing of assets and liabilities reduces the flexibility of financial institutions and ignores the advantages of looking at the statistical properties of the overall portfolios, but it reduces some of the risks of variations in credit market conditions.

QUESTIONS FOR DISCUSSION

1. Illustrate the concept of transmutation as it applies to the sources and uses of funds for some type of financial institution.
2. Give some specific examples of loans that might show some positive covariance with respect to default risk. How can a financial institution with a substantial degree of positive covariance in its loan portfolio protect its depositors from the dangers of this risk?
3. What probability of default would you assign to your checking account?

How would that value compare with the default risk on the bank's loan portfolio? What explains the differences, if any?

4. How is it possible for the demand deposits of all banks to show nearly perfect negative covariance? Can you think of an exception?

5. Imagine that you have been asked to sort a random pile of checks, which came into an individual bank on any given day, into separate piles: (1) those that indicate statistical independence, (2) those that indicate positive covariance for your bank, and (3) those that indicate negative covariance for your bank. How would you proceed?

6. Develop a list of steps that you might take as a bank manager to reduce the dangers of insolvency by changing the asset structure and loan policies of the bank. Discuss the implications of each step for the bank's earnings and the frequency distribution that applies to its default risk.

7. Most of the loans of a bank cannot be called even if the bank is desperately in need of money. Can you think of any ways in which its loan portfolio can be used to meet urgent liquidity needs?

SELECTED REFERENCES

Cohen, Kalman J., and Frederick S. Hammer, eds., *Analytical Methods in Banking*. Homewood, Ill.: Richard D. Irwin Inc., 1966.

Goldfeld, S. M., *Commercial Bank Behavior and Economic Activity*. Amsterdam: North-Holland Publishing Co., 1966.

Gurley, John G., and E. S. Shaw, *Money in a Theory of Finance*. Washington, D.C.: Brookings Institution, 1960.

Markowitz, Harry M., *Portfolio Selection*. New York: John Wiley and Sons, 1959.

Porter, Richard C., "A Model of Bank Portfolio Selection," *Financial Markets and Economic Activity*, eds., Donald D. Hester and James Tobin. New York: John Wiley and Sons, 1967.

Van Horne, James C., *Function and Analysis of Capital Market Rates*, chapter V. Englewood Cliffs, N.J.: Prentice-Hall, Inc., 1970.

Sharpe, William F., *Portfolio Theory and Capital Markets*. New York: McGraw-Hill Book Company, 1970.

Commercial Banks

10

Commercial banks play a central role in the intermediation process. They handle a large share of the funds that flow from lenders to borrowers, and their checking accounts provide most of the country's payment system. Their authority to accept checking accounts gives them nearly exclusive rights to accounts that can be used as a means of payment. It assures them of a large block of low cost funds and places them in a strategic position in the financing process. It also gives them quasi-public responsibilities that expose them to close regulatory attention.

Banks are creatures of government regulations. Their economic power and their competitive strength arise from their role as custodians of the money supply. Their authority to use this strength as a base for expanding their functions into other types of financial and economic activities is limited by restrictions imposed by law and by regulatory authorities. The scope of banking activities differs widely from one country to another and the history of banking in the United States has been dominated by the revisions and modifications of its banking laws.

The first section of this chapter looks at banks in their primary role as checking-account or note-issuing institutions. The second looks at a more realistic and broader version of a bank that accepts time and savings accounts and raises open market funds. The third section examines the current role of commercial banks in the intermediation process. The fourth examines the bank as the central institution of a holding company structure that extends the role of the bank beyond its institutional shell. The last section looks at the nature and role of supervisory controls that are applied to banks.

Demand Deposit Banking

An individual commercial bank in its simplest form consists of a privately owned institution authorized to accept demand accounts. These accounts shape its profit opportunities and its operating problems. As an institution, its sources of funds consist of equity supplied by stockholders and the fixed value claims of depositors. It can lend or invest these funds and capture the spread between the rate it receives on its loans and its costs. The most serious threats to successful operations arise from (1) the potential liquidity problems that would accompany sizable deposit withdrawals and (2) the potential losses on the loans and investments that it makes with the depositors' funds. Both of these problems are statistical in nature. They have to be viewed in terms of probabilities and frequency distributions, and the safeguards have to be formulated in statistical terms.

A bank has very little direct control over its demand accounts. It must design its asset portfolio in a way that gives it the liquidity it needs to meet potential deposit withdrawals. The problem becomes one of reconciling the potential need for liquidity with the profitability of the asset portfolio. Very few banks find it necessary to hold funds in money balances or in deposits with other banks. Their deposits with correspondent banks may serve this purpose to some extent but they are usually justified as part of the costs and benefits of the correspondent relationship rather than as a source of liquidity.

The first line of defense against deposit withdrawals lies in the bank's portfolio of short-term marketable securities or its *secondary reserves.* These securities provide liquidity in two ways. First, the regular turnover of funds provides a stream of cash flows that can also be diverted to cover deposit withdrawals. Second, the securities can be sold to cover deposit losses, if necessary.

The *operating liquidity* provided by the cash flow from the bank's secondary reserves can be measured by the periodic flow of funds that it produces. Almost any pattern of cash flows can be built into an investment portfolio by the timing of purchases and by the selection of maturities. The secondary reserves can, in this way, be used to provide funds for expected seasonal losses or other predictable movements of funds (positive covariance). They can also be used to cover random fluctuations by providing for the regular roll-over of these securities. A portfolio of $12 million can be used to produce a monthly cash flow of a million dollars when it is invested in one-year maturities, or a flow four times that large when it is invested in three-month maturities. The cost of liquidity in this form consists of the high transactions and opportunity costs associated with turnover and lower returns on short-term securities.

The adequacy of the bank's operating liquidity can be measured by comparing it to the frequency distribution of the bank's deposit fluctuations. The ratio (l_1) of the weekly turnover cash flow (c_1) to the standard deviation of the distribution of weekly deposit fluctuations (σ_d) provides a direct statistical measure of the effectiveness of the normal operating liquidity:

$$l_1 = \frac{c_1}{\sigma_d} \tag{1}$$

When l_1 is equal to or greater than 3, 99.87 percent or more of the normal deposit losses are covered by the normal turnover liquidity operations. Since the size of the roll-over cash flow relative to total deposits is determined by the portion of total assets held in secondary reserves and by the average maturity of the secondary reserve portfolio, the banker can adjust these features to obtain the degree of protection that he wants. The size of the l_1 ratio can be increased by either an increase in the size of the secondary reserve portfolio or a decrease in the average maturity of the securities held in that portfolio. Both of these changes imply some loss of earning power for the asset portfolio as a whole. The choice must be made by the banker, and the final decision depends on his attitude toward risk and the importance of the earnings involved in the tradeoff. A bank with a comfortable profit margin has greater freedom in planning for liquidity.

If the turnover cash flow from the bank's secondary reserves does not provide enough liquidity, some of the securities in the reserve can be sold. This approach, however, introduces the new problem of market risk. The liquidation of the bank's investment portfolio is likely to involve capital losses. Liquidity needs usually arise during periods of tight money when security prices are depressed. The dangers of market risk can be reduced by the selection of the securities held in the reserve portfolio, but the avoidance of market risk is also likely to reduce the return on the portfolio. Figure 10-1 gives the composition of the secondary reserves of large commercial banks on one date.

The *reserve liquidity* of a bank's assets is often measured by the ratio of its liquid assets—secondary reserves—to total assets or to total deposits. This measure can be made statistically more meaningful by relating the expected value of the secondary reserves (S) to the standard deviation of deposit fluctuations (σ_d). This ratio ($l_2 = S/\sigma_d$) produces a liquidity measure similar to the one used to measure operating liquidity in equation (1). If the value of l_2 is greater than 3, the secondary reserves will cover all but a deposit loss that exceeds three times the standard deviation of deposit variations, or 99.87 percent of the possible outcomes. A more conservative approach might also provide for the reduction of the value of

FIGURE 10-1
SECONDARY RESERVES OF LARGE COMMERCIAL BANKS,
DECEMBER 31, 1975

	Amount (billions)	Percent of total
Total investments	$100.3	100.0
U.S. Treasury:		
Bills	13.7	13.7
Notes and bonds maturing:		
within a year	6.7	6.7
1 to 5 years	17.0	16.9
After 5 years	2.8	2.8
State and political subdivisions:		
Tax warrants	6.5	6.5
Other	39.5	39.4
Certificates of participation, U.S. agencies	2.3	2.3
Other	11.8	11.7

Source: *Federal Reserve Bulletin* (January 1976), p. A-19.

secondary reserves by some estimate of the market risk. If one standard deviation of the frequency distribution associated with security price (σ_m) is used as an estimate of the potential capital loss, the total liquidity provided by secondary reserves would be

$$l_2 = \frac{S - \sigma_m}{\sigma_d} \qquad (2)$$

Since the bank's loans are continuously turning over, some *emergency liquidity* is provided by the loan portfolio itself. The flow of funds from loan repayments could be used to meet deposit withdrawals, but the extension of liquidity adjustments to these funds would involve the gradual liquidation of the bank's loan business and would seriously disturb its customer relations. Traditional banking theory emphasizes the need for short loan maturities, and many banks require their customers to pay down their loans at least once a year. This requirement should produce an average weekly cash flow of 1/52th of the total loan portfolio. These funds (c_2) can be included in a measure of a bank's ability to meet emergency deposit withdrawals:

$$l_3 = \frac{c_2 + S - \sigma_m}{\sigma_d} \qquad (3)$$

This approach has the advantage of relating loan repayments to the bank's liquidity problems, but it deals with the third or fourth line of liquidity defense.

From this discussion, it is evident that the special features of demand deposits play an important role in shaping the asset structure of the banks that accept these accounts. In addition to the secondary reserves, banks must hold funds in a variety of accounts associated with their check clearing and deposit functions. These accounts include (1) legal reserves against deposits, (2) balances with correspondent banks to compensate them for services of various types, and (3) funds that are due but not received—"cash items in process of collection." These accounts reduce the share of assets that can be placed in loans, and represent a cost of accepting demand deposits.

Even the bank's loan portfolio is conditioned by the nature of its liabilities. Both traditional theory and regulatory pressure have encouraged banks to make only short-term commitments and to provide for a relatively rapid turnover of their loans so that their assets can be readily adjusted to the movements of deposits. Banks are also expected to avoid market risks because of the fixed-value nature of their demand deposit claims. Any financial institution that makes loans or buys securities has to be concerned with default and/or market risk. Its ability to absorb risk depends on its commitments to its suppliers of funds. Since demand accounts are fixed-value claims, the ability of the bank to absorb losses without endangering its solvency is limited to the amount of its reserves for losses and its capital funds. The relationship of these funds to the frequency distributions of losses provides a statistical measure of risk exposure. The ratio of reserves for losses plus capital funds (E) to the standard deviation of the loss distribution (σ_e) provides an index of the institution's protection from insolvency.

$$k = \frac{E}{\sigma_e} \qquad (4)$$

Since the coverage ratio (k) can be adjusted by changing either term on the right side of equation (4), the desired degree of risk coverage can be achieved either by changing the amount of reserves and equity or by the selection of assets to control the nature of the loss distribution.

Since the equity ratios (E) are relatively small at the typical bank (between 5 and 10 percent), the bank cannot expose itself to a very high degree of market risk and must be relatively careful even about default risk. Banks are usually prohibited from investing funds in assets like common stock or real estate. They also usually try to limit the market risk on their secondary reserve portfolio by confining their purchases to short maturities. Banks are in a good position to control default risk. They can be selective, and usually do not have to accept high-risk loans.

A bank restricted to demand accounts as a source of funds has a very special set of operating problems that can be observed in the structure of its assets and liabilities. However, banks are seldom restricted to demand accounts, and in practice their operations involve a more complex mix of risk and liquidity problems.

Commercial Banks as Multipurpose Institutions

Commercial banks in most countries are permitted to raise funds with a wide variety of instruments and from a wide variety of markets. These alternatives supplement the demand accounts that serve to distinguish commercial banks from other types of financial institutions and give them a more important and more versatile role in the intermediation process.

The ability of banks to compete for savings is limited in the United States by legal ceilings on the rates they can pay on time and savings accounts. The relaxation of these ceilings that began in the 1950's led to expansion of the role of commercial banks and has given them greater flexibility in their financing arrangements. They can compete with savings institutions directly for time and savings accounts, and they can raise funds in the money market by selling negotiable certificates of deposit (CDs).

These new sources of funds have changed both the liquidity problems faced by individual banks and the approaches they can use in handling these problems. Savings accounts can be redeemed on demand, but the individual accounts tend to be much less volatile than demand accounts. Time accounts have specific maturities and can be redeemed in advance of the maturity date only by some sacrifice of interest. The addition of these accounts to the bank's deposit portfolio has tended to reduce the relative size of the overall day-to-day deposit fluctuations. But the vulnerability of these accounts to disintermediation has introduced a new liquidity problem for banks. The problem appears in the most acute form whenever short-term market rates move above the ceiling rates the bank can pay on time or savings accounts This problem could be solved by the removal of the ceilings but, as will be seen, this solution merely shifts the problem to savings institutions. The issues and problems of the competition for savings will be discussed later. A temporary compromise solution has been to remove the ceilings on the rates that banks can pay on large CDs. This solution permits them to raise funds in the money market without directly competing with the savings institutions for smaller accounts.

Direct access to money market funds introduced a new approach to bank liquidity problems. It had always been possible for banks to solve their short-run liquidity problems by borrowing from other banks or from the central bank. But these loans had to be repaid. Banks with access to the money market can use CDs as a continuing source of short-term funds that can be turned on or off almost at will. This new flexibility was used not only to adjust for losses of deposits but to expand loan activities. A bank that is limited in its sources to demand accounts may have very little control over the funds it can make available to its customers. If it doesn't have the money, it has to turn them down. A bank with access to the money market can act as an agent for its customers in raising funds. The CD, and the access to the money market that it has given the large banks, has greatly expanded the role of banks in the intermediation process and has altered the concept of liquidity management.

These changes in the scope of bank activities have been recorded in the changes in structure of their assets and liabilities. Time and savings accounts increased as a share of total deposits from 23 percent in 1950 to 57 percent in 1975 (see Figure 10-2). CDs grew from negligible amounts before 1960 to 11 percent of total deposits by 1975. On the asset side, secondary reserves dropped from 60 percent of total loans and investments in 1950 to 30 percent by 1975.

Liquidity management at a modern bank is concerned primarily with the problem of obtaining the funds that it wants or needs for loan expansion. The term *shiftability approach* is used to describe the use of secondary reserves to meet new loan demands. The scope of this approach is obviously limited by size of those reserves and by need for some minimum amount of secondary reserve balances. The term *liability management* is used to describe the use of money market instruments to finance loan expansion or to offset deposit losses.

Since liability management can be used to offset deposit withdrawals as well as to raise funds for new loans, the concept of operating liquidity can be extended to include the funds that can be raised by selling CDs. If it is assumed that there is some limit to CDs that an individual bank can sell (d^*), the spread between that limit and the actual amount of CDs that the bank has outstanding (d) represents a potential source of operating liquidity. Equation (1) can be changed to

$$l_1' = \frac{c_1 + (d^* - d)}{\sigma_d} \tag{5}$$

Similar adjustments can be made to the measures of reserve liquidity. It is unlikely, however, that CDs can be used for emergency liquidity, because the events that lead to an emergency are likely to impair the bank's ability to sell CDs.

FIGURE 10-2
CHANGING STRUCTURE OF COMMERCIAL BANK ASSETS AND DEPOSITS,
1950–1975

A. Distribution of Total Loans and Investments

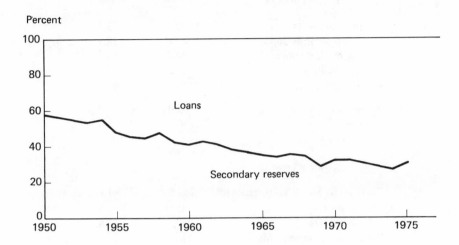

B. Distribution of Total Deposits

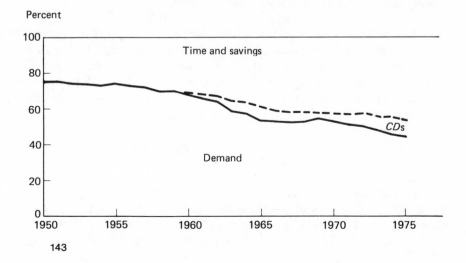

FIGURE 10-3
Sources and Uses of Funds at All Commercial Banks,
June 30, 1975

Sources of funds	Amount (billions)	Percent of total
Demand deposits	$309.7	33.3
Time and savings deposits	362.6	38.9
Money market sources[a]	144.7	15.5
Other liabilities	38.5	4.1
Total liabilities	855.5	91.9
Reserves for losses	9.0	1.0
Capital	66.6	7.1
Total	931.1	100.0
Uses of funds		
Total loans and investments	747.9	80.3
Loans	535.8	57.5
Investments	212.1	22.8
Reserves and cash items	128.7	13.8
Other assets	54.5	5.9
Total	931.1	100.0

[a]Includes large certificates of deposit, Federal Funds purchased
and borrowing.
Source: *Federal Reserve Bulletin* (January 1976), pp. A 16–17.

Commercial Banks as Financial Intermediaries

Figure 10-3 gives a picture of the scope and range of commercial banks in the process of financial intermediation. One-third of their funds come from demand accounts. The largest share, 39 percent, is obtained from the savings markets. A substantial and volatile share, 16 percent on June 30, 1975, is obtained from the money markets. This share identifies the role of banks in actively seeking funds for their borrowers and assisting with money market adjustments.

On the other side of the process, they supply funds in nearly all of the primary markets (see Figure 10-4). Less than a fourth of their funds are used in their traditional role as supplier of loans for commercial and industrial purposes. They supply funds to every sector of the economy and to all the short-term and intermediate-term financial markets. Some of these loans can be made with marketable financial instruments so that they can also serve the bank as secondary reserves. A substantial share (12.3

FIGURE 10-4

COMMERCIAL BANKS AS SUPPLIERS OF FUNDS IN PRIMARY MARKETS

Classification		Amount (billions)	Percent of total
Total loans and investments		$747.9	100.0
Commercial and industrial loans		179.0	23.9
Loans to farmers		19.1	2.6
Loans to other financial institutions		91.7	12.3
Nonbank financial	32.4		
Other banks	11.2		
Money market loans	38.8		
Brokers and dealers	5.5		
Purchase securities	3.8		
Real estate loans		131.4	17.6
Secured by—			
Farmland	6.1		
Residential property	81.3		
Other	44.0		
Loans to individuals		101.8	13.6
Passenger automobiles	32.1		
Residential repairs	5.6		
Credit cards	10.8		
Mobile homes	8.8		
Other consumer goods	6.5		
Other	38.0		
Securities of U.S. Treasury and U.S. agencies		102.1	13.7
Securities of state and political subdivisions		101.5	13.6
Other securities and loans		21.3	2.8

Source: *Federal Reserve Bulletin* (January 1976), p. A-16.

percent) of their loans is to other banks and financial institutions. These loans assist with the intermediation process by providing liquidity for the day-to-day adjustments at those institutions.

Bank Holding Companies

Traditional banking theory looks at a bank as a single legal and economic unit. It assumes that the bank's managers and representatives try to negotiate contracts and terms that serve the best interests of the bank. Problems of personal conflict of interest may arise, but the legal and moral obligations of the bank's representatives are usually clear. When a bank becomes a member of a holding company, both the legal and behavioral issues become more complex. The two limiting positions can be used to illustrate the problem. At one extreme, it can be assumed that the holding company is merely one of the stockholders whose interests in the bank's performance and success are consistent with the objectives and needs of the bank as a separate economic unit. At the other extreme, it can be assumed that the bank is merely a part of a larger economic unit where the objectives and needs of the larger unit are dominant. In this case, the holding company, and not the bank, is the behavioral unit. A holding company can, in this way, extend the range and scope of the bank's function and activities into nonbanking operations. Within the scope of banking activities, a holding company can alter the control structure by substituting a centralized system of banks for separate, individual banks.

Neither of these extreme positions provides a completely accurate description of reality. The bank retains its separate legal status as part of a holding company. It theoretically has the same operating responsibilities and is subject to the same regulations as a separate bank. But when the management and control of the bank and the other parts of the holding company are in the same hands, issues involving a choice between the best interest of the bank as a unit and the best interest of the holding company are likely to be resolved in favor of the holding company. The funds and reputation of the strongest unit are likely to be used to support new, weak, or more risky units. The legal issues of the independence of the bank as a unit of the holding company have not been clearly resolved. The functional interdependence of the units seems to be clear in many cases. For purposes of the following discussion, the bank holding company will be viewed as an extension of the bank as an economic unit. As such, it broadens the functions and activities of the bank and makes it possible for the bank to play a broader role in the process of financial intermediation. It also leads to important changes in the nature of competition and economic control in the financial market.

The 1970 amendment to the Bank Holding Company Act limited bank holding companies to activities "closely related to banking or managing or controlling banks." The Board of Governors of the Federal Reserve System was given the authority to define the range of permissible activities. A list of approved activities is given in Figure 10-5. The approved list is comprehensive and covers nearly all types of financial activities and services. The principal exceptions lie in the exclusion of investment banking and the actual operation of open-ended mutual funds. The banks may provide the advisory service for those funds.

Nearly all major banks have formed holding companies and have used this arrangement for extending their activities into a wide range of financial markets, activities, and geographic regions that were not accessible to the bank as a legal unit. Figure 10-6 gives information, obtained from the annual report of one holding company, that illustrates the range of its activities. Many holding companies are less willing to disclose the

FIGURE 10-5
APPROVED ACTIVITIES FOR BANK HOLDING COMPANIES

Mortgage banking
Consumer financing, personal and sales
Commercial financing
Credit cards
Factoring
Industrial and Morris Plan banking
Loan servicing
Trust services
Investment and financial advisory services
Leasing of real or personal property
Investing in community service projects
Data processing and bookkeeping services
Insurance agent or brokerage services
Underwriting of credit insurance
Courier services
Management consulting for unaffiliated banks

Source: *Federal Reserve Regulation Y*, Section 225.4(a)

extent of their activities. The bank holding company, viewed as an economic unit, presents a picture very different from the individual bank as a unit. It is able to provide a broader range of loans and financial services. It is able to obtain funds from a wide range of sources. Many of its subsidiary activities escape the regulatory restrictions that would be imposed upon the same activity within the bank. The impact of the growth of bank holding companies is difficult to assess because of the lack of comprehensive information. The following statement from an article in the *Federal Reserve Bulletin* gives some indication of the extension of their activities into three specialized fields.

> In 1974, BHC's controlled 27 of the 86 largest noncaptive finance companies, 34 of the top 100 mortgage banking companies, and 13 of the largest 30 factoring firms.[1]

A footnote to that statement reveals some of the problems of fully identifying interlocking controls.

> It should be noted that some relatively large mortgage banking and factoring companies are also controlled by bank subsidiaries of holding companies.

[1]Robert J. Lawrence and Samuel H. Talley, "An Assessment of Bank Holding Companies," *Federal Reserve Bulletin* (January 1976), pp. 15–21.

FIGURE 10-6

HOLDING COMPANY AND THE EXPANDED ROLE OF BANKS IN THE
INTERMEDIATION PROCESS, AN EXAMPLE*

	As suppliers of funds (As percentage of bank item)		
	Loans	Investments	Total
Bank	100.0	100.0	100.0
Subsidiaries			
Securities	7.8	48.7	18.9
Leasing and investment	.7	1.6	.9
Loan and finance	9.9	.3	7.4
Total, holding company	118.4	150.6	127.2

	Sources of funds (As percentage of bank item)				
	Deposits	Other debt	Other lia.	Equity	Total
Bank	100.0	100.0	100.0	100.0	100.0
Subsidiaries					
Securities	—	116.6	20.0	—	16.2
Leasing and investment	—	6.8	—	—	.9
Loan and finance	—	22.9	9.8	—	3.5
Parent		29.4	1.1	9.9	4.3
Total, holding company	100.0	275.7	130.9	109.9	124.9

*Based on material in the *Annual Report* of First Pennsylvania Corporation for 1975.

The bank holding company does not appear in the statistics of the intermediation process as an identifiable economic unit. Its parts are distributed among the statistics for different types of institutions. But it exists as a potential source of centralized economic power. The discussion and description of nonbank financial institutions in the next chapter will treat them as separate economic units, but it should be recognized that many of them are part of bank holding companies.

Regulation of Banking

The traditional justification for the regulation of banks stems from their role as the custodians of the country's money supply. But the complex structure of state and federal regulations that apply to modern commercial banks cannot be characterized by any single regulatory objective or any simple set of objectives. A safe and efficient financial system is essential for economic and social welfare, and the public recognition of this role invites public regulation. The major changes in the banking laws have been attempts to correct problems and abuses that have developed in the functioning of the banking system. These reforms have generally imposed new restrictions on the scope of bank activities and have made changes designed to improve performance of the system. All of the major reforms have included restrictions on speculative activities. The interim amendments to the laws and the regulatory interpretations have, in general, tended toward the relaxation of the restrictions and the expansion of the scope of bank activities. For purposes of discussion, governmental regulations will be divided into three types: reserve requirements, selective controls on bank activities, and organizational restrictions on the control and structure of banking.

Banks in the United States are faced with a complex variety of controls from many sources. One large group of banks is chartered under state laws and is subject to the supervision of the state banking departments. Another large group is chartered under the National Banking Act and is supervised by the Comptroller of the Currency. Most of the banks in both groups have deposit insurance with the Federal Deposit Insurance Corporation and must meet its requirements and face its examinations. Some of the state banks and all of the national banks are members of the Federal Reserve System which is responsible for controlling the country's money supply and for supervising many aspects of banking. In addition, the banks must conform to special laws and regulations that apply to the financial instruments and markets they use. Efforts are made to avoid conflicts and duplication in the supervisory process, but the overlapping structure of authority produces a great deal of confusion and complexity in the rules and regulations that banks must follow. Figure 10-7 indicates the scope and coverage of the major supervisory systems. It should be noted that the monetary controls of the Federal Reserve System apply to only 40 percent of the banks by number and 75 percent by total deposits.

Reserve requirements

Reserve requirements against bank deposits require the bank to hold some fraction of its deposits in the form of currency, in deposits with other banks or on deposit with the Federal Reserve Banks. In the days before central banks, these requirements were designed to provide funds for the redemption of notes or to meet deposit withdrawals. Since reserves are only a fraction of deposits, use of these funds to meet withdrawals brings the level of reserves below the amounts required on the remaining deposits, so they never provide a long-run solution to liquidity problems. But they served to reduce the volume of loans that could be made from a given volume of deposits and in this way served as a restriction on bank lending.

FIGURE 10-7
SUPERVISORY STRUCTURE OF U.S. BANKING, JUNE 30, 1975

Supervisory classifications	Number of banks	Total deposits (billions)	Percent of total	
			Number	Deposit
All commercial banks	14,573	$754.3	100.0	100.0
Members of Federal Reserve				
System	5,794	573.3	39.8	76.0
National	4,730	431.6	—	—
State	1,064	141.7	—	—
Nonmembers	8,779	181.0	60.2	24.0
Insured, total	14,320	746.0	98.3	98.9
Members of Federal Reserve System	5,794	573.3	—	—
Nonmembers	8,526	172.7	—	—
Noninsured	253	8.3	1.7	1.1

Source: *Federal Reserve Bulletin* (January 1976), pp. A 14–15.

In this latter role, they were adopted by the Federal Reserve System as the principal tool for controlling the money supply and aggregate bank expansion.

In their theoretically perfect form, reserve requirements can be used to control the aggregate size of bank deposits. In practice, the application of these controls has been more complicated. These issues will be discussed in Chapter 14.

One of the problems of using reserve requirements to control the money supply stems from their attractiveness for various types of selective controls. The impact of a reserve requirement is similar to that of a tax on deposits. The bank must raise more money in deposits than it can use for loans, and the cost of the extra funds adds to the cost of the money used for loans. For example, 20 percent reserve required adds 25 percent to the cost of the loan funds. If the bank's deposits cost $2 per hundred, the reserve requirement increases the effective cost of loan funds to $2.50 per hundred. As a device for selective controls, differential reserve requirements can be used to encourage or discourage various types of deposits or classes of banks. Savings accounts have typically held lower reserve requirements than demand accounts, and the deposits of small banks have typically been subject to lower requirements than those of large banks. Figure 10-8 gives some indication of the size and range of reserve requirements. These differentials can be and have been rationalized or justified by regulatory objectives or by various types of arguments about the equity of requirements. They have been used to encourage or discourage selective types of bank activities. As will be seen later, the problem with using

FIGURE 10-8

RESERVE REQUIREMENT ON BANK DEPOSITS

Requirements in effect on member banks December 31, 1975:	Reserve requirement (percent)
Net demand deposits:	
Deposit size (millions of dollars)	
0–2	$7\frac{1}{2}$
2–10	10
10–100	12
100–400	13
Over 400	$16\frac{1}{2}$
Savings deposits	3
Time deposits:	
Size (millions of dollars)	
0–5, maturing in:	
less than 4 years	3
4 or more years	1
Over 5, maturing in:	
30–179 days	6
180 days to 4 years	3
4 years or more	1
Requirements in selected states:[a]	
Alaska	
Demand	20
Time	8
Illinois	
Demand	0
Time	0
Indiana	
Demand	10
Time	3

[a]In effect on March 20, 1973 as recorded in the *Business Review* of the Federal Reserve Bank of Philadelphia, June 1974, p. 7. Many of the states permit reserves to be held in part or totally in the securities of the state government or in those of the U.S. government.

reserve requirements for selective purposes arises from the fact that it reduces their effectiveness as a tool for controlling the monetary aggregates.

Selective controls

A wide variety of selective controls have been used to influence the activities of banks. Ceiling rates on time and savings accounts have been used by the Federal Reserve System to control the participation of its member banks in these markets. The ceiling set under Regulation Q after World War II was so low that the member banks were virtually excluded from active competition in those markets. Ceilings have been used since that time in a more permissive way, but they are still used to achieve a variety of selective results. These controls, together with differential reserve requirements, can be used to effectively control the sources of funds available to banks.

Capital requirements are usually imposed at the time the bank is organized or when it wants to establish new branches. After the initial requirements are met the supervisory agents have less specific authority over the amount of capital used by banks. However, they can exert considerable pressure on individual banks, through the bank examination process, to expand their capital base. The supervisory authorities can also determine the amounts and type of debt financing that can be used.

On the asset side, banks may be restricted by law from making certain types of loans or investments. In general, they are not permitted to invest in common stock or in real estate. The share of their assets that can be placed in certain types of loans or investments may also be restricted. They are subject to a variety of interest rate ceilings that may be imposed by the banking authorities or by other agencies. Most states have legal ceilings on the rates that can be charged on mortgage loans and on consumer loans. They may also be subject to restrictions on the terms of the loans that they can make. For example, the amount they can lend for the purchase of securities is determined by the Federal Reserve System under its authority to control the use of credit to purchase securities.

These regulations affect the ability of banks to compete in the specific types of market to which they apply. Although they are usually imposed for other reasons, they also limit bank participation in the intermediation process. Banks usually press for the relaxation of these regulations and their competitors press for further restrictions. The control of banking is a political as well as an economic process.

Organizational restrictions

The structure of banking in the United States is determined primarily by the state banking laws. Banking institutions, with minor exceptions, are confined to a single state, and the national authorities accept the state laws with respect to the bank offices and facilities. Some states, such as California, permit statewide branching. Other states impose various types of restrictions on the scope of branching. The structure of banking reflects these differences in the laws. Banking in branch-banking states is highly concentrated in a small number of banks with offices throughout the state. Banking in restricted-branching states is distributed among a larger number of banks serving separate cities and communities. The comparative performance of the different systems is controversial. The large branch banks gain in efficiencies of size and scale of operations, but the reduction in the numbers of separate institutions introduces potential imperfections in the markets in which they operate.

The trend in the last 25 years in the United States has been towards a sharp rise in the number of banking offices, with relatively slight growth in the number of banks. These developments reflect both acquisition and mergers of existing banks and the establishment of both new branches and new banks (see Figure 10-9). About one-eighth of the banks, counted in the statistics of separate banks, are members of multibank holding companies. These banks together accounted for one-fourth of banking offices and 38 percent of the deposits of all commercial banks at the end of 1974.[2]

FIGURE 10-9
NUMBER OF COMMERCIAL BANKS AND ADDITIONAL BRANCHES AND OFFICES, 1950–1975

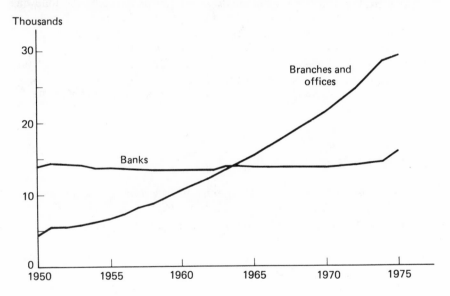

QUESTIONS FOR DISCUSSION

1. How would you expect the frequency distribution that describes the variations in a bank's deposits for a bank that accepts only demand deposits to differ from one for a bank that accepts all types of deposits?

[2]*Federal Reserve Bulletin* (June 1975), p. A-79.

2. Judging from the changes in the structure of bank assets and liabilities shown in Figure 10-2, have the liquidity management problems of commercial banks improved or worsened since 1950?

3. If it is assumed that the overall quality of loans and investments is the same, is the typical commercial bank in a better or worse position for avoiding insolvency than it was in 1950?

4. Compare the liquidity and solvency of the bank and the entire holding company treated as a single institution in the example given in Figure 10-6.

5. Discuss the advantages and disadvantages of the right to accept demand deposits from the point of view of an individual bank.

6. What would you expect from nationwide branch banking? Would there be any disadvantages?

7. What are some of the advantages to a bank in setting up a one-bank holding company?

8. Under what economic conditions would you expect the ratio of loans to the total of loans and investments at banks to increase? What changes in the composition of deposits would you expect to accompany this change? Why?

9. As a banker, which source of funds would you prefer under the following circumstances: demand accounts that cost you $2 a hundred to handle and are subject to a 25 percent reserve requirement, or savings accounts at 3 percent interest that are subject to a 3 percent reserve requirement?

10. What regulatory techniques could be used to discourage commercial banks from competing with savings institutions for savings accounts? What regulatory techniques could be used to discourage them from competing for mortgage loans?

SELECTED REFERENCES

CROSSE, HOWARD D., and GEORGE H. HEMPEL, *Management Policies for Commercial Banks* (2d ed.), Englewood Cliffs, N.J.: Prentice-Hall, Inc., 1973.

GIES, THOMAS G., and VINCENT P. APILADO, eds., *Banking Markets and Financial Institutions.* Homewood, Ill.: Richard D. Irwin, Inc., 1971.

HODGMAN, DONALD, *Commercial Loan and Investment Policy.* Urbana, Ill.: University of Illinois Press, 1963.

JESSUP, PAUL E., ed., *Innovations in Bank Management.* New York: Holt, Rinehart and Winston, 1969.

NADLER, PAUL S., *Commercial Banking in the Economy.* New York: Random House, 1968.

ROBINSON, ROLAND I., *The Management of Bank Funds* (2d ed.). New York: McGraw-Hill, 1962.

Nonbank Financial Institutions

11

The first nonbank financial institution in the colonial United States was a fire insurance company, the Philadelphia Contributionship, which began operations in 1752. The first life insurance company, the Pennsylvania Company for Insurance on Lives and Granting Annuities, opened in 1812. Three savings institutions appeared between 1816 and 1819 in Philadelphia, Boston, and New York.[1] These institutions signaled the beginning in the United States of the creation of financial institutions to solve specialized financing problems. They have proved to be very versatile. Some have survived centuries of changing economic and financial developments. Others have appeared in response to special opportunities or needs and have disappeared just as quickly.

A financial institution, in its simplest form, is a pool of financial assets shared by the participants in the pool. The shares offer safety and liquidity that could not be obtained by direct investment in the same assets. The pool may also offer efficiencies or economic power arising from its size.

Many types of financial institutions take the simple form. The participants share in the success or failure of the institution in direct proportion to their contribution. The initiative for the formation of these institutions can be traced either to the cooperative efforts of some of the participants or to the guiding hand of an entrepreneur who detects the need for the services of the institution and is rewarded for his efforts by management or advisory fees.

[1]Herman E. Krooss and Martin R. Blyn, *A History of Financial Intermediaries* (New York: Random House, 1971), p. 11.

155

Nonbank financial institutions are the specialists of the intermediation process. Their origins can be traced to the development of specialized financial opportunities or problems. The early savings institutions were designed to offer savings alternatives to the poor. The application for the charter of the Bank for Savings in the City of New York was requested by the Society for the Prevention of Pauperism in the City of New York. The charter of the Philadelphia Savings Fund Society described it as a "benevolent institution...to aid and assist the poor and middling classes of society in putting their money out to advantage."[2] The forerunners of the modern savings and loan association appeared as building and loan associations designed to assist in the financing of housing, and were initiated largely by builders and real estate agents.[3] Credit unions and personal finance companies appeared under the sponsorship of charitable organizations concerned with offering the poor an alternative to loan sharks. Automobile finance companies were developed and encouraged by the automobile companies themselves as a means of promoting and financing their sales. These institutions developed and grew outside of the traditional financing channels. They were and are encouraged by legal restrictions on existing institutions and by the conservatism of established institutions. Many of the types of financing now routinely handled by commercial banks originated with nonbank financial institutions.

The existence and survival of a specialized financial institution depends upon its ability to (1) offer contracts that serve the needs of its specialized customers, (2) maintain a spread between the rate it pays for funds and the rate it receives that will support its costs, and (3) meet its commitments to its suppliers of funds. All financial institutions operate in two sets of markets, and the details of their operations are largely determined by the features of the market in which they specialize. A savings institution has to provide the liquidity, safety, and return required by the savings market. An insurance company has to meet the claims on its policies. A finance company has to design its operations to accommodate its borrowers. Each of these institutions plays a special role in the intermediation process and the discussion in this chapter centers on the functions they perform and the implications of these functions for their operations and behavior. Together they hold three-fourths of outstanding mortgages and corporate bonds, one-third of the consumer credit, and about one-fifth of all corporate stock and obligations of state and local government (see Figure 11-1). Figure 11-2 shows the sources and uses of funds by these institutions and gives some insight into the nature of their operations and relative size.

[2]*Ibid.*, p. 61.

[3]Edward C. Ettin, "The Development of American Financial Intermediaries," *Quarterly Review of Economics and Business*, vol. 3, no. 2 (1963), 51–69.

FIGURE 11-1

Share of Major Types of Financial Assets Held by Nonbank
Financial Institutions, End of 1973

Type of security	Share of outstanding amount held by:					
	All nonbank financial institutions	Savings institutions	Insurance companies	Pension and investment funds	Finance companies	Federally sponsored agencies
U.S. govt. securities	13.4	7.7	1.8	2.4	—	0.9
State and local obligations	19.6	0.5	17.8	0.7	—	—
Corporate:						
bonds	75.3	5.0	37.7	31.6	—	—
equities	20.5	0.4	4.7	15.1	—	—
Mortgages	73.7	47.9	12.7	3.8	2.0	7.3
Consumer credit	37.3	13.3	—	—	24.0	—

Source: Board of Governors of the Federal Reserve System, *1974 Supplement—Flow of Funds Accounts*, 1965–1973 (September 1974).

Savings Institutions

All financial institutions look to savings for their funds but the term *savings institution* is generally applied only to those institutions that offer savings accounts. These accounts promise the supplier of funds withdrawal privileges, the safety of the institution's backing, which frequently includes government insurance, and an interest rate competitive with other outlets for savings. The institution has to be prepared to meet potential withdrawals, protect its depositors, and be able to compete for funds.

The institutions permitted to offer savings accounts are usually classified into three types: mutual savings banks, savings and loan associations, and credit unions. They are chartered under different laws and are subject to somewhat different types of regulations. The mutual savings banks were established to invest the funds of their shareholders and were given considerable flexibility in the types of loans and investments that they could make. The savings and loan associations were originally designed to assist in the financing of housing, and they have been limited essentially to mortgage financing. The credit unions were established to provide a source of personal loans for their members and they have, in general, confined their activities to these loans. The operations of these three types of institutions are reflected in the composition of their assets (see Figure 11-3). Savings and loan associations have 85 percent of their

FIGURE 11-2
Sources and Uses of Funds at Nonbank Financial Institutions,
End of 1973
(Billions of Dollars)

	Total	Savings institutions	Insurance companies	Pension and investment funds	Finance companies	Federally sponsored agencies	Brokers and dealers
Uses of funds, total	1181.0	403.5	313.4	278.3	88.4	79.0	18.4
U.S. government securities	56.4	32.4	7.8	10.2	—	4.0	2.0
State and local obligations	37.3	0.9	33.8	1.4	—	—	1.1
Corporate-bonds	198.7	13.1	99.6	83.4	—	—	2.6
-equities	198.0	4.0	45.5	146.1	—	—	2.4
Mortgages	471.6	306.3	81.3	24.5	12.5	47.0	—
Consumer credit	67.4	24.0	—	—	43.4	—	—
Money market instruments	6.8	2.1	3.0	1.6	—	—	—
Other loans	76.0	—	20.2	1.9	29.0	24.9	—
Other financial assets	68.8	20.7	22.1	9.4	3.4	3.1	10.2
Sources of funds, total	1181.0	403.5	313.4	278.3	88.4	79.0	18.4
Savings accounts	348.2	348.2	—	—	—	—	—
Marketable securities	104.6	—	—	1.9	33.9	68.9	—
Money market instruments	29.7	—	—	4.0	25.7	—	—
Insurance reserves	246.0	—	246.0	—	—	—	—
Bank loans	37.9	—	—	7.0	20.5	—	10.3
Other debt	27.6	22.0	—	—	—	—	5.7
Other liabilities	43.8	8.6	31.6	1.4	0.4	1.7	0.2
Net worth and unclassified item[a]	343.2	24.7	35.8	264.0	7.9	8.4	2.2

[a]Item was obtained by subtracting liabilities from total financial assets.

Source: Board of Governors of the Federal Reserve System, *1974 Supplement—Flow of Funds Accounts, 1965–1973* (September 1974).

FIGURE 11-3

USES OF FUNDS AT SAVINGS INSTITUTIONS, DECEMBER 31, 1973

Type	Savings and loan associations	Mutual savings banks	Credit unions
Total financial assets (billions)	$272.4	$106.6	$24.6
Percentage distribution	100.0	100.0	100.0
Home mortgages	69.1	41.5	4.1
Other mortgages	16.2	27.2	—
Personal loans	1.0	1.6	79.7
U.S. government securities	8.4	6.7	10.6
State and local obligations	—	0.8	—
Corporate bonds	—	12.3	—
Corporate equities	—	3.8	—
Demand deposits and currency	1.2	1.1	4.1
Other	4.1	5.0	1.5

Source: Board of Governors of the Federal Reserve System, *1974 Supplement—Flow of Funds Accounts*, 1965–1973 (September 1974).

assets in mortgage loans. Mutual savings banks have somewhat more diversity but also hold the largest share of their assets in mortgages. Credit unions hold 80 percent of their assets in loans to their members.

Savings institutions have faced severe tests of their ability to survive in recent years. They have been faced with large-scale withdrawals of funds during recurring periods of tight money, and they have had difficulty in meeting these withdrawals. Their secondary reserves, in general, have not been large enough and the slow turnover rates on their long-term mortgage contracts made it difficult for them to liquidate their assets fast enough to provide the cash for the withdrawals. Many of the individual institutions could not have handled this problem without assistance. Most of the assistance came from another set of nonbank financial institutions, federally sponsored credit agencies. They were able to raise funds during tight money periods and they used the funds they obtained to relieve the liquidity problems of the savings and loan associations. The Federal Home Loan Bank, which acts as the central bank for savings institutions, raised funds for advances to the individual savings institutions by selling its securities. The Federal National Mortgage Association raised funds which it used to provide a secondary market for the mortgages individual institutions were forced to sell. These institutions provided the emergency access to the money and capital markets that was essential for the survival of some of the individual savings associations.

The safety of the deposits in savings institutions has been assured in a number of ways. The accounts at all three types of institutions are eligible for insurance under various federal deposit insurance programs. All three types of institutions are required by law to set aside reserves for losses and to build up net worth as a cushion to protect the savings accounts from losses on loans. These funds appear in accounting statements as paid-in surplus, undivided profits, and the book value of equity shares when the institutions are owned by stockholders. They appear as general or special reserves in the statements of mutually owned institutions. Net worth funds amounted to 5.8 percent of the total assets of savings and loan associations at the end of 1975 and 6.5 and about 9 percent, respectively, of the assets of mutual savings banks and credit unions. These ratios compare with a ratio of 7.1 percent for commercial banks on the same date.

Insurance Companies

An insurance company's ability to attract funds and its principal operating obligations are determined by the nature of its commitments to its policyholders. Its growth depends on its ability to offer attractive forms of insurance contracts. Its continued success and survival depend on its ability to meet the claims on its policies. It has to select loans and investments that give it the pattern of cash flows needed to meet expected claims and that give it enough liquidity to handle unexpected claims. Its asset portfolio has to be compatible with the statistical features of its insurance commitments.

Insurance companies, as such, are not really intermediaries in the borrowing and lending process. The funds they receive are payments for protection against risk and, with the exception of life insurance premiums, they are not part of the net worth or savings of the policyholders. The insurance company places the funds it receives into the primary markets only as an obvious way of handling the reserves that it must keep to meet its policy commitments.

Fire and casualty insurance companies face widely different patterns of risk. A list of some forms of insurance indicates the variety of protection they provide:

1. Insurance against property damage from natural and man-made hazards of all types.
2. Medical insurance and protection from loss of income.
3. Insurance against legal liability.
4. Insurance against theft, burglary, forgery, and embezzlement.
5. Surety bonds that protect against contract default.
6. Title insurance.
7. Insurance against credit losses.

Each type of insurance coverage has its own pattern of risks, and the operations of these companies must be designed to provide for the statistical implications of these risks. The assets of these companies are invested in marketable securities and relatively short-term obligations to provide for the potential variations in claims.

Large life insurance companies, like large banks, cannot be described in terms of a single function. They handle a substantial block of pension and retirement funds, and they offer related investment services as part of their life insurance programs. They place the funds they receive into nearly all money and capital markets (see Figure 11-4). They hold a major share of outstanding corporate bonds. They hold large amounts of corporate stock. They make direct loans to corporations and they have substantial amounts invested in mortgages. Their investment policies reflect the special needs created by the pattern of their claims.

FIGURE 11-4

DISTRIBUTION OF FINANCIAL ASSETS OF INSURANCE COMPANIES, DECEMBER 31, 1973

Type	Life insurance companies	Other insurance companies
Total financial assets (billions)	$224.6	$68.8
Percentage distribution:	100.0	100.0
U.S. government securities	1.8	4.9
State and local obligations	1.4	44.2
Corporate bonds	37.8	10.4
Corporate equities	10.6	28.5
Mortgages	33.2	0.2
Money market paper	1.2	—
Demand deposits and currency	0.8	2.2
Other	13.2	9.6

Source: Board of Governors of the Federal Reserve System, *1974 Supplement—Flow of Funds Accounts*, 1965–1973 (September 1974).

Pension and Investment Funds

A wide variety of private and public pension funds, retirement funds, investment trusts, and investment companies have been developed to handle specialized investment problems. These institutions are designed to match investment policies with the needs and wishes of the suppliers of funds. They usually involve direct sharing in the success or failure of the pool of assets. They may involve long-run contracts between the supplier of funds and the institution, as in the case of pension funds, or they may permit the supplier to add to or withdraw his contributions at will, as in the case of open-end mutual funds. They provide investors with the advantage of professional advice and management skills, and access to the financial features of large portfolios. On the borrower's side, they offer an important source of direct funds, and they have contributed to the strength of the markets for secondary securities (see Figure 11-5). These institutions now hold about a third of all outstanding corporate bonds and about a sixth of all corporate equities.

FIGURE 11-5

Distribution of the Financial Assets of Pension and Investment Funds—End of 1973

	Private pension funds	State and local govt. employee retirement funds	Real estate investment trusts	Open-end investment companies
Total financial assets (billions)	$133.3	$81.6	$17.0	$46.5
Percentage distribution	100.0	100.0	100.0	100.0
U.S. government securities	3.2	5.7	—	2.5
State and local obligations	—	1.7	—	—
Corporate—bonds	22.4	60.5	—	9.0
—equities	67.0	22.8	—	82.4
Mortgages	2.0	8.2	89.0	—
Other financial assets	5.4	1.1	11.0	6.1

Source: Board of Governors of the Federal Reserve System, *1974 Supplement—Flow of Funds Accounts*, 1965–1973 (September 1974).

The versatility of this institutional form has been demonstrated by the fairly recent appearance of the *real estate investment trust* (REIT) and the *liquidity asset management funds*. These institutions developed in response to special financial needs and opportunities arising from tight money market conditions and from the speculative prospects in real estate and land development. The real estate investment trusts were designed to raise funds for land development and construction and to permit the participants in the trust to share in the profits of the boom. The initial high returns on the mortgages held by these trusts were supplemented by the leverage of funds obtained from banks and from the sale of bonds and open-market paper. The acceptance of these debt issues in the public markets was made possible, at least in part, by the support of bank letters of credit and guarantees. Some of the major bank holding companies served as advisors to these trusts. The collapse of the land development boom in 1973 changed the outlook for their investments and created serious default and loss problems for many of these trusts and for their bank advisors.

The liquid asset management funds developed in response to high short-term interest rates. These organizations invest the funds made available to them in high quality, short-term money market instruments—primarily CDs, commercial paper, and short-term U.S. government securities. They, in turn, give their shareholders the right to purchase or withdraw shares on demand and provide for withdrawal by check or telegraphic transfer. Since they permit transactions in relatively small amounts ($500 is typical), they give small investors and businesspeople access to the money market and make it possible for them to keep their cash balances fully invested at all times.

Finance Companies

Finance companies are typically organized to handle some specialized financing problem that is not adequately being handled by banks and other institutions. In most cases, they serve as financial intermediaries between the borrowers and other financial institutions rather than between borrowers and lenders. They add an additional stage to the intermediation process and, in doing so, add to the transmutation effects of the entire process. They may add an additional stage of risk protection or provide specialized and high-cost service functions.

State usury laws, which establish legal ceilings on the rates that can be charged on loans to consumers, imposed a barrier to many types of legal lending activities that were too costly to be profitable under these laws. The widow of a man who had accumulated a fortune in moneylending used some of the money to establish the Russell Sage Foundation, which sponsored studies that led to the development of small-loan laws. These studies demonstrated the fact that the cost of lending to consumers often exceeded the legal rates that could be charged. They served as a support for the development of small-loan laws that provided legal ceilings high enough to cover these costs. The adoption of these laws by many states led to the establishment of small-loan companies, later called consumer finance companies. These companies borrow a large part of their funds from banks or other financial institutions. Their equity capital provides the protection required by their suppliers, and the leverage provided by debt financing assures the owners of a return on their capital that justified their costs and risks.

Other types of finance companies originated as part of the marketing of automobiles and other expensive durable goods. The early sales finance companies were encouraged or formed by automobile manufacturers to assist in their sales. General Motors Acceptance Corporation and earlier versions of Chrysler Acceptance and Ford Motor Acceptance Corporations were formed to handle this financing. A rash of these captive finance companies appeared again in the mid-1950's in reaction to a partial withdrawal of commercial banks from the financing of household durables. Nearly all manufacturers of major durable items, including boats, airplanes, and farm equipment have finance company subsidiaries that can assist them in financing their products.

Factoring and commercial finance companies also developed to handle specialized business financing problems that were too expensive or risky to attract bank financing. The specialized finance company, in most cases, obtains a large share of its funds from banks, but it gives the bank an extra degree of protection.

Many of the companies that developed as specialized lenders in one field have diversified into other types of lending so that it is no longer possible to classify the companies by type of lending activities. Figure 11-6 gives the financial assets of these companies in mid-1975. They engage in all types of loan activities and specialize in handling problems and risks that other institutions won't accept. Their interest rates reflect their costs and risks.

The liabilities of finance companies provide a case study of use of priorities in the allocation of risks. The summary of the sources of funds for these companies, as shown in Figure 11-7, does not differentiate clearly among risk distinctions, but it can be used to illustrate the nature of these arrangements. Bank loans and other senior obligations have the best protection against losses. The outstanding commercial paper, in most cases, is supported by bank credit lines. Various degrees of subordination may be introduced in the subordinated debt category. Capital and surplus accounts, amounting to 16 percent of total assets, provide the residual protection for debt obligations. Banks typically look to the capital and subordinated debt for protection in making their decisions about the amounts that they will lend to these companies.

Federally Sponsored Financial Institutions

Two types of federally sponsored financial institutions are currently important in the financing process: (1) the farm credit institutions, and (2) the mortgage-related institutions. Both sets of institutions have been developed to overcome special problems and gaps in the private intermediation process.

Farmers, even more than consumers, present difficult financing prob-

FIGURE 11-6

FINANCIAL ASSETS OF FINANCE COMPANIES, JUNE 30, 1975

Item	Amount (billions)	Percentage of total
Consumer:		
Automobile paper	$9.9	10.1
Mobile homes	3.5	3.6
Revolving credit	5.8	5.9
Personal cash loans	16.7	17.0
Other consumer loans	6.9	7.0
Business:		
Wholesale paper		
Automobiles	7.7	7.9
Other consumer goods	1.3	1.3
Other	2.0	2.0
Retail paper		
Commercial vehicles	5.0	5.1
Business, industrial and farm equipment	6.1	6.2
Lease paper	8.1	8.3
Loans on accounts receivable	3.4	3.5
Factored accounts receivable	1.4	1.4
Advances and other	4.4	4.5
Other loans and investments	10.6	10.8
All other assets	5.2	5.4
Total assets	98.0	100.0

Source: Evelyn M. Hurley, "Survey of Finance Companies, 1975," *Federal Reserve Bulletin* (March 1976), pp. 197–207.

lems. They need large amounts of all types of financing and their ability to repay is exposed to the vagaries of volatile agricultural prices and weather. The federal government's effort to assist with their financing problems began in the early 1900's. These programs have developed into the Farm Credit System, which is made up of three specialized types of financial institutions. Except for the federal sponsorship, they are similar in function and form to private finance companies. The Federal Land Banks provide mortgage loans. The Federal Intermediate Credit Banks provide short- and intermediate-term credit to farmers through local Production Credit Associations. The Banks for Cooperatives provide the financing for farm cooperatives that have developed as service organizations for farmers. The entire system is now owned and capitalized by the farmers, who are also the borrowers. The system gives the farm sector direct and efficient access to the money and capital markets (see Figure 11-8).

FIGURE 11-7

Sources of Funds for Finance Companies, June 30, 1975

	Amounts (billions)	Percentage of total
Bank loans	$8.6	8.8
Commercial paper:		
Directly placed	23.7	24.2
Dealer placed	2.2	2.2
Other short-term debt	4.3	4.4
Senior debt, long-term	23.4	23.9
Subordinated debt, long-term	5.6	5.7
Other liabilities	6.9	7.0
Reserves for losses and unearned income	9.3	9.5
Capital surplus and undivided profits	14.0	14.3
	98.0	100.0

Source: Evelyn M. Hurley, "Survey of Finance Companies, 1975," Federal Reserve Bulletin (March 1976), pp. 197–207.

FIGURE 11.8

Principal Sources and Uses of Funds at Selected Federally Sponsored Credit Agencies, December 30, 1975

	Uses	Sources
Federal Home Loan Banks		
Advances to members	17.8	
Investments	4.4	
Bonds and notes		18.9
Members' deposits		2.7
Capital stock		2.7
Federal National Mortgage Association		
Mortgages	31.9	
Debentures and notes		30.0
Banks for Cooperatives		
Loans to cooperatives	4.0	
Bonds		3.6
Federal Intermediate Credit Bank		
Loans to farmers	9.9	
Bonds		9.2
Federal Land Banks		
Farm mortgages	16.6	
Bonds		14.8

Source: Federal Reserve Bulletin (March 1976), p. A-37.

Federal mortgage agencies have been developed to assist and support the private financial institutions engaged in mortgage financing. The Federal Home Loan Bank (FHLB) serves as the lender of last resort for savings institutions. It introduces an extra stage in the intermediation process by obtaining funds from the money and capital markets that it, in turn, makes available to private savings institutions when they are having difficulties in raising funds. Its principal assets are in the form of advances to member associations, and most of its funds are raised by capital and money market issues (see Figure 11-8). The Federal National Mortgage Association maintains a secondary market in mortgages that serves as a source of liquidity for holders of mortgages. Its funds are also raised in the money and capital markets.

Brokers and Dealers

Brokers and dealers in securities do not normally enter into the primary borrowing and lending process. They play an important role in the marketing of seasoned securities. They can act as agents for buyers and sellers or purchase securities for their own accounts and hold them for resale. The inventories of securities that they accumulate in the second role must be financed either by their own funds or by borrowing, and a simple type of financial institution results.

The securities held by brokers and dealers range from U.S. government securities to common stocks of all types. The riskiness of their portfolios varies with the volatility of the prices of the securities that they hold, and so does the opportunity for trading profits (and losses). When debt is used to finance their inventories of securities, the direct opportunities for profits and losses are multiplied by the leverage involved in using debt. The risks faced by securities dealers who use bank credit to support their operations are sizable as are the opportunities for profits.

QUESTIONS FOR DISCUSSION

1. Why might it be to the advantage of a corporation to establish a separate finance company to finance sales of its products rather than to handle financing with the organization of the corporation itself?
2. Credit unions and consumer finance companies both make loans to consumers but they use different sources of funds. How is the risk of the loans distributed in both cases? Compare their liquidity management problems?
3. Savings institutions have been trying to get authority to offer some form of checking account. What advantages would these accounts offer? How would the liquidity management problems of savings institutions be altered by responsibility for these accounts?

4. Brokerage firms frequently assist other financial institutions in their portfolio adjustments by buying large blocks of securities, which they hold for resale. Discuss the nature of the risks involved in these transactions and describe the ways in which the transactions are financed, and the assignment of responsibility for the risk.

5. Design a finance company to provide the financing for a very large number of relatively small contracts (a few thousand dollars each). How would a company designed for that purpose differ from one of the same overall size that was engaged in financing a small number of very large contracts?

6. Give a number of examples where the introduction of additional steps in the intermediation process may add to its effectiveness.

7. Compare the sources of funds for pension and retirement funds with those for investment funds and savings institutions. Comment on some of the economic and financial forces that would affect the relative stability of various sources.

8. If one of the objectives of mutual funds is to provide diversification, how can the existence of mutual funds that specialize in industries or special types of securities be explained?

SELECTED REFERENCES

CHAPMAN, JOHN M., and ROBERT P. SHAY, eds., *The Consumer Finance Industry, Its Costs and Regulation*. New York: Columbia University Press, 1967.

COMMISSION ON MONEY AND CREDIT, *Federal Credit Programs*. Englewood Cliffs, N.J.: Prentice-Hall, Inc., 1963.

———, *Federal Credit Agencies*. Englewood Cliffs, N.J.: Prentice-Hall, Inc., 1963.

ETTIN, EDWARD C., "The Development of American Financial Intermediaries," *Quarterly Review of Economics and Business*, vol. 3, no. 3 (Summer 1963), pp. 51–69.

FRIEND, IRWIN, ed., *Study of the Savings and Loan Industry*, vol. 1-N. Washington, D.C.: Federal Home Loan Bank Board, 1969.

GOLDSMITH, RAYMOND W., *Financial Intermediaries in the American Economy Since 1900*. Princeton, N.J.: Princeton University Press, 1958.

GUP, BENTON E., *Financial Intermediaries: An Introduction*. Boston: Houghton Mifflin Company, 1976.

JACOBS, DONALD P., LORING C. FARWELL, and EDWIN NEAVE, *Financial Institutions* (5th ed.). Homewood, Ill.: Richard D. Irwin, Inc., 1972.

KROOSS, HERMAN E., and MARTIN R. BLYN, *A History of Financial Intermediaries*. New York: Random House, 1971.

Life Insurance Fact Book. New York: Institute of Life Insurance, n.d.

McGILL, DAN M., *Fundamentals of Private Pensions*. Homewood, Ill.: Richard D. Irwin, 1964.

ROZEN, MARVIN E., "The Changing Structure of Financial Institutions," *Quarterly Review of Economics and Business*, vol. 11, no. 4 (November 1962), pp. 69–80.

Behavior
of
Financial Institutions

12

Each financial institution operates in at least two markets, one for its borrowers and one for its suppliers. The demand function for its loans records the prices its borrowers are willing to pay. Its supply function records the prices it has to pay for funds. Each institution has some features that cannot be duplicated by any other institution. These features, such as its location, size, and reputation, are an inseparable part of its image and operations. They are observed by its customers. They shape its demand and supply functions and determine its competitive position in various markets.

Demand and supply schedules can be drawn for an institution, describing the opportunities available to it and identifying the limits to its operations. Each institution is also constrained by its operating costs. If these costs are allocated to its demand and supply operations, the limits to the institution's operations can be adjusted to obtain a net revenue function (AR), derived by subtracting the appropriate operating costs from the demand function, and a cost function (AC), derived by adding the appropriate operating costs to the supply function (see Figure 12-1). The institution can select any scale of operations within these limits by adjusting the rates that it charges for loans and the rates that it pays for funds. It can attain size T by paying the rate k for its funds and charging the rate r for its loans. The spread between r and k measures the cost of financial intermediation. The share of this amount that falls between the AR and AC functions (s) represents a surplus or a potential source of excess profits. The remainder represents the expenses (e) associated with the given scale of operations. The size of these two components indicates the

FIGURE 12-1

OPPORTUNITIES AND CONSTRAINTS FACED BY A FINANCIAL INSTITUTION

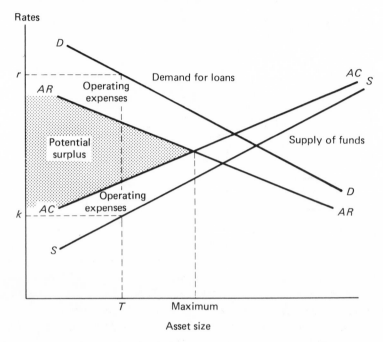

efficiency of the process of financial intermediation. Alternative market structures and arrangements can be compared in terms of their ability to reduce or eliminate the surplus (*s*) and to minimize operating expenses (*e*).

The first section of this chapter examines the relationship between the accounting statements of financial institutions and this simple economic model. The second section discusses the choice of the equilibrium size, and the third discusses the factors that affect the shapes of the cost and revenue functions. Throughout the discussion in this chapter, it will be assumed that the revenue and cost functions are given. This assumption implies that all the external forces of competition and changing economic events are held constant and that all internal policies that could affect the shapes and positions of the functions are unchanged. The role of competition and other factors that can shift the revenue and cost functions will be considered in the next chapter.

Accounting Data and Economic Concepts

The loans and investments that appear on accounting statements as assets generate the income for financial institutions. The income (R) from these sources can be divided by total assets (T) to obtain an average return

(r). The average return will also be equal to the weighted average of the rates on different types of loans and investments:

$$r = \frac{R}{T} = \sum_{i=1}^{n} r_i p_i \qquad (1)$$

where:
R = total revenue
T = total assets
r = average return
p_i = proportion of total assets in type of asset i
r_i = market rate on type of asset i

The average return (r) on the assets of a financial institution as obtained from accounting records represents one point on its demand curve. The remaining points on the curve describe the relationship between the amount of total assets and the rates charged on loans. The shape of the function depends on the borrowers' response to changes in the interest rates and on the availability of competitive sources of loans. The function as drawn in Figure 12-1 reflects the imperfections in the market that can be traced to the uniqueness of each institution.

The claims against assets that appear on accounting statements as liabilities and net worth identify the sources of funds. The cost of these funds (k) appears in the income and expense statement as interest payments and as the share of net income (or profit) that can be identified as *normal profits*. Normal profits are defined as the amount that would have to be earned under competitive market conditions to attract and hold the capital. Figure 12-2 indicates the relationship between the accounting terminology used in commercial bank statements and the economic concepts used in this model. In a simple institution with a single source of funds, the cost of funds is the rate paid to the supplier. In a complex institution, the cost of funds is the weighted average of the rates paid on different types of funds:

$$k = \frac{K}{T} = \sum_{j=1}^{m} k_j w_j \qquad (2)$$

where:
K = total cost of funds
T = total assets
k = average cost of funds
k_j = rate paid on source j
w_j = proportion of the total sources of funds
obtained from source j.

The average cost of funds (k), represents one point on the institution's supply curve. The full supply curve (see Figure 12-1) gives the relationship between the amount supplied and the average rate (k). Its shape depends on the response of its suppliers to changes in rates and to

FIGURE 12-2

ACCOUNTING DATA AND ECONOMIC CONCEPTS

Income and expenses[a]	Economic concept	As percent of total assets
Operating income ——————— Total revenue (R)		r
Operating expenses:		
Salaries and wages		
Interest paid		
Other	Operating expenses (E)	e
Income taxes		
	Net operating income (N)	n
Gains or losses on		
loans and securities	Cost of funds (K)	k
Additions to reserves		
Net income:		
"Normal profits"		
Other ——————————— Surplus		s

[a]Terminology used in published statistics for income and expenses of banks, *Federal Reserve Bulletin* (June 1974), pp. A 84–85, detail omitted.

the competitive alternatives, and reflects the uniqueness of each financial institution.

When total operating expenses (E in Figure 12-2) are divided by total assets, they can be plotted as a point on an expense function (see Figure 12-3A). Since many types of operating costs are fixed and do not vary with the size of total assets, we would expect the operating expense function to slope downward as the size of the institution increases, at least through some range of sizes. Ideally, the expenses associated with lending operations should be assigned to the management of assets and deducted from the gross income to obtain a net return or net operating income that reflects the net yield on the assets of the institution (AR in Figure 12-1). And the expenses associated with raising funds and servicing deposits should be added to the rate paid for funds to obtain the total cost of funds that includes the allocation of this expense (AC in Figure 12-1). In practice, many of the operating expenses of a financial institution cannot be allocated accurately to specific functions. For simplicity, it will be assumed in most of the following discussion that all operating expenses are charged to the lending operation.

Under this assumption, the operating expenses are subtracted from the demand curve to obtain a curve that measures the net operating income from lending activities (n) (see Figure 12-3B). The net operating

FIGURE 12-3
ALTERNATIVE TREATMENT OF OPERATING EXPENSES

A. Operating Expenses as Separate Function

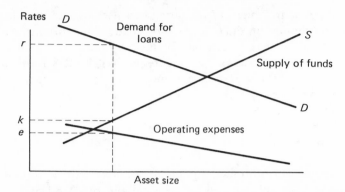

B. Operating Expenses Subtracted from the Demand Function

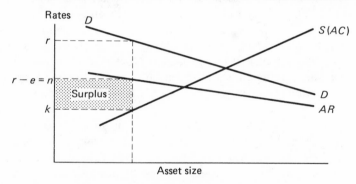

C. Operating Expenses Added to Cost of Funds

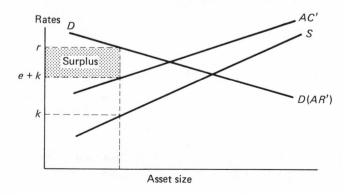

income curve corresponds to the average revenue function (AR) in the normal economic model, and the cost of funds corresponds to the average cost function (AC). The spread between n and k then measures the surplus (s).

A different treatment of operating expenses will be used in Chapter 13 to focus attention on the total costs of financial institutions. An average total cost function (AC') can be obtained by addition of operating expenses to the cost of funds (see Figure 12-3C). In this formulation the demand function (D) corresponds to the average revenue concept, and the surplus is measured by the spread between average revenue (r) and average total costs ($k + e$).

Choice of Asset Size

A financial institution can adjust its asset size by appropriate adjustments in the rate it charges on its loans (r) and the rate it pays for funds (k). If it selects any position to the left of the point where average costs equal average revenue, its operations generate an economic surplus or excess profits. The ability to extract a surplus depends upon the inelasticities that were built into its demand and supply functions and that can, in turn, be traced to the features of the institution that distinguish its loans and money-raising contracts from those of other institutions. The potential size of the surplus depends on the nature of the demand and supply functions. The actual surplus depends on the institution's decision about the scale of its operations.

Traditional theory assumes that the institution will select the size that maximizes profits. Modern behavioral theory, however, suggests that the choice is more complicated and that profit maximization may be only one of a number of possible objectives. Survival is often suggested as the goal that shapes the actions of business and social organizations. This view focuses on the long-run success of the organization and emphasizes the control of the decision process and the complexity of alternatives.

Modern financial institutions take many different forms and are owned and controlled in many different ways. Some are cooperatives or mutuals, some are owned by the borrowers, and some are owned by the holders of equity funds. In all of these cases, the decision process is likely to be dominated in varying degrees by the managers.

The manager of an institution would be expected to identify his or her personal success with the success of the institution. But the success of the institution from the manager's point of view is not necessarily measured by the amount of excess profits. A manager is likely to be concerned with job security and with various measures of business and personal achievement. He must reconcile the interests of all the groups that contribute to the institution's success. From an economic point of view, the maximum surplus position measures this success in extracting the best possible bargain from everyone involved with the institution; the suppliers of funds, including the stockholders; the borrowers; and the other employees. But, from a managerial point of view, it may not be desirable to pay the stockholders the lowest possible dividend, the employees the lowest possible wages, or charge good customers the highest possible rates. The behavioral approach to the decision process recognizes the possibility that a variety of objectives may affect the manager's decisions.

Surplus maximization

The maximum surplus (or excess profits) size is reached when the revenues from any new loans are equal to the cost of the new funds required to support those loans, or where marginal revenue (MR) equals marginal costs (MC). Figure 12-5 gives a hypothetical numerical example of the calculation of these amounts. This position maximizes the area between the average revenue (AR) and average cost (AC) functions (see Figures 12-4A and 12-5) and leaves the manager with an operating surplus in excess of the amount he needs to pay the suppliers of funds and to cover the necessary operating expenses.

It is usually assumed that these excess funds are paid to the stockholders or owners, but this assumption creates both theoretical and practical problems when it is applied to financial institutions. In some cases, the supply of funds obtained from the owners changes in the short-run in response to the rate they are paid, as it does in the supply function shown in Figure 12-4, and as it does in fact for mutually owned financial institutions. The nature of these problems can be illustrated by examining the implications of profit maximization for mutually owned institutions. The owners of such institutions are also the suppliers of funds. The amounts they will supply will increase as the rate paid on these funds is increased.

Under these conditions, the maximum surplus position is not a stable position even in the short-run.[1] The suppliers of funds will respond to the excess profits by supplying more funds than are needed for the loan volume consistent with the maximum profit position. Faced with an inflow of funds, the manager will have to either lower loan rates to make profitable use of the funds or refuse to accept new funds. In the first case, he will be forced toward the maximum size position. In the second case, the supply function is altered by the restrictions. Profit maximization in the

---

[1]Short-run stability in the standard model of the firm arises from the assumption that the time is not long enough for capital adjustments. This assumption, which is appropriate for industrial firms, does not apply to many types of financial ownership.

FIGURE 12-4
SHORT-RUN EQUILIBRIUM POSITIONS

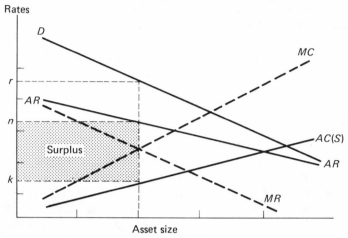

A. Maximum Surplus (Excess Profits)

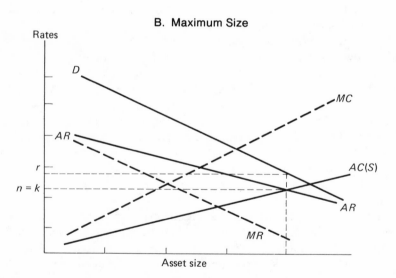

B. Maximum Size

traditional form can only result in a stable short-run equilibrium when there are restrictions on the supply of funds that will be accepted from the suppliers receiving the excess profits or where the supply of funds is fixed in the short run.

Under the behavioral approach to the theory of the firm, the manager can use the surplus for a variety of other purposes. He could use it (1) to reduce lending rates below the normal competitive rates indicated

FIGURE 12-5
Hypothetical Short-Run Revenue and Cost Relationships

				Max. profit MC=MR				Max. size AR=AC
(1) Asset size (T)	100	200	300	400	500	600	700	800
(2) Total revenue (R)	12	22	30	36	40	42	42	40
(3) Operating expense (E)	4	7	9	10	10	9	7	4
(4) Net operating income (N) (line 2 − line 3)	8	15	21	26	30	33	35	36
(5) Marginal revenue (MR) (Δ line 4)	7	6	5	(4.5)	4	3	2	1 ↑
(6) Cost of funds (K)	1	3	6	10	15	21	28	36
(7) Marginal cost (MC) (Δ line 6)	2	3	4	(4.5)	5	6	7	8 ↑
(8) Surplus (S) (line 4 − line 6)	7	12	15	(16)	15	12	7	0
Related averages (percent)								
(9) Revenue (r) (line 2/line 1)	12.0	11.0	10.0	9.0	8.0	7.0	6.0	5.0
(10) Operating expense (e) (line 3/line 1)	4.0	3.5	3.0	2.5	2.0	1.5	1.0	.5
(11) Net operating income (n = AR) (line 9 − line 10)	8.0	7.5	7.0	6.5	6.0	5.5	5.0	(4.5)
(12) Cost of funds (k = AC) (line 6/line 1)	1.0	1.5	2.0	2.5	3.0	3.5	4.0	(4.5)
(13) Surplus (s) (line 11 − line 12)	7.0	6.0	5.0	4.0	3.0	2.0	1.0	(0)

by the firm's demand function or (2) for expenditures or payments of various types that would increase effective operating expense beyond the required amounts indicated by the firm's operating expense function. His choice will depend on the nature of the institution and its objectives as the manager sees them.

Some financial institutions are controlled by the borrowers rather than the suppliers of funds. The clearest examples appear among the farm credit agencies, which are owned by the borrowers and are oriented to the needs of the borrowers. Less obvious cases are found where the borrowers have effective representation on the board of directors or among the trustees. In these cases, the surplus developed at the profit maximization position could be used to reduce loan costs or to make interest refunds. The statements of farm credit agencies and credit unions frequently show such refunds. The reduction in the effective loan charges would, however, lead to an expansion in the loan demand as indicated by the firm's demand function. In response to the new loan demand, the manager would either have to borrow more to meet the new demand or refuse to make any new loans. If he tries to accommodate the new demand, he will be forced out of the maximum surplus position toward the maximum size position. He cannot maintain the maximum surplus position unless he refuses to accommodate the loan demand.

The terms *organizational slack* or *managerial slack* are sometimes used to describe the absorption of surplus in expenses of various types. The advantages to a manager of a block of funds that can be used for almost any purpose are obvious. He can use them to make concessions to important employees or labor groups or to hire nonessential personnel. He can use them to enhance the status or image of the institution, or he can use them for more personal benefits. These expenditures all appear as operating expenses in the institution's accounting statements. The term *business consumption* might be used to describe these expenditures that are not essential to normal business operations. Any businessperson or administrator recognizes the existence of expenditures of this type, but they are hard to identify in accounting data.

Theory suggests that we should be able to find evidence of an association between nonessential expenditures and market power. R. E. Caves has suggested that a share of the surplus may be used to protect the firm from risk, and that financial conservatism may be related to market power.[2] This hypothesis has not been thoroughly tested but it does appear to be useful in explaining some of the observed behavior of financial institutions. For example, risk and liquidity precautions often appear to be

---

[2] R. E. Caves. "Uncertainty, Market Structure and Performance: Galbraith as Conventional Wisdom," *Industrial Organization and Economic Development*, J. Markham and B. Papanek, ed. (Boston: Houghton Mifflin, 1970), pp. 284–300.

directly related to the competitive strength of the financial institution, rather than inversely related, as might be expected.

The traditional maximum surplus size position has survived as the short-run equilibrium position in modern behavioral theory but the implications of that position are less predictable than in the traditional version. It seems most likely to appear in some form of organizational slack where the form of the expenditure is determined by the objectives and preferences of the manager.

Size maximization

The maximum size of a firm is reached when its average revenue (AR) just covers its average cost (AC) (see Figures 12-4B and 12-5). Size maximization has some important and interesting implications for the efficient use of the given short-run structure of a financial institution:

1. It gives the largest volume of loans at the lowest possible rate.
2. It absorbs the largest volume of savings at the highest possible rate.
3. It minimizes the cost of financial intermediation.
4. It eliminates any excess profits or surplus that might attract competitors.
5. It permits the manager to make loans where the marginal costs exceed the marginal revenue.

The maximization size position offers a number of social advantages that can normally be achieved only by competitive pressures. However, it is not clear how important it is as a realistic short-run equilibrium position. It is one of a set of possible alternatives under the behavioral theory of the firm, but it implies special attitudes and objectives on the part of the manager. He must be willing to forego the managerial advantages of control over the surplus funds. He must be either idealistic or innocent in not taking advantage of the institution's economic bargaining power.

As was indicated earlier, size maximization is the natural short-run equilibrium position for financial institutions being managed to maximize the return to the suppliers of funds or to minimize the cost of borrowing when there are no restrictions on the amounts that can be supplied or borrowed. It is also the position that would best satisfy the objectives of organizations, such as credit unions, that are dedicated to the two-way objectives of encouraging saving and of providing low cost funds to their borrowers. A conscientious credit union manager should be trying to reach the maximum size position. Even in this case, however, it is easy to imagine examples of apparently legitimate organizational slack, including larger-than-necessary reserves or conservative loan policies, that could lead to an equilibrium position short of the maximum size position.

The prestige associated with the published rankings of banks and other institutions by size may provide some incentive for size maximization. There is also some evidence that decisions about new business are frequently based on average cost concepts, which could lead to size maximization rather than profit maximization.

The behavioral approach to the theory of the firm has introduced an important element of realism into discussions of the behavior of financial institutions. But the complications that it requires cannot be incorporated directly into the simple revenue and cost model to produce a short-run equilibrium solution. The precise solution that followed from the traditional assumption of profit maximization has to be replaced by a range of possible solutions. A more precise solution requires the identification and specification of the objective function being used by the manager in reaching his decision. This, in turn, introduces complex empirical and behavioral questions that are not easily resolved.

Figure 12-6 illustrates some of the variations in accounting data that could reflect differences in policy objectives. It shows income and expense information for four institutions with identical revenue and cost functions that have selected different short-run positions. The first has selected the maximum size position (see Figures 12-4 and 12-5). The others have selected the size that maximizes surplus but have used the surplus in

FIGURE 12-6

IMPLICATIONS OF DIFFERENT POLICY OBJECTIVES
FOR ACCOUNTING STATEMENTS

Item (as percentage of total assets)	Policy Objective				
	Maximum asset size	Maximum surplus			
		Economic version	Accounting version, excess to:		
			Suppliers	Borrowers	Organizational slack
Income (revenue, r)	5.0	9.0	9.0	5.0*	9.0
Operating expenses (e)	0.5	2.5	2.5	2.5	6.5*
Net operating income (n)	4.5	6.5	6.5	2.5	2.5
Cost of funds (k)	4.5	2.5	6.5*	2.5	2.5
Surplus (excess profits, s)	0	4.0*	—	—	—

*Location of hidden surplus or excess profits in financial statement.
Note: Examples were developed from the data given in Figure 12-5.

different ways. It is assumed that the firms that allocated the surplus to the owners and the borrowers adopted policies that would restrict the expansion of the sources of funds and loans so the position could be maintained. Accounting statements do not provide footnotes to indicate the presence of an economic surplus, but an expert familiar with the industry could probably detect any sizable variations that a large surplus would produce. It seems likely that some of the variations in earnings and expenses observed among financial institutions can be traced to policy differences of the type identified in Figure 12-6.

Fixed Components of Revenue and Cost Functions

Major size adjustments of a financial institution have to be made gradually. During any period of time only a fraction of its loans and debt contracts will be replaced or renewed. The remaining assets and liabilities are fixed elements of its revenue and cost functions. The size of the fixed components will depend on the composition of the assets and sources of funds, on the turnover rate on the various components, and on the time period covered by the analysis. The ability of the institution to adjust its size in the current market depends in part on these fixed components, and they must be built into its revenue and cost functions.

The average cost and revenue functions represent weighted averages of various components (see equations (1) and (2)). If it is assumed that the sources of funds (or assets) are divided into two components—X_1, which is fixed for the time period of the analysis and carries a contract rate of k_1; and X_2, which is determined by current revenue and cost functions and carries an average rate of k_2—the average cost of funds (k) can be derived by

$$k = w_1 k_1 + w_2 k_2 \qquad (3)$$

where:
$$w_1 = \frac{X_1}{X_1 + X_2}$$

$$w_2 = \frac{X_2}{X_1 + X_2}$$

The average cost of funds (k) decreases with an increase of X_2 whenever k_2 is less than k_1, and increases whenever k_2 is greater than k_1. These relationships are illustrated in Figure 12-7 with the assumption that k_2 does not vary with changes in X_2, i.e., the supply of X_2 is perfectly elastic. Several types of financial behavior can be explained by the presence of a fixed component in the revenue or cost functions.

FIGURE 12-7

FIXED COMPONENTS AND AVERAGE REVENUE AND COST FUNCTIONS

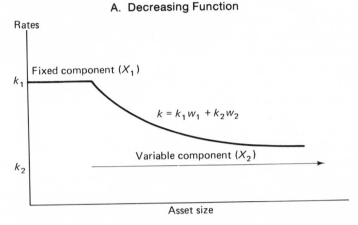

A. Decreasing Function

B. Increasing Function

Net worth and the average cost of funds

The implications of changes in the debt–equity mix for the average cost of funds can be illustrated by assuming that the amount of funds obtained from equity sources is held constant. Equity then becomes a fixed component (X_1) of the supply function, and the shape of the average cost function depends on the relative cost of debt and equity sources. The privately owned institutions and the mutually owned institutions provide very different examples. The cost of equity at banks and other privately owned institutions has been assumed to be equal to the normal profit rate (k_e). This rate is higher than the rate banks have to pay implicitly for demand accounts and higher than the rates on most other debt sources. The average costs, obtained by equation (3), will decrease as the proportion of debt to equity increases and will approach the average cost of debt sources as a limit. At some point the assumption of perfect elasticity will have to be dropped, and the cost of deposits and debt will begin to increase as the banks have to compete for deposits with more expensive services and have to increase the rates they have to pay for savings accounts and money market funds. But until those effects are registered on the average cost function, the institution will be in a decreasing cost situation (see Figure 12-7A). At mutually owned institutions, the net worth that has been accumulated over time serves much the same function as the equity funds at privately owned institutions, but these funds are not specifically assigned to anyone. They do not create any claims against current income (unless the institution is short of the legal requirement and is required to add to its general reserves). The accounting cost of the funds in net worth to the institution is zero. The average cost of funds for these institutions will tend to increase as the ratio of debt to net worth increases and will also approach the average cost of the debt sources as the limit (see Figure 12-7B).

The relative size that can be achieved by institutions with these two types of cost function depends on the amounts and rates involved. The bank faces some range of decreasing money costs as it spreads the higher cost of equity funds over the lower demand deposit costs. The savings institution starts with an initial cost advantage from the availability of historically accumulated free funds, but it faces increasing money costs at all stages of its operations.

Throughout this discussion it has been assumed that changes in the distribution of risks, or in the overall level of risk, have not affected the cost of funds. This assumption is not likely to be correct, although the precise impact of an increase in the debt—equity ratio is subject to debate. An increase in the debt-to-equity ratio may lead to an increase in the cost of equity capital (the normal profit rate) because of the added risk exposure. This would offset some of the cost advantages of debt financing. There may also be some reduction of risk with the expansion in portfolio size.

Portfolio turnover and average revenue and cost functions

Long-term contracts on either assets or liabilities introduce a fixed component into the average revenue and cost functions. During any period of time, some share (X_2) of loans and deposits will be turned over and replaced by contracts at current market rates. The remaining share (X_1) will be retained at the old rates, and the institution's average revenue and cost functions will reflect this mixture of old and new contracts as in equation (3). The size of the fixed component depends on the time period

FIGURE 12-8

PORTFOLIO TURNOVER AND AVERAGE COST AND REVENUE FUNCTIONS

A. Higher Rates and Average Costs

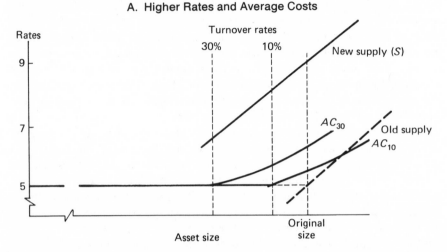

B. Higher Rates and Average Revenue

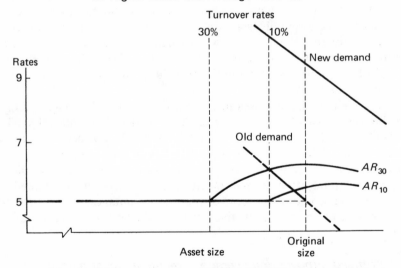

used and the portfolio turnover rates. Figure 12-8 illustrates the effects of a sizable increase in current market rates on the average cost and revenue functions with different turnover rates. The turnover rate is indicated as a subscript to the appropriate function. For example AC_{30} indicates that the average cost function was based on an assumed turnover rate of 30 percent among the sources of funds.

The fixed component of revenue and cost functions dampens the impact of fluctuations in market rates on the institutions' earnings and

FIGURE 12-9

HIGHER INTEREST RATES AND THE COMPATIBILITY OF PORTFOLIO
TURNOVER RATES

A. Incompatible Turnover Rates

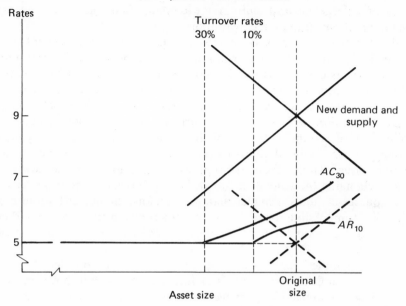

B. Compatible Turnover Rates

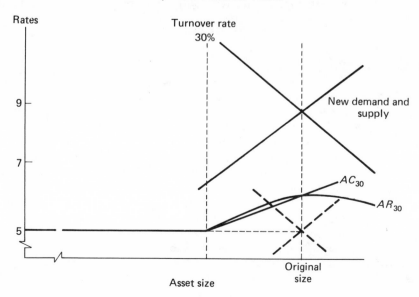

expenses, but it can also create problems if the turnover rates on assets and liabilities are greatly different. Figure 12-8A illustrates the effects of a large upward shift in the supply function on the average cost functions of institutions with different turnover rates; Figure 12-8B illustrates the effects of a large upward shift in the demand function on the average revenue functions of the same institutions.

If the turnover rates on assets and liabilities are consistent, even sizable changes in interest rates will not create problems for the institution. It can adjust its current loan and deposit rates to the amounts required to maintain its position without adversely affecting the relationship between average cost and average revenues. Figure 12-9B illustrates this adjustment for an institution with 30 percent turnover rates on both assets and liabilities. It is assumed, for simplicity, that the institution is trying to maximize in size and will adjust its size until average revenue and average costs are equal. Under these assumptions, it can adjust to the new rates without changing the scale of its operations. If, however, the turnover rate on its sources of funds is higher than on its loans, the higher level of rates will make it impossible for it to compete for funds in the current markets, as its average cost function will be above its average revenue function (see Figure 12-9A).

This example illustrates one aspect of the liquidity problem faced by savings institutions in periods of rising interest rates. The turnover rates on their mortgages are likely to range between 10 and 15 percent per year while the turnover rates on their savings accounts may be 30 to 40 percent a year. Long-term debt contracts can create a similar but inverted problem for institutions with short-term loan contracts during periods of declining interest rates.

QUESTIONS FOR DISCUSSION

1. List some important types of operating costs faced by commercial banks. Which of these items can be assigned directly as a lending cost or as a cost of raising funds? Suggest an appropriate way of allocating the expenses that cannot be directly assigned.

2. Place yourself in the position of the manager of a financial institution who learns that the net income for the year is going to be larger than expected. How might that information affect your decisions?

3. If the revenue and cost functions as shown in Figure 12-4 are assumed to correctly reflect the short-run market conditions faced by the financial institution, show that the traditional theory of profit maximization that assumes that the excess profits are paid to the owners (suppliers in this case) will not lead to a stable equilibrium at the point of equality between marginal revenue and marginal costs.

4. Any comparison of the financial ratios of financial institutions will reveal sizable variations in individual ratios. What evidence would you regard as indicating that the manager was trying to maximize the size of the institutions? What market conditions would tend to produce the same type of results?

5. How should the cost of capital (K) for a cooperative or mutually owned financial institution be calculated? Can the net worth be given a zero cost? What would be the implication for a growing institution of not allocating any of the current income to net worth?

6. Distinguish between the fixed and variable components of a financial institution's revenue and cost functions when the time span being considered is one day.

7. Consider the nature of the cost functions of various types of operating expenses faced by a financial institution. How many types of fixed-cost relationships can you find where costs are fixed with respect to some type of financial variable? For example, loan set-up costs can be thought of as fixed relative to the maturity of the loan. Draw the appropriate average cost functions for the examples you have identified, and comment on their significance for related financial policies.

8. How will a decision to relax loan quality standards without changing rates affect the institution's revenue function (AR)?

SELECTED REFERENCES

CAVES, R. E., "Uncertainty, Market Structure and Performance: Galbraith as Conventional Wisdom," *Industrial Organization and Economic Development*, eds., J. Markham and B. Papanek. Boston: Houghton Mifflin, 1970.

COHEN, K. J., and FREDERICK S. HAMMER, eds., *Analytical Methods in Banking*. Homewood, Ill.: Richard D. Irwin, Inc., 1966.

EDWARDS, FRANKLIN R., "Managerial Objectives in Regulated Industries: Expense-Preference Behavior in Banking," *Journal of Political Economy*, 85 (January 1977), 147–62.

GOLDFELD, S. M., *Commercial Bank Behavior and Economic Activity*. Amsterdam: North-Holland Publishing Co., 1966.

SHULL, BERNARD, "Commercial Banks as Multiple-Product Price Discriminating Firms," *Banking and Monetary Studies*, ed., Deane Carson. Homewood, Ill.: Richard D. Irwin, Inc., 1963.

WHITE, C. MICHAEL, "Multiple Goals in the Theory of the Firm," *Linear Programming and the Theory of the Firm*, eds., Kenneth E. Boulding and W. Allen Spivey. New York: Macmillan Company, 1960.

WILLIAMSON, O. E., "A Model of Rational Managerial Behavior," *A Behavioral Theory of the Firms*, eds., Richard M. Cyert and James G. March. Englewood Cliffs, N.J.: Prentice-Hall, Inc., 1963.

Competition
Among
Financial Institutions

13

Competition among financial institutions is not a one-on-one contest between institutions. Each institution has to compete in a variety of markets, and it faces a different set of competitors in each market. Similar institutions may find themselves as competitors in several markets, but they will be sharing the markets with others.

The full set of markets available to financial institutions ranges from demand deposits to equity on the supply side and from consumer loans to U.S. Treasury securities on the borrowers' side. Each market is characterized by the specialized needs of its borrowers and lenders and is differentiated by special contract features and geographic considerations. The institution's access to a market depends on the nature of its charter and the regulatory restrictions on its activities. Only commercial banks can offer demand accounts. Only insurance companies can write insurance. But many types of institutions can compete for savings accounts, mortgages, or corporate bonds.

The competitive conditions in the markets in which the institution is permitted to operate (or chooses to operate) determine its revenue and cost functions. Its success or failure depends on its ability to work within the constraints imposed by the markets. It thrives if the conditions are favorable. It fails if they are unfavorable. Increased competition in any of the markets in which it operates will be reflected unfavorably in its cost and revenue functions. It either has to pay more for funds or receives less for its loans. These changes affect its ability both to extract a surplus and to survive.

The first section of this chapter deals with the relationship between the competitive conditions in individual markets and the revenue and cost functions of the institutions that serve those markets. The second section discusses the nature of competition and its implications for the equilibrium position of individual institutions. The third section deals with the relationship between competition and the performance of financial markets. The fourth describes some of the changes in the competitive positions of various types of institutions.

Price and Nonprice Competition

The market alternatives available to financial institutions include some in which they can borrow or lend at the going market rate and others in which they can set their own rates. The differences in their ability to influence rates measure the competitive differences in the markets. In highly competitive markets, individual institutions have very little control over rates, and their demand and supply functions will be perfectly elastic. In less perfect markets, they are able to influence rates, and their demand and supply functions will show some inelasticity. Whenever any real or imagined differences exist among institutions or contracts, some inelasticities will appear in their demand and supply functions. Some inelasticities can be observed in nearly all the primary markets.

The role of nonprice considerations in shaping the demand and supply functions at individual institutions can be illustrated by an example of two institutions (A and B) that share an otherwise closed market. It will be assumed that they offer identical services except for their locations. It will also be assumed that they are located so that they will share the market equally when they pay and charge the same rates. This example will be applied only to the demand for loans, although it could be developed in the same way for the supply of funds.

When both institutions charge the same rates for their loans ($r_a = r_b$), their demand functions will have the elasticity of the market demand function and their shares of the market will be equal ($p_a = p_b$). When they charge different rates, their demand schedules will be functions of the differentials in rates. For simplicity it will be assumed that the total market demand for loans is perfectly inelastic so that the aggregate demand is unaffected by rate differential and the demand for A's loans (as a share of the market p_a) can be expressed as a function of the spread in rates:

$$p_a = f(r_a - r_b) \qquad (1)$$

When location is the only form of product difference, the spread in rates also measures the inconvenience and expense of travel. Some rate differential (c) will exist that makes it worthwhile for all of the borrowers to go to the institution with the lowest rate. If A's rates are higher than those at B by the amount of the differential c, B will have all the loans ($p_a = 0$) and if A's rates are lower by the same differential, A will have all the loans ($p_a = 1.0$). Figure 13-1 shows the market distribution of loans as the rate differential moves from c to $-c$ and A's share of the market (p_a) moves from zero to 100 percent. The spread in rates can be expressed as a function of A's share of the market (p_a):

$$r_a - r_b = c - 2cp_a \qquad (2)$$

FIGURE 13-1

A. Rate Differentials and the Distribution of Market Shares

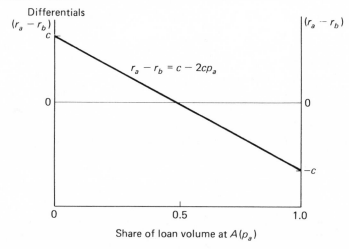

B. Derived Demand for Loans at A ($r_b =$ constant, r^*)

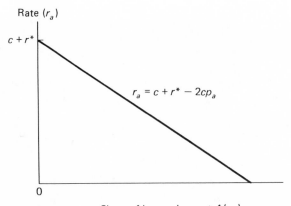

If B's loan rate is assumed to be given as a constant (r^*), equation (2) also provides A's demand schedule (expressed as a share of the total):

$$r_a = c + r^* - 2cp_a \tag{3}$$

The slope and position of A's demand function is determined by the value of c, which is also a measure of the only difference between a loan at A and a loan at B.

The impact of changes in market conditions on the demand and supply functions of individual financial institutions can be illustrated by changing the r^* and c parameters of equation (3). If the value of c increases, i.e., transportation becomes more expensive, the slope of A's demand function increases. If the value of c decreases, the slope decreases. If c is set equal to zero, i.e., if both institutions are in the same location, the product difference is eliminated and A's demand function becomes perfectly elastic and the market is perfectly competitive (see Figure 13-2B). In this example, c measures only the cost and inconvenience of transportation. If any other type of product difference were introduced, the effects on the demand and supply functions of the two institutions would be similar to the effects of changes in the value of c. In practice, product differences appear in many forms, and, as long as any customer is willing to pay for the difference or does not know that different rates exist, some inelasticity will be observed in the demand and supply functions of individual institutions.

Changes in a competitor's rates will have the effect of shifting the institution's demand and supply functions. A decrease in the rate that B charges for loans (decrease in r^*) will shift A's demand function to the left (see Figure 13-2A). In practice, every institution will be competing with different institutions for different types of contracts. The term r^* in equation (3) can be thought of as representing the rates charged on all loans that are potential substitutes for the institution's loans. The term *cross-elasticity* is used to describe the relationship between a change in rates (prices) at another institution and the loan volume of institution A. Some cross-elasticity exists as long as a change of rates anywhere in the market affects the r^* parameter in A's demand function.

Nature of Competition

Competition starts with a short-run equilibrium position that permits an economic surplus or excess profit. The surplus attracts competitors and leads to changes in the demand and supply conditions that are reflected in unfavorable changes in the revenue and cost functions of the established institutions. The competition may appear in either the price (r^*) or the

FIGURE 13-2
MARKET CONDITIONS AND THE DEMAND FOR LOANS
AT FINANCIAL INSTITUTIONS

A. Effects of Changes in Competitor's Rates (r^*)

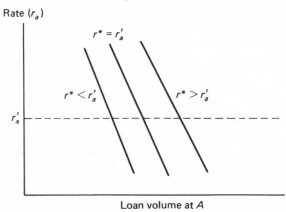

B. Effects of Changes in Nonprice Features (c)

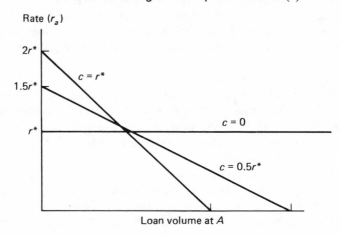

nonprice (c) parameters of the institution's demand and supply functions. The process continues as long as a surplus exists and access to the market is available.

Since the surplus at financial institutions reflects the spread in rates between at least two markets, competitive pressure can develop in several ways. It can come from a new institution that operates in the same set of markets, or it can come from the entry of other financial institutions or other participants into either or both of the markets in question. Entry for purposes of financial competition does not necessarily require the establishment of a new financial institution.

Many types of financial markets are essentially local in nature and require direct personal contact between the financial institution and its customers. The local nature of these markets adds a geographic dimension to the definition of a market for competitive purposes. Barriers to entry may appear either in the form of geographic restrictions or as functional limitations. Both types of barriers are required to prevent competitive attacks on surpluses that may appear at individual institutions. If the institution is not protected by geographic barriers, similar institutions from other areas can invade its territory. If it is not protected by functional barriers, other types of institutions may be able to move into its markets.

The story of competition among financial institutions centers around commercial banks. An attack on the surplus position of a bank requires the ability to enter markets that make the surplus possible. Many types of financial institutions are free to enter the loan markets serviced by banks, but since they are likely to be using more expensive funds, it is unlikely that they will be able to offer very effective competition. The most effective competition is likely to come from other banks. Despite the restrictions on the payment of interest on demand deposits, competition among a group of banks in the same geographic area can lead to the elimination of excess profits. The competition can take place in any or all of the loan and deposit markets, but it has to be conducted largely along nonprice lines in the demand deposit market.

An attempt by any bank to expand its position in any of the loans or deposit markets affects the revenue and cost functions of its competitors. Price competition in loan markets leads to a reduction in excess profits through the downward shifts in revenue functions of the type illustrated in Figure 13-2A. Price competition in deposit markets leads to the reduction of excess profits by an upward shift in the cost of money functions in much the same way. Competition of this type will stabilize into a long-run equilibrium when the average revenue and the average costs of the marginal banks are brought into equality (see Figure 13-3).

Nonprice forms of competition are somewhat more difficult to trace because they can affect both the slope and the position of the revenue and cost functions (see Figure 13-2B). They also involve some shifts in the operating expenses of the initiating bank. The bank can compete in several loan and deposit markets by opening new branches, keeping longer hours, or advertising; or it can compete in specific markets by selective changes in contract terms or related services. If these attempts are successful, they will shift the initiating institution's supply and demand functions and add to its operating expenses. Retaliation by competitors may reverse the gains in volume achieved by the initiating bank, but they will not reverse the effects

FIGURE 13-3
COMPARISON OF SHORT-RUN AND LONG-RUN EQUILIBRIUM POSITIONS

A. Short-run equilibrium

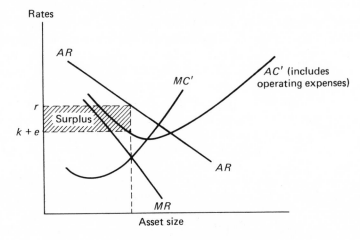

B. Long-run equilibrium

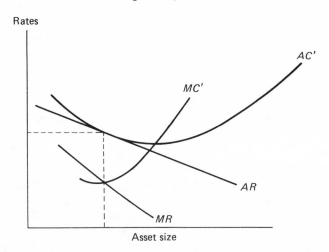

on operating expenses. Nonprice competition moves banks toward the long-run equilibrium position illustrated in Figure 13-3, but some share of the eliminated surplus will go to cover the higher costs of more banking facilities or more expensive nonprice services.

Banks and other financial institutions are competitors in most loan and deposit markets. Nonbank competition can even affect the market for demand accounts to some extent. All types of savings accounts are good substitutes for demand accounts for many purposes. New forms of negotiable instruments, such as the NOW accounts, that can be used for transactions purposes have been developed. These accounts, and the withdrawal drafts provided by liquid asset management funds, are direct substitutes for demand accounts. The boundaries between bank and non-bank competition are set by a wide variety of regulatory controls that are constantly changing.

Competition and the Cost of Intermediation

The cost of financial intermediation is measured by the spread between the rate paid to the supplier of funds and the rate charged for loans. It consists of operating expenses (e) and surplus or excess profits (s). Competition can, in theory, minimize both of these cost components. The description of the competitive process in the preceding section traced the effects of competition on the revenue and costs functions of individual institutions as they were pushed by competition from their short-run equilibrium position into a long-run equilibrium position. The long-run position assumes that the institutions are trying to maximize their surplus position but that market conditions have forced them into a position that eliminates the surplus.[1] The long-run position also implies a minimum level of operating expenses under the constraints imposed by the demand and supply functions. These are reassuring results, but they follow from a number of assumptions that have to be examined more closely to obtain a realistic picture of the competitive process.

Potential barriers to competition

The success of competition depends on the existence of potential competitors with the ability to detect surplus and with the motives and opportunities to set the competitive process in motion. These conditions are usually assumed to exist, but, as a practical matter, it is very hard to detect their presence or absence. Surplus may be hard to detect. Some of the ways in which it is hidden in accounting statements were discussed earlier. The practical problem of detecting surplus is made more difficult by the inadequacy of published information.

The motives for profit maximization are always assumed to exist, but in markets where there is personal and direct contact among competitors,

[1]The elimination of the surplus controlled by the financial institution is one aspect of the question of the *allocative efficiency* of the intermediation process. The broader question is concerned with the justification for rate differentials that are charged to various borrowers and paid to various suppliers. These issues involve judgments about the economic value of various types of nonprice differences and are beyond the scope of this chapter.

explicit collusion or implicit restraints may discourage the competitive process. Trade associations and other business groups that involve social and personal contacts tend to reduce the pressures for direct competition. The smaller the number of participants in the market, the greater the likelihood of cooperative behavior.

There is a wide variety of legislative and regulatory controls that imposes explicit barriers to the entry in some cases. The charters of all types of financial institutions place some limits on the scope of their financial activities. Most types of financial institutions are also supervised by various state and federal agencies, which impose a variety of selective controls. Rate ceilings, restricted investment lists, geographic limits, and a variety of other restrictions serve as barriers to entry into various markets. However, money is a very mobile commodity and tends to be attracted to profitable opportunities. Entry into a finalcial market does not require the establishment of a new financial institution. Most entry takes the form of expansion of the activities of established institutions. Wealthy individuals, finance companies, and investment companies also serve as versatile and flexible financial forces. New finance companies and new investment companies are relatively easy to establish and have historically appeared at the frontiers of new financial needs and opportunities.

The most effective barriers to competition have typically surrounded the demand deposit activities of banks. The combination of geographic and functional barriers provides the potential for highly protected situations. However, the problem of encouraging competition for demand accounts gets involved in the question of the effectiveness of monetary controls. The controls over demand deposits are also the tools of monetary policy. Relaxation of barriers to the acceptance of demand deposits can reduce the effectiveness of monetary controls. These problems will be discussed in Chapter 14.

Optimum size and problems of concentration

The assumption of the stability of long-run equilibrium solutions implies that the markets are large enough to permit financial institutions to reach their optimum size. The number of institutions that can best serve any set of markets depends on the size of the markets and the relationship between costs and the scale of operations. As long as any institution can reduce its costs by expansion, open competition leads to a reduction in the number of competitors and to the concentration of financial power that can be a threat to effective competition. The solution to the problem of optimal financial structure has to reconcile the cost advantage of size with the need for enough independent competitors to preserve competition. The issues are often clouded by the difficulty of distinguishing between attempts to protect the sheltered position of small institutions and the desire to protect the competitive process.

The list of economies of scale at financial institutions is impressive, and in most cases it is difficult to detect any size at which the relationships are reversed. Studies of the economies of scale at commercial banks have produced evidence of the advantage of scale on nearly every aspect of the bank's operations.[2] The evidence indicates that the operating costs can be expected to decrease with bank asset size up to the very largest size group where the evidence is difficult to interpret.[3]

Less attention has been paid to some of the purely financial economies of scale, but they may be potentially even more important than the economies of operating expenses. All of the statistical financial advantages of pooling increase with the size of the pool. These improvements can, in turn, be related to specific cost reductions. The relative size of the reserves needed for protection against default risk decreases with the number of loans; the relative size of secondary reserves needed for a given degree of liquidity decreases with the number of deposit accounts; and the equity ratios required for the given level of protection against insolvency decrease with the size of the institution. Size may also contribute to the reduction of certain types of financing costs. Large institutions have direct access to the money and capital markets and to the related cost advantages. Size can also contribute to the marketability and acceptability of securities and to lower financing costs.

It is harder to find diseconomies of scale at financial institutions. It seems likely that a financial structure made up of a small number of very large institutions will be more efficient than one made up of a large number of small institutions. The principal danger in encouraging growth in size and concentration lies in the danger of reducing the competitive potential essential for maintaining efficient performance.

Changing Shares of the Market

The United States emerged from World War II with a financial system that had been conditioned and shaped by a prolonged depression and by the controlled economy of the war years. Commercial banks and insurance companies dominated the intermediation process and held three-fourths of the assets of all financial institutions. The financial system, as well as the economy, had to adjust to the transition to peacetime activities and postwar expansion.

[2]Frederick W. Bell and Neil B. Murphy, "Economies of Scale in Commercial Banking, Part I: The Measurement and Impact," *New England Business Review* (March 1967).

[3]Jack M. Guttentag and Edward S. Herman, *Banking Structure and Performance* (New York: Graduate School of Business, New York University, 1967), pp. 115–125.

New demand pressure came from all sectors. Industry needed funds for conversion and expansion of facilities. Construction of all types had been delayed and postponed by the depression and the war. Consumers were anxious to improve and replace their housing, automobiles, and other durables. These demands were regarded as a mixed blessing by the monetary authorities who were concerned about the potential inflationary impact of financing these pent-up demands with an expansion of the money supply. They kept tight control over both the money supply and total bank credit. Low ceilings on rates that banks could pay on time and savings accounts were maintained to prevent them from expanding their funds from those sources. The banks were not able to handle their share of the new demand pressure and other financing channels had to be developed.

The 1950's

During the decade of the 1950's, commercial banks grew at an annual rate of only 4.3 percent in contrast to the GNP growth rate of 5.9 percent and the average growth rate of 10 percent at other types of financial institutions. The bank share in total assets held by financial intermediaries dropped from 50.8 percent in 1950 to 37.7 percent in 1960 and to an eventual low of 36.3 percent in 1965.

The savings institutions, and particularly the savings and loan associations, were in an excellent position to fill the gap. They specialized in mortgage financing and were able to offer rates high enough to attract new funds. They grew at an annual rate of 15.5 percent during the 1950's and doubled their share of the assets of financial intermediaries.

Development of retirement and pension programs as employee benefits introduced an important new feature into the pattern of savings flows during the postwar years. These agreements created a large, predictable, and relatively stable flow of savings. The pension funds of corporations and state and local governments grew at an annual rate of 17.4 percent during the 1950's. They provided funds for long-term corporate needs and, indirectly, for many other types of financing through their purchases of the securities of finance companies and federally sponsored credit agencies.

The growth in retirement plans also contributed to the decline in the role of life insurance in family savings programs. High-savings forms of life insurance (endowments, retirement income, and prepaid life insurance) declined in importance relative to total insurance. Life insurance companies continued to grow at about the same rate as the GNP, but their share of the total assets of financial intermediaries declined (see Figure 13-4).

Finance companies of various types appeared to handle the demands

FIGURE 13-4

GROWTH OF FINANCIAL INSTITUTIONS IN 1950's

A. Selected Growth Rates (annual rates)

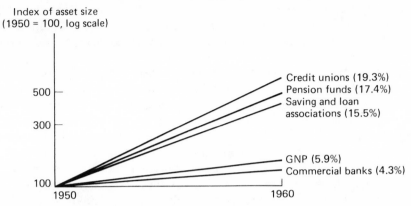

B. Shares of Financial Assets

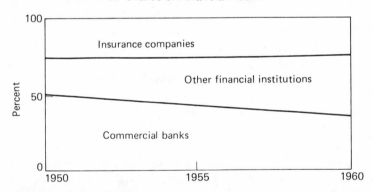

of consumers and businesspeople that could not be met by banks. Sales finance companies provided a large share of the funds for consumer purchases of automobiles and durable goods. Factoring companies and commercial credit companies helped businesses with their receivables and with various forms of relatively high-risk financing. These companies grew at an annual rate of 11.3 percent during the 1950's.

In a period of impressive growth rates, the credit unions recorded the most impressive rate of all, 19.3 percent. Their activities, which are subsidized to some degree by sponsoring organizations, by volunteer help, and by their frequent exemptions from taxation, were stimulated by the strong consumer demand for loans and by the enthusiasm of supporters of the movement. The assets of credit unions, which were less than a billion dollars in 1950, grew to 5 billion dollars by 1960.

The Investment Company Act of 1940 set the stage for revival of the role of the investment company in the financing process. Open-end mutual funds grew at a rate of 17.7 percent during the 1950's and, together with pension funds, became an important force in the capital markets. The marketing procedures of investment underwriters and the structure of the secondary markets became more and more oriented toward institutional investors.

The decade of the 1950's was characterized by the exuberant growth of all forms of financial intermediation except for the two types of institutions that had dominated the process prior to 1950 (see Figure 13-4). Insurance companies held their own, relative to the growth of the economy; but the commercial banks declined, relative to the economy as well as to other types of financial institutions. Their loss of position set in motion two interrelated developments that continued into subsequent years. First, the banks began to press for the relaxation of some of the barriers to their participation in a broader range of financial activities. Second, economists became interested in the economic role of nonbank financial intermediaries. Gurley and Shaw recorded this new awareness of nonbank financial institutions in an article that appeared in 1956.[4] Joint interest of the banks and the academic community contributed to the formation of the Commission on Money and Credit by the Committee for Economic Development to study the financial structure of the United States and make recommendations for changes.

The Commission's report, published in 1961, marked the beginning of a prolonged debate about the structure of the financial system and, more specifically, about the competitive role of various types of institutions. The Commission recommended

> ...that the existing statutory reserve requirements against savings and time deposits be repealed and that pending repeal of such requirements, those banks and competing thrift institutions subject to them be permitted to hold reserves in the form of either cash or Treasury securities with maturities up to five years.[5]

They also recommended that banks be subject to restrictions on the rates that they could pay for time and savings deposits

> ...only when in the opinion of the appropriate authorities further interest rate competition for these deposits is deemed not in the public interest, and that when applied, consideration be given to maintaining appropriate but not necessarily identical interest rate maxima for competing institutions.[6]

---

[4]John G. Gurley and Edward S. Shaw, "Financial Intermediaries and the Savings-Investment Process," *Journal of Finance,* vol. XI (May 1956), pp. 257–77.

[5]Commission on Money and Credits, *Money and Credit: Their Influence on Jobs, Prices and Growth* (Englewood Cliffs, N.J.: Prentice-Hall, Inc., 1961), p. 69.

[6]*Ibid.,* p. 168.

These recommendations supported the banks in their effort to expand their sources of funds.

The seesaw results of the efforts of banks and savings institutions to influence the Congress, state legislatures, and relevant regulatory authorities dominated developments in the 1960's and complicated the problems of the monetary authorities, as will be seen in the discussion later in the book.

The 1960's

The strong demand pressures continued into the 1960's. The Federal Reserve Board strengthened the competitive position of commercial banks by raising the legal ceilings on time and savings accounts. These changes permitted the banks to compete directly with savings institutions for funds, and the large banks began to use negotiable certificates of deposit (CDs) to raise funds directly from the money market. During the 1950's the savings institutions had raised twice as much in the form of savings accounts as the commercial banks. In the early 1960's, their positions were about equal, and by 1965 the banks were raising more funds from the savings account markets than all types of savings institutions combined. The competitive tide for savings had turned.

The near financial crisis that developed in 1966 revealed some of the problems that had been built into the financial structure by rapid postwar growth. When loan demands exceeded the existing supplies, as they did in 1966, the ability to compete for funds became a matter of survival rather than merely a question of relative growth rates. The savings institutions that were unable to raise their rates to match the money market rates lost funds to the banks and money market instruments. The events of 1966 introduced the concept of *disintermediation* into the competitive debate and demonstrated the vulnerability of savings institutions to liquidity problems. Congress moved quickly to restore the spread between the rates that could be paid by commercial banks and savings institutions. Later in 1966, the commercial banks themselves felt the effects of disintermediation as money market rates moved above the legal ceiling on the rates they could pay for CDs. The financial system had experienced the first of a series of recurring credit crunches that intensified the debate about competitive issues.

The demand pressures continued through the 1960's, and the growth patterns that had been established for financial institutions in the early 1960's continued but at a somewhat reduced rate (see Figure 13-5). The commercial banks were able to maintain their position relative to other financial institutions but did not gain. The insurance companies continued to grow with the economy but lost ground relative to other financial institutions. The most rapid growth rate during the 1960's was recorded by

FIGURE 13-5
Growth of Financial Institutions, 1960 to 1975

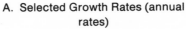
A. Selected Growth Rates (annual rates)

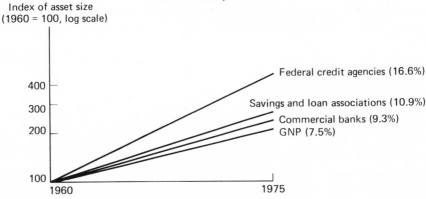

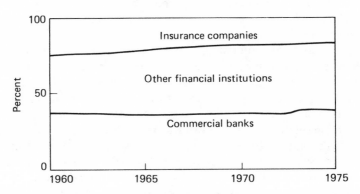
B. Shares of Financial Assets

the federally sponsored credit agencies as they became involved in support operations for the savings and loan associations.

The growth of one-bank holding companies during the 1960's added a new force to the competitive scene that is not revealed by the data based on institutional classifications. The commercial banks expanded their role in the intermediation process by acquiring control over a variety of other types of institutions that continued to appear in the statistics under their functional classifications. An important, but unmeasured, share of the financial activities of nonbank financial institutions is controlled by banks through their holding companies.

There is also very little information on the other changes in the concentration of control in the financial process. Widespread mergers and acquisitions of individual companies have reduced the number of competing institutions in most sectors of the industry. There appears to have been a marked trend toward the concentration of control within the financial system during the postwar years, both through a decline in the number of institutions and through the harder-to-identify holding company device, but the information is not available to measure these changes accurately.

Concern over inflation pressures that developed in the late 1960's led the monetary authorities to adopt very restrictive policies in 1969. These policies checked the growth of the commercial banks, particularly those that were members of the Federal Reserve System. The new ceiling on the rates the banks could pay on CDs proved to be inadequate as money market rates rose sharply. The banks were unable to sell CDs and were faced with the pressures of disintermediation. They were forced to turn to the Eurodollar markets and to repurchase agreements for funds. After gaining important regulatory concessions to improve their competitive position, the banks found themselves faced with new and serious liquidity problems as the decade ended.

The erratic functioning of the financial system in the 1960's, which had produced record interest rates, recurring financial crises, and marked swings in competitive positions, led to widespread demands for reforms. The President's Commission on Financial Structure and Regulation was set up to recommend changes. Its report reflected the objectives of all sectors of the industry to improve their respective competitive positions.[7] The commission supported commercial banks in their efforts to compete for money market funds by recommending removal of the ceiling rates on large certificates of deposit. They supported the efforts of savings institutions to expand into the demand deposit market (third party payment services). They recommended that both savings institutions and banks be permitted to compete in a wider range of financial markets and to provide a wide range of financial services—many of the distinctions between savings institutions and banks would be eliminated by their recommendations. And they included a recommendation that all institutions that "offer third party payment services" be required to become members of the Federal Reserve System.[8]

Early 1970's

The decade of the 1970's began with the removal of the ceiling on rates that banks could pay for CDs, and the competitive strength shifted back toward commercial banks in the next credit crunch in 1974. However,

---

[7]*Report of the President's Commission on Financial Structure and Regulation* (Washington, D.C.: U.S. Government Printing Office, 1971).

[8]*Ibid.,* p. 65.

both banks and savings institutions grew more rapidly than the economy as a whole during the first half of the 1970's. The activities of both types of institution were characterized by the diversification of their activities as they obtained concessions from regulatory and legislative bodies to expand the types of services they could offer. Savings institutions in several states began to offer transactions facilities competitive with those of commercial banks. These services took several forms: Electronic funds transfer systems were introduced at retail outlets in several states; negotiable orders of withdrawal or NOW accounts were adopted in several states; and telephone bill payment services were permitted in other states. The role of banks as the center of the money transfer system was being challenged. The banks, on the other hand, were actively engaged in adding other types of financial services and were pressing to be permitted to enter more actively into the investment and brokerage fields.

The exuberant growth of pension funds and open-end investment companies was dampened by the sharp drop in security prices in 1973. A steady stream of funds continued to flow into pension funds, but the growth in the value of these assets slowed. Investment companies showed almost no net growth in the first half of the 1970's as the value of their assets declined and as they became less attractive to investors. The most rapid growth was again recorded by the federally sponsored credit agencies.

QUESTIONS FOR DISCUSSION

1. Compare the effects of price and nonprice competition on the supply functions of two institutions that share the same market. Illustrate the theoretical results with examples of competition as observed in practice.

2. Discuss the advantages and disadvantages that a commercial bank is likely to have in competing with a savings bank for loans of the same type and quality.

3. From the customer's point of view, what are the advantages and disadvantages of price competition as compared with nonprice competition? Would a customer ever prefer nonprice competition?

4. Many types of financial institutions have to obtain state or federal charters before they can open offices or conduct business in given areas. Under what circumstances are these requirements barriers to competition?

5. Develop a list of general conditions essential for effective competition among financial institutions. Use the list to appraise the effectiveness of competition in the primary markets for mortgages and business loans. If some of the desirable conditions are not met, what recommendations would you make to improve competition?

6. What information would you need to decide whether a given market is or is not competitive?
7. Define the concept of cross-elasticity of demand, and describe the cross-elasticity in perfectly competitive markets. Do most financial markets meet this test of perfect competition?

SELECTED REFERENCES

ALHADEFF, DAVID A., *Monopoly and Competition in Banking.* Berkeley, Calif.: University of California Press, 1954.

——, "A Reconsideration of Restrictions on Bank Entry," *Quarterly Journal of Economics*, 76 (May 1963), 246–63.

BENSTON, GEORGE, "Branch Banking and Economies of Scale," *Journal of Finance*, XX (May 1965), 312–31.

CARSON, DEANE, "Bank Earnings and the Competition for Savings Deposits," *Journal of Political Economy*, LXVII (December 1959) 580–88.

EDWARDS, FRANKLIN R., *Concentration and Competition in Commercial Banking: A Statistical Study.* Boston: Federal Reserve Bank of Boston, 1964.

GRAMLEY, LYLE E., *A Study of Scale Economies in Banking.* Kansas City, Mo.: Federal Reserve Bank of Kansas City, 1962.

GUTTENTAG, JACK M., and EDWARD S. HERMAN, *Banking Structure and Performance.* New York: New York University, Graduate School of Business Administration, 1967.

HORVITZ, PAUL M., *Concentration and Competition in New England Banking.* Boston: Federal Reserve Bank of Boston, 1958.

KOHN, ERNEST, *Branch Banking, Bank Mergers and the Public Interest.* Albany, N.Y.: New York State Banking Department, 1964.

PHILLIPS, ALMARIN, "Competition, Confusion, and Commercial Banking," *Journal of Finance*, XIX (March 1964), 32–46.

MACROECONOMICS OF FINANCE

Part TWO

The economic process in its stable form is self-financing. Income provides the funds for consumption and the replacement of capital, and these outlays provide the new source of income. Financial markets play an important but neutral role in this process by assisting in the conversion of savings into loan funds. They can become a force for expansion when they are used to generate new funds, or they can be a force for contraction if they fail to convert savings into loans. This part of the book is concerned with the role of the financing process as a force for economic change.

Two new sets of institutions have to be introduced. First, the monetary authorities, as custodians of the money supply, can contribute to either an expansion or a contraction. Chapter 14 deals with their role in controlling the money supply and with the impact of their actions on the overall supply of funds. Second, the secondary markets do not enter directly into the primary financing process but they add flexibility to the process and serve as the focal point for the financial adjustments. They are sensitive indicators of demand and supply pressures and of the nature of the events that are creating these pressures. Chapters 15, 16, and 17 examine the role of these markets in the adjustment process and interpret the information they provide.

The last six chapters focus on the role of financial institutions and markets in meeting the aggregate demand for funds. Chapters 18 and 19 deal with the nature of the aggregate supply function and the interaction of the supply function with aggregate demand in the determination of the level of interest rates. Chapters 20, 21, and 22 deal with special structural and institutional forces that affect the aggregate supply function. The last chapter looks at the recent changes in the financial system in the United States in the context of economic events.

Control of the Money Supply

14

Newly issued money plays a special role in the financing process. It provides a supply of new funds that does not have to be obtained from the savings markets. The purchasing power it represents is a claim on goods and services that has not been earned by productive contributions to the supply of goods and services. New money has often been used by governments to finance social or political objectives that could not be paid for by more conventional techniques. Galbraith called money an "instrument of revolution" in describing the role of note issue in the financing of the American, French, and Russian revolutions.[1] Nearly all wars have been financed in part by newly created money and numerous social reforms have been eased by the liberal use of monetary devices.

New money created by banks provides the same new source of purchasing power, but the obvious inequities of unearned purchasing power are avoided when new money is introduced into the economy as a loan. The borrower has to earn the funds for repayment. He is unaware of the subtleties of the differences in the source of the funds. Banks have achieved their dominant role in the money-issuing function because they can introduce new money into the economy in response to shifting pressures of demand without giving anyone the windfall benefits of newly issued money. Some may regard the bank's right to the income from loans based on new money as a windfall, but except for the possibility of excess profits, the income from loans can be appropriately allocated to the costs associated with making loans and the other banking activities, including some share to a "normal profit" on the private capital used.

[1] John Kenneth Galbraith, *Money: Whence it Came, Where it Went* (Boston: Houghton Mifflin Co., 1975), pp. 58–67.

D. H. Robertson summarizes a chapter on the merits and drawbacks of money with the statement:

> ...money, which is a source of so many blessings to mankind, becomes also, unless we can control it, a source of peril and confusion.[2]

Governments recognize the necessity and advantage of controlling the country's money supply. One of the few explicit economic provisions of the Constitution of the United States gives Congress the power "to coin money, regulate the value thereof, ..."[3] The control of money is a power too great to be yielded to private interests. It is even dangerous to expose it to political temptations. Most money control systems are designed to insulate the control process from direct political pressure. In the United States, the control of the money supply has been placed in the hands of the Federal Reserve System, which was established as an independent agency that reports to Congress. It is not a part of the administrative branch of the government.

Control of the money supply is not a simple matter. Long-run objectives may be sidetracked by political considerations or by specific short-run control problems. Even when there is agreement on the objectives of the controls, there is frequently disagreement on the techniques for achieving those objectives. Economic stability is a widely accepted objective of monetary policy, but economists do not agree on the role of money in the stabilization process. The expansionary effects of an increase in the money supply are generally acknowledged, but the similarities between the effects of new money issues in the traditional sense of the word and the effects of increases in other types of financial instruments has led to a debate about the definition of the monetary aggregate that should be used for control purposes.

The traditional discussions of money and monetary policy have focused on money defined as a means of payment, which includes only coins, currency (either government notes or private bank notes), and the checking accounts of banks. The unique feature of all of the conventional components of the money supply is their acceptance in direct payment for goods and services. This concept and definition would be appropriate for accounts that might be used for the proposed systems of electronic transfers of funds without the use of checks. It does not include credit cards, which require the use of another form of payment for settlement purposes. Nor does it apply to passbook accounts or certificates of deposit, which have to be converted into a means of payment before they can be spent. This definition of money has become M_1 in the hierarchy of monetary aggregates.

---

[2]D. H. Robertson, *Money* (New York: Harcourt, Brace and Co., 1929), p. 17.

[3]*Constitution of the United States*, Article 1, Section 8.

After World War II the national income expanded much more rapidly than the money supply (M_1). During this period nonbank financial institutions were also expanding rapidly, and the growth of their liabilities, which were similar to money in terms of their safety and liquidity, seemed to be contributing new funds to the expansion in much the same way as an expansion of the money supply. Some economists suggested that monetary controls should focus on a monetary aggregate that included some or all of the near-monies. Several combinations of M_1 and near-monies have been suggested as the target for monetary policy.[4]

The problem of the choice of a monetary aggregate for control purposes can be illustrated with the algebraic truism that equates income (Y) with the product of the money supply (M) and the velocity (V) with which the money supply is used ($Y = MV$). In this truism any increase in income can be attributed to an increase in either the money supply or the velocity of circulation. When money is defined as M_1, the effects of changes in near-monies are treated as contributing to the changes in the velocity of circulation. If the definition of the money stock is expanded to include various near-money components (M_x), the effects of changes in near-monies and the M_1 money stock appear in the same term and are measured directly from the changes in the outstanding amounts of those assets. The choice of definitions becomes largely a question of the usefulness of the concept for control purposes. The issues involved in this choice will be discussed in Chapter 21. This chapter is concerned with the technical problems of controlling monetary aggregates. Fortunately the techniques and problems are similar for any or all of the aggregates that appear as the liabilities of financial institutions.

Control Techniques

The problem of controlling monetary aggregates is one of controlling the selected liabilities of some group of financial institutions. The controls for purposes of monetary policy are concerned with the total size of the specified liabilities at all of these institutions. They are not directly concerned with the distribution of those liabilities among individual institutions in the controlled group. In any effective control system, the expansion of one institution must be offset by a contraction of another.

The standard control technique consists of requiring individual institutions to hold some fraction (r) of their deposits (D) in assets of some specified type (A). The assets that are eligible as reserves for deposits are usually called the *reserve base*. If the size of the reserve base can be controlled, the total deposits of the controlled group of institutions can be

[4]For example, see Leonall C. Anderson, "Selection of a Monetary Aggregate for Economic Stabilization," *Review, Federal Reserve Bank of St. Louis* (October 1975), pp. 9–15.

limited by the following relationship:

$$A = rD \qquad (1)$$

The controlled segment of the financial system is thus limited to liabilities equal to (D) and assets equal to the required asset (A) plus the loans (L) that can be made with funds not held to meet the reserve requirement.

Uses of funds	Sources of funds
Loans or investments (L) Reserve base ($A = rD$)	Notes or deposits (D)
$L + A$	D

Totals will be smaller than the limit only when some of the assets eligible to meet the reserve requirements are not used to support deposits. When such an excess (E) exists, the total deposits of the system will be smaller than the maximum by the amount of the potential expansion on the basis of the reserves (E/r). The amount of the reserve base will appear as two components:

$$A = rD + E \qquad (2)$$

This type of control can be applied to any set of financial institutions and to any set of the liabilities of those institutions. The reserve base used for control purposes can be defined in many different ways.

Historically, when banks were authorized to issue notes they were frequently required to hold some fraction of their notes in specie (gold or silver). Since these notes were in most cases redeemable in specie, these requirements were designed to assure some degree of liquidity at individual banks. They also served as an overall constraint on the total supply of notes but not as a specific control device. The total amount of note issue possible under this system was determined by the total amount of available specie and the share of that total held by the banks. Both the total and the share available to banks were subject to the vagaries of economic circumstance and to the public's confidence in bank notes. These systems were characterized by violent fluctuations in the amount of outstanding notes. These fluctuations were, in turn, associated with alternating periods of inflationary prosperity and financial crisis.

Government securities have also been used as the required asset for bank note issue. The advantages of this form of monetary control for a government in need of a market for its securities are obvious. The disadvantages of this technique for control purposes are also obvious. The aggregate amount of the note issue can vary with the total supply of acceptable securities and with the share of these securities held by the banking system. This form of bank control has been a favorite of governments faced with urgent expenditures and a reluctance to increase taxes. It has been less successful as a technique for effective monetary control. But under properly controlled conditions that restrict and control the securities used for this purpose, it could theoretically be used to create an effective control system.

The modern version of the asset requirement control system requires banks to keep some fraction of the deposits (which may be specifically defined in many ways) in the form of deposits (reserves) in a central bank. In its simplest form, the banks are required to hold a given fraction (r) of their deposits (D) in the form of reserves or deposits in the central bank (A). The simple relationship of equation (1) holds only when all types of deposits are subject to the same reserve requirement. In this form, the total amount of the controlled deposits is limited to a multiple (m) of the reserve base (A). This multiple, which is the reciprocal of the reserve ratio ($m = 1/r$), is often called the *money multiplier*. A 20 percent reserve requirement produces a money multiplier of 5, and a 5 percent reserve requirement produces a multiplier of 20.

The precision of the control over the relevant deposit total (D) in practice depends on (1) the ability to control the size of the reserve base (A), (2) the stability of the relationship between the reserve base and the deposit aggregate to be controlled (which is affected by the timing of the adjustments and the structure of the reserve requirements), and (3) the inclusion in the regulated system of all of the institutions that have deposits of the type to be controlled. The next three sections of this chapter examine these problems as they apply to the control of money in the United States.

Control of the Reserve Base

Only banks that are members of the Federal Reserve System are subject to their direct monetary controls. This group includes the largest banks in the country and accounts for the largest share of banking activity, although the share of deposits held by member banks has been declining in recent years. At the end of 1975, member banks held 71 percent of the country's demand accounts.

Member banks are permitted to hold their required reserves either in currency or as deposits in their reserve accounts with a Federal Reserve bank. The reserve accounts, which also serve as interbank clearing accounts, are the principal component of the reserve base. The total amount of these accounts can be controlled by the Federal Reserve System with considerable precision, and therefore the total amount of reserves available to a member of the system can be controlled. Although the currency component of member bank reserves cannot be controlled, the effect of shifts in currency holdings on a bank's total reserves can be offset by changing the reserve account component so that the combined total can be controlled.

Control over the amount available for member bank reserves is achieved by making the reserve accounts the exclusive clearing accounts for checks of the Federal Reserve banks and for drafts against the accounts themselves. Limited access to the funds in these accounts, called *Federal Funds*, creates a closed accounting system where transfers among accounts are possible, but the sum of the amounts in all of the accounts is not changed by the normal range of transactions. Only banks that are members of the Federal Reserve System hold deposits in the Federal Reserve banks. These accounts are, in effect, an exclusive form of money that is held only by member banks, the U.S. Treasury, and the small group of foreign central banks that are permitted to hold deposits in the Federal Reserve banks.

Since the reserve accounts appear as liabilities on the accounting statements of the Federal Reserve banks, the other accounts in these statements identify the sources of changes in reserves. By the immutable laws of accounting, a debit (or credit) to member bank reserves must appear as a counterpart credit (or debit) somewhere else in the statement. A listing of the transactions provides a complete list of the factors that can affect member bank reserves.

The accounting statements of the Federal Reserve System cannot be used directly for this purpose, however, because some of the essential items are carried on the Treasury Department's books.[5] The problem is easily solved by the preparation of a consolidated statement of the assets and liabilities of the Federal Reserve System and the Treasury's items that relate to the money supply. This statement, which is regularly prepared and published by the Federal Reserve System under the caption "Member Bank Reserves, Federal Reserve Bank Credit, and Related Items," is the

---

[5]The discussion of the factors that affect bank reserves is complicated by some residual responsibility for currency that was left with the U.S. Treasurer by the Federal Reserve Act. Some forms of currency appear in the official accounting statements as a liability of the Treasury Department; and, officially, all gold is held by the Treasury and not by the Federal Reserve System. But these technical distinctions are of minor importance except for the complications they introduce into the description.

key to the understanding of the factors that affect the level of member bank reserves.

The statement is easier to understand if it is thought of as the simplified asset and liability statement of a central bank (see Figure 14-1). The basic accounting relationships make it possible to summarize the factors affecting bank reserves in a simple algebraic equation, sometimes called the *reserve equation*, where reserves are regarded as the dependent variable and all other assets and liabilities are treated as independent variables. Any increase in an asset item will increase member bank reserves (assuming that other items are unchanged). Any increase in a liability item will decrease bank reserves. The net changes in these items can be summarized for any given period to identify the sources of change. Figure 14-2 shows the net changes in these items for December, 1975 and the effects of those changes on member bank reserves. In that month, the principal changes came from an increase in the public's holding of currency and coin, which reduced member bank reserves, and from the purchases of securities by the Federal Reserve System, which increased member bank reserves.

Any payment by the Federal Reserve banks to the public or to the banks adds to the member bank reserve base. Payments to the Federal Reserve banks by the public or by member banks contract the reserve base. The most important transactions of this type are those arising from

FIGURE 14-1

MEMBER BANK RESERVES, FEDERAL RESERVE BANK CREDIT, AND RELATED ITEMS, DECEMBER 1975 (AVERAGES OF DAILY FIGURES IN MILLIONS OF DOLLARS)

Assets		Liabilities	
Reserve Bank credit outstanding:		Currency outside member	
U.S. government securities	$92,108	banks	$78,037
Loans (to member banks)	127	Treasury cash	452
Float	3,029	Deposits of:	
Other F.R. assets, net	1,140	Treasury	3,955
Gold stock	11,599	Foreign and other	1,165
Special drawing right account	500		
Treasury currency outstanding	10,094		
		Member bank reserves (A):	34,988
		With F.R. $27,215	
		Currency and coin 7,773	
Total	$118,597	Total	$118,597

Source: *Federal Reserve Bulletin* (April 1976), p. A2.

FIGURE 14-2

FACTORS CHANGING MEMBER BANK RESERVES, DECEMBER 1975
(AVERAGES OF DAILY FIGURES IN MILLIONS OF DOLLARS)

	Change in accounting item	Effect on member bank reserves
Member bank reserves (A)	+ 418	+ 418
Federal Reserve operations:		
Purchases of securities	+ 1,174	+ 1,174
Float	+ 549	+ 549
Other, net	+ 76	+ 76
Member bank borrowing	+ 66	+ 66
Treasury and foreign operations:		
Gold stock	—	—
Treasury currency outstanding	+ 84	+ 84
Treasury cash holding	+ 37	− 37
Treasury deposits	− 378	+ 378
Foreign and other deposits	+ 219	− 219
Public holdings of currency and coin	+ 1,653	− 1,653

Source: *Federal Reserve Bulletin* (April 1976), p. A2.

the *open market operations* (purchases and sales of securities) of the Federal Reserve System. These transactions have become the principal tool for controlling the size of the reserve base.

When a Federal Reserve bank buys securities, it pays for them with a check drawn on the Federal Reserve bank itself (signed by one of its officers). The accounting implications of this transaction are shown in step 1, Figure 14-3A. The security dealer deposits this check in his account with a commercial bank, which sends it to a Federal Reserve bank for collection and credit to the bank's reserve account (step 2). If the check were deposited at a nonmember bank, it would have been sent to a member bank for credit in the nonmember bank's account with a member bank. The member bank would then send it to the Federal Reserve bank and the effects of step 2 would be the same as in the illustration. Note that if anyone other than a member bank were permitted to hold deposits at Federal Reserve banks, the transaction, which is intended to increase the reserves of member banks, would not necessarily succeed, and the ability of the system to control the reserves of a member bank would be weakened. Sales of securities by the Federal Reserve System reverse these transactions and are illustrated in Figure 14-3B.

The public affects the reserves of member banks by asking for their money in the form of currency or coin. The U.S. monetary system gives

FIGURE 14-3

OPEN MARKET OPERATIONS AND MEMBER BANK RESERVES

    A. Open market purchase of $100 million of U.S. government securities.
        (1) Check issued by Federal Reserve bank on itself to security dealer who deposits it in a member bank.
        (2) Member bank sends the check to the Federal Reserve bank for credit to its reserve account.

Federal Reserve System		Member Bank	
Assets	*Liabilities*	*Assets*	*Liabilities*
(1) U.S. govt. sec. + 100	(2) Member bank reserves + 100	(2) Reserves with F. R. bank + 100	(1) Customer deposits + 100

    B. Open market sale of $100 million of U.S. government securities.
        (1) Payment made to security dealer by customer and in turn made by security dealer to Federal Reserve bank.
        (2) The security dealer's check is returned to member bank for collection and the amount is deducted from member bank's reserve account.

Federal Reserve System		Member Bank	
Assets	*Liabilities*	*Assets*	*Liabilities*
(1) U.S. govt. sec. − 100	(2) Member bank reserves − 100	(2) Reserves with F. R. bank − 100	(1) Payment from customer's deposit − 100

the public complete freedom in the amount of currency and coin that it wants to use—they merely have to trade a deposit in a member bank for currency or they can reduce their currency by accepting a deposit in a member bank. These transactions complicate the problem of controlling the reserve base and the money supply, but they do not present a serious barrier to effective control. The currency demands of the public are largely seasonal in nature, and their effects on the reserves of member banks can be anticipated by the Federal Reserve System and offset by open market operations. Figure 14-2 provided an example of an outflow of cúrrency that was largely offset by the open market operations of the Federal Reserve System. The accounting implication of changes in the currency holdings of the public are illustrated in Figure 14-4.

    The Federal Reserve System's role as banker for the U.S. Treasury complicates its monetary control problem slightly, but if the Treasury keeps the Federal Reserve advised of its payments and transfers of funds,

FIGURE 14-4

CHANGES IN THE AMOUNT OF CURRENCY HELD BY THE PUBLIC

(1) Depositors cash checks for $100 thousand to obtain currency and vault cash reserves decline.

Member Bank

Assets	Liabilities
Reserves in currency − 100	Deposits − 100

(2) If the bank replenishes its cash, its balance at the Federal Reserve bank is drawn down in exchange for new notes issued by the Federal Reserve System.

Federal Reserve System

Assets	Liabilities
	Member bank reserves − 100
	F. R. notes outstanding + 100

Member Bank

Assets	Liabilities
Reserves: In currency + 100 With F. R. − 100	

(3) If the Federal Reserve System wishes to offset the effects of the currency withdrawal on the reserves of member banks it can buy securities of an equal amount and replenish the reserves as in Figure 14-3.

Federal Reserve System

Assets	Liabilities
U.S. govt. sec. + 100	Member bank reserves + 100

Member Bank

Assets	Liabilities
Reserves + 100	Deposits + 100

the effects of the Treasury's operations on the reserves of member banks can be offset and the desired level of reserves can be maintained. The U.S. Treasury keeps most of its deposits in "tax and loan accounts" in commercial banks, but all of its payments are made from its deposits in Federal Reserve banks. When the Treasury shifts funds from its accounts in member banks to the Federal Reserve accounts, the reserves of member banks are reduced (see Figure 14-5A). As the U.S. Treasury writes checks and makes payments, the checks are deposited in member banks, and member bank reserves are increased (see Figure 14-5B). The effects of these changes on the reserves of member banks can be offset by the Federal Reserve if the changes have undesirable implications for the reserve positions of member banks.

FIGURE 14-5
CHANGES IN U.S. TREASURY DEPOSITS AND MEMBER BANK RESERVES

A. When the Treasury shifts funds from its deposits in member banks to its accounts in Federal Reserve banks, member bank deposits and reserves are reduced.

Federal Reserve Banks		Member Banks	
Assets	*Liabilities*	*Assets*	*Liabilities*
	U.S. Treasury deposits + 100 Member bank reserves − 100	Reserves − 100	U.S. Treasury deposits − 100

B. When the Treasury writes checks on its Federal Reserve accounts, member bank deposits and reserves are increased.

Federal Reserve Banks		Member Banks	
Assets	*Liabilities*	*Assets*	*Liabilities*
	U.S. Treasury deposits − 100 Member bank reserves + 100	Reserves + 100	Private deposits + 100

Although many of the factors that affect the reserves of member banks are beyond the direct control of the Federal Reserve, the system can theoretically control the total amount of available reserves by using open market operations to offset any undesirable changes. The practical problem of accurate control involves the correct anticipation of changes in the uncontrolled items. It may be quite difficult for the Federal Reserve to anticipate day-to-day variations in the factors affecting reserves, but it can move quickly to offset any undesired effects. Day-to-day variations of the reserve base from their targets may be sizable but average variations over a few days can be kept within narrow limits.

Note on alternative targets: This discussion has focused on total member bank reserves (A) as the target for control purposes. This concept has some theoretical and practical advantages, but a variety of other targets has been suggested. The basic control techniques are the same, but the objectives and results are somewhat different. Three definitions of the target for control purposes have obtained considerable support:

1) The concept of *unborrowed reserves* (total member bank reserves minus member bank borrowing) has been widely used as a measure of Federal Reserve policy actions on the grounds that the member banks themselves determine the amount they want to borrow and that such amounts are, to a considerable extent, beyond the direct control of the system. This point is correct, but the Federal Reserve can, if it wishes, offset the effects of the member banks' actions. It is also argued that the borrowed proportion of the reserve base is somehow different from the unborrowed share because it is temporary and would not be used by the banks so freely. This argument is relevant for the borrowing bank but lacks conviction from the perspective of the member bank system as a whole. During periods of tight money, member bank borrowing has at various times provided a sizable and continuing amount of reserves for the system as a whole. The fact that the borrowing banks are forced to make temporary adjustments does not alter the fact that the system as a whole is using the reserves on a continuing basis.

2) The St. Louis Federal Reserve Bank has developed the concept of the *monetary base*, which has gained some support as a potential control target.[6] It consists of total member bank reserves plus currency outside the banks. It is also adjusted for changes in reserve requirements. It was designed to improve the relationship between the reserve base, which can be controlled, and the total amount of member bank credit. It does make some progress toward recognizing the role of the shift of funds among accounts with different reserve requirements, but it does not accurately provide for these changes to be reflected in the monetary base. It also introduces a new source of slack in the relationship between the controlled base and the monetary aggregate that is not present in the other base concepts. Shifts between currency outside the banks and the reserves of the banks do not change the size of the monetary base, but they do materially change the aggregate related to a given base. The currency in the circulation component of the monetary base has a one-to-one relationship with the currency in the monetary aggregate to be controlled, but the member bank reserve component has a fractional relationship to the deposit component of the aggregate, however defined.

3) A third concept, called *reserves available to support private nonbank deposits* (or, more briefly, *available reserves*), has been adopted by the Federal Reserve System. It excludes the reserves that are required against

---

[6]Federal Reserve Bank of St. Louis, "The Monetary Base. Explanation and Analytical Use," *Review* (August 1968), pp. 7–11.

U.S. government deposits from the base that is used for control purposes. It removes one element of variability between the reserve base and any monetary aggregate that excludes the deposits of the U.S. government.

Linkage Between the Reserve Base and Monetary Aggregates

The next stage of the control problem involves the linkages between the reserve base and the appropriate monetary aggregate. Any change in the reserve base (ΔA) in a simplified model of the control problem will be related to the changes in deposits (ΔD) by the following difference equation based on equation (2):

$$\Delta A = r\Delta D + \Delta E \qquad (3)$$

In this simplified form, the linkage between the change in the reserve base and the change in deposits depends on the amount of new reserves held as excess reserves (ΔE) and the reserve requirement ratio (r).

The ideal control situation exists when excess reserves are zero and when there is a stable relationship between the changes in the reserve base and changes in the aggregate deposits so that any change in the reserve base will be reflected in a multiple change in deposits:

$$\Delta D = m\Delta A \qquad (4)$$

where:
$$m = \frac{1}{r}$$

When the reserve requirement is 0.10, the multiplier (m) will be 10, and a $1 increase in the reserve base (ΔA) will produce a predictable $10 change in deposits. In the real world, however, this relationship is not direct and instantaneous. The bank that receives the reserves can make loans or buy securities up to the amount of the reserves. But any of its actions are likely to result in the withdrawal or loss of deposits equal to the amount of the new loan. Few borrowers plan on leaving the funds from the loan on deposit. The full expansion is achieved only after a series of loans and transfers of funds that may involve a number of banks. The implications of this expansion process for the member bank system as a whole can be described, but the actual process itself cannot be specifically identified in the complex clearing process. New reserves are being added or subtracted every day, and the expansion or contraction on the basis of earlier changes may be in various stages of completion.

The accounting implications of the expansion can be illustrated by following the new funds as they move into new loans or are used to purchase securities and are transferred into other banks as the process continues. The process is started by any transaction that creates new reserves. The illustration in Figure 14-6 is based on the assumption that the new reserves were created by open market operations (as in Figure 14-3), so that the events in Figure 14-3A represent the first stage of the expansion process. The bank or banks with the $100 million of new deposits and new reserves can make loans or purchase securities with the share of the new reserves that is not needed to meet the requirements on the new deposits (see stage 2, Figure 14-6A). As payment is made, the amount of excess reserves is lost to the bank making the loans or buying the securities but these funds reappear as deposits in the same bank or other banks (stage 3). The process continues until the full multiple is reached or until some bank decides to hold excess reserves.

The enumeration of the steps in this simplified version of the expansion process describes the mechanism of the process, but it does not cover the complexities of the process in practice. The *transition matrix* of a Markov chain will be used in the following discussions to identify and specify the complex set of paths that can be taken by the expansion process in a modern banking system. This approach, which may appear difficult at first to those not familiar with Markov chains, is used only as a descriptive device for identifying and controlling the assumptions used in the discussion. The transition matrix provides a compact specification of various expansion paths. The implications of any matrix are quickly revealed by converting it into a flow diagram (see Figure 14-6B).

Bank expansion as an absorbing Markov chain

The details of the expansion process can be represented by a flow chart similar to a probability tree (see Figure 14-6B). The new reserves can be traced from the initial deposit into reserves and then into loans and investments. After each new deposit, some fraction of the funds is absorbed into required reserves, and the amount available for loans in successive stages is decreased. When the parameters of the process are constant, the notation and transition matrix of an absorbing Markov chain can be used for specifying the features of this flow process. The transition matrix for the simple expansion model is shown in Figure 14-6C. Each row of this matrix gives the disposition of the funds that enter the state indicated by the row name. The sum of the values in each row must be equal to 1.0. In this example the expansion starts with open market operations of the Federal Reserve System that give member banks new deposits (D) of $100 million. The values in row D of the transition matrix indicate that 10 percent of these funds must be held in required reserves (R) and 90 percent are available as excess reserves (E). The rows for R and E specify the next stage of the process. All of the funds that move into required reserves (R) are held to meet the reserve requirements on deposits. The value of 1.0 in the R column indicates that funds moving into the R state are retained in that state. This is the absorbing state of the

FIGURE 14-6

BANK DEPOSIT EXPANSION (IN MILLIONS OF DOLLARS)

A. Expansion Stages

	Initial	1	2	3	4	5	6	7	8	...	Sum[a]
Deposits:	+ 100	—	—	+ 90	—	—	+ 81	—	—		+ 1,000
Reserves:											
Req.	—	+ 10	—	—	+ 9	—	—	+ 8.1	—		+ 100
Excess	—	+ 90	− 90	—	+ 81	− 81	—	+ 72.9	− 72.9		0
Loans	—	—	+ 90	—	—	+ 81	—	—	+ 72.9		+ 900

[a]The fully expanded position will be reached when excess reserves are equal to zero and the change in deposits is equal to $\Delta A / r$ or 1,000.

BANK EXPANSION AS AN ABSORBING MARKOV CHAIN

B. Path of Expansion

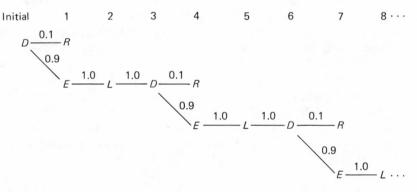

C. Transition Matrix

	R	E	D	L
R	1.0	0	0	0
E	0	0	0	1.0
D	0.1	0.9	0	0
L	0	0	1.0	0

Where: D = deposits

R = required reserves[b]

E = excess reserves

L = loans

[b]Reserve requirement = 0.1

expansion process. The disposition of the funds held as excess reserves is shown by the values in the E row. In this example, it has been assumed that they are placed entirely into new loans and investments. This is not a necessary assumption. If the banks involved decided to hold some fraction of these funds as excess reserves, this decision could be reflected in the values in the E row. Some fraction (x) would be in the E column and $(1-x)$ would be in the loan column. The excess reserve state then would be a partial absorbing state, and the effects on the expansion would be similar to an increase in the reserve requirement of the same amount.

The values in the loan (L) row are of special importance in describing the realities of the expansion process. In this example, it is assumed that 100 percent of the funds are redeposited in some bank in the system and the process continues. This assumption is essential for the completion of the expansion process, but the validity of the assumption depends on the nature and structure of the banking system. The values used in the matrix in Figure 14-6C specify the assumptions implied by the simplified expansion process.

The simple model of bank expansion just described will produce a predictable expansion in deposits (ΔD). The actual value of the multiplier (m) is the reciprocal of the value of the reserve requirement as indicated in position (D, R) in the transition matrix. The completion of the expansion process is assured by the assumption that 100 percent of the funds are redeposited in the system, which is indicated by the value of 1.0 in position (L, D) in the matrix, and by the assumption that banks do not want to hold excess reserves—i.e., the value in position (E, E) is zero.

As a practical matter, the bank expansion process is complicated in a number of ways that affect the linkage between the reserve base and monetary aggregates and that create difficulties in using the reserve base to control the money supply. These complications can be classified into four general types:

1) *Time lags in the expansion process.* The precision of the process for control purposes depends, in part, on the speed of the expansion process. If the process were instantaneous, a given change in the reserve base would produce the predicted change in deposits as soon as the reserve base were changed. In this ideal case, the money multiplier, as measured by the ratio of new deposits to new reserves, would be constant. If there is a long time lag in the completion of the process, the money multipliers calculated at various stages of the process will vary, depending on the timing of the changes in reserves and the stages of the expansion process. A model that assumes long time lags will produce wide variations in the money multipliers. In general, the faster the expansion (relative to the time interval for which the multipliers are computed), the greater the stability of the money multiplier.

Some judgments can be made about the speed of the process from the amount of excess reserves in the system. As can be seen from Figure 14-6, the amount of excess reserves decreases as the bank expansion process proceeds, and becomes zero when the expansion is complete. If all banks tried to keep fully invested, the amount of excess reserves in the member bank system at any given time would indicate the stage of the expansion on the basis of recent additions to reserves. Although it is impossible to trace the expansion process from a given increase in reserves, statistical studies suggest that the process occurs rapidly. Time lags leave a telltale mark in the form of excess reserves. The absence of large amounts of excess reserves at member banks and the absence of any significant relationship between the variations in these reserves and changes in total reserves is evidence of the rapid utilization of funds made available in member bank reserve accounts.

The evidence of the speed of the process is supported by observations of the actual reserve adjustments. The federal funds market permits banks to buy and sell reserves rapidly and to transfer funds telegraphically so that excess reserves can be placed into the market quickly. If it were assumed that each stage of the bank expansion process took one day, 70 percent of the full expansion could be achieved in two weeks. A close examination of the evidence of the ability of the modern banking system, and the markets they have developed, to take care of excess reserves suggests that the process may even be faster. Time lags in the bank expansion process do not appear to be a serious barrier to the effective control of a selected monetary aggregate. If time lags were the only complication, we would expect a stable relationship between changes in the reserve base and the amount of demand deposits of member banks. Since this relationship is not very stable, other complications must be important.

2) *Accumulation of excess reserves.* The availability of good substitutes for excess reserves and the efficiency of the short-term markets make it possible for banks, even in the most remote locations, to be fully invested without endangering their liquidity positions. Bankers deliberately hold excess reserves only when they do not have safe, liquid, and profitable alternatives. These conditions can arise. But it can be assumed that, under normal conditions, bankers will seek a zero excess reserve position, i.e., the (E,E) position in the transition matrix will be zero, and that excess reserve policies will not appreciably affect the linkage between the reserve base and monetary aggregates.

3) *Leakages in the expansion process.* Any leakage of reserves during the expansion process reduces the expansion potential. The withdrawal of currency by the public has been the standard example of this type of leakage. Since currency is accepted as part of the reserve base, any loss of currency reduces the expansion that can be achieved from any initial input

of new reserves. Some of the textbook examples of bank expansion assume that some fraction of the potential expansion is automatically lost to the public's need for currency. This type of leakage can be introduced into the transition matrix used to describe bank expansion in Figure 14-6 by the addition of another row and column to provide for the absorbtion of funds from reserves into currency withdrawals. The Federal Reserve can prevent these leakages from affecting the reserve base by replacing the funds by open market operations. Special care has to be used in the analysis of currency withdrawals at member banks to avoid duplication of treatment, since currency changes are also introduced as a factor affecting the reserve base. We will assume in the following discussions that the Federal Reserve does not let currency leakages affect their policy objectives. The assumption is the same as assuming that there are no currency leakages at member banks, i.e., that the reserve base is effectively controlled and that currency leakages are offset.

4) *Shifts of funds among accounts with different reserve requirements.* The current structure of reserve requirements in the United States provides for a variety of reserve requirements on different types of accounts. Shifts of funds among these accounts can release excess reserves or absorb excess reserves depending on the direction of the movement. Since these changes can occur without any changes in the reserve base, they also affect the relationship between the reserve base and any deposit variable that the authorities may be attempting to control. Shifts of this type are the principal source of instability in the linkage between the reserve base and monetary aggregates under the present structure of controls in the United States. Since these movements lead to very difficult and complex control problems, they will be discussed separately in the following section.

Differential reserve requirements
and the control of monetary aggregates

Although reserve requirements are most familiar as a device for controlling the money supply, they can also be used to reward or penalize various types of fund-raising activities or institutional arrangements. These selective results are achieved by differentials in the requirements. County banks traditionally have had lower reserve requirements than those imposed on large city banks, and savings accounts have been given preferential treatment over demand accounts. Currently, many of the differentials are determined by size of the bank. Even when these differentials can be justified in terms of selective control objectives, they introduce serious problems for the use of the reserve base for controlling monetary aggregates.

The nature of the problem depends on the nature of the control objective. If the only objective of the monetary authorities is to control the total deposits (of all types subject to reserve requirements), the effects of shifts in funds among accounts with different reserve requirements can be offset by changing the reserve base the right amount to compensate for the shift. For example, movements of funds between large banks in the money market centers and banks in outlying areas tend to ease or tighten the market merely because of the differentials in the reserve requirements. The movement of a billion dollars from large banks with reserve requirements of 16.5 percent to banks in the lowest reserve requirement category of 7.5 percent provides the system, as a whole, with excess reserves of 9 percent of a billion dollars, or 90 million dollars. The reversal of this movement contracts the system by the same amount. Some movements of this type are a regular and recurring feature of the payments system. Many of the so-called seasonal problems of the monetary authorities can be traced to movements of this type. These developments as they affect the total deposits of member banks can be offset by appropriate adjustments in the reserve base if they can be anticipated or if they can be detected quickly enough.

If the objective of the monetary authorities is to control the demand deposit (M_1) component of member bank deposits, the simple offset approach may not work. If they want to offset a shift that produces a drop in demand deposits, they can supply new reserves, but they cannot control the growth in deposits that will accompany the new reserves. The problem can be illustrated by considering an example of bank expansion for a system that has only two types of accounts: demand deposits (D) and savings deposits (S). The transition matrix (see Figure 14-7) for such a system would be similar to that in Figure 14-6 except that a new row and new column would have to be added to provide for savings accounts (S). Funds moving into savings deposits (row S) would be distributed between required and excess reserves according to the reserve requirement (t). The total expansion of the system on the basis of a given amount of reserves then depends on the values of the reserve requirements and on the distribution of the deposit growth as indicated by the values in the loan (L) vector. This vector might be called the *reentry vector* because it describes the assumptions made about the return of loan funds to the system covered by the matrix.

The possibilities for the growth of a controlled system with two types of deposit accounts are illustrated in Figure 14-7B. At one extreme, when the proportion of the deposit growth in savings accounts (p) is zero, the expansion process will be the same as that already described for a demand deposit system. One dollar of excess reserves will produce an expansion of $10 in demand deposits (and total deposits) with a 10 percent reserve requirement. At the other extreme, when the proportion of deposit growth in savings is 100 percent, the expansion of total deposits and savings

FIGURE 14-7
DIFFERENTIAL RESERVE REQUIREMENTS AND DEPOSIT EXPANSION

A. Transition Matrix

	R	E	D	S	L
R	1.0	0	0	0	0
E	0	0	0	0	1.0
D	0.1	0.9	0	0	0
S	0.05	0.95	0	0	0
L	0	0	$(1-p)$	p	0

Where: R = required reserves

E = excess reserves

D = demand accounts

S = savings accounts

L = loans

B. Deposit Expansion (per dollar of excess reserves)

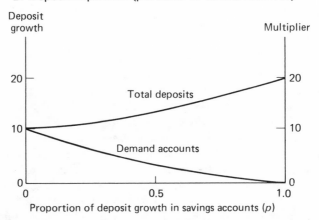

Proportion of deposit growth in savings accounts (p)

deposits will be 20 times the amount of excess reserves when the reserve requirement on savings accounts is 5 percent. The total deposit multiplier in this case can range between 10 and 20 and the demand deposit multiplier can range between zero and 10. The monetary authorities can be sure of some expansion in total member bank deposits when they provide new reserves, but they cannot be sure of the form or the amount. The values of the reentry vector (L) are determined by credit market conditions and by the objectives of the banks.

An important example of this type of control problem has arisen from the development of liability management techniques by commercial banks. During periods of tight money, banks respond to the demand for loans by selling certificates of deposit or by raising rates on their savings accounts. Their success in raising funds is accompanied by a hidden substitution effect that arises from the nature of the reserve requirements. The successful bank acquires reserves, but, in the absence of any net additions to the reserve base, some other bank or banks within the system must lose reserves and must contract accordingly.

The aggregate amount of funds that can be raised by the banking system as a whole is considerably less than the initial amount raised by the individual banks. The funds raised by sales of CDs are offset by the reductions in some other type of account—most likely demand accounts. These offsets are examples of the *intra-bank substitution effect*. If there are no excess reserves in the system, the addition of new deposits will lead to a reserve deficiency somewhere within the system. An aggregate expansion can take place only if the reserve requirement (d) on the accounts being replaced is larger than that on CDs (t). The reserves required for the new CDs ($t\Delta CD$) must be equal to the reserves made available from the reduction in other deposits ($d\Delta D$):

$$t\Delta CD = d\Delta D \qquad (5)$$

The net expansion in the total deposit of member banks (ΔT) will be equal to the amount obtained from the sale of CDs (ΔCD) minus the contraction forced by the intra-bank substitution effect, or

$$\Delta T = \Delta CD - \Delta D \qquad (6)$$

According to equation (5),

$$\Delta D = \frac{\Delta CDt}{d} \qquad (7)$$

or

$$\Delta T = \Delta CD \left(1 - \frac{t}{d}\right) \qquad (8)$$

Member banks can expand without any change in the reserve base by shifting deposits to lower reserve requirement categories. However, the amount of the expansion is considerably less than it appears to the individual banks involved, and the expansion in the total is accompanied by a contraction in demand accounts (M_1). If the reserve requirement on demand accounts is twice that on CDs ($d = 2t$), the expansion in total deposits will be equal to one-half the amount of CDs sold. The expansion in CDs will be offset by a contraction of the M_1 money supply equal to one-half of the amount of the sale.

Since attempts of member banks to sell CDs are made during periods when loan demand is strong, the movement into and out of CDs produces a cyclical pattern in changes in the M_1 money stock that is inversely related to interest rates and independent of the amount of the reserve base. The supply of M_1 will be contracted during periods of tight money and expanded during periods of easy money. Figure 14-8 illustrates the

FIGURE 14-8
SALES OF CDS AND AGGREGATE CHANGES IN MEMBER BANK DEPOSITS

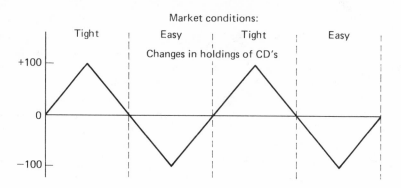

Market conditions:

Tight | Easy | Tight | Easy

Changes in holdings of CD's

+100

0

−100

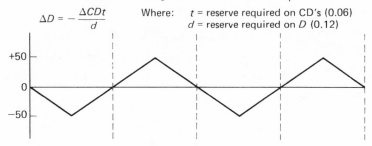

Resultant changes in demand accounts (M_1)

$$\Delta D = -\frac{\Delta CDt}{d}$$

Where: t = reserve required on CD's (0.06)
d = reserve required on D (0.12)

+50

0

−50

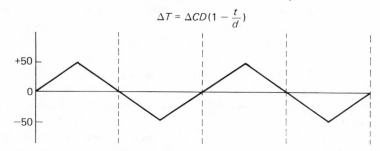

Resultant changes in total deposits (M_4)

$$\Delta T = \Delta CD(1 - \frac{t}{d})$$

+50

0

−50

Note: Assumes no excess reserves and no changes in total reserves.

230

hypothetical variations in total member bank deposits (M_4 concept) and changes in demand deposits (M_1 concept) that would accompany a cycle of sales and run-offs of 100 million of CDs in response to tight and easy money conditions when it is assumed that the reserve base is held constant. This cyclical pattern cannot simply be offset by changes in the reserve base. An attempt to prevent the decline in demand accounts by making more reserves available may not work. The banks are likely to use the new reserves as a base for more CDs as long as the demand for loans persists. As a result of these shifts in deposits, the Federal Reserve System's attempts to maintain stability in the growth of the M_1 money stock have resulted in exaggerated swings in the growth of total member bank deposits and in a failure to achieve the desired rate of growth in demand accounts. These shifts of funds have been, at least in part, responsible for charges by critics of the Federal Reserve System that it has overreacted to changing credit conditions.

The practical problem of controlling the member bank demand deposit component of the money supply is more difficult than this example illustrates. Shifts of funds among other reserve classifications can introduce variations into the multipliers as well as shifts between demand and savings accounts. At the time this was written, there were ten different reserve ratios applied to different types of accounts and different classes of banks. Any shifts among these accounts introduce variability in the control multipliers. A study of the 10-year period from 1962 to 1972 indicates that the actual monthly changes in demand deposits varied from the changes projected by a stable multiplier by 100 percent or more a third of the time. Seventeen percent of the time the changes were in the opposite direction from the apparent intent of the monetary authorities. In only 10 percent of the cases were the changes within plus or minus 10 percent of the target as indicated by the changes in the reserve base.[7]

If the only objective of monetary controls were to control the total member bank deposits, the effects of shifts of funds among different deposit classifications could theoretically be offset by appropriate changes in the reserve base, although practical problems of anticipating or detecting the changes probably would still lead to sizable variations from target objectives. If, however, the objectives are focused on some component of the total, changes in the reserve base will not assure the adjustments required to reach the control targets.

Under the present organization and structure of the Federal Reserve System, the monetary authorities have the tools and the authority to control the reserves available to member banks. They cannot control the

---

[7]Unpublished tabulations prepared in the research for a paper by Paul F. Smith, "Bank Liability Management and the Efficiency of Financial Intermediation," Working Paper No. 15-75, Rodney L. White Center for Financial Research, 1975.

deposits of member banks with the same degree of precision, however, because of the variability in the linkages between the reserve base and various deposit aggregates.

The most important source of variability can be traced to shifts of funds between demand and time accounts. These problems could be largely eliminated by improvements in the structure of reserve requirements. A system designed to control either the demand accounts of member banks or the total deposits of member banks with considerable precision could be developed, but the same reserve base cannot be used for both objectives.

Controlled and Uncontrolled Parts of the Financial System

Only banks that are members of the Federal Reserve System are subject to the direct impact of the attempts to control various monetary aggregates. In early 1976, member banks held about 70 percent of demand deposits, and about 40 percent of the time and savings accounts covered by the broader monetary aggregates. This leaves a substantial share of the monetary aggregates beyond the control of the monetary authorities.

The growth of banks and other financial institutions that are not members of the Federal Reserve System is not restricted by ties to a controlled reserve base. These institutions are subject to reserve requirements and other forms of regulation but their growth is limited only by their ability to attract and hold the funds needed to meet their reserve requirements. There are no quantitative limits to the reserve base.

The reserve requirements at nonmember banks and savings institutions can normally be satisfied by currency or by deposits with other banks or financial institutions. The expansion process can therefore be started for these institutions by any new additions to their currency or demand deposit holdings. Because the leakage problems are slightly different for banks and savings institutions, the two groups will be discussed separately. The complete monetary sector will be treated as three separate but interacting systems for purposes of this discussion: (1) banks that are members of the Federal Reserve System, (2) nonmember banks, and (3) savings institutions.

Deposit expansion at nonmember banks

Deposit expansion at nonmember banks can start with any increment of new reserves for the system as a whole, in the form of currency or of any deposit that can be used to meet the reserve requirements. A transition matrix similar to that used for member banks in Figure 14-6 can be used to specify the parameters of the expansion except that an additional row and column have to be added to provide for the possibilities of leakages from the system as the process proceeds. This vector will be designated as K and will represent an absorbing state for this system. The separate vector for savings accounts has been omitted to simplify the discussion. The implications of a savings alternative for the expansion process will be similar to those already described for member banks. The transition matrix for the nonmember bank system would then appear as follows:

	K	R	E	D	L
K	1.0	0	0	0	0
R	0	1.0	0	0	0
E	0	0	0	0	1.0
D	0	d	$(1-d)$	0	0
L	k	0	0	$(1-k)$	0

where: d = reserve required on demand accounts

k = proportion of loan funds lost to system.

The expansion potential of the nonmember banking system is determined by the values of the reserve requirements (d) and of the leakage ratio (k). If k is zero, the expansion process is identical to that described for member banks, and the amount of the expansion would be a multiple of the increment of new reserves where the multiplier is the reciprocal of the reserve ratio $(m = 1/d)$. If k is equal to 1, the expansion process is halted at the first stage, and the full expansion is equal to the amount of new funds received at the initial stage of the process. The important questions obviously center around the actual value of k and the forces that determine its value.

The value of k for the nonmember banking system as a whole will be one unless the proceeds from its loans and investment outlays are redeposited with the same bank or another nonmember bank. If the borrower wants his funds in currency, or if the check he draws for the proceeds of the loan is deposited in a member bank, the value of k for the system will be one. The incidence of currency withdrawals would probably be much the same for nonmember banks as for member banks, except that the nonmember banks cannot expect the Federal Reserve System to replace their currency losses. In the nonmember banking system, currency losses have to be regarded as a possible leakage that will add to the positive value of k (as well as to the variability of its reserve base).

The most important potential source of leakages, however, arises from losses of deposits to member banks. This contribution to the value of k depends on the competitive position of nonmember banks in the payments process. The almost perfect negative covariance associated with the checking account process assures the return of loan proceeds to some bank. The question for the potential expansion of the nonmember system is whether or not it will be in a nonmember bank. The likelihood that the expansion process can proceed with a relatively small leakage value (k) will increase with the size and availability of nonmember banks and their ability to compete for deposits. The value of k is likely to be smaller when nonmember banks hold 30 percent of the demand deposits than when they hold 5 percent. Thus the expansion multiplier as well as the size of their reserve base depends on their ability to attract funds from member banks.

The ability of the nonmember banks to expand their loans and deposits depends on the reserves available to meet their requirements and on the parameters of the expansion process that they can achieve on the basis of those reserves. Their expansion capacity differs from that of member banks in two fundamental ways: (1) there is no limit to the size of the reserve base that can be used as a base for expansion, other than their ability to attract deposits from member banks or currency from the public, (2) the potential leakage of reserves (k) in the expansion process is large, while the leakage of reserves at member banks is zero.[8]

Member banks are limited in their expansion by a controlled reserve base, but since they have the exclusive use of the reserve base, the system as a whole can expand to the full multiple as determined by the reserve requirements and the deposit mix without any concern about leakages during the expansion process. Since nonmember banks and other financial institutions cannot hold deposits in Federal Reserve Banks, claims on those funds must be deposited with member banks. The system developed for the control of member banks also gives the system as a whole independence from the competitive inroads of the nonmember banks and of other types of institutions. The expansion of the nonmember banking system is based on its ability to attract deposits in competition with member banks. But its success in attracting deposits does not force a contraction on the member banking system. The competitive success of nonmember banks cannot alter the member bank reserve base.

Direct control over the monetary aggregates at nonmember banks and other financial institutions could be achieved by some arrangement that would provide for a reserve base in some form that could be controlled as a supplement to the reserve requirements. In practice, the unlimited theoretical capacity for expansion of the nonmember banks is restrained by their ability to compete as individual institutions with member banks. Supervisory or regulatory changes that give nonmember banks any comparative advantages in attracting and holding deposits will act to weaken the effectiveness of controls over monetary aggregates. Lower

---

[8]This assumes that the Federal Reserve System tries to achieve some reserve position and offsets any currency withdrawals with new reserves.

reserve requirements, the authority to pay interest on deposits, or any other competitive advantages compared to the member banking system will weaken effective monetary controls. Complete parity between the two systems may work to the disadvantage of the nonmember banking system because of the advantages of size and prestige held by member banks. In the absence of formal controls over this segment of the monetary aggregates, the battle for control has to be fought at the supervisory and legislative levels. The member banks tend to aid in this process by pursuing a self-interest position.

Deposit expansion at savings institutions

The growth of thrift and savings institutions depends on their ability to attract and hold funds in the savings and money markets. The ability of these institutions as a system to expand on the basis of an increment of new reserve funds can be analyzed by the same techniques used to trace the expansion at member and nonmember banks. The same type of transition matrix can be used by substituting a savings account vector for the demand deposit vector used for banks. The transition matrix for savings institutions would appear as follows:

	K	R	E	S	L
K	1.0	0	0	0	0
R	0	1.0	0	0	0
E	0	0	0	0	1.0
S	0	s	$(1-s)$	0	0
L	k	0	0	$(1-k)$	0

where: s = reserve requirement

k = proportion of loan funds lost to the system

The expansion potential of the system on the basis of some increment of new funds depends on the reserve requirements (s) and the leakages from the system (k). If k is zero, the expansion process is similar to that of the member banking system, and the limit to the expansion would be a multiple of the increment of reserves where the multiple is the reciprocal of the reserve requirement ($m = 1/s$). If k is equal to 1, the expansion process is halted at the first stage, and the fully expanded position is equal to the increment of funds received at the initial stage of the process.

The central question about the multiple expansion potential of the savings system lies in the value of k. Since savings institutions are assumed not to have checking accounts, none of the loan proceeds will return automatically to the system as part of the check clearing process, as in the case of commercial banks. If an atomic tracer could be placed on the proceeds of the loans of these institutions, some fraction might be returned more or less directly to some savings institution. But such an event would be part of the regular spending–savings decisions of the people involved. It would not be a purely mechanical step in the clearing process. It can be argued that some fraction of the loan proceeds is returned ($k \neq 1.0$) and that the savings system is capable of some multiple expansion in much the same way as the banking system. The extension of the theory of multiple deposit expansion to the thrift system is something of an academic exercise, however, because the system must succeed in the market competition for funds at every stage of the process. The series of events that can be described as multiple expansion can also be described as a series of direct financing successes. It is likely that the leakage in any multiple expansion (k) will be large (close to 1) and the description as a process of multiple expansion adds very little insight into the actual events. In fact, it suggests an automatic result that may be misleading.

The ability of the thrift system to expand its loans and deposits depends on its ability to attract funds in the marketplace. If this process is treated as a multiple expansion process, it is similar to that of the nonmember banking system in that (1) there is no limit to the size of the reserve base for the expansion, other than its ability to attract funds, and (2) the potential leakage of reserves in the expansion process is likely to be large, and this value depends on its ability to continue to attract funds from the marketplace.

There are no direct controls over the growth of the deposits of thrift institutions in the United States at the present time. The reserve requirements that have been imposed make attempts to raise funds more expensive, but as long as market conditions permit thrift institutions to expand there are no absolute limits on their ability to do so. Direct controls over the amount of their deposits would have to include arrangements for a reserve base that could be controlled. However, their growth can be indirectly controlled by supervisory or legislative changes that affect their ability to compete for funds. During periods of tight money it may be difficult for thrift institutions to compete with banks and direct borrowers for savings because of the long-term contractual nature of their income receipts. The expansion of savings institutions can be limited by regulatory changes that permit or encourage member banks to compete for funds with the savings institutions. By this indirect technique, the member banks, whose expansion can be limited by the reserve base, can be used as an indirect tool for controlling the expansion of savings institutions. The potential for the control of the entire system of monetary aggregates, with only direct controls over member banks, is better than it would seem from direct examination of control functions. Changes in selective controls that affect the ability of the controlled segment (member banks) to compete can turn on or off the expansion in the uncontrolled segments. Unfortunately, the selective control process is dominated by considerations other than those of monetary control.

Summary

The effectiveness of reserve requirement as a technique for controlling monetary aggregate requires the ability to control the reserve base and the ability to control the linkage between the reserve base and the appropriate monetary aggregate (or the multiplier). Of the three basic classes of banking and savings institutions, only the banks that are members of the Federal System are subject to direct controls. The reserves available to member banks can be controlled with precision, but the linkages between the reserve base and the monetary aggregate, M_1, M_2, or M_4 components, are quite unstable. This instability can be traced largely to the use of the reserve base for multipurpose objectives so that shifts of funds from one class of deposit to another may either frustrate or reinforce control objectives. The current structure of controls does not provide for very accurate control over any of the components of monetary aggregates held by the controlled segment of the financial system.

There are no direct controls over the components of the monetary aggregates held by nonmember banks and by thrift institutions. Their ability to expand depends solely on their ability to attract and hold funds in competition with the controlled segment, the member banks. This process can be controlled indirectly by supervisory or legislative acts that affect the ability of these institutions to compete with member banks. Changes that reduce their ability to compete strengthen the control system. Changes that improve their competitive positions reduce the effectiveness of controls.

Actual problems of monetary control by indirect techniques become entangled with controversial questions of the self-interest of various pressure groups and with issues that confuse the discussion of monetary policy. In general, the political strength of the large banks that are members of the Federal Reserve System is allied with an attempt to reduce the competitive capabilities of the nonmember banks and thrift institutions. But there is no reason to think that decisions based on the resolution of competitive disputes will also produce the best results for monetary policy.

The monetary authorities have the authority to release or withdraw member bank reserves and, in this way, to introduce massive stimuli or constraints into the financial system. But with the present control structure this should not be conceived as a precise system of control over either the money supply (M_1) or any broader monetary aggregate. It is merely a source of funds to the member banks that may or may not be used to build the M_1 money supply. The money markets are affected by these actions, but the nature of the effects will depend on the strength of loan demand and other market conditions. These results have to be examined in the context of the market pressures. This problem will be discussed in later chapters.

QUESTIONS FOR DISCUSSION

1. Since any level of expenditures can be expressed as the product of the money stock M_x times the velocity with which that stock is used, what difference does it make how the money stock is defined?

2. Proposals have been made from time to time that U.S. Treasury bills be accepted as satisfying the reserve requirements for banks. Compare the effectiveness of these securities with the current reserve base as a technique for controlling the deposits of commercial banks.

3. Describe the procedure by which the public can increase its stock of currency. How do these actions affect the deposits of the banking system? In view of your answer, how can it be argued that the public's demand for currency is not an important problem for the monetary authorities in their efforts to control the money supply?

4. If the bank expansion process always proceeds to its ultimate limits, how can the speed of the process be a matter of concern for the monetary authorities? What direct evidence can be introduced that gives an indication of the speed of the expansion process?

5. Construct a transition matrix that will produce a total deposit multiplier of 25. Modify the matrix so that the multiplier might vary between 12.5 and 25, and describe the forces that would determine the actual expansion when the options you have built into the system exist.

6. Design a transition matrix that provides for two types of deposit accounts that will always yield the same total deposit multiplier.

7. Comment on the statement: "The expansion of nonmember banks depends on their ability to attract deposits in competition with member banks. But their success does not force a contraction in the member banking system." Can the role of member and nonmember banks be reversed in that statement?

8. Comment on the statement: "The differences that exist between commercial banks and savings institutions have little intrinsically to do with the monetary nature of bank liabilities."

9. Suggest selective controls that might be applied to member banks that would encourage the growth of nonmember banks. How would this competitive growth of nonmember banks affect the potential growth of member banks considered as an aggregate?

10. What changes in the structure of reserve requirements can you suggest that would eliminate some of the instability in the M_1 money multiplier? What related problem would your suggestion entail?

SELECTED REFERENCES

ANDERSEN, LEONALL C., "Selection of a Monetary Aggregate for Economic Stabilization," *Review: Federal Reserve Bank of St. Louis*, 57 (October 1975), 9–15.

AXILROD, STEPHEN H., and DARWIN L. BECK, "Role of Projections and Data Evaluation and Monetary Aggregate as Policy Targets," *Controlling Monetary Aggregates II: The Implementation*. Boston: Federal Reserve Bank of Boston, 1972, pp. 9–26.

BOARD OF GOVERNORS OF THE FEDERAL RESERVE SYSTEM, "Monetary Aggregate and Money Market Conditions in Open Market Policy," *Federal Reserve Bulletin*, 57 (February 1971), 79–104.

BRITO, D. L., and DONALD D. HESTER, "Stability and Control of the Money Supply," *Quarterly Journal of Economics*, 88 (May 1974), 278–303.

FORTUNE, PETER, "The Effectiveness of Recent Policies to Maintain Thrift-Deposit Flows," *Journal of Money, Credit and Banking*, 8 (August 1975), 297–316.

FROST, PETER A., "Short-Run Fluctuations in the Money Multiplier and Monetary Control," *Journal of Money, Credit and Banking* (February 1977), 165–181.

PIERCE, JAMES L., and THOMAS D. THOMPSON, "Some Issues in Controlling the Stock of Money," *Controlling Monetary Aggregates II: The Implementation*. Boston: Federal Reserve Bank of Boston, 1972.

RASCHE, ROBERT H., "A Review of Empirical Studies of the Money Supply Mechanism," *Review: Federal Reserve Bank of St. Louis*, 54 (July 1972), 11–19.

SMITH, WARREN L., "Time Deposits, Free Reserves, and Monetary Policy," *Issues in Banking and Monetary Analysis*, eds., Pontecorvo, Shay and Hart. New York: Holt, Rinehart and Winston, Inc., 1967.

Secondary Markets

15

The most active and best-known secondary markets are those used for buying and selling common stocks. The New York Stock Exchange and the American Stock Exchange, both located in New York City, are the largest trading centers. These exchanges, together with 8 regional exchanges, handled an average of 500 million shares a month in 1975 with an average total value of 13 billion dollars. In addition to these centralized exchanges, a large share of common stock transactions, perhaps as much as a third, are handled in over-the-counter markets by brokers and dealers. Large over-the-counter markets are also available for trading in U.S. government securities, obligations of state and local governments, and various types of money market instruments. The transactions of dealers in U.S. government securities alone averaged over 6 billion dollars a day in 1975.

These markets play an important and complex role in the financing process. They facilitate the flow of funds from savings into investments without being a direct part of that process. They provide liquidity and reduce borrowing costs. They also serve as sensitive indicators of the demand and supply pressures in primary markets. The first section of this chapter deals with the role of secondary markets in providing liquidity, the second looks at the special features of pricing in secondary markets, and the last section discusses the role of these markets in shaping economic events.

Marketability as a Source of Liquidity

The ability of secondary markets to provide liquidity can be measured by their ability to reduce the selling costs that serve as a barrier to the liquidation of financial contracts. In perfect markets, the only barrier to liquidity would be the cost of the transfer or the transactions costs. In practice, the costs of liquidation, as measured by the spread between the equilibrium price and the price received by the seller, include (1) the costs of transferring the securities, (2) costs arising from the imperfections in the secondary markets, and (3) costs that represent the duplication of investigation or processing costs on the initial loan.

Secondary markets do not offer much help with costs of the third type. Contracts that must be investigated are virtually excluded from the secondary marketing process. This includes nearly all of the direct loans made by banks and other financial institutions. These contracts can be sold only if some device is used to relieve the buyer of the necessity of repeating the costly initial processing steps. Some consumer and commercial loan contracts are sold, but these sales are usually accompanied by agreements that assign some, or all, of the risk to the seller and that often provide for the servicing of the loans by the seller. For example, Sears, Roebuck and Company sells large blocks of its installment loans to banks, but continues to service and collect the loans; and it replaces any bad contracts, which it may have sold, with good ones.

The secondary marketing process in the pure form, which does not leave the seller with any residual obligations, starts with securities that have known risk features and that do not require any costly handling or processing. Only the securities of large and well-known corporations and governmental units qualify for secondary market transactions.

The potential selling costs on these securities center around the problem of the "double-coincidence of wants" or the problem of matching buyers and sellers. Each sale requires a buyer who is looking for a security exactly like the one being offered for sale. If a buyer is not immediately available, the seller faces a choice of not selling or of incurring the costs of market imperfections. These costs depend on the technique used to find a buyer. The seller can (1) reduce the price, (2) search for a buyer, or (3) wait for a buyer to show up. Matching costs can seldom be measured directly. They appear in exchange markets as deviations from the equilibrium price. They appear in the over-the-counter (OTC) markets as some combination of search or waiting costs or as deviations from the equilibrium price. The success of a secondary market in reducing or eliminating these costs is a measure of its ability to provide liquidity.

The ability of a secondary market to reduce matching costs depends in part on the features of the securities being traded and in part on the structure and organization of the market. A successful market requires the participation of large numbers of buyers and sellers. The potential number of sellers is directly related to the outstanding number of shares, to the number of shareholders and to their willingness or interest in trading. The actual number involved in trading in any particular market will also depend on the degree of centralization of the trading. The major security exchanges and the arbitrage among exchanges provide the centralization for listed securities in the U.S. markets.

A security that is listed on the major exchanges has access to the efficiency offered by centralized trading, but it is not guaranteed the elimination of all of the costs of market imperfections. Substantial differences can be observed in the performance of listed securities. Measuring the costs of market imperfections in exchange markets is complicated by the problem of identifying the equilibrium price. The concept of *continuity* has been used as a rule-of-thumb approach to the problem. A *continuous market* is one that can be depended upon to offer the seller (and buyer) a price close to the prices on other recent transactions (a proxy for the equilibrium price). The concept is used in much the same way as the concept of a continuous variable in mathematics. A market is continuous when the prices in the market move in the minimum interval as they increase (or decrease) from one level to another. When securities are quoted in eighths, successive price changes are never more than an eighth in a perfectly continuous market.

Listing does not guarantee the continuity of the market for securities. Large purchases or sales can disrupt even the best markets. To avoid some of these problems, the exchanges provide specialists who are assigned the task of reducing the short-run variations in prices by buying (or selling) for their own portfolio. The specialist reduces the trading costs that arise from extreme price variations, but incurs the cost of maintaining an inventory of the securities. He solves the problem of short-run imperfections in the market by extending the time period in which the market can be cleared, and incurs the cost of waiting for it to happen.

The exchange markets, even with the assistance of specialists, cannot always maintain satisfactory markets. In these cases, the OTC (over-the-counter) markets offer a number of alternatives. They provide for sales on a commission basis where the broker looks for a buyer (or seller) and charges his customer for the search costs. They also provide for direct purchases of securities by dealers who hold them in inventory until a buyer is found. The search and waiting costs are assumed by the dealer and passed on to his customers. The OTC markets handle securities not listed on the exchanges, and large block transactions in listed securities that might create disruptive price movements in the exchange markets. Most of the transactions of the large mutual funds are handled by the OTC markets.

Modern developments in electronic computing and communications equipment have important implications for the future efficiency and structure of secondary markets. They promise major improvements in the centralization of trading and in access to markets and to market information. It is easy to imagine a centralized market that provides easy access to the demand and supply information for all potential buyers and sellers of a broad range of securities. The technical problems for the development of such a market can be solved. The difficulties center around the potential disruptive implications of such a market for the current market structure and around the rights to the access and control of such a system.

Pricing in Secondary Markets

Newly issued securities and the seasoned securities that are bought and sold in secondary markets are competitive alternatives for the investor. If the capital markets were perfectly competitive, the prices and yields on new and seasoned issues with identical characteristics should be identical. Empirical studies of corporate bonds show that the yields on newly issued bonds are slightly higher than those on similar seasoned issues.[1] Studies of common stocks, however, show that the yields on newly issued stocks are below those on seasoned stocks.[2] The question of the efficiency of competition in capital markets cannot be answered completely by these statistical tests, however, because of the problems of matching securities. Newly issued securities are unique because they are in large blocks that carry features and coupon rates necessary to sell the securities in the immediate market.

The spread between yields on newly issued and seasoned bonds is usually attributed in part to the desirability of "sweetening" the new issues to ease their introduction into the market. Part of the spread can also be traced to differences in coupon rates. After an extended period of rising interest rates, the yields on seasoned issues will be substantially above their coupon rates, and their prices will be below the face value of the bonds.

[1]Joseph W. Conard and Mark W. Frankena, "The Yield Spread Between New and Seasoned Corporate Bonds, 1952-63," *Essay on Interest Rates,* Jack M. Guttentag and Philip Cagen, eds. (New York: National Bureau of Economic Research, 1969), pp. 143–222.

[2]Irwin Friend and J. R. Longstreet, "Price Experience and Return on New Stock Issues," *Investment Banking and the New Issues Market* (New York: World Publishing Co., 1967).

Newly issued bonds will have to carry higher coupon rates to match the yields on similar seasoned securities, but the tax treatment of the income from new and seasoned securities purchased at the same price may be different. Part of the income from the seasoned securities can be treated as capital gains, but all of the income on the new securities will be taxed at the normal income-tax rates. Other differences can frequently be found that account for some, but not all, of the observed spread between the yields on new and seasoned securities. However, the evidence suggests that the markets are more nearly competitive than the observed spreads appear to indicate. Capital market theory does not distinguish between primary and secondary markets but assumes that they are perfect markets for purposes of determining overall prices and yields.

Modern capital market theory has been shaped by two developments that have added new insights into both the pricing of individual securities and the nature of market averages. The development of evidence of the random behavior of security prices stimulated work on the role of information in the pricing of securities. The development of portfolio theory paved the way for the inclusion of risk in theoretical models of the capital markets.

Random behavior in security prices

The possibility of random behavior in stock prices has unfortunate implications for many stock market practitioners because it casts doubt on the usefulness of *technical analysis*—a widely practiced art devoted to forecasting prospective trends in stock prices from patterns or configurations of past prices. If successive changes in stock prices are independent, the history of prices cannot be used to forecast future prices. Early studies of the randomness of stock prices were largely neglected until it became clear that the evidence was too strong to be ignored.[3] The demonstration by Samuelson that random price behavior was not only consistent with efficient markets but that it could be expected in such markets led to the development of the *efficient market hypothesis* and to a great deal of empirical work in testing that hypothesis.[4] The efficient market hypothesis transforms the Samuelson argument into an assumption that random price behavior can be used to identify an efficient market.[5] The presence of nonrandom movements in stock prices is used as evidence of market

---

[3]The initial evidence appeared in a paper by Louis Bachelier in 1905; it has been reproduced, along with a number of the other early papers on the subject, in *The Random Character of Stock Market Prices,* ed. by Paul H. Cootner (Cambridge, Mass.: The MIT Press, 1964).

[4]Paul A. Samuelson, "Proof That Properly Anticipated Prices Fluctuate Randomly," *Industrial Management Review,* vol. 6 (Spring 1965), pp. 41–49.

[5]To students of classical logic this may suggest the affirmation of the consequent.

inefficiencies. Under the efficient market hypothesis, an efficient market is defined as

> ...one in which a large number of buyers and sellers react through a sensitive and efficient mechanism to cause market prices to reflect fully and virtually instantaneously what is knowable about the prospects for companies whose securities are being traded.[6]

A number of empirical studies have tested the market reaction to specific types of information, such as changes in dividends and earnings. These studies, which are sometimes referred to as tests of the semistrong version of the efficient market hypothesis, have generally been interpreted as indicating that the stock market is relatively efficient in reacting to items of information, i.e., the information is quickly reflected in stock prices. Other studies have been designed to test the efficiency of the market in adjusting to information not generally available to the public (the strong version of the efficient market hypothesis). Some of these tests have involved comparing the performance of professionally managed portfolios with the performance of the market as a whole. The finding that the professionally managed funds have not performed significantly better has been interpreted as evidence of the efficiency of the stock market in reflecting all types of information.

The efficient market hypothesis is concerned primarily with the ability of the market to adjust to relevant information. It does not say anything about the accuracy of the information; and it does not deal directly with the questions of the efficiency of secondary markets in allocating funds among alternative uses, minimizing operational costs of trading, or in handling various types of imperfections that appear at the fringes of the major exchange markets.

Portfolio theory

Markowitz's pioneer work in portfolio theory led to the incorporation of risk into capital market models and to a new approach to the pricing of individual securities.[7] Since the contribution of a security to the riskiness of the portfolio depends in part on its relationship to other securities, the market price of the security should reflect its usefulness to portfolio builders as well as its intrinsic features. The average prices of all of the securities in the market should also reflect the individual prices of securities as they are combined into some most efficient portfolio. The average

---

[6]James H. Lorie and Mary T. Hamilton, *The Stock Market: Theories and Evidence* (Homewood, Ill.: Richard D. Irwin, Inc., 1973), p. 97.

[7]Harry M. Markowitz, *Portfolio Selection, Efficient Diversification of Investments,* Cowles Foundation, Monograph No. 16 (New York: John Wiley and Sons, 1959).

return on the portfolio of risky assets and the return on riskless assets determines the overall cost of funds in the risk-adjusted view of capital markets.

The concept of an efficient portfolio involves the hypothetical construction of portfolios of all of the possible combinations of securities. Since the prices of individual securities will be interrelated in a variety of ways, the portfolio risk on these combinations will vary widely (see the discussion of the role of market risk in portfolio risk in Chapter 9). The risk and return parameters of this large set of portfolios can be plotted as illustrated in Figure 15-1. The portfolios that appear on the upper boundary of the entire set (line *AB*) are the most efficient because they offer the maximum return for a given risk. This boundary is called the *efficient frontier*.

If it is assumed that there is also a riskless asset, the range of possible portfolios is extended to include all combinations of the riskless asset with efficient portfolios. A straight line drawn between the return on the riskless asset (*r*) and the point of tangency with the efficient frontier (*m*) will describe a set of the most efficient portfolios that can be constructed from the riskless asset and the risky portfolio assets at point *m*.

FIGURE 15-1
Security Portfolios and the Efficient Frontier

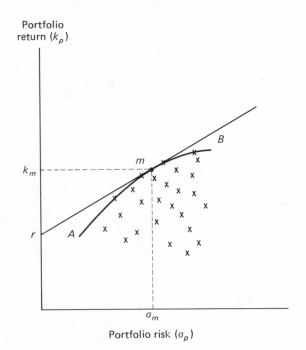

Portfolio return (k_p)

k_m

r

σ_m

Portfolio risk (σ_p)

It can be demonstrated that any combination of the riskless asset with any portfolio of risky assets will be linear with respect to portfolio risk (σ_p). The equation for the variance of a portfolio of two assets, given as equations (3) and (4) in Chapter 9, is

$$\sigma_p^2 = X_a^2\sigma_a^2 + X_b^2\sigma_b^2 + 2X_aX_b\rho\sigma_a\sigma_b \tag{1}$$

If the riskless asset is represented by a, and the portfolio of risky assets is represented as b, the values of the first and third terms become zero (the variance on the riskless asset is zero). The combined portfolio variance will be

$$\sigma_p^2 = X_b^2\sigma_b^2 \tag{2}$$

and the standard deviation will be

$$\sigma_p = X_b\sigma_b \tag{3}$$

Thus the portfolio risk of the mixed portfolio will be linearly related to the proportion invested in the risky portfolio (X_b).

For the market as a whole, it is assumed that the optimal portfolio of risky assets (m) is the portfolio that includes all assets in proportion to the market value. The line describing the expected return (k_p) on various combinations of the riskless asset with the optimal risky portfolio becomes the *capital market line*. It can be described in terms of the risk-free rate (r) and the portfolio risk (σ_p) as

$$k_p = r + \beta\sigma_p \tag{4}$$

where: $$\beta = (k_m - r)/\sigma_m$$

The capital market line can be theoretically extended beyond m for the individual investor by borrowing (at the riskless rate) and using the funds to purchase more of the risky asset portfolio.

Individual investors can select the combinations of risky and riskless assets that best meet their needs and their attitudes toward risk. Their optimal position will occur at the point of tangency between their risk-return indifference map and the capital market line (see Figure 15-2). The choice is similar to that described in the discussion of Tobin's liquidity preference model in Chapter 8. The return on the riskless asset (money) was assumed to be zero in the Tobin model.

The capital market model in this form provides a simplified picture of the role of risk in the pricing process. It describes a financial world with two critical average rates: (1) the riskless rate (r), which in practice will be an average of the rates on all riskless assets where any rate differentials can

FIGURE 15-2
ATTITUDE TOWARD RISK AND THE OPTIMAL PORTFOLIO

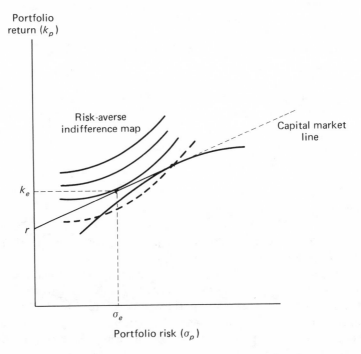

Portfolio risk (σ_p)

be explained by other contract features, and (2) the average return on the market portfolio of risky assets (k_m).

Economic Role of Secondary Markets

When the flow of funds from savings into investment is traced for the economy as a whole, secondary markets do not enter into the process at all. Yet the events in secondary markets can affect the flow of funds in primary markets in a variety of ways that can alter the overall level of economic activity and the performance of the economy. These effects are indirect and difficult to trace. They are even more difficult to measure and to evaluate, but they cannot be ignored.

Changes in the prices and yields in secondary markets stimulate two types of reactions that affect primary markets. First, they alter the relative attractiveness of various types of real and financial assets that assist with the allocation of real resources and that facilitate adjustments in primary markets to changing pressures of supply and demand. Second, they alter the value of the huge superstructure of financial wealth which, in turn, is likely to affect the spending plans of consumers and businesses.

Allocative effects

The liquidity that secondary markets give to the holders of marketable securities also adds an important element of flexibility to the economy as a whole. In aggregate, current income must provide the funds for current outlays. Sales of seasoned securities do not release any net funds for expenditures because the transactions absorb as much cash as they release. But they do shift the control of the cash from one investor to another. These shifts add to the ability of the market to accommodate new demand pressures and to the allocation of funds in response to these pressures.

If primary markets were perfectly competitive, and if there were no constraints on the free and quick movements of savings from one type of loan to another or from one geographic market to another, the appropriate responses to changing demand pressures could be achieved without help from the secondary markets. In practice, the flow of savings moves through paths that are not completely flexible. For example, it may be difficult to shift funds from commercial loans to home mortgages. When special demand pressures develop in any segment of the market, the primary markets can and do adjust to these pressures. Loan rates and terms respond to the pressures, and funds are shifted from other loan categories or from other localities to meet the new demands. But, in practice, a variety of selective regulations and internal policies limit the ability of financial institutions to respond to new demands, and the adjustment may be slow. The adjustment process is greatly facilitated if the lending institution has marketable securities that it can sell to raise the funds to meet the new loan demands.

Secondary markets provide this flexibility. The secondary market accepts the securities, which can be resold to someone with savings that would not be available for loans of the type required to meet the new demand pressures. In doing so, it channels the funds into the correct market by this two-stage process. An individual or a portfolio manager may be willing to buy government securities at the right price when he would not be willing to put money into the mortgage market in Arizona.

Secondary markets add to the ability of primary markets to adjust to new demand pressures by expanding the sources of funds that can be used in achieving the adjustment. In doing so, they assist with the economically important process of allocating real resources. The most obvious cases arise when financial institutions sell their secondary reserve assets to obtain funds to meet new loan demand. The buyers of the securities in the secondary markets would, in all likelihood, not be willing or able to make loans of the type required to meet demand pressures, but they are interested in some of the assets the financial institution can sell. The huge post-World-War II demand for business and consumer loans was met in part by the liquidation of the government securities that the banks had accumulated during the war. The same type of adjustment occurs daily on a smaller scale and in many different ways. The secondary markets make these adjustments possible.

Wealth effects

A ten-dollar increase in the price of a security adds a million dollars to the wealth of the individual or corporation that holds 100,000 shares of the security. Day-to-day changes in the market value of securities are real for the holders of those securities. They add to their net worth, and the amounts involved can be converted to other types of wealth or can be used for expenditures. The amount of the wealth effect is the product of the change in price and the number of outstanding shares. It is an interesting but not very useful exercise to calculate the wealth effects of daily changes in security prices. Many holders of securities may not be aware of the day-to-day changes, but prolonged periods of price appreciation or depreciation can lead to wealth effects that are potentially important for both business and consumption decisions.

For investors, the wealth effect can be translated into a change in the cost of capital, which, in turn, is used as a guide to investment decisions. High stock prices mean a reduction in the cost of capital and the encouragement of business outlays. Stock prices also affect the flexibility of business managers in a very practical way. Rising stock prices strengthen their position in dealing with their stockholders and other suppliers of funds. They will find it easier to press plans for expansion, to retain earnings, and to raise new funds by debt financing. Falling stock prices have the opposite effects, and even excellent investment plans may be difficult to justify when the company's stock prices are falling.

The potential impact of changes in wealth on consumption decisions are intuitively obvious, although the results of statistical tests designed to measure the effects have been mixed. The wealth effect represents one path by which the psychological implications of good and bad times can be transmitted into concrete expenditure decisions.

QUESTIONS FOR DISCUSSION

1. Find a copy of the requirements for listing a security on the New York Stock Exchange, and comment on the relationship of those requirements to efficiency (in terms of the ability of the market to minimize trading costs) of the secondary market for that security.

2. Compare the economic features of the market for the securities of a large well-known corporation with those of the market for some familiar consumer product such as a clock-radio.

3. Outline specific proposals for an "ideal" secondary market that will use modern electronic computing and communications equipment. The proposals should cover all the essential mechanics of trading and should provide rules for ownership, control, and access to the system. Discuss the implications of your proposals for the existing institutional arrangements.

4. What implications does portfolio theory have for the theoretical market price of a defensive security that frequently moves against the general index of stock prices?

5. Using the F–H model, illustrate the effects of an increase in stock prices on the level of investment.

6. Discuss the cyclical pattern of the wealth effect on consumption expenditures. What type of commodities are most likely to be affected by the wealth effect?

SELECTED REFERENCES

BAUMOL, W. J., *The Stock Market and Economic Efficiency.* New York: Fordham University Press, 1965.

BLUME, MARSHALL E., "Portfolio Theory: A Step Toward Its Practical Application," *Journal of Business*, 43 (April 1970), 152–73.

COOTNER, P. H., ed., *The Random Character of Stock Prices.* Cambridge, Mass.: M.I.T. Press, 1964.

FAMA, E. F., "The Behavior of Stock Market Prices," *Journal of Business*, 37 (January 1965), 34–105.

———, and Merton H. Miller, *The Theory of Finance.* New York: Holt, Rinehart and Winston, 1972.

LEFFLER, GEORGE L., and LORING C .FARWELL, *The Stock Market.* New York: The Ronald Press Company, 1963.

LORIE, JAMES H., and MARY T. HAMILTON, *The Stock Market: Theories and Evidence.* Homewood, Ill.: Richard D. Irwin, Inc., 1973.

SHARPE, WILLIAM F., *Portfolio Theory and Capital Markets.* New York: McGraw-Hill, 1970.

Structure of Interest Rates

16

Interest rates play a dominant role in the adjustment of individual markets to demand and supply pressures and in the allocation of the aggregate supply of funds among different markets. If financial contracts were identical, and if markets were perfect, the equilibrium would be represented by a single rate in all markets. In practice, interest rates differ widely. These differences testify to the complexity of the financial process and to the variety of contracts used. Differences in risk, liquidity, and contract terms contribute to the observed differences in rates. Market imperfections may also add to these differences. If r^* is used as a standardized measure of the level of rates, the rate on any individual contract (r_i) can be expressed as the sum of the standard rate, the premium or premiums for special nonpecuniary features (p), and the differences that reflect any imperfections in the trading markets or temporary disequilibrium conditions (d):

$$r_i = r^* + p + d \tag{1}$$

This chapter is concerned with the last two terms of equation (1), or the components that explain the structure of rates. The factors that determine the level of rates (r^*) are the subject matter of the theory of interest and are discussed in Chapter 19. Attempts to identify and measure the differentials in rates that can be attributed to risk or other contract features (those included in p of equation (1)) will be discussed in the first section of this chapter. The special role of market segmentation or other barriers to rate adjustments (those included in d of equation (1) will be considered in the second section. The last section will deal with the complex mixture of forces involved in shaping the term structure of rates.

Premiums for Special Contract Features (p)

The mathematical and subjective considerations associated with risk premiums of various types were discussed in Chapter 7. Special liquidity considerations were discussed in Chapter 8 and other specialized contract features were covered in Chapter 6. All these features can give rise to differentials in rates. The measurement of these premiums in practice involves the complex statistical problem of trying to isolate the effects of a single contract feature among the mix of factors that can contribute to differentials in rates.

Default risk

The widely used quality ratings of Standard and Poor's and Moody's investor services are designed to measure default risk. The highest-grade securities are given triple-A ratings to indicate a negligible degree of default risk (see Figure 16-1). The others are ranked by lower letter combinations to indicate higher chances of default risk. These ratings are widely accepted by investors, and tests seem to support their ability to discriminate among different levels of risk.[1] The spreads between the yields on different risk categories and the yields on U.S. government securities are widely used as measures of default premiums. Comparisons of the yields on U.S. Treasury long-term bonds and those on corporate bonds with Moody ratings of Aaa and Baa are shown in Figure 16-2.

The spreads between the yields on U.S. government securities and those on other risk classes of securities have increased with the increases in the level of interest rates. They have also shown a cyclical pattern that is related to business and money market conditions. The spreads tend to increase during periods of strong loan demands and rising interest rates and to decrease as conditions ease. These changes may reflect changing attitudes toward the likelihood of default, but it seems more likely that they reflect the "crowding-out" effects of tight market conditions that permit the suppliers of funds to be more selective.

Liquidity premium

Liquidity is important to many investors, and they are willing to pay for it by accepting lower returns. The premium appears as a cost reduction to the borrower who can offer contracts that provide liquidity. From the borrower's point of view, the liquidity premium is the added cost of contract features that do not offer liquidity. For example, a savings

[1]W. Braddock Hickman, *Corporate Bond Quality and Investor Experience* (New York: National Bureau of Economic Research, 1958).

FIGURE 16-1

QUALITY RATING BY INVESTOR SERVICES

Moody's

Aaa	Best quality
Aa	High quality
A	Higher medium grade
Baa	Lower medium grade
Ba	Passes speculative elements
B	Generally lacks characteristics of desirable investment
Caa	Poor standing; may be in default
Ca	Speculative in high degree; often in default
C	Lowest grade

Standard and Poor's

AAA	Highest grade
AA	High grade
A	Upper medium grade
BBB	Medium grade
BB	Lower medium grade
B	Speculative
CCC } CC }	Outright speculation
C	Reserved for income bonds
DDD-D	In default, with rating indicating relative salvage value

institution expects to pay more on 3-year certificates of deposit than on its normal savings accounts that can be withdrawn on demand.

The concept of a liquidity premium has been most widely used in discussions of the term structure of rates. In these discussions, it is assumed that the liquidity premium increases with the maturity of the contract. The premium, in this case, reflects the loss of turnover liquidity and the potential increase in market risk that accompany the lengthening of the contract maturity.

When liquidity depends on marketability, the cost of liquidity includes the transactions costs and the risk of price variations, or the market risk. The price variations associated with a given change in yield can be calculated directly from the present value equations for the securities. Malkiel has expressed the relationship between price changes and maturities as follows:

> ...For a given change in yield from the nominal yield, changes in bond prices are greater, the longer the term to maturity.[2]

[2]Burton G. Malkiel, *The Term Structure of Interest Rates: Expectations and Behavior Patterns* (Princeton: Princeton University Press, 1966), p. 54. He also points out some reservations to this theorem when yield changes are measured from a base other than the nominal yield, pp. 79–81.

FIGURE 16-2

A. Yields of Different Risk Classes of Securities

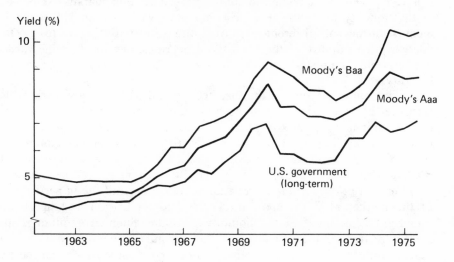

B. Spread Between Aaa Bonds and U.S. Government Bonds

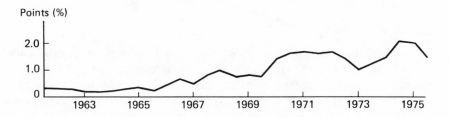

C. Spread Between Baa Bonds and U.S. Government Bonds

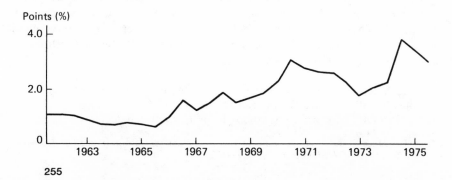

Although the calculation of the actual market risk is complicated by imperfections in the market and by other factors affecting marketability, it is likely to be directly related to contract maturity; thus market risk is part of the liquidity premium. The observed price variations in U.S. government securities of different maturities are shown in Figure 16-3. The relative price stability of the short-term securities, despite the wide variation in yields, emphasizes the usefulness of these securities in providing liquidity.

The liquidity premium that has been identified on readily marketable securities is a measure of rising costs of liquidation where these costs are defined to include the risk of price fluctuations, transactions costs, and the costs of market imperfections. In the discussion of the liquidity premium on U.S. government securities, the transactions costs and the costs of market imperfections are usually ignored. But the concept can be extended to other types of securities where transactions costs and the imperfections of the market may be important barriers to liquidation and hence an important component of the liquidity premium. Such a premium is inversely related to the efficiency of the secondary markets in reducing liquidation costs. The price advantages of marketability are recognized by market practitioners but are hard to measure. Fisher used the outstanding value of the bonds of a corporation as an index of marketability and found a significant and inverse relationship between yield spreads and this measure of marketability.[3]

Other premiums

Any feature of a financial contract that is important to either the borrower or the lender will contribute to interest-rate differentials. The exemption of the income from the securities of state and municipal governments from federal income taxes creates a widely recognized basis for yield differentials. Some differentials can be traced to handling costs. The high legal ceiling under the state small-loan laws is justified in large part by the high per-dollar cost of making and servicing small loans.

Call provisions on bonds give the borrower the right to redeem the debt prior to maturity. These provisions make it possible for the borrower to reduce interest costs if the market yield falls below the coupon rate on the bonds. They also expose the lender to the reversal of the original agreement at a disadvantageous time, and they limit the possibilities of price appreciation. One empirical study found that

> ...On seasoned bonds with intermediate and high coupon rates, deferments (call deferments) reduced yields to maturity by five to nine basis points during the period from 1957 to 1961, and they reduced yields by

[3]Lawrence Fisher, "Determinants of Risk Premiums on Corporate Bonds," *Journal of Political Economy,* LXVII (June 1959), pp. 217–37.

FIGURE 16-3
Yields and Prices on U.S. Government Securities

A. Yields

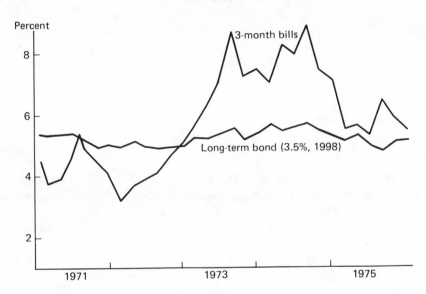

B. Prices

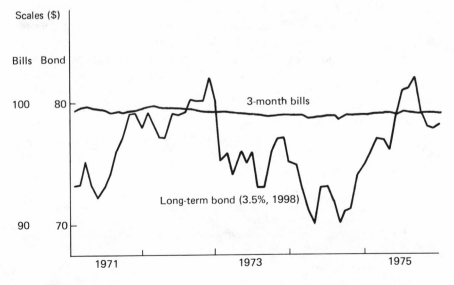

more than twice that when price appreciation on the callable bonds was limited by the call price and the prices of the deferred bonds rose a few points above the call prices.[4]

Even the marketing channels used in the placement of securities can contribute to interest-rate differentials. Cohan summarizes the difference in yields on direct placements and on public offerings as follows:

> The findings suggest that yields on direct placements were higher, on the average over the whole period, than yields on public offerings, even after the latter were adjusted for cost of flotation. The difference in favor of public offerings is not, however, constant for all types of issues. For the smaller issues alone, the difference appears to be negative for industrials (i.e., direct placements have lower yields) and close to zero for utilities.[5]

There is good evidence that many of the observed differentials in interest rates can be explained by specific contract features. The diversity of individual contracts, however, makes it difficult to measure the premiums associated with specific features accurately, or even to distinguish clearly between the role of market imperfections and contract features in explaining specific rate differentials.

Market Imperfections and Yield Differentials (d)

If market adjustments were always perfect and instantaneous, differentials in yield would reflect only the premiums justified by differences in contract features. Any barriers to the movement of funds among markets will create differentials that reflect the imperfections in the adjustment process. Short-run changes in yield differentials can be attributed either to factors that lead to changes in premiums or to rigidities in the market structure that impede the natural adjustment to market pressures.

Changes in the demand or supply of funds are likely to be selective in their initial impact. A sudden shift in the demand for housing affects the mortgage market. Changes in the demand for inventories affect the business loan market. After the initial impact, the effects will be transmitted to other markets unless there are barriers to this process. The inability of a specialized market to adapt to new pressures will lead to yield differentials that reflect these imperfections.

---

[4]Mark W. Frankena, "The Influence of Call Provisions and Coupon Rate on the Yields of Corporate Bonds," Jack M. Guttentag, ed., *Essay on Interest Rates*, vol II (New York: National Bureau of Economic Research, 1971), p. 137.

[5]Avery B. Cohan, *Yields on Corporate Debt Directly Placed* (New York: National Bureau of Economic Research, 1967), p. 22.

Specialized financing needs tend to be handled by specialized institutions. When the market is in equilibrium, new loans are financed by the flow of repayments from old loans. New funds are needed only when the new loan demands exceed the flow of repayments. The problem of raising the new funds has to be faced by the institutions involved. Diversified lenders may be able to divert funds from one channel to another. If not, they must either liquidate some portfolio assets or try to raise new funds in the money or capital markets. Barriers to this process lead to segmentated market effects and to differentials in yields. Proof of the role of market segmentation in contributing to yield differentials requires (1) evidence of unique demand or supply conditions that account for the market pressures and (2) evidence of barriers to adjustments that could eliminate the differentials. The role of market segmentation as one explanation of the observed term structure of rates will be discussed in the next section.

Term Structure of Rates

Yields on securities with different maturities differ widely from time to time (see Figure 16-4). The yields on long-term securities are generally above those on securities with shorter terms, and they tend to fluctuate over a narrower range. *Yield curves,* or cross-sectional plots of yields at any given time, reveal the structure of the relationships. A yield curve taken at peak rates tends to slope downward; a yield curve taken in the middle range of rates may have a hump in the intermediate maturities; and a yield curve taken at low levels of rates slopes upward throughout the entire range of maturities (see yield curves *A*, *B*, and *C*, respectively, in Figure 16-4).

Two theories, the *market segmentation theory* and the *unbiased expectations theory*, have been advanced to explain the pattern of changes revealed by yield curves. These two approaches will be presented separately in the following discussion, but they should be regarded as complementary rather than competitive theories. They both contribute to a realistic description of the motives and behavior of various segments of the markets. The role of liquidity premiums in shaping yield curves is discussed separately as a supplement to the expectations theory.

Market segmentation

The market segmentation approach emphasizes the distinctive features of the markets for securities with different maturities. Each market is characterized by some participants who operate within a preferred maturity range. These participants prefer to conduct their business within a rather narrow range of maturities, and they are willing to pay a premium

FIGURE 16-4

A. YIELDS ON U.S. GOVERNMENT SECURITIES

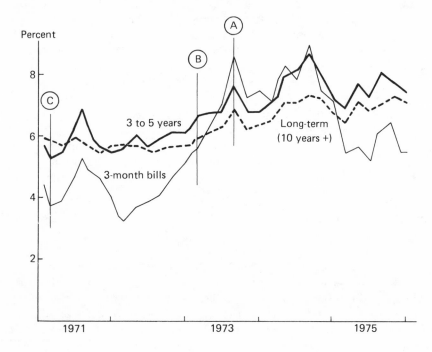

B. YIELD CURVES

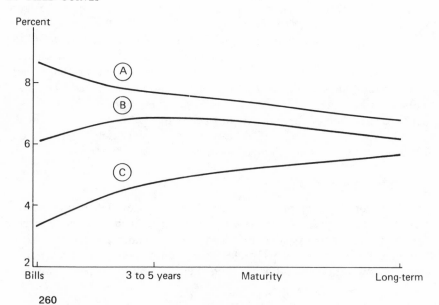

to do so. Economic events that affect this group of borrowers and lenders will be recorded in the markets they prefer to use.

Short-term funds are used primarily to finance inventories or receivables. Both of these demands are highly cyclical in nature. The demand for funds in both cases increases more rapidly than sales during the expansionary phase of the cycle, and decreases more rapidly than sales during the contraction. These variations add to the volatility of the pressures on short-term rates.

This natural volatility in the demand for short-term funds is accentuated by the role of the short-term secondary markets in providing liquidity for financial institutions. Demand or supply pressures that originate in any market are likely to exert pressure on the short-term secondary markets. New demands for funds that cannot be met immediately by the normal supply channels are likely to be transmitted into the short-term markets. Borrowers who do not have direct access to the money markets turn to banks or other financial institutions. These institutions, in turn, try to raise funds in the short-term markets by selling some short-term portfolio assets or by selling new money market instruments.

The special role of short-term secondary markets in implementing monetary policy is also a potential source of volatility in short-term rates. The open market operations of the Federal Reserve System are conducted primarily in short-term securities. The temporary adjustments of commercial banks to changes in their reserve position are usually made in short-term loans or in the liquid asset portfolios. Even the changes in the supply of funds, traced to reduction in idle cash balances, are most likely to occur in the short-term markets that provide the best substitutes for cash. The potential changes in the aggregate supply of funds that are initiated in the short-term markets can be a source of either volatility or stability in short-term rates, depending on the nature of the changes. Monetary policies designed to check expansion will accentuate the effects of demand pressures on short-term rates and add to the volatility of these rates. On the other hand, the ability of an increase in short-term rates to attract idle balances into active use will ease some of the demand pressures.

The short-term markets are exposed to a variety of special demand and supply pressures that can potentially contribute to the volatility of short-term rates observed in the changing pattern of yield curves. The differential impact of these forces on rates, however, involves the further assumption that there are some imperfections in the markets which prevent these pressures from being arbitraged into other markets. The proponents of the segmentation theory argue that many of the participants in the short-term markets, both on the demand and supply side, will not be willing to accept long-term securities as substitutes and that they are willing to pay (or forego) the rate differentials to accommodate their specific maturity needs. A close look at the special financial needs and objectives of corporations, consumers, and governmental units supports this argument and suggests that the segmentation theory does play a role in explaining the volatility of short-term rates.

On the other hand, it is possible to find many corporations, financial institutions, and individuals that have considerable flexibility in the maturity structures of their asset and liability portfolios. They should be willing and able to take advantage of disequilibrium rate differentials, and, in doing so, should be able to eliminate any unjustified spreads in rates. The existence of large amounts of funds that can be shifted to take advantage of profitable rate differentials suggests that the market segmentation theory alone cannot explain the observed patterns in the term structure and that some approach that is more sensitive to arbitrage opportunities is also needed.

Expectations theory

Borrowers who have flexibility in the maturity structure of their financing may be able to save money by borrowing long when rates are expected to rise, and by borrowing short when they are expected to fall. In the same way, investors with some flexibility in their portfolio maturities may be able to increase their average return by lending short when rates are expected to rise, and by lending long when they are expected to fall. If the expectations of borrowers and lenders are the same, they will be attempting adjustments at opposite ends of the maturity scale, and their efforts will tilt the yield curve. When an increase in rates is expected, the borrower demand for long-term funds will put upward pressure on long rates, and lender preference for short-term securities will put downward pressure on the short rates. Thus, the yield curve will be given an upward slope when increases in rates are expected, and a downward slope when decreases are expected.

If future rates were known with certainty, a yield curve could be constructed that would eliminate the possibilities of reducing costs or increasing returns by maturity adjustments. Such a curve represents an equilibrium set of rates that anticipates future rates. It also measures the premium that will be paid for different maturities with any given set of expectations. If the market yield on any maturity falls below the equilibrium rate, it will be to the borrower's advantage to borrow at that maturity. If the market yield on any maturity moves above the equilibrium rate, it will be to the investor's advantage to buy that maturity. The actions of borrowers and lenders in seeking the best maturity structure for their portfolios will keep market rates on the equilibrium yield curve.

This hypothetical equilibrium yield curve can be constructed from any set of expected one-period future rates as the geometric average of the expected rates (r_i).:

$$R_1 = (1 + r_1) - 1$$

$$R_2 = \sqrt[2]{(1 + r_1)(1 + r_2)} - 1$$

$$R_3 = \sqrt[3]{(1 + r_1)(1 + r_2)(1 + r_3)} - 1$$

$$\cdots$$

$$R_n = \sqrt[n]{(1 + r_1)(1 + r_2)\ldots(1 + r_n)} - 1 \qquad (2)$$

where: R_i = current rate for an ith period loan

r_i = future rate for a one-period loan

$$R_1 = r_1$$

Figure 16-5 illustrates the equilibrium yield curves derived under three sets of assumptions about future rates. Expectations of lower rates will produce a downward sloping yield curve (A). Expected stability will produce a flat curve (B), and expectations of higher rates will produce an upward sloping curve (C). The expectations premium can be measured by the difference between the stable expectation curve and the other curves. The premium is a function of the maturity and gives the yield curve its distinctive slope.

The unbiased expectations theory assumes that the observed yield curves correspond to these hypothetical equilibrium curves and that the current long-term rates are unbiased estimates of the future short-term rates expected to prevail during the term of the long-term obligations. The theory implies that the one-period rates expected in some future period (n) can be calculated from the current yield curve.

$$r_n = \frac{(1 + R_n)^n}{(1 + R_{n-1})^{n-1}} - 1 \qquad (3)$$

In the example used in Figure 16-5, it was assumed that one-period rates were expected to increase by 40 percent per period. With an assumed one period rate of 3 percent in the first period, the derived yield structure rates (R_i) and the expected future rates in curve C are as follows:

Period	Expected future one-period rates (r_i)	Current rates (R_i)
1st	0.03000	0.030000
2nd	0.04200	0.035983
3rd	0.05880	0.043533
4th	0.08232	0.053098

FIGURE 16-5

A. HYPOTHETICAL YIELD CURVES WITH UNBIASED EXPECTATIONS*

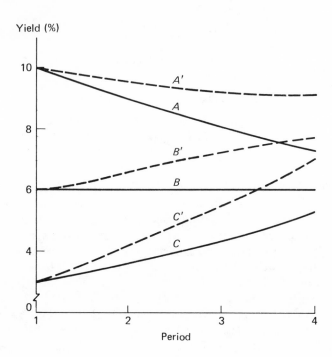

B. LIQUIDITY PREMIUM

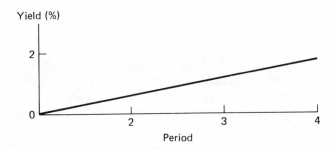

*Assumptions
  A = current rate of 10%, expected decrease at 20% per period.
  B = current rate of 6%, no changes expected.
  C = current rate of 3%, expected increase of 40% per period.
  A' = A + Liquidity premium.
  B' = B + Liquidity premium.
  C' = C + Liquidity premium.

If only the current rates were known, the unbiased expectations theory indicates that it would be possible to derive the market's expected one-period rate for any future period from equation (3) above. For example, the one-period rate for the fourth period can be obtained as follows:

$$r_4 = \frac{(1 + R_4)^4}{(1 + R_3)^3} - 1 = \frac{(1.053098)^4}{(1.043533)^3} - 1 = 0.08232$$

The expectations theory is capable of explaining both upward- and downward-sloping yield curves. More importantly, the motivations captured by the theory are realistic and familiar to both borrowers and lenders. The theory correctly forecasts the downward slopes observed at peak rates when it seems plausible for borrowers and lenders to expect declining rates. It also forecasts the upward slopes when rates are low and borrowers and lenders expect them to increase. However, in the simple form presented in Figure 16-5, it suggests a symmetry in the upward and downward slopes that is not observed in practice.

Hicks and others have pointed out that the unbiased expectations theory does not provide for the greater market risk and reduced liquidity on long-term securities.[6] When liquidity premiums are added that are positively related to maturity, the adjusted equilibrium yield curves appear to conform more closely to those observed in practice. The broken lines in Figure 16-5 show the expectations yield curves as modified by the inclusion of a given liquidity premium function. The upward sloping curves are even more steeply sloped (C'). The flat (or normal) curve has the slope of the liquidity premium function (B'), and the downward sloping function (A') becomes flatter. All these changes bring the theoretical results closer to the observed pattern of yield curves.

As we have seen, the observed yield on any security can be thought of as being made up of a number of separate components: the equilibrium level of interest rates (r^*), the set of premiums that is uniquely related to the features of the security (p), and a residual component that reflects imperfections in market adjustments (d). Some of these components are thought to be relatively stable. Others are more volatile and are affected by money market conditions. The most important components can usually be identified. The less important ones may be difficult to isolate.

QUESTIONS FOR DISCUSSION

1. Look at the yields that are published in the financial pages of daily newspapers, and suggest explanations for the differentials that you observe on different issues.

[6] J. R. Hicks, *Value and Capital*, 2nd ed. (London: Oxford University Press, 1946), p. 147.

2. Assume that you have been assigned the problem of grading the securities of two corporations by potential default risk. What criteria would you use?

3. Assume that you are the treasurer of a corporation that is urgently in need of funds and that the market rates on the normal sources of corporate funds are so high that they create serious cost problems. Suggest techniques that might be used to obtain funds at lower costs, and comment on the practicality and desirability of various alternatives.

4. Can you think of any practical example or situation that might give rise to differentials in yields that reflect market segmentation? What evidence can you use to support your position?

5. If the unbiased expectations theory correctly describes the day-to-day yield curves, and the current curves are upward sloping, would it be possible for a portfolio manager to improve the yield on his portfolio by shifting to longer-term securities?

6. From the earlier discussion of financial institutions, indicate those institutions that might be willing and able to assist in arbitraging rates on securities with different maturities.

7. What types of financial institutions must, by the nature of their business, speculate on expected changes in interest rates? How can you infer the interest rate forecasts that they are making from the changes in their statements?

8. Assume that as a corporate borrower you can use either very long- or very short-term debt for your inventory financing. If the rates are identical, which would you use? Why? If the rates are different, what premium would you pay for your preferred maturity?

SELECTED REFERENCES

BRIMMER, ANDREW J., "Credit Conditions and Price Determination in the Corporate Bond Market," *Journal of Finance*, XV (September 1960), 353–70.

CAGAN, PHILLIP, *Changes in the Cyclical Behavior of Interest Rates.* New York: National Bureau of Economic Research, 1966.

COHAN, AVERY B., *Yields on Corporate Debt Directly Placed.* New York: National Bureau of Economic Research, 1966.

CONARD, JOSEPH W., *Introduction to the Theory of Interest.* Berkeley, Calif.: University of California Press, 1959.

————, *The Behavior of Interest Rates.* New York: National Bureau of Economic Research, 1966.

CULBERTSON, JOHN M., "The Term Structure of Interest Rates," *Quarterly Journal of Economics*, LXXl (November 1957), 485–517.

EDERINGTON, LOUIS H., "The Yield Spread on New Issues of Corporate Bonds," *Journal of Finance*, XXIX (December 1974), 1531–43.

FISHER, LAWRENCE, "Determinants of Risk Premiums on Corporate Bonds," *Journal of Political Economy*, LXVII (June 1959), 217–37.

GUTTENTAG, JACK M., ed., *Essays on Interest Rates*, vol. II. New York: National Bureau of Economic Research, 1971.

―――― and PHILLIP CAGAN, eds., *Essays on Interest Rates,* vol. I. New York: National Bureau of Economic Research, 1969.

HICKMAN, W. BRADDOCK, *Corporate Bond Quality and Investor Experience.* New York: National Bureau of Economic Research, 1958.

HICKS, J. R., *Value and Capital* (2nd ed.). London: Oxford University Press, 1946.

HOMER, SIDNEY, *A History of Interest Rates.* New Brunswick, N.J.: Rutgers University Press, 1963.

JEN, FRANK C., and JAMES E. WEST, "The Value of the Deferred Call Privilege," *National Banking Review*, 3 (March 1966), 369–78.

JOHNSON, RAMON E., "Term Structures of Corporate Bond Yields as a Function of Risk of Default," *Journal of Finance,* XXII (May 1967), 313–45.

KESSEL, REUBEN H., *The Cyclical Behavior of the Term Structure of Interest Rates.* New York: National Bureau of Economic Research, 1965.

LUTZ, FRIEDRICH A., "The Structure of Interest Rates," *Quarterly Journal of Economics*, LV (November 1940), 36–63.

MACAULAY, FREDERICK R., *The Movement of Interest Rates, Bond Yields and Stock Prices in the United States Since 1856.* New York: National Bureau of Economic Research, 1938.

MALKIEL, BURTON G., *The Term Structure of Interest Rates.* Princeton, N.J.: Princeton University Press, 1966.

MEISELMAN, DAVID, *The Term Structure of Interest Rates.* Englewood Cliffs, N.J.; Prentice-Hall, Inc., 1962.

VAN HORNE, JAMES C., *Function and Analysis of Capital Market Rates.* Englewood Cliffs, N.J.: Prentice-Hall, Inc., 1970.

The Money Market

17

Bagehot called his classic book on the English money market *Lombard Street* because as he says,

> ...I wish to deal, and to show that I mean to deal, with concrete realities. A notion prevails that the Money Market is something so impalpable that it can only be spoken of in very abstract words, and that therefore books on it must always be exceedingly difficult.[1]

No street name can be used to adequately identify the physical location of the U.S. money market, but this chapter shares Bagehot's concern for concreteness in describing the role of the money market. It is the central mechanism of the financial system. It provides one of the major links between the monetary authorities and the financial system, and it absorbs the day-to-day pressures of adjustments that cannot be handled by the normal financing channels.

The money market is not easy to identify or define. It consists of the set of markets for financial instruments that are normally used by financial institutions and others to adjust their cash positions. The instruments used may vary from time to time, and the nature and structure of the markets may change. In the United States and other countries with highly developed secondary markets, many types of government or private securities may be traded as money market instruments. In less well-developed countries, money market transactions may be confined to negotiated adjustments among banks and with the central bank or monetary authori-

[1]Walter Bagehot, *Lombard Street: A Description of the Money Market*, reprint of 1873 ed. (Homewood, Ill.: Richard D. Irwin, 1962), p. 1.

ties. The first section of this chapter describes the principal money market instruments used in the United States. The second section deals with the nature and objectives of the major participants in the money markets. The third section deals with the money markets as a link between monetary policy actions and the financial system. The fourth discusses the role of the money markets in absorbing the demand and supply pressures from other sectors of the economy. The last section discusses the use of the regularly published statistics on money market events as early indicators of changing economic conditions.

Money Market Instruments

Money market instruments must meet all the requirements for easy secondary trading and, in addition, must carry very little market or default risk. The definition of money market instruments is usually limited to securities with maturities of less than a year, but U.S. government securities, with somewhat longer maturities, may serve much the same function.

The shortest contracts are those used for trading in *Federal Funds*. Federal Funds are accounts with Federal Reserve Banks. Since the Federal Reserve Banks only accept deposits from commercial banks, foreign governments, the U.S. Treasury, and a few other special depositors, the trading in Federal Funds is limited primarily to banks that are members of the Federal Reserve System. A bank with an excess in its reserve account can sell it to another bank through the Federal Funds market. The transaction could take place between any two banks, although in practice the market is concentrated in the principal banking centers. The major banks make a market for Federal Funds and will, as a rule, either buy (borrow) or sell (lend) Federal Funds to accommodate smaller banks. Trading is conducted by wire or by telephone. The most common transactions are unsecured. However, they may be secured by pledges of collateral or may involve repurchase agreements, which are, in effect, sales of U.S. government securities with an agreement to repurchase them at a later date. The transfers in the Federal Funds market are predominantly bookkeeping transfers. Amounts in reserve accounts at Federal Reserve Banks are transferred from one account to another. If collateral is involved, the ownership of securities held by Federal Reserve Banks as custodians is shifted from one bank to the other.

U.S. Treasury bills have traditionally served as the principal money market instrument. They are sold as part of the Treasury's regular financing program. A Treasury bill is an obligation of the U.S. government to pay the bearer a fixed sum after a specified number of days from the date of issue. They typically carry maturities of 91, 182, and 365 days and are offered in regular weekly auctions. They are issued in denominations of from $10,000 to $1,000,000. They offer excellent temporary outlets for funds, since they carry no default risk and little or no market risk. The outstanding amount of bills, which has ranged between 100 and 200 billion dollars in recent years, provides a major component of liquid asset portfolios.

Tax anticipation notes of the U.S. government and other governmental units, and other types of government securities, serve as money market instruments to a lesser degree. Their usefulness can be measured directly by their freedom from default risk and by their marketability, which is related to the issue size, the issuer, and the nature of the trading market.

Commercial paper is a term used to describe short-term negotiable promissory notes issued by large corporations to raise money in the public markets. These notes are the private counterpart to Treasury bills. They offer some of the same features but carry somewhat greater default risk and may be less marketable. Only the largest and best-known corporations have access to the commercial paper market.

The banks entered the market as issuers of money market instruments in 1961 when the First National City Bank of New York announced that it would issue *negotiable certificates of deposit* in large denominations and that a major government securities dealer had agreed to make a market in them.[2] These instruments are similar to regular time certificates of deposit, but they offer marketability as an added liquidity feature. They have become an important type of money market instrument.

Federal agency securities, banker acceptances, Eurodollar accounts, and other suitable short-term instruments may be part of the money market from time to time. Any security that is readily marketable and that can meet the very high quality requirements can qualify as a money market instrument.

Participants

The money market is both a primary and a secondary market. But access to the money market as a source of new funds is limited to a relatively small number of large, well-established borrowers, such as the U.S. Treasury, government agencies, and large well-known financial and business organizations. A buyer's access to the market is limited only by the large denominations involved. Anyone with enough money can buy money market securities.

Borrowers use money market securities as an alternative to other sources of funds when flexibility is needed or when they reduce borrowing costs. They are most attractive when they are less expensive than longer

[2]Federal Reserve Bank of Richmond, *Instruments of the Money Market* (1974), pp. 51–53.

term funds or when the issuer does not want to get locked into high long-term rates.

Potential buyers of money market securities can be classified into two types. The first group consists of those who have cash (M_1) balances and whose financing needs impose strict limitations on the terms and quality of the securities they can use as substitutes for their cash balances. The second group faces less restrictive financing needs, and can use money market securities as part of their asset portfolios to achieve the desired mix of liquidity and yield.

The first group includes anyone who holds or manages cash. They will be willing and happy to invest their cash balances if their conditions can be met. They have to be assured access to the funds when they need them, and rates that are high enough to cover their transactions costs. These buyers are of special economic importance because they control a source of funds that would otherwise not be available. They provide the elasticity that is built into the aggregate liquidity preference function and the aggregate demand for money function.

The new liquid asset (money management) mutual funds provide a concrete illustration of the role of the money market in activating idle money balances. These institutions appeared when money market rates were high enough to justify the expense of trying to reach holders of small amounts of idle balances. By serving as intermediaries between the money market and cash manager who would not otherwise have access to the market, they added to the effectiveness of the money market in mobilizing idle balances. They also illustrate a type of institutional change that can affect the velocity of circulation of money.

The second group of buyers of money market instruments includes banks, financial institutions, governments, corporations, and anyone else who uses money market instruments as part of an investment portfolio. These buyers provide the regular demand for money market instruments and absorb the newly issued instruments as part of the turnover of their portfolios. When they move into or out of money market instruments, their moves will be from the longer-term, lower-quality, less-liquid end of the spectrum as they shift from one type of security to another. These shifts provide the arbitrage that brings rates in different markets into line, but they do not affect the aggregate supply of funds or the overall level of rates.

Federal Reserve System

The responsibility for control of the money supply assures the monetary authorities of an important role in the money market. In the United States, the Federal Reserve System deals directly in the money market through its open-market operations, and affects it indirectly in a variety of ways through its regulatory operations. Riefler classified the effects of the System's open market operations on the prices and yields of securities in secondary markets into three types:

> (1) They affect the volume of securities available for trading and investment, (2) they change the volume of reserves available to member banks for making loans and investments or paying off debts, and (3) they influence the expectations of market professionals and other investors regarding market trends.[3]

The Federal Reserve System has tremendous resources for buying and selling, and its transactions are likely to have an impact on any market it uses. It can, and does, buy and sell U.S. government securities of all maturities, federal agency securities, and bankers' acceptances. Figure 17-1 gives the gross volume of the Federal Reserve's outright purchases and sales in 1975. Three-fourths of their purchases, and all of their sales, were in short-term money market securities. Their day-to-day operations are conducted primarily in Treasury bills, in large part because it is the only market large enough to absorb major transactions without disruptive

FIGURE 17-1

OPEN MARKET TRANSACTIONS OF THE FEDERAL RESERVE SYSTEM IN 1975

Type of security	(In millions of dollars)	
	Gross purchases	Gross sales
U.S. government securities:		
Treasury bills	11,562	5,599
Others within 1 yr. mat.	3,886	—
1–5 yr. mat.	2,863	—
5–10 yr. mat.	1,510	—
Over 10 yr. mat.	1,070	—
Federal agency obligations	1,616	246
Banker acceptances, net	163	—
Total[a]	22,670	5,845

[a]Outright transactions only. Excludes repurchase agreements, matched sale–purchase transactions and redemptions.
Source: *Federal Reserve Bulletin* (March 1976), p. A9.

[3]Winfield W. Riefler, "Open Market Operations in Long-Term Securities," *Federal Reserve Bulletin* (November 1958), pp. 1260–74.

market effects. The average daily transactions of the dealers in government securities are shown in Figure 17-2 to give some indication of the relative depth of these markets. The average for daily transactions in securities of maturities of less than one year was over $4 billion, while the average for securities with maturities of more than ten years was only $138 million.

The Federal Reserve's purchases of securities add to the free reserves available to member banks, and their sales reduce the reserves available to these banks. Many of the adjustments by banks to the changes in their reserve positions are likely to be made, at least in the short-run, in the money markets. Free reserves, if they cannot be used immediately for loans, will be used to buy money market securities. The impact of these purchases may be several times as large as that of the initial purchase by the Federal Reserve System because of the multiple expansion potential arising from the fractional reserve requirements. In the modern money market, where excess reserves are traded in the Federal Funds market, the full expansion is likely to appear very rapidly.

Any net contraction of reserves by open market operations is almost certain to force some adjustments in the money market. Banks in a deficit reserve position may be able to buy Federal Funds. If they can't, they will be forced either to sell some of their holdings of money market securities or to try to sell CDs. Either action shifts the pressure to the money market and adds to the impact of the initial open market operations.

The actions of the Federal Reserve System are so important that they are watched closely by market practitioners for clues to the System's policies. Information about the Federal Reserve's activities is analyzed as soon as it becomes available, as a potential guide to financial decisions. The problems of analyzing and interpreting the information available, regarding events in the money market, will be discussed in the last section of this chapter.

FIGURE 17-2
DEALER TRANSACTIONS IN U.S. GOVERNMENT SECURITIES IN 1975

	Daily averages (Par value, in millions of dollars)
U.S. government securities, total	$6,027
By maturities	
Within 1 year	4,112
1–5 years	1,414
5–10 years	363
Over 10 years	138
U.S. government agency securities	1,043

Source: Federal Reserve Bulletin (March 1976), p. A36.

Arbitrator of Demand and Supply Pressures

Despite the highly specialized and selective nature of the money market, it plays a central role in resolving the demand and supply pressures that originate in all sectors of the economy. The special role of money market securities as substitutes for idle money balances gives the money market access to, and control over, the only private source of new funds. It meets the net demands for funds that are not met by the monetary authorities.[4] It also absorbs net surpluses that appear in any sector of the economy.

The special demand pressures that originate for business loans in Oregon or Alaska may seem pretty remote from the money market, but if these pressures are large, they will be reflected quickly in the rates and terms on money market securities. When businesspeople or consumers need money they turn to financial institutions. Since a well-run financial institution seldom has idle cash reserves, these demands have to be turned down or passed on to the money market. The bank can raise the funds temporarily by buying Federal Funds. It can make longer-term adjustments by selling some of its holdings of money market securities or it can sell CDs to raise new funds. All these adjustments involve the money market and will be reflected in money market rates.

The ability of the money market to accommodate new demands depends on its ability to persuade the holders of idle balances to invest them in money market securities. The supply of funds available to the money market is determined by the elasticity of the aggregate demand for money function. If the supply of idle balances is inelastic, the demand pressures transmitted into the money market will merely lead to higher money market rates without meeting the new demands for funds. Its failure to supply new funds will result in an upward adjustment of rates in all sectors and a reallocation of funds among the existing demands.

A similar process is observed when surplus funds appear in any market. The surplus enters the financial system as loan repayments or as deposits in financial institutions. The excess funds available to banks are quickly placed into the Federal Funds market, used to buy money market securities, or used to let CDs run off. All of these actions shift the funds into the money market with a corresponding softening in the rates and terms on money market securities. If holders of idle balances are responsive to the drop in rates, they may absorb the funds by building up their balances. If they are not, the decreases in market rates will be shifted into other markets as an overall decline in the level of rates.

[4]The savings accounts at financial institutions may also assist in this process.

Interpretation of Money Market Events

Financial publications carry a variety of new items about events in the money markets. These events can be used as early indications of financial and economic pressures that may not be confirmed in the regular statistics until weeks or months later. The money market rates are the most sensitive indicators of the basic ease or tightness of money in the economy as a whole. The U.S. Treasury bill rate has long been used as the standard measure of money pressures. It has been supplemented by the Federal Funds rate, which reacts even more quickly to changing pressures.

Changes in money market rates provide evidence of the presence or absence of special pressures, but they do not give much insight into the reasons for the changes. The problem of interpreting changes in short-term rates is one of identifying the nature of the demand and supply pressures.

Since the monetary authorities are a regular and important participant in the money market, and since reasonably prompt information can be obtained about their actions, the interpretation of changes in the money market usually starts with the weekly statements of the "Factors Affecting Bank Reserves and Condition Statements of F. R. Banks."[5] These statements are released to the press weekly, and are republished either completely or in part by the major newspapers. A description and analysis of the items in these statements appears in Chapter 14 and in Figures 14-1 and 14-2. These statements give a complete accounting of all of the events that affect the reserves available to member banks and the amount of the changes in those reserves.

The Federal Reserve System can use open market operations to offset the effects of any factors affecting member bank reserves and to supply the amounts it feels are appropriate. If its offset operations are effective, the change in total member reserves as reported in the weekly statement will represent the policy objectives of the Federal Reserve System. In practice, they also include some amounts that measure the failure of the Federal Reserve to achieve its policy objectives. The interpretation of the weekly statement requires some judgment about the share of the change in reserves that reflects policy objectives and the share that represents operational problems or errors.

The nature of the offset problems faced by the Federal Reserve can be seen by a closer look at the factors that affect member bank reserves. In the statement shown in Figure 17-3 for the week ending December 17, 1975, the Federal Reserve System bought $1,616 million worth of securities

---

[5]Board of Governors of the Federal Reserve System, "Factors Affecting Bank Reserves and Condition Statement of F. R. Banks," weekly statistical release H.4.1.

and let $522 million in repurchase agreements run off, to add a net amount of $1,094 million to the reserves of member banks. If they were trying to expand bank reserves by exactly $720 million, the remainder of their open market activities, or $374 million, could be regarded as offsets to other factors. The principal offset problem in that week was the increase of $462 million in the currency holding of the public. Since currency movements can be estimated with some degree of accuracy, part of the system's open market operations was probably intended to offset these changes. Some offset problems, such as changes in float, are harder to anticipate. Large changes attributed to float are likely to be reversed in subsequent weeks. The items in the statement that are controlled by the U.S. Treasury can be anticipated by good communications with the Treasury. The size and nature of the changes in factors affecting reserves can usually give some insight into the size of offset errors as opposed to policy objectives. In the statement for the week ending December 17, it seems likely that the Federal Reserve tried to increase the reserves available to its member banks during the week; but accurate judgments require information for more than one week.

FIGURE 17-3

FACTORS AFFECTING BANK RESERVES (AVERAGES OF DAILY AMOUNTS IN MILLIONS OF DOLLARS)

	Week ending December 17, 1975	Change from previous week
Member bank reserves, total	35,139	+ 720
Reserve Bank credit:		
U.S. government securities:		
Bought outright	90,625	+ 1,616
Held under repurchase agreements	—	− 522
Member bank borrowing	44	+ 16
Float	2,626	+ 279
Other accounts	4,790	+ 26
Gold stock	11,599	—
Treasury currency outstanding	10,087	+ 6
Total, factors supplying reserves	119,771	1,421
Currency in circulation	85,686	
Minus amount held as bank reserves	7,827	
Currency held by public	77,859	+ 462
Deposits of U.S. Treasury	1,943	+ 78
Other deposit and liability items	4,830	+ 160
Total, factors absorbing reserves	84,632	+ 700

Source: Federal Reserve Bulletin (March 1976), p. A2.

The weekly reports of condition for the large commercial banks give some further clues to the nature and intensity of both demand and supply pressures.[6] The intensity of the demand pressures on this particular set of banks can be judged by the financial adjustments that they make.

Demand pressures for loans should show up as an increase in loans relative to investments in securities. In the sample statement shown in Figure 17-4 for the week of December 17, 1975, the total loans and investments of large commercial banks increased by $3.4 billion. Two-thirds of the increase was in loans, but a closer look at the nature of the loan demand indicates that half of the increase was in loans to brokers, dealers, and others for the purchase of securities. This suggests that the dealers are building inventories of securities, which they are reluctant to do unless they are expecting higher security prices, i.e., a decline in rates. The

FIGURE 17-4

ASSETS AND LIABILITIES OF LARGE COMMERCIAL BANKS (IN BILLIONS OF DOLLARS)

Item	Outstanding amounts on December 17, 1975	Change from preceding week
Total loans and investments	402.4	+3.4
Federal funds sold	18.8	−0.1
Commercial and industrial loans	120.1	+0.6
For purchasing or carrying securities	9.3	+1.2
To nonbank financial institutions	27.3	—
Real estate	59.5	—
Consumer credit	34.9	+0.1
All other loans	31.7	+0.7
U.S. Treasury securities	40.3	+1.3
Other securities	60.5	−0.4
Reserves and cash accounts	75.6	+3.8
Other assets	39.2	−1.1
Total assets	517.2	+6.1
Demand deposits	171.9	+7.1
Time and savings deposits	226.2	+0.1
Federal funds purchased	47.8	−1.5
Borrowing	4.4	—
Other liabilities	24.7	+0.5
Capital accounts and reserves	42.2	−0.1

Source: *Federal Reserve Bulletin* (January 1975), p. A21.

[6] Board of Governors of the Federal Reserve System, "Weekly Condition Report of Large Commercial Banks and Domestic Subsidiaries," weekly statistical release H.4.2.

demand pressures from the business and consumer sectors did not appear to be unusually strong. The ratio of loans to total loans and investments can be used as a general index of demand pressure relative to the funds available to banks. This ratio which usually moves with interest rates, remained almost unchanged during the week.

Attempts to sell CDs or other efforts to raise new funds usually indicate loan demand pressures. In the sample statement in Figure 17-4, there was no increase in borrowing, and time and savings deposits, which include CDs, increased by a much smaller amount than demand accounts. When the banks are making a serious attempt to raise funds, their efforts to sell CDs will shift funds from demand accounts into CDs, and the changes will appear as an increase in the ratio of time accounts to total deposits. In the sample week, this ratio declined, indicating relatively easy money conditions.

Since the large banks make a market for the smaller banks in Federal Funds, the changes in the Federal Funds items are suggestive of the shortages or surpluses at the smaller banks. In the sample week, the net Federal Funds purchased by the large banks declined, suggesting a reduction at the surplus in the smaller banks.

The events recorded in the statements of the Federal Reserve Banks and of the large commercial banks tell only part of the story, and interpretations of the type suggested in the preceding paragraphs have to be used with caution. But these statements do provide information quickly on an important range of financial activities, and can give valuable preliminary insights when they are interpreted carefully in the background of longer-run information and events.

QUESTIONS FOR DISCUSSION

1. Develop a short list of the titles and employers of the people who are active participants in the U.S. money markets.
2. Under what conditions might the treasurer of a large, well-known corporation find it desirable to try to raise funds in the money market?
3. If short-term riskless rates are used as an index of the interest rate (r^* in the notation of Chapter 16), what special role does the money market play in the determination of the level of interest rates?
4. What alternatives do cash managers have to money market securities for purposes of cash management? Compare the advantages and disadvantages of money market securities and their alternatives.
5. What institutions are likely to be the most important in the arbitrage between money market rates and the rates in other markets.
6. Some of the critics of the Federal Reserve System policy of conducting open

market operations in "bills only" have urged them to extend their operations into longer-term issues. Comment on the desirability of this policy and on the practical problems that it raises.

7. Obtain copies of the weekly statements on the operations of the Federal Reserve System and the large commercial banks, and discuss the implications, for money market conditions, of the changes observed in these statements. (These statements are usually published in the *Wall Street Journal* and other financial papers.)

SELECTED REFERENCES

BAGEHOT, WALTER, *Lombard Street: A Description of the Money Market*. Reprinted. Homewood, Ill.: Richard D. Irwin, Inc., 1962.

BOARD OF GOVERNORS OF FEDERAL RESERVE SYSTEM, *The Federal Funds Market*. Washington, D.C., 1959.

———, *Open Market Policies and Operating Procedures—Staff Studies*. Washington, D.C., 1971.

HEEBNER, A. GILBERT, *Negotiable Certificates of Deposit: The Development of a Money Market Instrument*. New York: New York University, 1967.

KLOPSTOCK, FRED H., "Euro-Dollars in the Liquidity and Reserve Management of United States Banks," *Monthly Review*, 50 (July 1968), 130–138. Federal Reserve Bank of New York.

MADDEN, CARL H., *The Money Side of the Street*. New York: Federal Reserve Bank of New York, 1959.

NADLER, M., SEPA HELLER, and SAMUEL SHIPMAN, *The Money Market and its Institutions*. New York: Ronald Press, 1955.

REIFLER, WINFIELD W., "Open Market Operations in Long-Term Securities," *Federal Reserve Bulletin*, 44 (November 1958), 1260–74.

ROOSA, ROBERT V., *Federal Reserve Operations in the Money and Government Securities Market*. New York: Federal Reserve Bank of New York, 1956.

SELDEN, RICHARD T., "Commercial Paper, Finance Companies, and the Banks," Deane Carson, ed., *Banking and Monetary Studies*. Homewood, Ill.: Richard D. Irwin, 1963, pp. 334–40.

YOUNG RALPH A., *Instruments of Monetary Policy in the United States*. Washington, D.C.: International Monetary Fund, 1973, chapters 3 and 4, pp. 54–96.

Tracing Moneyflows

18

When the financing process is proceeding normally, current income provides the financing for current expenditures. Funds that are not used directly for consumption or internal financing are placed into financial markets and are used by borrowers. In equilibrium, the supply of funds from current income permits a current level of expenditures, which in turn generates a stable level of income. The self-financing stability of this process is destroyed whenever funds that are not spent are not placed into the loan markets or when barriers develop in the financing process.

The act of saving by an individual businessperson or consumer involves a decision to not use all of his income for consumption or current outlays. It is reflected in the balance sheet as an increase in net worth and by the appropriate counterpart item, either an increase in assets or a reduction of debt. If all forms of savings guaranteed the availability of the funds for spending by someone else, the stability of the flow of funds would be assured. If, however, anyone wishes (or is required) to increase his holdings of cash balances, some leakages from the income stream can occur. Keynes' liquidity preference function identifies these leakages as an increase in the demand for idle money balances.

The most obvious example arises from the hoarding of currency. Currency hoards are a form of savings. They add to the hoarder's assets and to his net worth. But they do not provide funds for loans. No one else can borrow and use currency hoards. Income diverted to idle currency balances reduces the supply of funds available in financial markets and, in the absence of any new sources of funds, the level of income. Currency hoards are normally not an important phenomenon in economically developed countries. However, other types of leakages can be traced to deposits in financial institutions. These leakages are more difficult to detect and depend, in part, on the structure and organization of the financial system. Forms of savings that appear to be very similar may, in fact, have very different implications for the level of moneyflows.

Potential Leakages from the Income Stream

It is customary to think of income as being used for either consumption or savings. When it is used for consumption, the flow of funds can be traced through the payment channels back into the income stream. Funds used to purchase food, clothing, and other items become available for wage payments, dividends, and other outlays. Some of these funds become income quickly, others may go through more elaborate steps, but there is no reason to assume that there will be any long-term leakages in this process. Delays in payments that result in temporary leakages will presumably be quickly reversed. In such cases, the presence of the leakage depends only on the time period used to trace the stages of the process. When the time period is extended, the leakage disappears.

The savings process is more complicated. Part of savings may be placed directly into investment expenditures for houses, capital equipment, etc. The moneyflows associated with such investment outlays are similar to those described for consumption expenditures. The funds used for these expenditures become available for wage payments, dividends, and other payments that will eventually become part of income. Temporary delays may develop, but again there is no reason to assume that there will be long-term leakages.

A large share of savings is channeled into financial institutions either as new deposits or as repayments on loans. Both add to the saver's net worth. The accompanying balance-sheet entries appear either as additions to assets or as reductions in indebtedness. Most of these funds find their way back into the income stream, but the path is less direct and the potential for leakage is greater. The return of this form of savings to the income stream depends on the ability of financial institutions to make the funds available to their borrowers.

Savings in the form of loan repayments comprise a substantial share of all financial moneyflows. Short- and long-term debt obligations are continuously being retired. These funds are normally used by financial institutions to make new loans or to buy new securities. The process converts the savings of one group into new sources of funds for another group and sends the funds on their way back into the income stream.

When savings are placed into savings accounts or other financial assets of various types, new funds usually become available for loans and investments. The process in its simplest form merely adds another step or two to the flow of funds back toward the income stream. However, in some cases, the initial act of saving may be offset completely or in part by leakages or substitution effects that follow from the movement of the funds through the intermediation process. The amount of these offsets depends on the nature of the controls applied to the financial system.

Reserve requirements and leakages

When funds are placed in a savings institution that is required to hold some fraction of its deposits in the form of a reserve, the reserve requirement may represent a small leakage of funds from the moneyflows stream. If the savings institution is required to hold a given percentage of its deposits in currency or in a demand account with a commercial bank, the reserve requirement fraction of the new funds is not available for loans. It represents a leakage of that share of the funds from the income stream. Where s is the reserve percentage, the amount of new loans (ΔL) will be equal to $(1-s)$ of the amount placed in the savings institution (ΔS), and the leakage will be equal to $s\Delta S$:

$$\Delta L = \Delta S(1-s) \tag{1}$$

The same type of leakage arises from savings deposits at commercial banks, but the effects are more complicated when the bank is a member of the Federal Reserve System and subject to its reserve requirements.

Control of the reserve base and leakages

Funds placed on deposit in banks that are members of the Federal Reserve System are subject to the leakages associated with reserve requirements and, in addition, are subject to leakages that arise from the intrabank substitution effects associated with the constraints on the reserve base. The first type of leakage is easy to see. The second type is concealed by the complexity of the clearing process.

Any new deposit in a member bank appears on its books as a new source of funds and in its reserve account as new reserves. The bank can loan out all of the funds except the fraction required as reserves for the new deposit (s). At this stage the leakage of funds at a controlled bank is the same as that at an uncontrolled institution with the same reserve requirements (see equation (1)).

The leakage that arises from the intra-bank substitution effect reflects the constraints on the reserves available to banks that are members of the controlled system. The gain in reserves at any one bank has to be exactly offset by a loss of reserves at another bank. The loss of lending capacity at the bank that loses reserves is equal to

$$\Delta L_X = \Delta S (1 - x) \tag{2}$$

where x is the reserve requirement on deposits that were withdrawn.

The implications of the intra-bank substitution effect for the ability of the controlled system as a whole to make new loans depends on the differential in the reserve requirements on the types of accounts involved. The effects can be classified into three types: two limiting cases, and the cases that fall between the limits.

1) If the reserve requirements on the two types of accounts are equal ($s = x$), the leakage arising from the intra-bank substitution effects is equal to 100 percent of the initial deposit. The net addition to the lending capacity of the controlled system from the new deposit is zero. From equations (1) and (2),

$$\Delta L - \Delta L_X = \Delta S (1 - s) - \Delta S (1 - x) = 0 \tag{3}$$

where: $$s = x$$

An important example of this type of effect arises in the case of the accumulation of idle balances in demand deposit accounts. When an individual deposits his pay check into his checking account at a member bank and doesn't spend all of it, he is saving money. His assets and net worth are increased. This type of saving appears to be very similar to other types of savings, from the individual's point of view. But the economic effects are like those of hoarding currency. The aggregate results reflect the intra-bank substitution effect involving accounts with identical reserve requirements. The depositor's check sets in motion the check-clearing process that results in an equal and opposite transaction somewhere within the banking system. If both accounts are held by the same bank, the bank has obviously not gained any new funds by the transaction. If it has not gained any new funds, it cannot make any new loans. Saving in this form does not produce loan funds for anyone else to spend. The same type of leakage develops when the two accounts are not held by the same bank, but the results are harder to see. The banker who gets the new deposit can make new loans. It is easy to forget about the banker who lost the deposit.

Theoretical discussions of the liquidity preference function assume that the relevant money supply is part of a controlled system so that accumulations of idle balances reduce the funds available for loans. This result does not necessarily follow when deposits are accumulated in accounts outside of the controlled system. Deposits in nonmember banks or in the checking type of accounts at savings institutions are subject only to the leakages associated with reserve requirements against those accounts.

2) The intra-bank substitution effect is weaker when the reserve requirements on the two types of accounts involved are different. The most important example of this type arises from new time or savings deposits in member banks (or with purchases of CDs). The initial effects of these deposits are identical to those of deposits in savings accounts at noncontrolled institutions. The bank can make new loans in the amount of the deposit minus the required reserves (see equation (1)). However, when the bank is a member of the Federal Reserve System, the restriction on the size of the reserve base sets in motion the intra-bank substitution effect. The initial deposit or purchase of the CD is most likely to be made with a check drawn on a member bank. When the check clears, it reduces the deposits and reserves of the bank on which it is drawn. The net reserve amount available to the member banks after the check has been cleared is equal to the difference in required reserves on the two types of accounts. Where ΔS is the amount of savings, and the reserve ratios are d on demand and s on savings, the change in excess reserves (ΔE) measures the amount available for new loans:

$$\Delta E = \Delta S (d - s) \qquad (4)$$

These reserves will support new loans (ΔL) for the banking system as a whole of

$$\Delta L = \frac{\Delta E}{d} = \frac{\Delta S (d - s)}{d} \qquad (5)$$

The difference between the amount of new loans that can be supported by the savings deposit and the amount of the initial savings deposits represents a leakage of funds from the moneyflow stream:

$$\text{Leakage} = \Delta S - \Delta L = \Delta S - \frac{\Delta S (d - s)}{d}$$

$$= \Delta S \frac{s}{d} \qquad (6)$$

The amount of the leakage appears in the balance sheet of the member banking system as a reduction in demand accounts, which, if not offset by other developments, will reduce the stock of money (M_1 concept) accordingly.

These calculations reveal the striking fact that a rather large fraction of new savings placed in member banks does not become available for new loans. The size of the leakage depends on the differentials in reserve requirements. When the reserve requirement is 12 percent on demand accounts and 3 percent on savings accounts, one-fourth of new savings in this form does not become available for new loans. This is in contrast to the leakage of 3 percent on a similar transaction with a savings institution with the same reserve requirement.

3) A third case arises when the new source of funds at controlled banks is not subject to reserve requirements. Under the current structure, this case applies only to new capital issues or to long-term capital notes. It would, however, apply to any source of funds not subject to reserves that are part of the controlled reserve base. In this case, no leakages are observed. All the new funds can be converted into loans or investments.

The range in leakages that can result from the intra-substitution effects arising from the restrictions on the reserve base of member banks is illustrated in Figure 18-1. They range between zero and 100 percent on transactions that appear very similar to the individual depositors and banks involved but that have very different economic implications.

Moneyflows Process

The complexity of the moneyflows process makes it desirable to use a formal descriptive device for tracing the paths that have significantly different economic and financial implications. Six categories (listed below in three groups) provide a comprehensive classification of the potential uses of income and serve as the starting point for tracing the flow of funds through financial markets and through the expenditure and distribution process into income (see Figure 18-2).

INCREASES IN MONEY BALANCES (H).   The decision to add to money balances, in the form of currency or of demand deposits at banks that are part of the controlled system, is of particular importance because it represents the principal leakage from the moneyflows process. Such decisions disturb the self-financing equilibrium that is implicit in the normal process of spending and saving. Keynes recognized the importance of these decisions with his concept of liquidity preferences. His discussion of the motives for holding money balances still serves as the standard description of the problem.

INTERNAL FINANCING DECISIONS.   Consumption decisions (C) and decisions to invest with internal funds (I) escape from some of the pressures of changing conditions in the money and capital markets. The detailed paths of such funds after the initial expenditure are complex, but it will be assumed that they move back into the income stream as wages, dividends, etc., without systematic leakages. Government expenditures of funds received from taxes will be treated as part of consumption for this discussion.

FIGURE 18-1
LEAKAGES AT MEMBER BANKS ARISING FROM INTRA-BANK SUBSTITUTION EFFECTS

Transaction	Moneyflows	Statement of Banking System		
A. Requirements equal ($d = s : d = 0.2$, $s = 0.2$)				
1) Deposit of $100 check in savings account	$\Delta S = +100$	1) Req. R.	+20	+100 S (1
		1) Ex. R.	+80	
2) Check is cleared		2) Req. R.	−20	−100 D (2
		2) Ex. R.	−80	
		Net: Req. R.	0	
		Ex. R.	0	
3) New loans with excess reserves (Ex/d)	$\Delta L = 0$	3) L	0	0 (3
		Total	0	0
4) Leakage	$\boxed{\Delta S - \Delta L = 100}$			
5) Change in money supply (M_1)	$= -100$			

B. Requirements on demand accounts greater than on savings accounts
$(d > s : d = 0.2, s = 0.05)$

1) Deposit of $100 check in savings account	$\Delta S = +100$	1) Req. R.	+ 5	+100 S (1
		1) Ex. R.	+95	
2) Check is cleared		2) Req. R.	− 20	−100 D (2
		2) Ex. R.	−80	
		Net: Req.	− 15	
		Ex.	+15	
3) New loans with excess reserves (Ex/d)	$\Delta L = +75$	3) L	+75	+ 75 D (3
		Total	+75	+ 75

4) Leakage $\boxed{\Delta S - \Delta L = 25}$

5) Change in money supply (M_1) $= -25$

C. No reserve requirements on savings accounts $(d = 0.2, s = 0)$

1) Deposit of $100 check in savings account	$\Delta S = +100$	1) Req. R.	0	+100 S (1
		1) Ex. R.	+100	
2) Check is cleared		2) Req. R.	− 20	−100 D (1
		2) Ex. R.	− 80	
		Net: Req. R.	− 20	
		Ex. R.	+ 20	
3) New loans with excess reserves (Ex/d)	$\Delta L = +100$	3) L	+100	+100 D (3
		Total	+100	+100

4) Leakage $\boxed{\Delta S - \Delta L = 0}$

5) Change in money supply (M_1) $= 0$

FIGURE 18-2
TRACING MONEYFLOWS

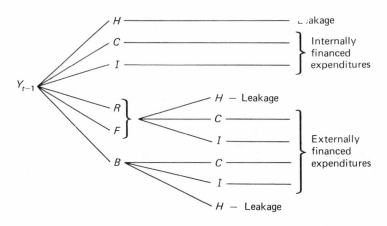

Where:

Y = Income
Y_{t-1} = Income for the previous period
$Y_t = C + I$
$Y_t = Y_{t-1} - H$
C = Consumption and governmental expenditures

Forms of savings

I = real investment
R = repayment of debt
F = financial savings at uncontrolled institution
H = increases in idle money balances (demand deposit or currency) or at banks as excess reserves
B = deposits in time, savings accounts or CDs at banks that are members of the Federal Reserve System

FINANCIAL TRANSACTIONS. It is desirable to separate financial savings that take the form of debt repayments on old loans (R) from savings that represent the creation of new financial assets (F). Repayments on loans provide a steady stream of funds for new loans without altering the structure of the source of funds of the institutions involved, and are not, therefore, subject to the potential leakages that arise from reserve requirements. They are also more stable and subject to somewhat different economic forces.

The funds that move into the institutional savings markets or directly into primary loan markets are subject to a variety of potential leakages depending on the nature of the path. It is essential to distinguish between the movement of savings into banks that are members of the Federal

Reserve System (B) and other financial institutions (F) because the different regulatory and institutional features lead to different moneyflow patterns.

The movement of funds into the financial system introduces a second stage of the moneyflows process. The diposition of those funds depends on the policies of the institutions involved and on regulatory provisions. Most of the funds will be placed into loans and securities that provide the funds for externally financed consumption (C) and investment (I). The leakages that occur within the financial system (H) are, to a large extent, related to reserve requirements that are controlled by regulatory authorities. To the extent that banks or other financial institutions accumulate idle balances (excess reserves), the process may be affected by the interest rate. When the leakage potentials are different in different parts of the system, the overall leakage depends on the share of funds moving through the relevant sectors. Competition between member banks and nonmember sectors will affect the size of the overall leakage. This problem will be discussed in greater detail in Chapter 20.

The Interest Rate and Leakages

Since the major potential source of leakage among businesspeople and consumers arises from the desire to build up cash balances, the leakage problem is closely related to liquidity preference motives. The interest rate plays a critical role in these decisions and can be thought of as the control valve of the moneyflows process. At an equilibrium rate (r^*), the standard Keynesian liquidity preference function (L) tells us that there will be no effort to add to or reduce cash balances (see Figure 18-3A). But when the rate drops below the equilibrium rate, the public will want to increase its cash balance by the amount H. The attempts to add to cash balances will divert the amount H into cash forms of savings and will reduce the income available for expenditures by that amount.

Since income provides the funds for current expenditures, a supply curve based on income in the previous period (Y_{t-1}) provides the starting point for the construction of a complete money supply function. The Y_{t-1} component is known (ex post) and therefore is not affected by the level of current interest rates (see Figure 18-3B). Higher interest rates cannot increase the supply of funds from the given level of income, but rates below the level required to attract the funds into financial markets could result in some leakages from this basic source of supply. One segment of the supply function can thus be obtained by subtracting the amount that is added to cash balances at various rates from the income available for expenditures. The leakage that occurs below the equilibrium rate is therefore merely a transformation of part of the standard liquidity preference

FIGURE 18-3
Leakages from Income and the Supply of Funds

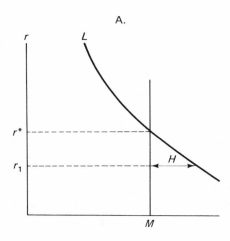

A.

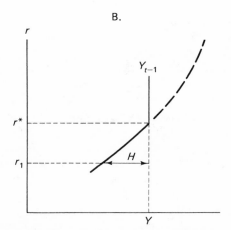

B.

function into a supply function expressed in terms of income.[1] The interest rate can also turn the process around and induce people to reduce previously accumulated balances. Thus idle balances are a potential source of growth. This side of the process will be discussed in the next chapter.

The notation and mathematics for finite Markov chains can be used for specifying and tracing moneyflows as they move from one state to another. This formalized descriptive approach has the advantage of identi-

---

[1]This transformation from a stock to flow measure implies some assumption about the speed of the process. It has been assumed for purposes of illustration that one dollar of idle balances reduces funds available for expenditures by one dollar during the time period under consideration.

fying explicitly the assumptions that are made about the process. However, the following section, which uses a Markov matrix to describe the money-flows process, is not essential for an understanding of the material in the rest of the chapter or in subsequent chapters.

Moneyflows as a Markov Chain

The familiar investment-multiplier principle can also be described as a Markov chain and serves as a simple illustration of the application of the tool. The multiplier principle states that an exogenous increase in invest-ment will have a multiple effect on the level of income:

$$\Delta Y = k\Delta I \tag{7}$$

$$k = \frac{1}{1-c} \tag{8}$$

where:　　　　　ΔY = change in income

ΔI = exogenous change in investment

k = the multiplier

c = marginal propensity to consume

The multiplier process can be traced through time by following the flow of funds from the initial investment transaction. The initial investment adds to income. Part of the new income is consumed and part is saved. The multiplier principle assumes that the part that is saved is not returned to the income stream. The leakages implied by the multiplier principle are the same as those discussed earlier. They have to take the form of individual savings that are not made available for others to use, i.e., of additions to idle money balances. Using an initial investment of $64 million and a marginal propensity to consume of 0.5, the detailed steps in the process can be calculated as shown in Figure 18-4.[2] It can be seen that the change in income induced by the new increment of investment will approach $128 million, or twice the amount of the investment.

The same process is plotted through the early stages as a flow chart in Figure 18-4B. The leakage of funds in the process is clear from the chart. It is also clear that it is assumed that the savings that take place are not available in financial markets for the use of potential borrowers. The multiplier process assumes the presence of financial leakages of the type identified earlier as the accumulation of money balances.

The Markov chain, as illustrated for the investment multiplier in Figure 18-4, can be described more succinctly by a transition matrix that

---

[2]The low value for the marginal propensity to consume was used for numerical convenience to obtain integers for the values in the early stages of the process.

FIGURE 18-4
INVESTMENT MULTIPLIER AS A MARKOV CHAIN

A. Stages of the Process

Change in	1	2	3	4	5	6	7		Total
Investment (I)	64	—	—	—	—	—	—	—	64
Consumption (C)[a]	—	32	16	8	4	2	1	...	64
Income (Y)	64	32	16	8	4	2	1	...	128

[a]Marginal propensity to consume equals 0.5.

B. Path of Process (income state omitted)

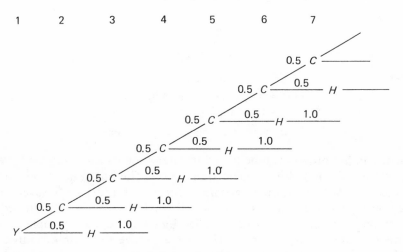

C. Transition Matrix

	H	C	Y
H	1.0	0	0
C	0	0	1.0
Y	0.5	0.5	0

gives the vector that specifies the movement of funds from one state to the next. Each row of the transition matrix gives the disposition of the funds that enter the state indicated by the row name. The sum of all the values in the row must equal 1.0. In this example, the funds can be in any three states after the initial investment: income (Y), consumption (C), or savings (leakage) (H). When the funds appear as income, the marginal propensity to consume (c) tells us that some proportion (in this case 0.5) will move into consumption and the remainder ($1 - c$) will be saved. The row vector for income is thus equal to

$$Y = \begin{array}{ccc} H & C & Y \\ (0.5 & 0.5 & 0) \end{array}.$$

When funds move from income (Y) into savings (H), it is assumed that they are absorbed and cannot move to any other state in the system. The vector for an absorbing state is characterized by the value of 1.0 in the column representing the state itself,

$$H = \begin{array}{ccc} H & C & Y \\ (1.0 & 0 & 0) \end{array}.$$

When funds move from income into consumption (C), they are returned completely to the income stream and to the Y state, and the process continues.

The transition matrix provides a road map for following the funds through the system. If the amount of $64 million is put into the Y row in the matrix, the information shown in Figure 18-4A will be produced as the path of the funds is followed through the matrix. In each round trip, a fraction of the amount is absorbed into savings, and the increments of income are gradually reduced. The mathematics of the process permit the manipulation of the matrix to obtain information on the process at various stages or on the accumulation of funds in the process. These manipulations are useful technical tools, but the transition matrix also plays an important descriptive role in identifying the paths of moneyflows.

We can develop a transition matrix for the moneyflows process that makes it possible to identify the assumptions made about the process and the potential leakages. The initial distribution of income sets the stage for the process. An income vector that provides for the alternatives specified in Figure 18-2 might take the following form:

$$Y = \begin{array}{ccccccc} H & C & I & R & F & B & Y \\ (0 & 0.6 & 0.1 & 0.2 & 0.1 & 0 & 0) \end{array}$$

This vector indicates that 60 percent of income is used directly for consumption (C), 10 percent is invested by internal financing (I), 20 percent is used to repay loans (R), and 10 percent is placed in uncontrolled financial institutions (F).

The process can be traced to the next stage by developing vectors that describe the paths followed in subsequent steps in the expenditure stream. In real life these paths would be quite complicated, and many states might be involved before the funds were eventually returned to income. These potential complexities will be omitted, and it will be assumed that the next step in the case of consumption and real investment is a return to income, so that the vectors for consumption and investment states will have zero values except for a value of 1.0 in the income column:

$$C \text{ and } I = \begin{matrix} H & C & I & R & F & B & Y \\ (0 & 0 & 0 & 0 & 0 & 0 & 1.0) \end{matrix}$$

The placement of funds in financial institutions or markets involves at least one additional step before the funds can be returned to income. The funds have to be made available for loans and investment by the institutions or markets involved, so that the vector for financial institutions or markets will intervene before the funds can be returned to consumption. The matrix at this point can be made as complex as is necessary to trace the steps and stages through financial institutions and markets. Simplified vectors, such as the following, will be used for purposes of discussion:

$$R \text{ and } F = \begin{matrix} H & C & I & R & F & B & Y \\ (0 & 0.2 & 0.8 & 0 & 0 & 0 & 0) \end{matrix}$$

Note that these vectors describe the portfolio decisions of financial intermediaries, where 80 percent of new funds are put into loans that result in investment expenditures, and 20 percent are put into consumer loans.

These vectors, together with those for the two absorbing states, are combined into a matrix. Since the financial intermediation paths involve an additional step, a problem arises in arranging the matrix so that the timing of all of the flows is coordinated. This is achieved in the matrix in Figure 18-5 by sending the direct consumption and investment expenditures (C_p and I_p) through a planning vector that merely serves to coordinate these one-stage decisions with the two-stage decisions involved in financial intermediation.

FIGURE 18-5
MONEYFLOWS MATRIX

	H	C_p	I_p	C	I	R	F	B	Y
H	1.0	0	0	0	0	0	0	0	0
C_p	0	0	0	1.0	0	0	0	0	0
I_p	0	0	0	0	1.0	0	0	0	0
C	0	0	0	0	0	0	0	0	1.0
I	0	0	0	0	0	0	0	0	1.0
R	0	0	0	0.2	0.8	0	0	0	0
F	0*	0	0	0.2	0.8	0	0	0	0
B	0.2*	0	0	0.1	0.7	0	0	0	0
Y	0*	0.6	0.1	0	0	0.2	0.1*	0*	0

Leakages will occur whenever the values in the absorbing state column (H) are greater than zero and when funds are moving through the rows in which those values appear. The critical cells in the sample matrix in Figure 18-5 are marked with an asterisk (*). Three different types of paths that can result in leakages can be identified. The values in those cells will determine the importance of the leakage.

1) *Liquidity preference decisions.* Some leakage appears when anyone decides to save some of his income by adding to money balances (either demand deposits at controlled banks or currency). This decision would be reflected in the matrix by a value greater than zero in the (Y, H) cell. This value will be a function of the interest rate and other factors that affect the desire to hold money balances.

2) *Nonbank financial savings.* A number of possibilities for some leakage appear in the nonbank financial paths. The most likely occurs when funds are placed in an institution subject to reserve requirements that involve the accumulation of demand deposit or currency balances. Voluntary additions to money balances might also result in leakages, but the existence of good money substitutes for portfolio purposes reduces the likelihood of leakages of this type. Delays in the income moneyflows might develop from active trading in secondary markets and the money balances required for purely trading purposes. All of these developments could lead to positive values in the (F, H) cell, but the most likely would seem to be the reserve requirements. The importance of these developments depends on the values in (Y, F) cell.

3) *Deposits in time or savings accounts of member banks.* Decisions to save by depositing funds in savings accounts or by buying certificates of deposit of banks that are members of the Federal Reserve System can result in leakages. The amount of the leakage is determined by the intra-bank substitution effects arising from the controls on the reserves available to member banks. The values in the (B, H) cell reflect the differentials in reserve requirements between different types of deposits. The value of 0.2 is consistent with a reserve requirement of 3 percent on savings accounts and 15 percent on demand accounts. The overall size of the leakage in this path also depends on the share of income moving into bank savings (Y, B), and, therefore, upon regulations and market conditions influencing the distribution of savings between member banks and other financial alternatives. Any additions to excess reserves would also appear in the (B, H) cell. These values will be a function of the interest rate and other factors influencing bank excess reserve positions.

The level of the interest rate affects the matrix values in many ways: it affects the decision to hold cash balances (Y, H), the decision to hold excess reserves (F, H) and (B, H), and borrowing or investment decisions

(Y, I_p) and (F, I). Government regulations or market conditions that affect the nature and path of the savings decision will affect the potential for leakage, and particularly the choice between member banks and other financial alternatives (Y, F) and (Y, B). Government regulations will specifically affect the values of the matrix that depend on the nature of reserve requirements (F, H) and (B, H).

Since the moneyflows matrix is limited to tracing the inputs into the process, the most optimistic result would be the stable self-financing of expenditures with no leakages from the income stream. Sources of funds for growth and expansion have to be introduced as exogenous elements (see Chapter 19). The values used in the sample matrix (Figure 18-5) provide for a stable nominal level of income by assuming that there are no motives for increasing money balances (values in H column are zero) and that no funds move into bank savings accounts $((Y, B) = 0)$. Any changes in these assumptions would imply a steady uninterrupted decline in the level of income. This obviously unrealistic result merely indicates that this description looks at only one side of the process. A complete view requires an examination of the potential sources of new funds that can offset leakages, and an understanding of the factors that may lead to changes in the matrix values that produce the leakages. These questions are discussed in Chapter 19.

Moneyflows and the Creation of Financial Assets

Financial transactions leave their imprint on the accounting records of society. Each new transaction creates a financial asset for the supplier of funds and an obligation for the borrower. The movement of funds from income to expenditures may leave a number of new financial assets in its wake. The purchase of a newly issued bond creates a new asset and obligation. The placement of the same funds in a savings institution creates one set of assets and liabilities at the time of the deposit and a second set when the funds are used to make a loan. Complex moneyflows paths can create several dollars of financial assets for each dollar of savings that moves through the process.

The existing structure of financial assets stands as a record of financial transactions that have taken place in the past. This edifice of wealth depends not only on the total real wealth of the economy but on the way in which expenditures were financed. In socialist countries, where a substantial proportion of the productive resources and housing are built by the government, the ratio of financial assets to real wealth may be quite small. In capitalist countries, where private capital expenditures are financed by borrowing or security issues and where private housing, consumer goods, and perhaps government expenditures are financed by borrowing, the ratio of financial assets to real wealth may be very high. Raymond W. Goldsmith has used what he calls the *financial interrelations ratio* or FIR to measure these differences. This ratio, which is defined as the value of all financial assets divided by the value of all tangible assets, ranged from 0.35 in the U.S.S.R., to 1.16 in the U.S.A., and to 1.64 in Great Britain, in 1967.[3]

The role of financial institutions in this process can be measured by the ratio of their assets to total wealth. This ratio, which also varies widely from country to country, serves as an approximation of the extent to which there is a duplication of assets arising from the multiple creation of financial assets in the moneyflows process.

The structure of financial assets is constantly changing as new loans are made and old ones are repaid. The total grows as long as part of income flows into new financial savings. Financial assets are more likely to grow when income is expanding, but their growth is not necessarily related to the growth of income. Some growth in financial assets is consistent with a stable level of money income and changing patterns of financing expenditures, either additions to the stages of the financing process or a decline in the relative importance of internal financing.

QUESTIONS FOR DISCUSSION

1. Compare the individual and aggregate implications of adding to currency balances, adding to demand balances, and adding to balances in a savings and loan association.

2. What features of the member banking system lead to leakages that do not arise among savings institutions? Would the same leakages be observed at nonmember banks?

3. How do regulations that give savings institutions a comparative advantage in the competition for savings accounts over member banks affect the efficiency of the moneyflows process in terms of minimizing the leakage of funds? How could the efficiency of the two paths be equalized?

4. Develop an example where $100 placed in some type of financial asset (other than money) could lead to an increase of $400 in the aggregate financial assets of the economy.

5. Show how a shift in the importance of internal financing could lead to a growth in financial assets in a stable economy.

[3]Raymond W. Goldsmith, *Financial Structure and Development* (New Haven and London: Yale University Press, 1969), p. 321.

SELECTED REFERENCES

COPELAND, M. A., *A Study of Moneyflows in the United States*. New York: National Bureau of Economic Research, 1952.

DUESENBERRY, JAMES S., "A Process Approach to Flow-of-Fund Analysis," *Flow of Funds Approach to Social Accounting*. New York: National Bureau of Economic Research, 1962, pp. 173–93.

GOLDSMITH, RAYMOND W., *Financial Structure and Development*. New Haven, Conn.: Yale University Press, 1969.

GRAMLEY, LYLE E., and S. B. CHASE, JR., "Time Deposits in Monetary Analysis," *Federal Reserve Bulletin*, 51 (October 1965), 1380–1406.

GURLEY, JOHN G., and EDWARD S. SHAW, *Money in a Theory of Finance*. Washington, D.C.: Brookings Institution, 1960.

Aggregate Demand
and Supply
and the Level of Interest Rates

19

Financial markets and institutions are the servants of real economic needs and desires. Under stable conditions, they play an essential but neutral role in converting savings into loans. Under changing conditions, they play an active and central role in activating the idle money balances that provide the major source of private financial elasticity. Since we are interested primarily in the financing process, we will be concerned with the ability of the financial system to supply the changing needs of the economy and with the role of the interest rate in reconciling demand and supply pressures. We will view the demand function as an exogenous variable that is pushed and pulled by economic forces and events, but that can be taken as given for purposes of our discussion.

Nature of the Aggregate Demand Function

The aggregate demand for funds includes the demand for all of the funds required for investment outlays, for consumption and for governmental expenditures. The amounts needed for these expenditures are expressed in terms of how much will be spent, rather than in terms of the size of money balances needed to support the expenditures. A million-dollar outlay requires control over a million dollars. The million dollars has to be in the form of an acceptable means of payment (either currency or a checking account) at the time of payment, although the average balance for the week in which the expenditure is made could vary from practically zero to the full million dollars.

The dollar demand for transactions purposes is equal to the real demand for goods and services times the prices of those goods and services. It is the sum of all of the individual demand functions of households, corporations, and governmental units for goods and services, regardless of the source of funds. It includes the demand that is internally financed as well as the demand that has to be financed externally.

The interest elasticity of the aggregate demand function reflects the elasticity of the individual functions. It is usually assumed that only investment decisions show any appreciable response to changes in interest rates, so that the elasticity of the aggregate demand function reflects the elasticity of investment demand functions (I_d) and the marginal efficiency of investment. Using this assumption, the aggregate demand function can be expressed as a linear function of the interest rate (r):

$$I_d = I_0 - ir \tag{1}$$

$$Y_d = C + G + I_0 - ir \tag{2}$$

$$Y_d = a - ir \tag{3}$$

where: Y = gross national income

C = consumption

G = governmental expenditures

I_0 = investment at a zero interest rate

$a = C + G + I_0$

i = slope of the investment demand function

Equation (3) measures the demand for funds that will be spent during the period (a flow concept). It corresponds to the *IS* function in the standard *IS–LM* analysis. It can also be expressed in terms of the average money balances (a stock concept) that will be needed to support the desired level of expenditures. If it is assumed that the ratio of money balances required for transactions purposes to income (k_1) is independent of the interest rate, the amount of transactions balances can be expressed as a constant ratio of income ($k_1 = b$), and the demand equation for transactions balances (a stock concept) can be expressed as a simple multiple of the flow equation (3):

$$L_1 = bY_d = b(a - ir) \tag{4}$$

Thus the aggregate demand function can be expressed either in flow terms with income (Y) as the specified variable or in stock terms with the amount of money balance required for transactions purposes as the specified variable (L_1).

Nature of the Aggregate Supply Function

A stable economy is self-financing. Income provides the funds for current expenditures, and the expenditures, in turn, generate income. Funds not used directly for internal financing are placed in financial markets and are used by borrowers. Since, in equilibrium, the level of income is given, any elasticity in the private financing process has to come from changes in holdings of idle money balances. Reductions in money balances can be identified in aggregate statistics either as (1) a decrease in the proportion of money balances required for a given level of income (k), or as (2) an increase in the velocity of circulation of money (V). These two alternatives can be expressed as simple ratios in terms of the money stock (M) and the nominal level of income (Y). The proportion of income held in money balances (k) times the level of income must be equal to the money stock,

$$Yk = M \text{ or } k = \frac{M}{Y} \tag{5}$$

The number of times each dollar of the money stock is used (the velocity of circulation, V) times the money stock must be equal to income,

$$MV = Y \text{ or } V = \frac{Y}{M} \tag{6}$$

If the money stock is controlled, the adjustment of the supply of funds to changing needs must be made by changes in the way the money stock is used, i.e., by changes in V or k. An understanding of the forces that lead to changes in V or k is at the heart of understanding the ability of the financial system to supply funds without changes in the money stock. The problem can be discussed either in terms of the forces that lead to a change in velocity or in terms of forces that lead to a change in money balances. The Keynesian tradition, which focuses on the desire to hold money balances (k), seems to give a better insight into the decision process and will be used in the following discussions.

Demand for money balances

Transactions balances are sometimes called *active balances* because they are in continuous use. The holder of transactions balances regards them as a necessary cost of achieving his expenditure objectives. He is happy to be offered satisfactory alternatives that reduce these costs or let him invest the funds until they are needed. But only a medium of exchange can be used for expenditures. Near-monies are acceptable only as temporary substitutes; they have to be converted into a medium of exchange before the transaction can be completed. The primary concern is the availability of the funds at the time payment is required. The time and energy spent on cash management is evidence of both the essential role of these balances for payment purposes and the desire to keep them as small as possible.

Transactions balances are rolled over as expenditures are made and as income is received. In equilibrium, aggregate transactions balances are self-financing in the same way that current income provides the financing for current expenditures. Every expenditure reduces transactions balances and every income receipt is an addition to cash balances. At any given interest rate the balances required for transactions purposes (L_1) can be expressed as a proportion (k_1) of nominal income (Y):

$$L_1 = k_1 Y \tag{7}$$

The size of k_1 is determined by payment procedures and practices and by the interest rate. Interest rates high enough to offset the transactions costs of short-term investment permit the more efficient use of transactions balances, and the proportion of planned expenditures that must be held in money balances (k_1) is reduced. Since the level of expenditures (Y) is also related to the interest rate, the demand for transactions balances becomes a complex function of the interest rate.[1,2]

$$L_1' = f[k_1(r), Y(r)] \tag{8}$$

If k_1 is assumed to be a linear function of the interest rate with a slope of m_1,

$$k_1 = b - m_1 r \tag{9}$$

the explicit relationship between transactions balances and the interest rate (L_1') can be obtained by substituting equations (3) and (9) in equation (7):

$$L_1' = (b - m_1 r)(a - ir)$$
$$L_1' = ab - bir - am_1 r + im_1 r^2 \tag{10}$$

The demand for money for asset balances (L_2) focuses on the properties of money as an asset, primarily its liquidity and safety. These

---

[1] The symbol L_1' is used in equation (8) to differentiate the concept from the standard transaction demand function L_1, which is assumed to be independent of the interest rate.

[2] It is incorrect to assume that income (Y) can be used as a parameter in a single demand-for-money equation that includes the interest rate as an independent variable when it is known that income is also related to the interest rate. This problem is avoided in multi-equation models that have separate demand equations for investment, but many presentations of the demand for money contain this implicit logical fallacy.

balances are held as part of a financial portfolio. The amounts held will depend on the alternatives available and the rates that can be obtained on those alternatives. The demand for money for asset balances as a function of the interest rate can be expressed in linear form as follows:

$$L_2 = c - m_2 r \tag{11}$$

In practice, asset balances are hard to distinguish from transactions balances. Over a period of time, they can be identified only by the fact that they have not been used. The smallest daily balance in a checking account is an asset balance, since it represents funds that were not used at any time during the period. In practice, the size of asset balances is affected by minimum balance or compensation balance requirements as well as by precautionary and speculative motives.

The combined demand for money balances (L') is the sum of the two types of demands:

$$L' = L_1' + L_2 \tag{12}$$

At the equilibrium level of interest rates (r^*), all money balance demands will be satisfied by the money supply (M) (see Figure 19-1). Those who want to hold money balances for asset purposes will be content with the amounts they hold. Those who are holding transactions balances will be able to meet their planned expenditures. While the economy stays at the equilibrium position, L_2 balances will remain constant and the L_1' balances will be turning over at just the right rate to finance the equilibrium level of income (Y^*).

If we imagine an interest rate that is higher than the equilibrium rate, we can study the adjustments that provide for flexibility in sources of financing when the money stock is constant. At rates higher than equilibrium rate (r_1), the total demand for money balances is smaller than the existing stock of money available to supply these funds. The excess (R), which can be measured from the amount demanded at rate r_1 to the amount of the money stock (M), represents a potential supply of funds from money balances that is the counterpart to the leakage of funds at rates below the equilibrium rate described in the preceeding chapter (see Figure 18-3A).

Holders of asset balances will find substitutes for money balances more attractive at the higher rate and will reduce their money balances by buying money substitutes. Holders of transactions balances will also find their balances larger than they need for two reasons. First, their needs for investment purposes will be less. Second, the higher rates will make possible more efficient cash management. In the first case, investors who would be borrowing at lower interest rates will not be seeking funds for new investments (they will not need transactions balances for expenditures

FIGURE 19-1

EXCESS MONEY BALANCES AT INTEREST RATES ABOVE THE EQUILIBRIUM
RATE

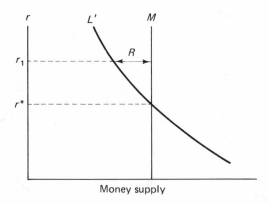

Money supply

they don't make). Those who would have financed marginal investments
with internal funds will have surpluses that they can put into financial
markets. In the second case, those who are maintaining their expenditures
will find that the higher interest rate permits them to place a larger share of
their transactions balances into short-term assets.

The same types of adjustments will be made in response to real
economic pressures that lead to higher rates. An exogenous increase in
demand for investment, consumption, or government expenditures will
increase the demand for transactions balances and will shift the L' function to the right (see Figure 19-2A). Higher rates will bring about the
adjustments described in the preceeding paragraph and will bring about a
new equilibrium at r^{**}.

The nature of the competition for the given money stocks and the
actual adjustment process can be illustrated by showing the L'_1 and L_2
demands for funds separately. In Figure 19-2B, the money stock M is
measured by the length of the base between the two vertical axes; the
demand for money for transactions purposes (L'_1) is measured from left to
right; and the demand for asset balances (L_2) is measured from right to
left. The exogenous shift in demand for real goods and services appears in
the L'_1 function and shifts it to the right. It immediately becomes clear that
any new funds will have to be obtained from idle, or asset, balances (L_2).

The nature of this process can be illustrated by the problems faced
by individuals or businesses as they try to finance new expenditures. If
they don't have idle money balances, they have to obtain the funds by
borrowing or by issuing securities. Sales of newly issued securities will put
downward pressure on security prices and upward pressure on interest

FIGURE 19-2
FINANCING NEW EXPENDITURE DEMANDS

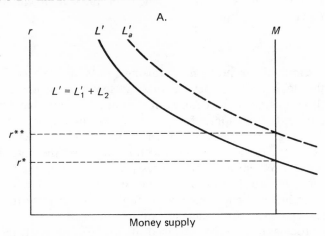

A.

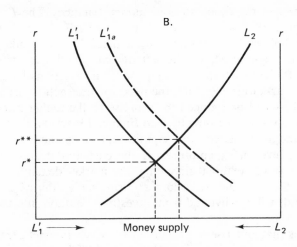

B.

rates. The higher interest rates will induce the holders of asset balances to accept money substitutes and to supply the additional funds. The new equilibrium position will be achieved at r^{**} after the adjustments have taken place. If the new expenditures are to be financed from the sale of seasoned securities accumulated as assets in anticipation of the expenditure, the results will be much the same.

The same types of adjustments will occur if the new funds are borrowed from financial institutions. The problem of raising the funds is merely shifted to the financial institution. It can raise the funds either by selling some of its secondary reserves (the shiftability approach) or by issuing new securities. The funds ultimately have to be obtained from holders of idle balances and by payment of rates that will induce the holders to give up their funds.

Demand becomes supply

Discussions of the problem of raising funds in financial markets in terms of the demand-for-money balances is somewhat awkward because, as Figure 19-2 illustrates, the demand-for-money functions have to be both the demand and the supply functions. When two types of demands compete for a given supply, the loser is the supplier. The problem is complicated in the case of the demand for money by the diversity of the demand motives. When the demand pressures increase on the transactions balance side, the new funds have to be obtained from holders of asset balances by inducing them to supply the funds by persuading them to shift their money balances into money substitutes.

The process has to be reversed if we assume that there is an exogenous change in the desire to hold money balances. The L_2 demand function in Figure 19-3 will shift to the left, and new funds have to be obtained from holders of transactions balances. These funds may be supplied in two ways. First, to the extent that the higher rates make possible more efficient cash management, some transactions balances can be moved into near-monies. Second, the need for transactions balances for investment outlays will be reduced in response to the higher rates. In the first case, funds are supplied directly into financial markets. In the second case, the demand is curtailed, and equilibrium is reached in part by a reduction in the level of expenditures. If the curtailment occurs at firms that would have to use external financing, the market demand is reduced accordingly. If the curtailment occurs at firms with internal sources of funds, those funds will be diverted from investment outlays into the money and capital markets.

Conditions that give rise to exogenous increases in asset demands for money balances are rare. They would be most likely to arise during a financial crisis when portfolio managers lose confidence even in short-term securities. If such a situation did arise, however, it would lead to a contraction of the funds available to meet transactions demand, to a corresponding increase in interest rates and reduction in income expenditures. The opposite situation has been observed in the 1960's and early 1970's, where the improvement of money substitutes and the improvements in the secondary markets for those instruments have lead to a reduction in asset demands for money balances and shift of the L_2 function to the right.

Figures 19-3 and 19-2B illustrate the role of the interest rate in resolving the competitive demands for the money stock. Figure 19-2B is especially important because it illustrates the way in which new expendi-

FIGURE 19-3

FINANCING THE DEMAND FOR ASSET BALANCES

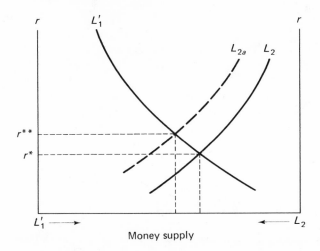

ture demands have to be financed in the absence of a change in the money stock (or when the growth in the money stock does not keep up with the growth in demand). The supply of funds rests in the hands of the holders of idle balances, and the asset demand for money balances becomes the supply function.

Aggregate Supply Function in Flow Terms

The theory of interest can be expressed either in terms of the money supply (stock version), as in the previous section, or in terms of the amounts of funds needed for expenditures during any period of time (flow version). When it is assumed that the ratio of transactions balances to income (k_1) is not a function of the interest rate, the comparison of these two approaches is relatively simple. Under this assumption, the aggregate demand function in stock terms can be expressed as a simple transformation of the flow equation, as indicated by equations (3) and (4) in the first section of this chapter. These two demand functions are shown in Figure 19-4A as the IS function and in 19-4B as the L_1 function. At equilibrium rates, the previous period's income will supply the funds needed for current financing in the flow analysis, and the rollover of transactions balances will supply the funds needed for current transactions in the stock analysis. The elasticity of supply in both cases has to come from changes in the holding of idle balances and, since k_1 is assumed to be constant, from L_2 balances. Rates above the equilibrium rate (r^*) will bring forth a supply of funds as balances are reduced (R in Figure 19-4B). Rates below the

FIGURE 19-4
COMPARISON OF STOCK AND FLOW VERSIONS OF
THE THEORY OF INTEREST

A.

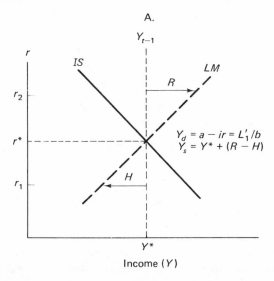

$$Y_d = a - ir = L_1'/b$$
$$Y_s = Y^* + (R - H)$$

Income (Y)

B.

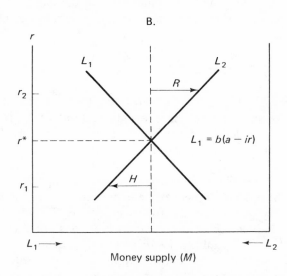

$$L_1 = b(a - ir)$$

Money supply (M)

equilibrium rate will lead to a buildup of money balances (H in Figure 19-4B).

If some assumption is made about the speed of the conversion of these balances, the amounts involved can be converted into demand and supply components in the flow analysis. This conversion on a one-to-one basis is shown in Figure 19-4A. At rates above the equilibrium rate, the amounts available from the reductions in asset balances (R) are available as a new supply to supplement income. The amounts withdrawn for income (H) reduce the funds available from income. The supply function in the flow version can be expressed in terms of the equilibrium level of income (Y^*) and changes in idle money balances:

$$Y_s = Y^* + (R - H) = Y^* - \Delta L_2 \tag{13}$$

The supply function in this form emphasizes the self-financing feature of the economic process where the current level of income $(Y^* = Y_{t-1})$ supplies most of the funds. Idle money balances provide the elasticity for any expansion. The supply curve is a locus of points indicating the equilibrium positions of the demand for money balances. It is a simple transformation of L_2 function. It is also conceptually the same as the *LM* function used in most textbooks on macroeconomics to represent the locus of equilibrium points between interest rates and the demand for money.

Both the standard *LM* function and the supply equation (13) have a serious disadvantage for discussions of current conditions in financial markets. They both assume that the transactions demand for money balances is a constant proportion of income $(k_1 = b)$. Developments in recent years suggest that this assumption is likely to be wrong and that variations in transactions balances may be the most important source of financial flexibility. Theoretical and empirical studies have pointed out the interest elasticity of transactions balances and the reduction of asset balances (L_2) with the availability of good money substitutes.

The relationship between the flow and stock versions of the demand and supply function becomes more complex when the assumption of a constant ratio of transactions balances to income (b) is dropped. The difference between the L_1 version in equation (4) and the L_1' version that provides for the interest elasticity of k_1 in equation (10) measures the reductions in transactions balances that are made possible by higher interest rates. This difference is represented by the shaded area between the two functions in Figure 19-5B.

As rates increase, the more efficient use of money balances for transactions purposes reduces the actual demand for balances associated with the dollar demand for funds-for-payment purposes. This reduction provides a further source of interest elasticity not represented in the supply equation (13). An increase in interest rates will reduce the proportion of money balances required for transactions purposes (k_1) as well as the actual demand for funds. The amount of this cash management effect (CM) is measured by the difference between the two equations representing the demand for transactions balances $(L_1$ and $L_1')$. The amounts made available to finance other expenditures will be equal to the relative changes in these balances (ΔCM) with changes in the interest rate. These amounts

FIGURE 19-5
CASH MANAGEMENT AND THE DEMAND FOR TRANSACTIONS BALANCES

A.

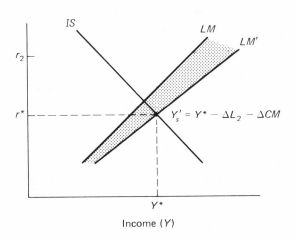

Income (*Y*)

B.

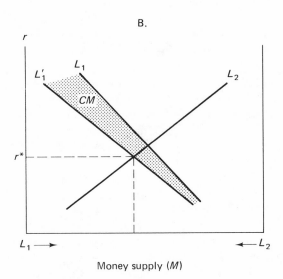

Money supply (*M*)

are plotted in Figure 19-5A as additions to the supply function, which takes the following form

$$Y'_s = Y^* - \Delta L_2 - \Delta CM \qquad (14)$$

The supply equation in this form is of special interest because it identifies the source of funds (other than changes in the money supply) that are available to finance expenditures. It represents the short-run flexibility of the financial system to adapt to variations in demand without changes in the money supply. The interest rate determines the amounts that will be made available in the short-run from idle money balances and from the efficiency of cash management provisions for transactions balances. It identifies the motives of the people who are in a position to make new funds available, and in doing so indicates the types of securities that have to be offered to activate these funds. Most of the money will have to be raised by the issuance of short-term substitutes for money. Cash managers and holders of idle asset balances will be attracted by such instruments.

Equations (13) and (14) can be converted into a variety of forms that relate the variables to money supply (assumed constant) and the demand for money balances by simple algebraic manipulations. These comparisons, which are discussed in the following note, give some insight into the role of the demand for money in the determination of interest rates, but they are not essential for an understanding of the rest of the chapter or other parts of the book. They may be helpful in attempts to reconcile this form of presentation with the *IS–LM* format used in most textbooks on macroeconomics.

Algebraic note: Various forms of the aggregate supply function: Most textbooks in macroeconomics use some version of the *IS–LM* analysis developed by Hicks to present the interaction between the demand and supply of funds and to discuss the determination of the level of interest rates and income.[3] The *IS* function, which represents the demands for funds from the real sector of the economy, appears as equation (3). It may be present in either real or nominal terms.

The *LM* function is usually derived by equating the exogenously controlled money supply ($\overline{M}$) to the demand for money (L). The transactions demand (L_1) and speculative demand (L_2) must necessarily be equal to the money supply, and the demand for money in nominal terms is often stated in the following linear form:

$$\overline{M} = kY - mr \tag{15}$$

With constant values for k and m, the *LM* function is derived as the locus of points of r and Y that satisfies the equality stated in equation (15). In this way, a stock equation for the demand for money (15) is converted into a flow equation, with income and the interest rate as the functional

[3]John R. Hicks, "Mr. Keynes and the 'Classics': A Suggested Interpretation," *Econometrica*, vol. V (1937), reprinted in *Readings in The Theory of Income Distribution* (Philadelphia: The Blakiston Company, 1946).

variables and the stock of money as a parameter. It is written with either Y or r as the dependent variable:

$$r = \frac{-\overline{M}}{m} + \frac{kY}{m} \tag{16}$$

$$Y = \frac{\overline{M}}{k} + \frac{mr}{k} \tag{17}$$

The demand for money is also presented as the sum of the transactions demand (L_1) and speculative demand (L_2), where the total is constrained by the money stock ($\overline{M}$):

$$\overline{M} = L_1 + L_2 \tag{18}$$

When the transactions demand is a constant proportion (b) of Y,

$$L_1 = bY \tag{19}$$

and the speculative demand is a linear function of the interest rate, as shown in equation (11),

$$L_2 = c - m_2 r$$

equations (19) and (11) can be substituted into (18) to obtain

$$\overline{M} = bY + c - m_2 r \tag{20}$$

The terms $bY + c$ are equivalent to the term kY in equation (15) and equation (20) is merely a restatement of equation (15) with the specific separation of the L_1 demand with the constant that relates it to income (b) and the addition of a constant term for the L_2 demand for money. Since the formulation of equation (15) provides only for the interest elasticity of the L_2 demand, m and m_2 are the same in both equations.

If Y^* and r^* are designated as equilibrium positions, equation (20) can be expressed as a difference equation, by subtracting the equilibrium values from the general equation to obtain:

$$0 = b(Y - Y^*) - m_2(r - r^*) \tag{21}$$

Solving for Y,

$$Y = Y^* + \frac{m_2(r - r^*)}{b} \tag{22}$$

The difference form of the speculative demand for money (11) can be obtained in a similar way

$$L_2 - L_2^* = -m_2(r - r^*)$$

or

$$\Delta L_2 = -m_2(r - r^*) \tag{23}$$

Equation (23) can be substituted into (22) to obtain

$$Y = Y^* - \frac{\Delta L_2}{b} \tag{24}$$

Equation (24) should be compared with the supply equation (13) derived earlier in the chapter. It is identical except for the appearance of b in equation (24). The constant b transforms the flow term Y into a stock measure. It was assumed in the derivation of equation (13) that new funds would be spent only once during the measurement period, or that b was equal to one. When b is set equal to one, equations (13) and (24) are identical and equivalent to the standard demand for money function (17). The demand for money function with the money stock as a parameter (17) looks to the turnover of transactions balances to provide the funds to meet current demand and to the elasticity of speculative balances to meet any new demand. In the difference equation form (24), the equilibrium level of income provides for its own financing, and the changes in idle (asset) balances provide the new funds in response to changes in the interest rate $(r - r^*)$.

If it is assumed that the system reaches an equilibrium position during a single period of time, equation (22) can be expressed in time periods where t is the current period and $t-1$ is the preceeding period:

$$Y_t = Y_{t-1} - \Delta L_2 \tag{25}$$

In a similar way, equation (14) can be derived as an extension of the demand-for-money functions to include the interest elasticity of transactions balances. The L_1 function is expressed in equation (10) as a complex function of the interest rate:

$$L_1' = bY - am_1 r + im_1 r^2$$

Equation (10) and the equation for L_2 balances (11) can be substituted into (18) to obtain

$$\overline{M} = b(a - ir) - am_1 r + im_1 r^2 + c - m_2 r \tag{26}$$

Equation (26) can then be converted into the following difference equation form:

$$Y_s' = Y^* - \Delta L_2/b - \Delta CM/b \tag{27}$$

Equations (14) and (27) are identical when b is assumed to be 1. Equation (27) expresses the *LM* function in a way that provides for the interest elasticity of the demand for L_1 balances. This form of the *LM* function will be designated as *LM'* in the rest of this discussion. The demand for money expressed in flow form as in equation (27) is consistent with the equations used in the discussion of the competition for existing money balances in stock form (see Figure 19-2).

The Theory of Interest

The interest rate is the link between the demand for funds for investment outlays and for consumer and governmental expenditures as recorded in the aggregate demand function and, in Keynes' words, the "reward for parting with liquidity" as recorded in the aggregate supply function.[4] Any economic or political force or event that leads to an increase in the transactions demand for funds will be reflected in a shift of the aggregate demand function (*IS*) to the right (see Figure 19-6). The interest rate plays the central role in inducing holders of idle balances to give up the liquidity of those balances and make them available to meet new demands. The ability of the private sectors of the financial system to accommodate these needs is indicated by the elasticity of the aggregate supply function (*LM'*).

The most dynamic and volatile forces leading to changes in the level of interest rates originate with changes in the demand for real goods and services. Any economic, social, or political event that alters consumption, investment, or government outlays shifts the aggregate demand function (see equation (2)). All sectors of the economy can contribute to these changes. Cyclical variations in investment plans and outlays are reflected in the demand for funds in capital markets. The highly volatile short-run changes in inventories are reflected in the short-term markets. Variations in consumer demands for houses, automobiles, and other durables and changes in governmental policies, plans, and financing techniques are reflected in many different markets. Inflationary fears and expectations, which have been recognized as a dominate force in the determination of interest rates, are also recorded as shifts in the demand function. Businesspeople, consumers, and speculators adjust their investment and

[4]J. M. Keynes, *The General Theory of Employment, Interest, and Money* (New York: Harcourt, Brace and Co., 1935), p. 167.

FIGURE 19-6
THEORY OF INTEREST

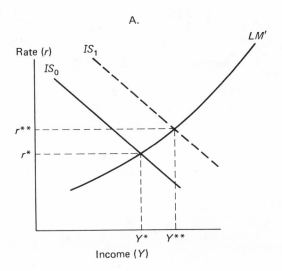

A.

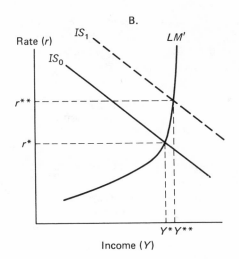

B.

spending plans to their price expectations. These adjustments are part of their overall dollar transactions demands for funds.

Spending plans that require external financing have an obvious impact on the demand function. The effects of internally financed plans are less obvious, but the results are much the same. In either event, the increased spending has to be financed. The spender who uses his own savings by liquidating money substitutes or by selling other securities puts upward pressure on interest rates, just as does the borrower who issues new securities. Demand pressures may appear anywhere in the vast complex of financial markets or in any region or geographic area, but new supplies can be obtained only from cash managers or other holders of idle balances. These suppliers are only interested in very good money substitutes —money market instruments or highly liquid deposit accounts. The cutting edge of the demand function, therefore, has to be applied in the money market and at the short-end of the maturity spectrum. The demand pressures that appear in other markets have to be shifted by banks and other financial institutions into those markets. Financial institutions perform this function by selling their own money market securities (the shiftability approach) or by issuing and selling new securities (the liability management approach).

As long as there is some elasticity in both the demand and supply functions, the new equilibrium will be reached by some reduction in holdings of money balances in response to the higher rates, and by some curtailment in the loan demand as a result of the higher rate required to raise the funds. The relative changes in income and in interest rates brought about by the shift in the demand function will depend on the relative elasticities of the two functions. If the aggregate supply function is highly inelastic, the higher interest rates brought about by attempts of borrowers to raise the funds will not add much to the aggregate supply of funds (see Figure 19-6B). Under these conditions, the borrowers face an unpleasant struggle for funds where the funds are allocated to the borrower willing or able to pay the highest rate. Such conditions exist during periods of short-run financial crisis when interest rates are very high and the demand for new funds exceeds the amounts being supplied by the monetary authorities.

In the standard textbook version of the theory of interest, shifts in the supply function (LM'), in the short-run, are traced primarily to changes in the money supply (see equation (16)). In this version, the story of the dynamics of the supply function rests largely on the actions of the monetary authorities. In practice, a number of complications have to be introduced to describe the actual behavior of the supply function: (1) shifts in the channels of financial intermediation can affect the elasticity of the aggregate supply function and can result in short-run changes in the function (see Chapter 20); (2) changes in the money supply as variously defined may not always lead to shifts in the supply function (see Chapter 21); (3) nonprice considerations may enter into the determination of both the aggregate demand and supply functions that can lead to both short- and long-run shifts in the functions and even to interaction between the two functions (see Chapter 22). A realistic view of either the short-term or long-term supply function requires a close look at the structure of the financial system and the adjustments being made to current conditions.

QUESTIONS FOR DISCUSSION

1. Give illustrations of specific decisions by individual or corporate treasurers that would lead to an increase in the aggregate supply of funds if they were not offset by other actions elsewhere in the economy.
2. Why is the demand for transactions balances related to the level of interest rates?
3. How can the demand for money appear as a supply function?
4. Compare the effect of an exogenous increase in demand on the level of interest rates in the stock version of interest rate theory with the effects of the same increase in the flow version. Which version provides the most useful information?
5. Assume that the exogenous increase in demand in Question 4 is exactly matched by an increase in the money supply (M). Illustrate the new equilibrium situation in both versions of interest rate theory.
6. Using the stock approach to the determination of the interest rates (Figure 19-2), show the effects of an exogenous increase in demand on the level of interest rates when the new investment is being paid for by the liquidation of bank CDs that have been accumulated for that purpose.

SELECTED REFERENCES

ACKLEY, GARDNER, "Liquidity Preference and Loanable Funds Theories of Interest: Comment," *American Economic Review*, 47 (September 1957), 662–73.

CONARD, JOSEPH W., *Introduction to the Theory of Interest*. Berkeley: University of California Press, 1959.

GURLEY, JOHN G., "Liquidity and Financial Institutions in the Postwar Period," *Employment, Growth and Price Levels*. Joint Economic Committee, U.S. Congress, Washington, D.C.: U.S. Government Printing Office, 1960.

LAIDLER, DAVID E. W., *The Demand for Money: Theories and Evidence*. Scranton, Pennsylvania: International Textbook Company, 1969.

LATANÉ, HENRY A., "Income Velocity and Interest Rates: A Pragmatic Approach," *Review of Economics and Statistics*, 42 (November 1960), 445–49.

LERNER, A. P., "Alternative Formulations of the Theory of Interest," *The New Economics* (S. Harris, ed.). New York: Alfred A. Knopf, 1950.

SELDEN, RICHARD T., *The Postwar Rise in the Velocity of Money—A Sectoral Analysis*. New York: National Bureau of Economic Research, 1962.

TEIGEN, R., "Demand and Supply Function for Money in the United States," *Econometrica*, Vol. 32, No. 4 (October 1964), 476–509.

TSIANG, S. C., "Liquidity Preference and Loanable Funds Theories, Multiplier and Velocity Analyses: A Synthesis," *American Economic Review*, 46 (September 1956) 539–64.

Financial Intermediation
and
the Aggregate Supply of Funds

20

Most borrowers do not have direct access to the savings and money markets. If they need funds, they have to turn to banks and other financial institutions for help. These institutions, if they do not have funds, must either turn down the request or act as the borrower's representative in obtaining the funds. They can raise the funds by selling securities from their own portfolios (the shiftability approach) or they can issue and sell their own obligations (the liability management approach). In either event, they have to deal with the same set of suppliers and they face the aggregate supply function (LM') described in Chapter 19. The impact of various approaches to the market should be identical when the quality and terms of the securities used are the same, but the supply of loanable funds developed by different approaches will depend on the nature of the regulatory structure under which the institutions are operating.

In practice, two distinct supply functions have to be identified. The first is the LM' or market supply function already specified. The other is the loan supply function (LM'_X) which measures the amount that will be supplied to eventual borrowers at different rates. Three different approaches to raising funds will lead to differences in the spread between the two functions. In the first case, when funds are raised directly by the borrower, the two functions will differ only by the amount of the transactions costs. In the second case, when the funds are raised by financial institutions, the two functions will differ by the cost of intermediation and by the amount of reserve requirements that prevent the complete conversion of the funds raised into loans. In the third case, when the funds are raised by banks that are restricted by a controlled reserve base, the intra-bank substitution effect may also reduce the aggregate loan funds that can be generated from any given amount of new funds raised in the market. The implications of these three approaches will be examined separately. For simplicity, it will be assumed that transactions costs and the costs of intermediation are the same in all three approaches and can be omitted from the discussion.

Direct Access to the Money Markets

Large corporations and governmental units have direct access to the savings and money markets. They can sell their securities and use (or lend) the funds at a rate that covers the transactions costs of issuing the securities. They can go directly to the best potential sources for new funds by selling securities that are good substitutes for money balances. Since it is assumed that the money supply is constant, the issuers of new securities will have to pay the rates indicated by the LM' function to obtain the funds they need (ΔF) (see Figure 20-1). The implications of this approach to financing can be read directly from the LM' function (transactions costs, assumed to be zero). Assuming that an exogenous increase in

FIGURE 20-1

LOAN SUPPLY FUNCTIONS ASSOCIATED WITH DIFFERENT APPROACHES
TO MONEY MARKETS

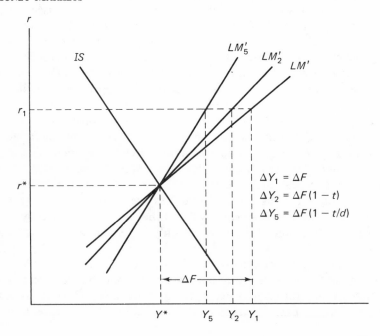

demand occurs that will support the change, income will increase to Y_1, and the interest will increase to a new equilibrium position at r_1. The full amount of funds raised will be reflected in an expansion of expenditures:

$$\Delta Y_1 = \Delta F \tag{1}$$

These funds will be raised only if new demands, as indicated by a shift in the *IS* function, make it desirable to do so.

The efficiency of this approach (e_1) can be measured in terms of the changes in income that accompany the changes in interest rates:

$$e_1 = \frac{\Delta Y_1}{\Delta r_1} \tag{2}$$

The same analysis applies to the attempts of banks or other financial institutions to raise new funds by the shiftability approach. They can sell securities that are good substitutes for money balances. If the quality is the same as in the previous case, they will have to pay the same rate to raise the same amount (ΔF). They will be able to convert the entire amount into loans (transactions costs assumed to be zero), and their efforts will result in the same change in the level of expenditures and income.

Liability Management Approach

If banks and other financial institutions are not willing to sell their portfolio asset to raise funds for loans, they may try to issue their own securities or raise the interest rate on their deposit accounts. These efforts are directed at the same sources of supply and, to the extent that the quality and terms of the securities are similar to those in the first case, they will be able to raise the same amount (ΔF) at the same rate (Δr_1) (see Figure 20-1). But if the institution raising the funds is subject to a reserve requirement (t), only the residual amount after the deduction of required reserves can be converted into loans and into expenditures:

$$\Delta Y_2 = \Delta F (1 - t) \tag{3}$$

The relative efficiency of this approach in financing new expenditures will be

$$e_2 = \frac{\Delta Y_2}{\Delta r_1} < e_1 \tag{4}$$

A loan supply function LM_2' that describes this approach can be derived that will be steeper than the market supply function:

$$Y_{s_2} = Y^* - (\Delta L_2 + \Delta CM)(1-t) \tag{5}$$

Intra-Bank Substitution Effects

Funds raised by banks that are subject to a limitation on the total reserve base (members of the Federal Reserve System) are further reduced by the intra-bank substitution effect. The theoretical size of the substitution effect can be calculated if it is assumed that the reserve base is held constant, but in practice it is hidden by the complexities of the reserve clearing and adjustment process.

When funds are raised by a bank that is a member of the Federal Reserve System, the new loans funds (ΔY_3) available at the individual bank can be measured by equation (3). But when there are no excess reserves in the system, the addition of the new deposits to the member bank total will result in a reserve deficiency somewhere else within the system. An aggregate expansion can take place only if the required reserve ratio (d) on the accounts that are replaced (ΔD) is larger than the required ratio on the new funds (t). The sum of the two reserve adjustments must be equal,

$$t\Delta F = d\Delta D \tag{6}$$

Some bank or banks within the Federal Reserve System will face a loss of reserves and must adjust their loans and investments accordingly. The resultant contraction of the loan supply (ΔY_4) will be

$$\Delta Y_4 = \Delta D (1-d) \tag{7}$$

The contraction can be expressed in terms of the amount of original funds raised (ΔF) by substituting from (6) to obtain

$$\Delta Y_4 = \frac{t\Delta F(1-d)}{d} \tag{8}$$

The net supply of loanable funds (ΔY_5) resulting from the initial attempts to raise funds will be

$$\Delta Y_5 = \Delta Y_3 - \Delta Y_4 = \Delta F(1-t) - \frac{t\Delta F(1-d)}{d}$$

or

$$\Delta Y_5 = \Delta F(1-t/d) \tag{9}$$

The relative efficiency of this approach will be

$$e_3 = \frac{\Delta Y_5}{\Delta r_1} < e_2 < e_1 \tag{10}$$

The associated loan supply function (LM_5') will also be steeper than the market supply function (see Figure 20-1):

$$Y_{s5} = Y^* - (\Delta L_2 + \Delta CM)(1 - t/d) \tag{11}$$

The size of the leakage resulting from the intra-member-bank substitution effect depends on the ratios of the reserve requirements involved in the substitution. It would be 18.2 percent if the new funds were raised in a form that carried a 3 percent reserve requirement and the substitution occurred from accounts with a 16.5 percent requirement. It would be 80 percent if the new funds carried a reserve requirement of 6 percent and the replaced funds carried a requirement of 7.5 percent. The limiting case of 100 percent leakage occurs when funds raised by one member bank result in a direct reduction of funds of the same type at another member bank.

When a group of banks is constrained in aggregate by a reserve base that can be controlled, the aggregate ability of the banks in the controlled group is not the simple sum of their individual effects, as it could be for noncontrolled institutions. The sum of the individual bank attempts must be reduced by the intra-bank substitution effects that are hidden and not apparent to the banks themselves or to outside observers that use the individual bank actions as an analogy for the aggregate effect.

Disintermediation and the Aggregate Supply of Loan Funds

The actual loan supply function (LM_X') will depend on the mix of approaches that are used to raise the new funds. As long as the mix remains stable, the LM_X' function will remain stable. Changes in the composition of the mix can shift the loan supply function even when the market supply function (LM') is stable. Shifts from less efficient to more efficient approaches will ease the market. Shifts from more efficient to less efficient approaches will tighten the market. Normally, we would expect financing to move toward the most efficient approaches, but regulations or market conditions that influence the ability of various institutions to compete for funds will affect the financing mix.

Savings institutions and banks may be limited in their ability to compete for new funds by legal restrictions on the rate they can pay or by fixed-interest income contracts. When open market rates go above their competitive limits, they find it more difficult to raise new funds and may face net losses of funds or disintermediation.

The implications of disintermediation can be illustrated by assuming that the market supply function (LM') is completely inelastic, i.e., no new funds can be obtained from idle money balances of any type. In this case, any new funds for growth would have to come from an expansion of the money supply, which we have assumed to be held constant for purposes of the discussion in this chapter. These severe assumptions mean that no new funds in aggregate could be obtained by higher interest rates. Successful financing attempts under these circumstances would involve competitive shifts of funds from one set of institutions and markets to another. For example, a successful attempt by the U.S. Treasury to sell bills might be accompanied by a run-off of commercial paper. Higher rates would not permit any expansion in the level of expenditures, but might change the pattern of expenditures.

The assumption of complete inelasticity of the LM' function may seem unrealistic, but something close to this situation develops in short-run financial crises when the demand for new funds greatly exceeds the growth in the money supply. At very high rates, there will be very little potential for improving cash management techniques, and the idle balances held for other purposes will have already been placed into money substitutes. The following discussion is more realistic if it is assumed that the changes in demand that produce pressure for high rates are relative to the growth of the money supply, than if it is assumed that the money supply is constant.

As long as competition for new funds occurs among borrowers who are equally efficient in raising funds, shifts in loan demand (IS to IS') will induce severely higher rates and shifts from one borrower to another with no net effects on the supply of funds or the level of income. The new equilibrium will be reached at r, Y^* (see Figure 20-2). If however, the new funds are raised by the U.S. Treasury by direct marketing techniques, and the funds are obtained from deposits in savings institutions that must hold reserves on those deposits, some slight increase in the funds available will be made possible by the release of the required reserves. The new funds raised in aggregate will be equal to only the fraction of the total funds raised by the Treasury (ΔS) that represented required reserves (t):

$$\Delta Y_1 = \Delta S - \Delta S (1 - t) = t \Delta S \tag{12}$$

The loan supply function associated with this type of disintermediation will be

$$Y_{s1} = Y^* + t \Delta S \tag{13}$$

If the disintermediation results in the loss of savings accounts by banks that are members of the Federal Reserve System, the results are more complicated. The loss of funds at member banks releases excess

FIGURE 20-2
DISINTERMEDIATION WITH AN INELASTIC MARKET SUPPLY FUNCTION

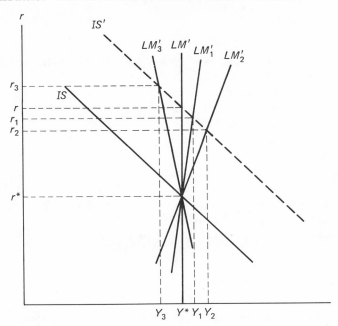

reserves that can be used by the Federal Reserve System as a whole to rebuild deposits so that the net addition to the aggregate funds available will include the bank expansion possible on the basis of the excess reserves,

$$\Delta Y_2 = \Delta S - \Delta S (1 - t/d) = \frac{t \Delta S}{d} \tag{14}$$

where d is the reserve ratio on deposits that are involved in the expansion.

Both of these illustrations indicate that disintermediation under tight money conditions serves to ease the market slightly. This theoretical result is not intuitively obvious, and the bankers affected by the disintermediation may be able to make a plausible case for changes in regulations that permit them to compete more effectively. If such regulatory changes are effective enough to make it possible for less efficient approaches to induce substitutions from more efficient approaches, the supply functions discussed in the previous section come into play. The success of one of the less efficient approaches can tighten rather than ease the market. If, for example, member banks are successful in selling CDs at the expense of savings accounts at savings institutions, the intra-bank substitution effect would lead to a net contraction of the funds available. Where the reserve requirements are the same at savings institutions (t) and on CDs at member banks, the aggregate amount of new funds (ΔY_3) will be

$$\Delta Y_3 = \Delta S (1 - t/d) - \Delta S (1 - t)$$

$$= t\Delta S - \frac{t\Delta S}{d} \tag{15}$$

The second term of equation (15) will always be larger than the first term since the reserve ratio d is always less than 1.

Policies that make it possible for member banks to attract savings from other types of institutions during periods of tight money can theoretically produce a backward sloping loan supply function so that the higher rates are self-defeating in aggregate. Since these effects arise from the intra-member-bank substitution effects, they are not apparent to the institutions involved and may be difficult to disentangle from the complex day-to-day flow of funds. They would occur in this extreme form only during periods of very tight money when the monetary authorities are under pressure to expand the money supply. Changes in the money supply both offset and obscure the effects of this type of substitution.

QUESTIONS FOR DISCUSSION

1. Compare the advantages and disadvantages of the shiftability approach to raising funds to meet new loan demands for individual member banks. Do the advantages and disadvantages apply in the same way for all member banks taken as a whole?

2. During tight money periods, which approach to raising new funds will produce the most funds with the smallest increase in interest rates? What type of regulatory actions would encourage financing by the most efficient path?

3. What techniques have been used by member banks to give their loan customers the advantages of the most efficient approach to raising funds during tight money periods?

4. Outline the arguments that you would make to a president of one of the big New York member banks in an attempt to persuade him that it would be a disservice to the economy for his bank to sell CDs during a very tight money period.

5. Give some examples of borrowers who have been excluded from the most efficient approaches to raising money during periods of tight money but who have been able indirectly to get the benefits of those approaches.

6. Compare the pattern of short-term interest rate changes you would expect during a period of shifting money market conditions, when member banks have a competitive advantage relative to savings institutions, with a situation where savings institutions have a competitive advantage. How would those competitive advantages be maintained?

SELECTED REFERENCES

DEWALD, W. G., "Free Reserves, Total Reserves, and Monetary Controls," *Journal of Political Economy*, 71 (April 1963) 141–53.

GRAMLEY, L. E., and S. B. CHASE, JR., "Time Deposits in Monetary Analysis," *Federal Reserve Bulletin*, 51 (October 1965) 1380–1406.

MEIGS, A. J., *Free Reserves and the Money Supply*. Chicago: University of Chicago Press, 1962.

SMITH, WARREN L., "Time Deposits, Free Reserves, and Monetary Policy," *Issues in Banking and Monetary Analysis*, eds., Pontecarvo, Shay, and Hart. New York: Holt, Rinehart and Winston, Inc., 1967.

Monetary Aggregates
in
the Financing Process

21

The "new view" of monetary economics, which has tended to blur the sharp traditional distinctions between money and other assets, has stimulated interest in the possibility that some broad monetary aggregate can be effectively used for purposes of economic stabilization. A great deal of empirical work has been done in the search for the aggregate with the most predictable relationship with nominal income.[1] Figure 21-1 defines six of the most commonly suggested measures. They range from M_1, the traditional money supply concept, to M_6, which includes nearly all short-term liquid assets. These assets are all created as part of the borrowing–lending process.

Creation of Monetary Aggregates

Monetary aggregates are created by the process of external financing. Whenever funds are raised directly or through financial intermediaries by issuing short-term instruments acceptable as money substitutes, monetary aggregates are created. The creation process is illustrated daily by success-ful sales of new issues of commercial paper or Treasury bills and by successful attempts by banks and other financial institutions to raise funds by liability management techniques. However, the success of individual corporations or financial institutions in raising funds may not result in a net growth of the monetary aggregates for the economy as a whole. Most

[1]For example, see Leonall C. Anderson, "Selection of a Monetary Aggregate for Economic Stabilization," *Review, Federal Reserve Bank of St. Louis* (October 1975), pp. 9–15.

FIGURE 21-1
MONETARY AGGREGATES

M_1	Demand deposits and currency held by the nonbank public.
M_2	M_1 plus time and savings deposits of commercial banks less large, negotiable certificates of deposit.
M_3	M_2 plus deposits at mutual savings banks and shares of savings and loan associations and credit unions.
M_4	M_2 plus large, negotiable certificates of deposit.
M_5	M_3 plus large, negotiable certificates of deposit.
M_6	Total liquid assets defined as M_5 plus commercial paper, savings bonds, and short-term U.S. government securities.

of the individual attempts to raise funds are accompanied by the run-off of other short-term securities that provide the funds. At an equilibrium level of income expenditures, there would be no net addition to monetary aggregates, or, in fact, other forms of debt.[2] The current flow of income provides the funds for new expenditures, and the repayments on existing financial obligations supply the funds for new obligations.

The net creation of monetary aggregates occurs when the demand for loan funds for consumption or investment is in excess of the supply of funds at the existing market rates. Borrowers need money for transactions and only M_1 balances can be used for this purpose. These funds have to be obtained from the holders of idle M_1 balances, either from cash managers who can economize on their needs or from portfolio managers with cash balances. The best technique for inducing the holders of these balances to relinquish them is to raise the rates paid on good substitutes for M_1 money balances. They may be willing to buy instruments that give them almost as much liquidity, as much safety, and some return (or a higher return when there is an explicit or implicit return on M_1 balances). Since the equilibrium implies that these holders of M_1 balances are satisfied with their position at current rates, an increase in demand financed by the net expansion of monetary aggregates other than M_1 requires an increase in the interest rate. The new equilibrium is reached by movement along the LM' function in response to the new demand for funds that is recorded as a shift in the IS function to IS_a in Figure 21-2.

This technique of financing new loan demand resembles the expansion of the M_1 money stock in that the stock of monetary aggregates has

[2]Shifts can occur in the composition and structure of financing, leading to increases or decreases in some of the components of the total. These increases or decreases are offset by changes in other components and do not reflect any changes in the aggregate amount of financing but may appear as changes in any specific component. For example, a net increase in monetary aggregates could reflect an offsetting reduction in long-term financing.

FIGURE 21-2

TWO CASES OF THE CREATION OF MONETARY AGGREGATES

A. Market-Induced Expansion of Monetary Aggregates

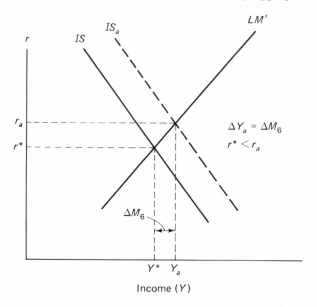

B. Parametric Expansion of Monetary Aggregates

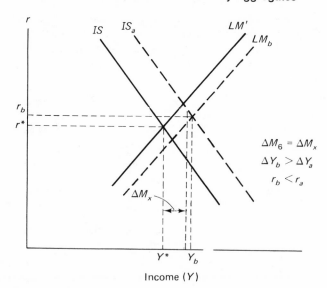

increased in direct proportion to the new funds supplied. It differs in that it involves movement along the *LM'* function rather than a shift in the *LM'* function. The standard analysis treats the M_1 money stock as a parameter of the *LM'* function where additions to the money stock (as defined in the parameter) are introduced into the economy at zero marginal costs.[3] The economic implications of an expansion of monetary aggregates by movement along the *LM'* curve and by a shift of the *LM'* curve are different. If the new loan demand in the previous example is financed by an increase in the money supply that can be correctly treated as a parameter of the *LM'* function (M_x) (see Figure 21-2B), the expansion of income will be larger, and the pressure for higher rates will be less.

A distinction has to be made between a market-induced expansion of monetary aggregates and one that is exogenous to the market process. The direct actions of the monetary authorities in supplying bank reserves and currency clearly fall in the exogenous (parametric) category. The bank expansion made possible by new reserves is more difficult to classify. The multiple expansion of deposits by member banks on the basis of new reserves does not necessarily lead to a costless addition to the supply of funds available for loans. The cost of the new funds arising from the expansion depends on the path of the expansion, which in turn depends on the strength of the demand for loans and on credit-market conditions. If loan demand is strong and member banks are actively trying to raise funds in the market by selling CDs or by raising their rates on savings accounts, the bank expansion will occur to some extent or entirely in a growth of time and savings accounts. In the bank expansion transition matrix presented in Chapter 14, the value of *p* (proportion of redeposits placed into time and savings accounts) will be 1 or close to 1. The banks will have to move along the *LM'* function to obtain new funds, and market conditions will dictate the rate that must be paid. Member bank expansion of the basis of new reserves will add to the monetary aggregates, but it will not be a costless addition. Member bank deposit expansion in this form depends on the market rate and cannot be treated as a change in a parameter of the *LM'* function.

When loan demands do not justify attempts at liability management by the member banks, the expansion on the basis of new reserves will tend to follow the traditional pattern. Banks with excess reserves will buy money market instruments or reduce their rates on loans, and the deposit expansion will continue until the excess reserves are eliminated. The resultant growth, in the form of demand deposits, will have zero marginal costs to the banks fortunate enough to get the benefits of the deposit expansion. The expansion in the monetary aggregates will appear as a

[3]William H. Branson, *Macroeconomic Theory and Policy* (New York: Harper and Row, 1972), p. 158.

costless growth in M_1 that will shift the LM' function to the right by the amount of the expansion. In terms of the expansion matrix, the value of p in the reentry vector will be zero or small, and at the limiting case the full expansion will be in demand deposits. The expansion, in this form, will take place only when the loan demand does not justify attempts at liability management. This version of the creation of monetary aggregates corresponds to the traditional view, but when the reserve base is used for multipurpose controls it is only a special case of the expansion possibilities.

The interest rate and expenditure implications of the two limiting cases of member bank expansion on the basis of a dollar of new reserves are illustrated in Figure 21-3. In both cases, the increase in the reserve base (ΔR) will be reflected in a shift in the LM' function to the right by the amount of the change in reserves. The events from that point on will depend on conditions in the money market. If the loan demand pressures are strong enough to sustain the full bank expansion by liability management, the expansion will proceed along the LM' function. The full expansion will lead to an increase in total member bank deposits by the multiple based on the reciprocal of the reserve requirement on the type of deposits used in the expansion $(1/s)$ (see Figure 21-3A).

When the market is in equilibrium, and demand and supply conditions are satisfied by the equilibrium rate (r^*), the member banks can either hold new reserves as excess reserves (unlikely under normal conditions) or use them to buy money market instruments or to make loans at lower rates. The member banks are now on the opposite side of the money market, and the expansion in their deposits will shift the LM' function to the right by the amount of the expansion multiple $(1/d)$ (see Figure 21-3B). Under easy market conditions, member bank expansion on the basis of new reserves will take the parametric form. Under tight market conditions, the expansion will be a mixture of market-induced and parametric expansion; the mixture will depend on the strength of the market pressures (the willingness of banks to use the expensive path—liability management).

A definition of money, based on its parametric role in the LM' function (M_x), would be similar to the M_1 definition, but would not be exactly the same. It would include currency and demand deposits, but it would also include the share of member bank reserves that is used to support non–M_1 types of accounts.[4]

The individual banker does not see the magic of parametric deposit expansion. The man in charge of the bank's reserve position may be aware of the open market operations of the Federal Reserve System, but it is

---

[4]Part of any member bank expansion on the basis of new reserves is parametric. The reserves against demand accounts are not included because it would represent double counting.

FIGURE 21-3
LIMITING CASES OF MULTIPLE EXPANSION IN MEMBER-BANK DEPOSITS

A. Response to New Loan Demand (shift in *IS*)

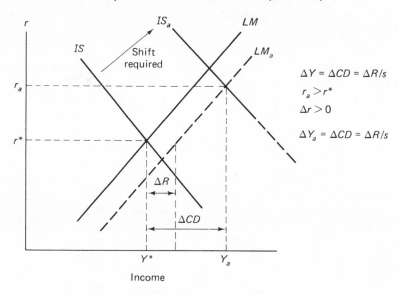

$$\Delta Y = \Delta CD = \Delta R/s$$
$$r_a > r^*$$
$$\Delta r > 0$$

$$\Delta Y_a = \Delta CD = \Delta R/s$$

B. Easy Money Market Conditions (no change in *IS*)

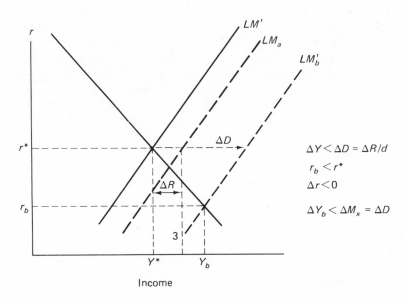

$$\Delta Y < \Delta D = \Delta R/d$$
$$r_b < r^*$$
$$\Delta r < 0$$

$$\Delta Y_b < \Delta M_x = \Delta D$$

unlikely that he can identify any specific deposit benefits from these operations. Yet the member banking system as a whole receives a windfall gain in deposits. These new amounts add to the M_1 component of monetary aggregates and, most importantly, they provide a one-time source of new loans for the banks. The parametric growth of monetary aggregates occurs when the member banks, as the instruments of the Federal Reserve System, supply funds to the money market. The market-induced expansion of monetary aggregates occurs when bank and other financial institutions raise funds for their customers. Both processes add to the funds available to individual institutions, and from their perspective it is impossible to tell the difference.

Special case of nonmember banks

The simplified approach to the theory of interest assumes that all banks are part of a homogeneous set of banks, so that the rules applying to banks apply to all banks. But, as was indicated in Chapter 14, the theory of bank expansion does not apply in the same way to banks under different control systems. The existence of a nonmember banking system does not alter the expansion discussion for member banks in the previous section because they cannot reduce the reserves available to member banks. However, under the assumption that nonmember banks are competitive equals of member banks, they can be expected to share, in a residual manner, in the demand deposit expansion of member banks. The additions to their demand deposits from this source would therefore be included in the costless expansion of the supply of loanable funds and would be part of the shifting LM' function. If, however, it is assumed that they have to compete with member banks for deposits by costly services that represent an implicit payment of interest (or if they are permitted to pay interest), the expansion of their deposits resembles the expansion of non-M_1 aggregates in that the expansion entails higher interest rates.

As a practical matter, it is not at all clear whether the demand deposit expansion at nonmember banks should be regarded as a component of the monetary aggregates that provide new loan funds at a zero marginal cost (a factor shifting the LM' function), or whether they should be treated as similar to the higher forms of money substitutes that can be expanded only by increases in the interest rate. It is simpler, for descriptive purposes, to treat the demand deposits of nonmember banks as part of the costless addition to the supply of loanable funds so that the entire M_1 can be used as part of the parameter of the LM' function. Shifts in the LM' function will then be induced by any change in M_1 and by changes in the member bank reserve base that are used to support higher types of monetary aggregates.

Economic Objectives and the Control of Monetary Aggregates

The control of monetary aggregates offers a potentially attractive technique for achieving various types of economic objectives. Most of the components of the aggregates are issued by financial institutions already subject to a variety of controls. New regulations can be introduced as modifications or extensions of the existing controls. Controls over the financing process are impersonal, and their selective effects on individual borrowers are likely to be hidden by the complexities of the financing process itself.

However, any simple analogy between the control of a broad monetary aggregate and the textbook version of the control of the money supply is misleading. All of the monetary aggregates (with the possible exception of M_1) cover components that behave differently and that affect economic activity in different ways. A simple link between a reserve base and a hetergenous aggregate cannot be expected to produce dependable results. First, intra-system substitutions among aggregates will hamper the control efforts, as they have in the Federal Reserve System's efforts to control the mixed deposits of member banks with the same reserve base. Second, the money substitute components of the broader monetary aggregate are part of a continuum of financial instruments that are all substitutes to some extent. Restrictions on any set of instruments encourages the substitution of uncontrolled instruments or the development of new instruments. For example, restrictions on the monetary aggregates issued by banks and savings institutions (M_5) encourage the use of commercial paper and other directly issued money market instruments. The disintermediation that has been observed during periods of tight money is evidence of the potential importance of this type of substitution.

At the present time, banks that are members of the Federal Reserve System are linked to a controllable reserve base that is used as a reserve base for all of the M_4 components issued by member banks. In addition, both the legal ceilings on rates and the differential reserve requirements are used to control individual components of that aggregate. Savings institutions and nonmember banks are subject to a variety of reserve requirements and selective controls, but they are not linked to any reserve base that can be controlled. Direct issuers of commercial paper and other instruments that qualify as money substitutes are not subject to quantity controls. The attempts to control monetary aggregates in practice have focused on selective reserve requirements and the regulation of rates and terms. The selective effects of these regulations on types of money substitutes that have been used can be observed directly. The effects on the aggregate amount of financing are harder to detect.

Interest Rate Ceilings and the Control of Monetary Aggregates

Interest rate ceilings on deposits and other instruments used to raise funds in the savings and money markets limit the ability of the institutions on which they are imposed to compete for funds. Since the potential supply of funds (as identified by the LM' curve) is independent of the channels that are used to convert it into loans, the aggregate effects of interest rate ceilings depend on the impact of those ceilings on the financing channels used and on the relative efficiency of those channels. If all channels were equally efficient, and if the markets were perfect enough to permit immediate substitutions, interest rate ceilings would have no aggregate effects unless they could be applied to all possible channels. Financing activities would merely be shifted from the controlled channel to uncontrolled channels. In practice, interest rate ceilings are likely to have some aggregate effects because of the imperfections in financial markets and the differences in the efficiency of alternative financing channels.

The structure of rates on various types of deposits and money substitutes reflects the preferences of the suppliers of funds. Demand deposits and other means-of-payment forms of money carry the lowest rates in any system that permits the payment of interest on those deposits. The other types of money substitutes are arranged at higher rates up the scale. The imposition of legal ceilings on any type of instrument in the scale will establish a limit to its use. At rates above the ceiling, less desirable alternatives will have to be substituted, and the substitution will be reflected in a shift of the effective supply function to the left. Higher rates will have to be paid for a given amount of savings, and the effective supply function will appear as a step function at the point of the rate ceiling. The size of the step will measure the added cost of the inferior type of contract.

Reserve requirements and transactions costs may further affect the ability of an institution to convert the funds it raises into loans. As was indicated in Chapter 20, the loan supply function may reflect differences in intermediation costs of this type. The imposition of legal ceilings that lead to shifts from more efficient to less efficient institutional paths will produce an inelastic step in the loan supply function at the ceiling rate, as financing is forced into more expensive channels.

The intra-system substitution effect is likely to be the most important complication in tracing the impact of specific types of rate ceilings. Rate ceilings imposed on members of an effectively controlled banking system (member banks in the case of the United States) will affect the ability of the members of that system to compete for funds in the market and, in addition, will affect the aggregate loan supply function by the amount of the intra-system substitution effect involved. The analysis of the impact of ceiling rates on a controlled system has to proceed in two stages. The first stage focuses on the implications of the ceiling for the ability of individual institutions to compete for funds. In the absence of parametric changes in the LM' function, the ceilings will induce interchannel substitutions, as the institutions restricted by ceilings lose funds to the unrestricted channels. The second stage requires an analysis of the implications of the success (or failure) for the mix of deposits within the controlled system. In the absence of additions to the reserve base, the intra-system substitution effects could be larger, the same as, or smaller than the amount of new funds raised by individual institutions under the protection of favorable ceilings, depending on the differentials in reserve requirements.

Recommendations for the removal of the interest rate ceilings on demand accounts have the appealing feature of permitting the substitution of these accounts for those with less attractive features in the competition for funds. Individual member banks would be able to compete for funds by offering interest on demand accounts. The success of individual banks would be easy to observe. The effects of the intra-system substitution effects would be harder to identify. Under a structure of reserve requirements that provided for higher reserve ratios on demand accounts than on savings accounts, the net results of the success of individual banks in expanding their demand accounts would be a contraction in the total amount of bank credit that the system could support. The aggregate effects of removing restrictions on the payment of interest on demand accounts are likely to be very different from those suggested by a simple demand and supply analysis. The analysis of these effects requires consideration of the interchannel substitutions that arise from the direct competition in the market and the intra-system substitutions that arise from the nature and structure of the controlled system.

QUESTIONS FOR DISCUSSION

1. Consider the circumstances that might give rise to an increase in M_6 monetary aggregate that would not reflect either an increase in the level of the interest rate or an increased level of income. Could a decreased in M_6 aggregate occur while the overall economy is in equilibrium?

2. Suggest a list of economic events that could shift the LM' function as defined in Chapter 19. Classify the items in the list into changes that could be originated by the monetary authorities, changes that appear as changes in assets and liabilities of financial institutions, and changes that do not appear in the asset and liability statements of financial institutions (these categories are not necessarily mutually exclusive).

3. Discuss the special problems of controlling monetary aggregates arising from a system designed to control an aggregate which includes some components that respond to market conditions and others that are parametric in nature. Can the controls be separated?

4. How is it possible for the aggregate effects of controls to be different from the effects of the controls on some important segment of the industry; for example, all the member banks in New York City?

SELECTED REFERENCES

BRITO, D. L., and DONALD D. HESTER, "Stability and Control of the Money Supply," *Quarterly Journal of Economics*, 88 (May 1974) 278–303.

BURGER, ALBERT E., "Money Stock Control," *Controlling Monetary Aggregates II: The Implementation*. Boston: Federal Reserve Bank of Boston, 1972.

CAGAN, PHILLIP, and ANNA J. SCHWARTZ, "Has the Growth of Money Substitutes Hindered Monetary Policy," *Journal of Money, Credit and Banking*, 7 (May 1975) 137–159.

COX, A. H., JR., "Regulation of Interest on Deposits: A Historical Review," *Journal of Finance*, 22 (May 1967) 274–96.

FORTUNE, PETER, "The Effectiveness of Recent Policies to Maintain Thrift-Deposit Flows," *Journal of Money, Credit and Banking*, 7 (August 1975) 297–315.

FRIEDMAN, BENJAMIN M., "Regulation Q and the Commercial Loan Market in the 1960's," *Journal of Money, Credit and Banking*, 7 (August 1975) 277–96.

LINDSAY, ROBERT, *The Economics of Interest Rate Ceilings*. New York: Institute of Finance, New York University, 1970.

MITCHELL, GEORGE W., "Interest Rates Versus Interest Ceiling in the Allocation of Credit Flows," *Journal of Finance*, 22 (May 1967) 265–73.

PIERCE, JAMES L., and THOMAS D. THOMPSON, "Some Issues in Controlling the Stock of Money," *Controlling Monetary Aggregates II: The Implementation*. Boston: Federal Reserve Bank of Boston, 1972.

RASCHE, ROBERT H., "A Review of Empirical Studies of the Money Supply Mechanism," *Review: Federal Reserve Bank of St. Louis*, 54 (July 1972) 11–19

SAMUELSON, PAUL A., "An Analytical Evaluation of Interest Rate Ceilings," *Study of the Saving and Loan Industry*, Vol. IV. Washington, D.C.: U.S. Government Printing Office, 1969.

TOBIN, JAMES, "Deposit Interest Ceiling as a Monetary Control," *Journal of Money, Credit and Banking*, vol. 2, pt. 2 (February 1970) 4–14.

Lending Policies
and
Other Nonprice Adjustments

22

Columbus' voyage to America was delayed six years by his search for financing. The availability of suitable financing does not affect desires or needs, but it often affects the ability to realize them. Nearly all major industrial projects and major consumer outlays require some external financing. The terms and features of financing contracts may be as important in the decision process as the rates paid for the funds. Some of the practical and institutional features of the financing process assumed to be given, for purposes of normal economic analysis, play an important role in understanding the relationship between the financing process and the level of economic activity.

When a banker devises a new credit plan or changes the terms of his contracts, he is trying to shift the demand or supply functions of his bank. Most of the business he gains is likely to be at the expense of his competitors. His actions affect the economy only insofar as they lead to shifts in the aggregate demand for loans, shifts in the aggregate supply of funds, or changes in the cost of financial intermediation. Most of the applied studies in finance are concerned with the use of nonprice techniques for competitive purposes, and it seems likely that only a small share of nonprice competition affects the aggregate level of economic activity. Nonprice changes affect the aggregate supply of funds only if they provide for the more efficient use of money balances. They affect the aggregate demand for funds only insofar as they alter the demand for products and services.

Financial Innovations and Economic Growth

Many types of financial innovations can lead to shifts in the aggregate demand and supply functions as well as to shifts in the competitive position of the innovator. For example, changes in mortgage terms may affect the demand for housing, and improvements in secondary markets can increase the liquidity of marketable instruments.

Innovations may appear on either the demand or supply side of the market or, in some cases, may affect both sides at the same time. The history of the savings and loan movement provides an example of two-sided innovation. The original savings and loan associations were organized by builders or real estate developers who realized that they could sell more houses if the buyers could get satisfactory financing. By forming a savings and loan association, they were able to shift the effective demand for houses and the demand for funds to the right. At the same time, they opened up a new source of supply by offering convenient savings facilities to a class of customers who did not have good outlets for their savings.

Comparisons of countries at different stages of financial development give us some indication of the role of financial markets and institutions. In financially backward countries, where the borrowing and lending that takes place is conducted directly between the two parties involved, we would not expect the volume of external financing to be very large. When savings institutions offer the lender greater liquidity and less risk, the prospects for external financing are clearly improved. The appearance of secondary markets adds another element of liquidity that further improves the prospects for external financing.

We can see the potential for differences in financial structures by comparing two hypothetical countries, A and B, with the same money stock and the same level of internal financing but at different stages of financial development. Country A, without institutional outlets for savings and without secondary markets, does not have very attractive alternatives to offer anyone with surplus funds. Country B, with highly developed savings institutions with convenient branches, liquid savings instruments and a good secondary market, can offer anyone with excess funds very attractive alternatives to idle money balances. At any given level of interest rates we would expect country B to make more efficient use of its money balances than country A. The more advanced institutional development in country B would be reflected in a supply curve (LM'_B) to the right of country A's (see Figure 22-1). With this same basic demand for funds, country B should be able to achieve a large volume of external financing and, accordingly, a higher level of transactions at lower interest rates.

FIGURE 22-1

FINANCIAL STRUCTURE AND THE SUPPLY OF FUNDS

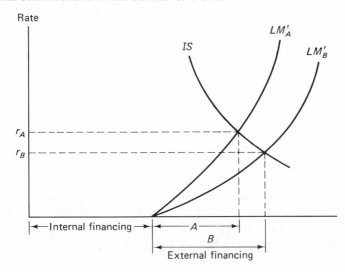

Goldsmith distinguishes three stages in the financial development of nonsocialist countries. The first stage is characterized by (1) a low financial interrelations ratio (which implies a low ratio of external to internal financing), (2) the predominance of claims over equity securities (which implies the absence of good secondary markets), (3) a relatively small share of financial institutions in all financial assets, and (4) the preeminence of commercial banks among financial institutions. The second stage is similar except for the

> greater role of the government and of government financial institutions.... In some cases the existence of a sector of large corporate enterprise constitutes a second difference. Since this sector is usually foreign owned and financed, it has, however, often little effect on the country's own financial structure.

The third stage is characterized by: (1) higher financial interrelations ratios, (2) higher ratios of equity securities to claims, (3) a higher share of financial institutions in total financial assets, and (4) increased diversification among financial institutions, leading to a decline in the share of the banking system and a corresponding increase in the importance of thrift and insurance organizations.[1]

Financial markets and institutions do not directly add to the productive capacity of a country. They do, however, widen the alternatives for

[1]Raymond W. Goldsmith, *Financial Structure and Development* (New Haven and London: Yale University Press, 1969), pp. 33–35.

financing growth. The development of attractive nonprice features can add to the available supply of funds without increasing rates. Financial innovations that led to more efficient use of the money supply are an alternative to increases in the money supply as a source of funds for expansion.

Nonprice Adjustments in Response to Money Shortages

When the growth of the money supply is slower than the growth in the demand for transactions balances, the pressure of the loan demand is quickly reflected in higher rates on short-term money substitutes. If the pressures continue and the money markets cannot supply the funds required to relieve the pressures, a variety of techniques may be used to increase the efficiency of the use of the money stock. Developments in the United States during the 1960's and early 1970's provide a number of excellent examples of nonprice adjustments and institutional changes that shifted the aggregate supply function to the right and that increased the velocity of circulation of the money stock.

1) The managers of cash balances developed techniques for speeding the flow of payments into bank accounts and into short-term investments. Lock-boxes were used to avoid delays in sending checks to banks. Cash accounts were centralized and controlled by telegraphic transfers, and various techniques were introduced to reduce the time involved in handling and processing payments. The new "point-of-sale" electronic terminals that provide for direct transfers of funds from the account of the buyer to the account of the seller are an extension of these attempts to speed up the handling of payments. The checkless society, if it comes, will be a by-product of pressures to reduce money balances. The appearance of a group of new professionals in the field of cash management is evidence of the savings that can be achieved by better cash management. Banks and other financial institutions have added cash management advisory experts as a service to their important customers.

2) Borrowers of short-term funds were stimulated by the high cost of these funds to seek the most efficient alternatives and to try to add features that reduce the cost of those funds. Issuers of commercial paper sought the endorsement of commercial banks to improve their credit standing. Federal agencies sought to improve the marketability of their securities by making them eligible for Federal Reserve open-market purchases. Commercial banks tried to improve the liquidity of their notes by making them negotiable.

3) The expansion in the outstanding amount of money substitutes improved the marketability of these securities and indirectly reduced the cost of issuing money substitutes.

4) Banks worked toward reducing their own transactions balances.

They tried to reduce or eliminate such cash items as "excess reserves" and "items in the process of collection." Electronic transfer systems and improvements in the check clearing process were developed. The Federal Funds market developed to the point that the daily investment of excess reserves became feasible. The Federal Reserve System assisted in the process by speeding up their clearing operations and by relaxing the technical provisions of reserve requirements so that the banks could manage their reserve positions more efficiently.

5) Nonbank financial institutions developed a variety of accounts that could be used as payment accounts and on which they paid interest. The accounts ranged from provision for the issuance of checks, drawn on the institution's accounts at the request of · the depositors, to formal demand accounts that provided check-writing facilities under different names. These accounts might properly be included as part of the M_1 money stock for some purposes. They fall between the issuance of a money substitute at the market interest rate as measured by the LM' function and the parametric expansion of the money stock. Savings institutions have taken the lead in developing point-of-sale transfer systems, which can serve as substitutes for checks.

6) Efficient cash management alternatives were brought to holders of small transactions and precautionary balances by the development of liquid asset mutual funds. These funds made it possible for anyone with surplus balances of $500 or more to invest in money market instruments with a high degree of safety and liquidity. The purchasers of shares in these liquid asset funds were assured both the safety of funds invested in U.S. government securities and certificates of deposit of major banks, and the liquidity of the right to draw checks on these funds without notice. With the appearance of these funds, anyone with excess balances of $500 or more could reduce their checking accounts to nominal amounts.

This list illustrates the major types of nonprice adjustments that were made in an effort to more efficiently use a scarce supply of transactions balances. Financial institutions and markets try to accommodate the real demands for funds. When they are assisted by free money from the monetary authorities, the financing can be achieved by standard procedures at low interest rates. When the monetary authorities are less generous, high interest rates and the ingenuity of financial experts and technicians must be used.

Nonprice Factors and the Effectiveness of Monetary Policy

A number of types of bank lending policies can be used to control the dollar volume of new loans. Credit policies can be tightened to exclude some borrowers or they can be expanded to include borrowers previously excluded. Compensating balance requirements can be increased or decreased to change the amount of the effective loan size and, of course, the effective costs. Borrowers may be encouraged to scale down or expand the amount of their requests. In face-to-face negotiations between bankers and their customers, the nonprice features of their loans may be easier to adjust than the interest rates.

The potential importance of changes in lending policies and practices in adjustments to changing market conditions has been widely recognized, but the effects are hard to measure. The Federal Reserve System has conducted a number of surveys in which banks have reported policy changes that appear to be directly related to credit market conditions.[2] A significant share of the reporting banks reported more restrictive lending policies on compensating or supporting balances, standards of credit-worthiness, and loan maturities during periods of tight money. They also reported greater reluctance to make term loans, mortgage loans, and other types of loans that were not related to their primary lending activities. If it can be assumed that the borrowers adversely affected by these policies cannot obtain funds at the old terms from other sources, lending policies add another dimension to monetary policy.

When banks adjust their loan policies to changes in their money positions, they shift the effective demand schedule for their loans. We can think of two demand schedules; one that gives the potential demand for their loans at different rates, and the other that gives the effective demand of borrowers who can meet their standards and requirements. The spread between the two schedules represents an unsatisfied demand that might be measured by loan rejections. A bank can alter the share of the potential demand for its loans that it accepts by adjusting its lending policies.

In terms of the *IS–LM* analysis, changes in lending policies establish a link between the supply function (*LM'*) and the demand function (*IS*). Changes in bank reserves and any accompanying parametric changes in money supply potentially can affect the level of income and interest rates in two ways: (1) by the changes induced by movement along the *IS* function in response to changes in the interest rate, and (2) by any changes in lending policies that shift the *IS* function. The extreme cases of these two alternatives are illustrated in Figure 22-2. Panel A shows the effects of a change in the money supply under the normal assumption that there are no changes in lending policies. An expansion of the money supply, in this case, leads to a reduction in the interest rate and some expansion in the level of income. The amounts involved depend on the elasticity of the functions. Panel B illustrates the effects of a change in the money supply of the same amount, when it is assumed that the banks prefer to relax their lending policies rather than to reduce their loan rates. These changes lead

---

[2] Paul W. Boltz, "Changes in Bank Lending Practices, 1974," *Federal Reserve Bulletin* (April 1975), pp. 221–29.

FIGURE 22-2
Two Reactions to Changes in the Money Supply

A. No Changes in Lending Policies

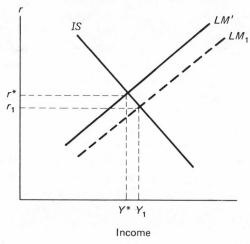

Income

B. Relaxation of Lending Policies

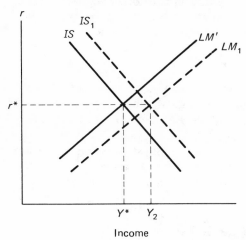

Income

to a shift of the *IS* function. When the shift is equal to the change in the money stock, these changes will lead to an expansion in income without a reduction in the interest rate. In this case, the expansion in expenditures will be equal to the amount of new funds and will be independent of the elasticities of the demand and supply functions.

The two classical cases of the ineffectiveness of monetary policy are based on assumptions about the elasticities of the demand and supply functions: (1) the perfect inelasticity of the demand for loan funds and (2) the perfect elasticity of the demand for money balances, or the "liquidity trap" condition. In both cases, it can be shown that, if it is assumed that lending policies are constant, changes in the money supply will have no effect on the aggregate level of expenditures (see left panels of Figure 22-3A and B). If, however, it is assumed that the banks that receive the funds relax their lending policies and, in so doing, shift the effective demand for loans (by reducing the unsatisfied demand), monetary policies would lead to an expansion of expenditures in both cases (see the right panels of Figure 22-3A and B).

Changes in lending policies can be observed at individual banks. The difficult question for aggregate theory is whether or not the effects of changes that are observed at individual institutions are offset in aggregate. If a rejected borrower obtains a loan from another source, the observed rejection would not be recorded in the aggregate demand. The theoretical results depend on the mobility of borrowers. Practical bankers tend to discount the widespread availability of alternatives. Theorists who believe in the effectiveness of market adjustments tend to assume that lending policies have no aggregate effects. The truth undoubtedly lies between the two extremes. This unfortunate conclusion removes some of the precision from the analysis of the effects of changing market conditions, but it should produce results that are closer to reality.

Selective Credit Controls

The importance of credit terms for some types of spending decisions has led to attempts to regulate these decisions by controls over credit terms. The Federal Reserve System was given authority, by the Securities Exchange Act of 1934, to set limits on the amount of credit that can be used for purchases of common stock. This provision was designed to discourage speculation in stocks by limiting the amount of debt that could be used for that purpose. The Federal Reserve Board has been setting margin requirements on stock under its Regulations T, U, and G since that time.

Selective controls have also been used in a variety of ways to stimulate or restrain consumer spending for houses, automobiles, and other durable goods. Various government credit programs have used credit terms (low down payments and small monthly payments) to stimulate expenditures that were regarded as socially desirable. Some of these programs have provided direct loans, and others have guaranteed private loans. During World War II and on several other occasions, controls on down payments and maturities were used in the reverse fashion to discourage expenditures.

FIGURE 22-3

LENDING POLICIES AND THE EFFECTIVENESS OF MONETARY POLICY

A. Inelastic Demand Conditions

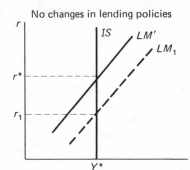

No changes in lending policies

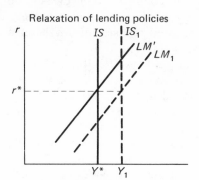

Relaxation of lending policies

B. Liquidity Trap Conditions

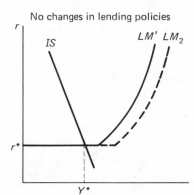

No changes in lending policies

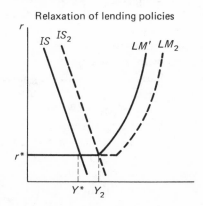

Relaxation of lending policies

Experience with selective controls suggests that they can be very effective in controlling expenditures that involve large outlays and the use of credit. The dispute about their effectiveness centers largely on their implications for the aggregate level of expenditures. The central issue in this debate revolves around the existence of substitution effects that partly or completely offset the direct and observable effects of the controls. The observable effects of these controls appear in a curtailment (or stimulation) of expenditures for housing or automobiles and in the credit that is extended for these purposes. If it is assumed that the aggregate effects are simply the sum of individual expenditures, any contraction (or expansion) will lead to a contraction (or expansion) in the total. This view, however, ignores the possibility that directly related and offsetting events may be set in motion by the response to the controls. If the credit that would have been used for the controlled expenditures is merely diverted to uncontrolled sectors, expenditures in the uncontrolled sector can increase, and the level of aggregate expenditures will be unaffected by the imposition of selective controls. Only the mix of expenditures will be changed. An analogy with a balloon is sometimes used to illustrate this possibility: You can push on one side of a balloon without changing its total size; only its shape is changed.

Since it is difficult to trace the impact of selective controls, individual positions on the effectiveness of selective controls on aggregate expenditures tend to reflect the individual's views about the speed and ability of economic markets to adjust to changes. If one thinks of different markets as being largely separate and noncompetitive, one will assume that the effects observed in a specific market will also be reflected in the aggregates. This position is found, in a naive form, among those who are not aware of the possibilities of the substitution effects or the interactions that may be created by selective events. This naive approach to aggregate economic problems is characterized by the now-famous quotation that "what is good for General Motors is good for the country." A more sophisticated version of the same position may be held by those who are aware of the possibilities of substitution effects but think that the imperfections in market adjustments will either delay or prevent offsetting events. Theorists who have confidence in the market mechanism are likely to conclude that effects of selective credit controls will be limited to changes in the product and credit mix with very little, if any, aggregate effect.

The extreme positions in this debate illustrate a recurring source of disagreement and confusion in aggregate economic theory. At one extreme the aggregative effects are viewed as a simple analogy of the effects observed at the individual bank or firm, i.e., the simple sum of these results can be assumed to be the aggregative effects. This approach is deceptive because it seems intuitively obvious, yet it may overlook substitution effects that may totally or partly offset the initial, easily observed effects. One of the major problems of applied aggregate economics lies in the identification and measurement of hidden substitution effects that can invalidate the intuitive arguments. The observation that a theory isn't much good unless it tells us something that isn't intuitively obvious is an appropriate warning.

QUESTIONS FOR DISCUSSION

1. Develop a list of the techniques of nonprice competition that might be used by a bank in trying to expand its share of the market. What effect, if any, will each item on the list have on the aggregate demand and supply functions?

2. Suggest a number of techniques that might be used in a developing economy to encourage the more efficient use of money stock. Compare the effects of this approach to financing new loan demand with the direct issuance of new money.

3. If changes in payment procedures and practices can increase the efficiency of the use of the money stock, why are these changes delayed until money market conditions are tight?

4. Suggest techniques that commercial banks could use to help their customers reduce their idle money balances and that would not result in the loss of deposits by the banks taking the initiative in such plans.

5. It is usually assumed that nonprice changes that improve the efficiency of the use of money are fixed in the short run. Discuss the time interval for the adoption of some changes of this type. Do any nonprice financial adjustments have time intervals that are short enough for them to appear as potentially important economic variables in analyzing month-to-month economic changes?

6. How can it be argued that the *IS* function might be inelastic with respect to changes in the interest rate?

7. Discuss the types of financial adjustments that might accompany selective credit controls that are effective in curtailing the demand for the products affected and the demand for credit to purchase them. Assume that the controls are imposed during a period of strong demand pressures and that no actions are taken to alter the reserves available to the banking system.

SELECTED REFERENCES

BACH, G. L., and C. J. HUIZENGA, "The Differential Effects of Tight Money," *American Economic Review*, 51 (March 1961) 52–80.

DAVIS, RICHARD G., "An Analysis of Quantitative Credit Controls and Related Devices," *Brookings Papers on Economic Activity*, No. 1. Washington, D.C.: Brookings Institution, 1971.

GOLDSMITH, RAYMOND W., *Financial Structure and Development*. New Haven, Conn.: Yale University Press, 1969.

HODGMAN, DONALD R., "Selective Credit Controls," *Journal of Money, Credit and Banking*, 4 (May 1972) 342–59.

KAMINOW, IRA, and JAMES M. O'BRIEN, eds., *Studies in Selective Credit Policies*. Philadelphia, Pa.: Federal Reserve Banks of Philadelphia, 1975.

MAYER, THOMAS, "Financial Guidelines and Credit Controls," *Journal of Money, Credit and Banking*, 4 (May 1972) 360–74.

ROOSA, ROBERT V., "Interest Rates and Central Banks," *Money, Trade and Economic Growth*. New York: Macmillan Co., 1961.

TOBIN, JAMES, "Monetary Restrictions and Direct Controls," *Review of Economics and Statistics*, 33 (November 1953), 196–98.

A Financial System
Under Pressure

23

The third quarter of the Twentieth Century provides an excellent example of the ability of the private financial system to handle demand pressures exceeding those that could be financed by the growth of the money supply. The gross national product in the United States increased at an average annual rate of 7 percent while the money supply grew at only about half that rate (see Figure 23-1A). The extent of the financing gap can be illustrated by the spread between the actual level of GNP expenditures and the level of expenditures (E^*) that could have been supported by the actual money stock at the 1950 velocity of circulation. These shortages had to be supplied by the more efficient use of the money stock, measured either as an increase in the velocity of circulation (V) or as a reduction in cash balances (k) (see Figure 23-1B).

The success of the financial system in handling these demand pressures was achieved only at the cost of a number of structural changes within the system itself. They include (1) a reduction in the elasticity of the loan supply function, (2) greater volatility in short-term interest rates, and (3) a reduction in the effectiveness of the traditional approach to controlling the money supply. The first section of this chapter examines the role of money substitutes and the money market in facilitating the more efficient use of money balances. The last three sections deal with the implications of the structural changes.

FIGURE 23-1

A. Growth of Gross National Product and the Money Supply

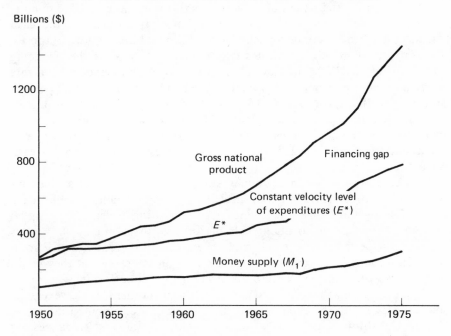

B. Efficiency of the Use of the Money Supply

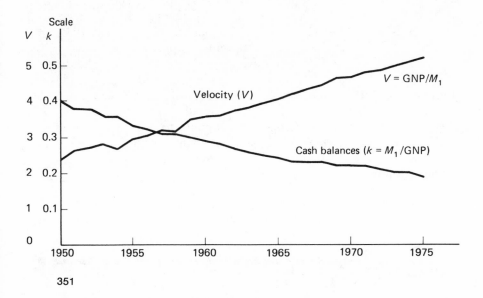

Growth of Money Substitutes

The more efficient use of the money stock was made possible in large part by the substitution of various types of near monies for the cash balances (M_1) that were being held for portfolio and transactions purposes. The growth of money substitutes $(M_6$ minus $M_1)$ parallels the financing gap (see Figure 23-2A). Money substitutes grew at an average annual rate of 10.6 percent as compared with the growth rate in GNP of 6.9 percent and that of the money supply (M_1) of 3.8 percent. Some of these instruments, such as negotiable certificates of deposit, were specifically developed to serve the needs of cash managers. Higher rates and improvements in secondary markets added to their attractiveness as substitutes for cash balances.

The early expansion of money substitutes developed at savings institutions as they raised funds to meet the growing demands for mortgage loans. During the 1950's, the savings accounts at thrift institutions tripled in size as they provided about half of the growth in money substitutes during that period. Commercial banks were excluded from effective competition for savings accounts by legal ceilings on the rates that they could pay. These ceilings, which were 2.5 percent on regular savings accounts and 1 percent on short-term accounts, had been set in 1937. However, the banks helped with the expanding loan demand and contributed indirectly to the substitution of money market securities for cash balances by reducing their own holdings of money market securities and using the proceeds for loans. Their actions added to the market supply of money substitutes and put upward pressure on their yields. The commercial banks reduced their holdings of securities from 59 percent of the total loans and investments, in 1950, to 41 percent in 1960, and to 29 percent by 1975.

The disadvantages of the "shiftability" approach to financing the new loan demand soon became obvious to the banks as their holdings of securities approached safety limits and as they watched the savings institutions grow in size and importance. The Federal Reserve System responded to pressure for higher rate ceilings by a small increase in 1957. In 1962, they raised the ceiling on long-term accounts to 4 percent, which was competitive with the rates being paid by savings institutions (see Figure 23-3), With a touch of understatement, the Board commented on their action as follows:

> For some time prior to this action, a number of commercial banks had contended that a 3 percent maximum rate restricted them in their efforts to compete for savings and time deposits.[1]

[1]*Forty-Eighth Annual Report of the Board of Governors of the Federal Reserve System* (1961), p. 102.

FIGURE 23-2
A. FINANCING GAP AND THE GROWTH OF MONEY SUBSTITUTES

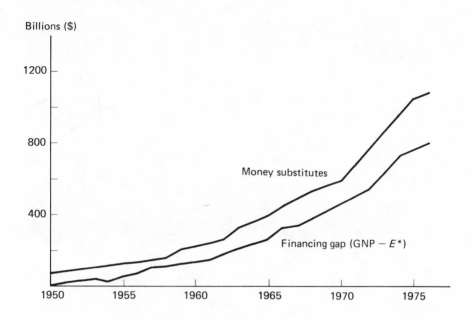

B. PERCENTAGE DISTRIBUTION OF MONEY SUBSTITUTES

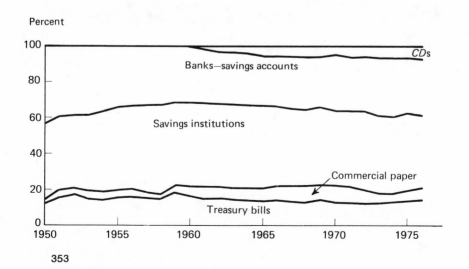

FIGURE 23-3
SELECTED INTEREST RATES AND REGULATION Q CEILINGS

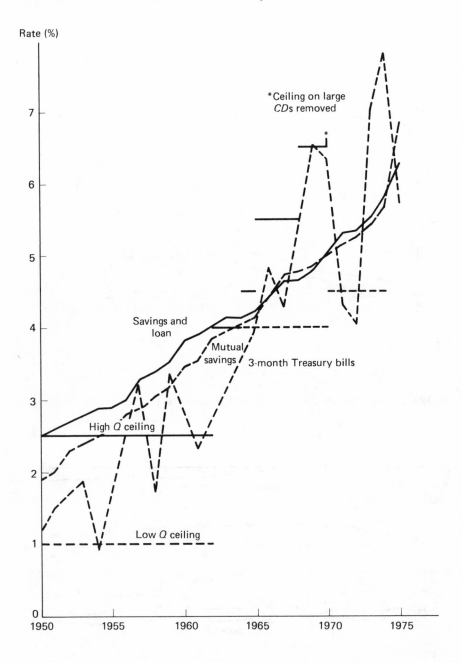

The new competition from commercial banks for savings accounts shifted the relative growth rates of the two types of institutions. By 1965, the commercial banks were attracting more savings than the savings institutions.

Appearance of negotiable certificates of deposit

The large banks were faced with two types of problems during the 1950's. They were having difficulty in raising the funds to meet the loan demands of their customers, and they were faced with a steady drain of demand accounts as their large customers placed their cash balances into money market securities. They faced the awkward problem of assisting some of their customers in the more efficient management of their surplus funds, while being unable to supply the loan demands of other customers. The negotiable certificate of deposit supplied the answer. They could sell CDs to their customers with surplus funds and use the proceeds to make loans.

The success of the program depended on the ability of the commercial banks to make CDs competitive with other money market securities. However, this did not prove to be a serious problem. The well-developed secondary market for U.S. government securities provided a ready-made organization for handling CDs. The announcement of the first major effort to sell CDs was accompanied by an announcement that a large dealer in government securities would make a market for them. The ceiling rates under Regulation Q were occasionally a problem, but the CD was quickly established as an important new money market instrument.

The CD gave commercial banks a versatile new tool for liability management. The supply was highly elastic to small rate differentials and could be controlled better than other types of deposit accounts. Its marketability and the existence of a good secondary market protected the bank from the redemption pressures that could develop on other types of accounts. It gave the banks direct access to the money market and enabled them to compete with the U.S. Treasury and the issuers of commercial paper for the surplus balances of cash managers.

Disintermediation and credit crunches

In mid-1966, interest rates on money market securities rose to new highs as a variety of special demand pressures converged on the credit markets. The inability of the money market to handle these demands led to the disruption of the normal patterns of moneyflows. Banks and savings institutions that had been using the money market as a source of reserve liquidity found that the money market was presenting them with liquidity problems. The servant had suddenly become the master. The banks and savings institutions lost funds as their depositors shifted into money market instruments. This movement of funds, called *disintermediation*, was a sign of the inelasticity in the supply of funds in the money market. The market could not handle the demand pressures and was forced to allocate the existing supplies to the highest bidders.

The problem for financial institutions was not simply the temporary one of paying more for their current needs. They were forced to raise rates on their other accounts to prevent withdrawals. These adjustments were difficult, or impossible, for institutions with long-term assets with fixed yields (see Figure 12-9). Many individual savings and loan associations were unable to face these liquidity problems without assistance. The banks were less seriously affected in the 1966 crisis. They were able to expand their share of the savings market and were able to sell CDs until late in the year when the market rates moved above the legal ceilings on their CD rates.

The savings associations sought relief through federal legislation. The events of 1966 led to temporary legislation that established a spread between the ceiling rates that could be paid by banks and by savings institutions. This protected the savings institutions from the direct competition of banks for certain types of savings accounts. A serious crisis was avoided only with the assistance of the Federal Home Loan Bank and by the easing of credit market conditions. The basic vulnerability of the savings institution to disintermediation had been vividly demonstrated.

The crisis of 1966 signalled the beginning of a period of high volatility in money market rates and of recurring cycles of market disruptions and disintermediation. The elasticity of the money market throughout the 1950's and early 1960's had been achieved in large part by the substitution of near-monies for cash balances. But that process approaches a limit as cash balances are reduced. By 1966 the largest and most accessible cash balances had already been reduced by the high level of interest rates and by improvements in portfolio and cash management techniques. The market was faced with less elasticity in the supply function.

The years that followed 1966 were characterized by rising interest rates and by the efforts of individual institutions and the regulatory agencies to adapt to the new market conditions. The experiences of 1966, with some variations, became a recurring feature of the financing process. The record short-term rates of 1966 were surpassed in 1968, again in 1969 and 1970; and all of the earlier highs were surpassed in late summer of 1974. When demand pressures exceeded supplies at equilibrium rates, the money market retained its role as the center of the adjustment process, but the nature of the adjustments changed. They consisted more and more of the reallocation of existing supplies, with the disruptions that this implies, and less and less of the generation of new supplies. The liquidity financial institutions provided to their suppliers of funds exposed them to the pressures of disintermediation. The ultimate winners in the reallocation process were the borrowers who could get the funds they needed. The losers were those who failed. Since most borrowers obtained their loans from financial institutions, their success or failure in raising funds depended on the success or failure of the institutions that served as their representatives in the struggle for funds. The vulnerability of the savings institutions had been demonstrated in 1966.The potential vulnerability of banks was demonstrated in 1969 and 1970.

The efforts of the monetary authorities to resist the inflationary pressures that were developing in 1968 and 1969 created serious problems for the banks that were members of the Federal Reserve System. Despite growing demands for loans, the monetary authorities permitted bank reserves to expand by less than 1 percent (at an annual rate) during the first half of 1969 and forced a contraction that averaged 2.2 percent (at an annual rate) during the second half of the year. These pressures were exerted at a time when market rates were rising sharply, and the ceiling rates on both savings accounts and CDs prevented the member bank from competing effectively for funds from these sources. Member banks were faced with a reduction in the reserve base, as well as with losses in savings and time accounts that reduced the volume of bank credit that could be supported by the reserve base. The disruptive market pressures that developed by the end of 1969 forced the monetary authorities to relax their restrictive position. They permitted member bank reserves to expand at an annual rate of 12.7 percent in the last two months of the year, in contrast to the average contraction at the annual rate of 9.7 percent in the preceeding four months.

The experience with disintermediation at member banks during 1969 led to the removal of the ceiling rates on large CDs in 1970. From that point on, the banks were free to compete for money market funds. The problem of disintermediation was handed back to the savings institutions for the next crisis.

Elasticity of the Loan Supply Function

The natural inelasticity of the short-run liquidity preference function, which followed the high level of rates and the reduction of cash balances, was accentuated on several occasions by the intra-member-bank substitution effects. As was seen in Chapter 20, the elasticity of the loan supply function depends in part on the path of the financing. Direct financing is most efficient from a moneyflows point of view because it avoids the leakages that can appear in the intermediation process. Any shift in the channels of financing toward member banks reduces the elasticity of the loan supply function. Shifts toward direct financing tend to increase its elasticity. In two of the tight-money periods, 1966 and 1974, the proportion of funds raised by member banks increased, relative to other channels of financing. In the 1969–70 crisis, the role of member banks declined. Thus, in two of the three tight-money periods between 1950 and 1975, the intra-member-bank substitution effect added to the disruptive pressures of the crises, and in the third it tended to mitigate the pressures.

The actual importance of the intra-member-bank substitution effect is difficult to measure. It is of special theoretical importance because its aggregate effects are opposite those that would be expected from the experiences of individual member banks. When individual member banks are successful in raising money in tight-money periods, it seems natural to assume that the supply of funds has been increased. But if the aggregate supply is inelastic, this can't be the case. If the data were complete, it would show that the member bank's gain was someone else's loss. In addition, since the member bank channel involves the leakages of the intra-member-bank substitution effect, the net results of using the less efficient approach may be to actually reduce the aggregate supply of funds. The large member banks are the center of the banking function in the United States, and it is hard to imagine the widespread acceptance of a theoretical argument that something good for the ability of these banks to raise new funds can, in fact, contract the aggregate supply of funds. But the theory has to speak for itself.

The longer-run elasticity of the supply function can be influenced by a variety of changes that lead to the more efficient use of money, including the continued use of money substitutes as potential substitutes for cash balances. The development of the liquid asset funds provides an example of an institutional development that extends the facilities of money market substitutes to holders of small cash balances. Several types of changes in payment procedures and practices have contributed to the more efficient use of the money stock in the transactions process and to the long-run elasticity of supply. The use of credit cards to synchronize money flows, techniques for speeding up transfers, and the elimination of float have reduced the required levels of cash balances. Efforts along these lines can theoretically lead to major long-run improvements in the efficiency of the use of the money stock and to further increases in the velocity of circulation of money. The ultimate stage appears to lie in the development of a nearly instantaneous electronic transfer system that would replace checks and currency for most payments. These developments will lead to long-run shifts in the supply function (*LM'*) but they are unlikely to add much to its short-run elasticity.

Struggle for Market Priorities

The higher rates accompanying financing techniques that involve the more efficient use of the money supply have also had allocative effects. They have precluded investment and expenditure projects that cannot support the high rates. As rates have moved higher and higher, the range of projects that cannot be financed and the difficulties of obtaining financing have increased. The problem received widespread publicity and attention in 1975 when the U.S. Treasury, the federally sponsored credit agencies, and state and local governments accounted for a record 65 percent of the total funds raised in the money and capital markets. Borrowers at the bottom of the priority scale were faced with improving their priority position or exclusion from the market by either impossibly high rates or outright credit rationing.

The construction industry, which is particularly vulnerable to the disintermediation that affects savings institutions, has been protected to some degree by the intervention of federal agencies. The Federal Home Loan Bank acts as the representative of the savings institutions in tight-money periods. It raises funds in both the money and the capital markets to replace some of the funds that are being lost by the savings institutions. The secondary mortgage agencies play essentially the same role. They use the funds they can obtain to buy the mortgages the savings institutions are forced to sell. The entire process protects the construction industry from some of the short-term reallocations in tight-money periods and stabilizes the flow of funds for the industry.

Banks have used a number of techniques for assisting their customers in obtaining funds when the banks themselves do not have them. They have established subsidiaries that can obtain access to the commercial paper market by virtue of their affiliation with the bank. They have also guaranteed the commercial paper of some borrowers who would otherwise be unable to sell their obligations. The banks have used both of these techniques to help real estate investment trusts (REITs) raise money. The reputation and name of the bank enhances the priorities of their customers and makes it possible for them to obtain the funds they need. These practices, however, also expose the banks to risks that are usually not apparent to their depositors and stockholders.

Implications for Monetary Policy

The inelasticity of the private financial system presents the monetary authorities with an unattractive set of alternatives during tight-money periods. They can either (1) supply enough funds to relieve the market pressures or (2) refuse to supply funds and let the existing supplies be allocated to the highest bidders under crisis conditions.

The first alternative accommodates inflationary pressures and is unlikely to be consistent with their policy targets. The second alternative is almost certain to lead to disruptive pressures and to disintermediation. The reduction in the elasticity in private financing sectors has added to the responsibilities of the monetary authorities and has, at the same time, reduced their freedom of action. The chairman of the Federal Reserve Board emphasized these problems in the following statement to Congress in early 1975:

> There is a school of thought that holds that the Federal Reserve need pay no attention to interest rates, that the only thing that matters is how this or that monetary aggregate is behaving. We at the Federal Reserve cannot afford the luxury of any such mechanical rule. As the Nation's central bank, we have a vital role to play as the lender of last resort. It is our duty to avert liquidity or banking crisis. It is our duty to protect the integrity of both the domestic value of the dollar and its foreign-exchange value. In discharging these functions, we at times need to set aside temporarily our objectives with regard to the monetary aggregates.
>
> In particular, we pay close attention to interest rates because of their profound effects on the workings of the economy.[2]

The reduction in the elasticity of the private financial sectors also led to the reduction in the effectiveness of the traditional tools of monetary policy. The Federal Reserve System can expand or contract the member bank reserve base with a high degree of accuracy, but the impact of those changes on the level of interest rates depends in part on credit market conditions and on the reactions of the member banks to the changes in the reserves. The traditional multiple expansion of the money supply that theoretically follows the introduction of new reserves does not develop when credit market conditions are tight and the supply function is inelastic. When demand pressures are strong, the member banks try to raise

---

[2]"Statements to Congress," *Federal Reserve Bulletin* (February 1975), p. 64.

new funds by selling CDs or by trying to attract other forms of savings. For the member banking system as a whole, any new reserves will supply the base for a multiple expansion of credit that will appear on the bank statements as new loans and as new time and savings accounts. The growth in member bank credit will be a multiple of the new reserves, but if the overall market supply function (LM') is inelastic, most of the expansion of member bank time and savings accounts will be at the expense of other money market borrowers. The only source of new funds will be the amount of new reserves provided by the Federal Reserve System. Under these conditions, the monetary authorities can reduce interest rates, but they have to provide the required funds. The apparent assistance from the expansion of member bank credit will be offset by a contraction somewhere else in the market. The member bank credit expansion is a correct measure of the net availability of new funds only if it can be assumed that it is not at the expense of others. This assumption is inconsistent with an inelastic supply function.

The nature of member bank response during a tight-money period can be observed in the first part of 1974. The Federal Reserve System permitted member bank reserves to expand at an average annual rate of 10.6 percent during the first seven months of the year. During the same period, their demand accounts grew at an annual rate of only 2.7 percent, their CDs expanded at an annual rate of 45 percent, and their time and savings accounts together expanded by 18 percent. Total member bank credit expansion at an annual rate of 12 percent was supported largely by the growth of savings and money market instruments, which the banks had to obtain in direct competition with other borrowers. There is no direct way of measuring the extent to which the member bank expansion was at the expense of other potential borrowers. However, the growth rate of time and savings accounts at member banks during the period was three times that of the nonbank savings institutions.

The traditional model of the multiple expansion of the money supply on the basis of new reserves is likely to occur only when credit market conditions are relatively easy and the member banks do not need the funds for loans. Under these conditions they will use excess reserves to increase their own holdings of money market instruments. The expansion will appear on bank statements as a growth in bank credit (usually money market securities) and a growth in demand accounts (since they are unwilling to try to compete for new time accounts). The growth in bank credit will be smaller than in the previous case, but it is achieved without competition with other borrowers and appears in the money market as a new source of funds rather than as a demand for funds. No substitution effects will reduce the impact of the member bank expansion. The expansion is achieved as a shift in the short-run supply function (*LM'*), rather than as a small shift in the supply function and movement along the supply function, as in the tight-money case.

The reduction of the effectiveness of the traditional monetary tools during tight-money periods stems largely from the more active role of commercial banks in the money market. In earlier periods, before member banks became active competitors in the money market, and when Regulation Q ceilings prevented them from competing for savings accounts, the inter-institution substitution effects were not large enough to seriously reduce the aggregative effects of their expansion.

A number of changes might be made in the structure of reserve requirements to increase the efficiency of the reserve requirement device as a tool of monetary policy. In 1961, the Commission on Money and Credit recommended that statutory reserve requirements against savings and time deposits be repealed and that, pending repeal, the banks be permitted to hold reserves in some other form.[3] In 1971, the President's Commission on Financial Structure and Regulation also recommended that "legally required deposit reserves in time and savings deposits, share accounts and certificates of deposit, be abolished."[4] These proposals have one feature in common: They would use the reserve base exclusively for the control of the demand deposits of member banks, rather than for the control of the total size of member banks. The inelasticity of the short-run supply function appears to be a permanent feature of an economy that functions at high levels of the interest rate, and individual financing operations and regulatory policies have to be adjusted to the problems imposed by this inelasticity.

QUESTIONS FOR DISCUSSION

1. Would the structure of our financial system have been the same if the demand pressures of the 1950's and 1960's had been financed by more liberal monetary policies? In what ways would it be different? Would the different method of financing have any effects on the growth of GNP?

2. Discuss the comparative advantages and disadvantages of long-term versus short-term debt financing in the financial environment similar to that prevailing in the late 1960's and early 1970's.

[3]Report of the Commission on Money and Credit, *Money and Credit* (Englewood Cliffs, N.J.: Prentice Hall, Inc., 1961), p. 69.

[4]*Report of the President's Commission on Financial Structure and Regulation* (Washington, D.C.: U.S. Government Printing Office, 1972), p. 65.

3. Does the growth of the banking system represent a demand for funds or a supply of funds in the money market?

4. Discuss the possibility that the *LM'* function could be backward sloping. What policy recommendations would you suggest to correct the problem if it occurred?

5. Could a "checkless society" function without money? Discuss the question of the elasticity of the *LM'* function in a checkless society.

6. Discuss the implications for savings institutions of the elimination of the reserve requirement on the time and savings accounts of commercial banks. What could serve as size constraints for member banks if this action were taken?

Index

365